Published for
OXFORD INTERNATIONAL AQA EXAMINATIONS

International AS Level
BUSINESS

Sandra Harrison
Brian Coyle
Peter Joyce
David Milner

OXFORD
UNIVERSITY PRESS

Great Clarendon Street, Oxford, OX2 6DP, United Kingdom

Oxford University Press is a department of the University of Oxford. It furthers the University's objective of excellence in research, scholarship, and education by publishing worldwide. Oxford is a registered trade mark of Oxford University Press in the UK and in certain other countries

British Library Cataloguing in Publication Data available

978-019-844541-8

11

Paper used in the production of this book is a natural, recyclable product made from wood grown in sustainable forests. The manufacturing process conforms to the environmental regulations of the country of origin.

Printed in Great Britain by CPI Group (UK) Ltd., Croydon CR0 4YY

Acknowledgements

The publishers would like to thank the following for permissions to use their photographs and extracts: https://trackit.teamknowhow.com/uk/deliver-and-install:

Cover: Nikada/iStockphoto; **p1, 2:** Tony Zelenoff/Shutterstock; **p15:** dpa picture alliance/Alamy Stock Photo; **p18:** JS Stone/Shutterstock; **p21:** Pixsooz/Alamy Stock Photo; **p25:** FXEGS Javier Espuny/Shutterstock; **p27:** Pixsooz/Alamy Stock Photo; **p31:** mertcan/Shutterstock; **p40:** PhotoTalk/iStockphoto; **p48:** Richard Levine/Alamy Stock Photo; **p65, 66:** michaeljung/Shutterstock; **p81:** Gwoeii/Shutterstock; **p84:** create jobs 51/Shutterstock; **p127:** michaeljung/Shutterstock; **p129:** Gareth Boden/OUP; **p132:** Noam Armonn/Shutterstock; **p153:** YASUYOSHI CHIBA/Getty Images; **p167:** © Lou Cypher/Corbis; **p173:** ndoeljindoel/Shutterstock; **p191:** PrinceOfLove/Shutterstock; **p204:** Fredrik Renander/Alamy Stock Photo; **p205:** michaeljung/Shutterstock; **p212:** cubephoto/Shutterstock; **p242:** Humpuugie/Shutterstock; **p249:** © Getty Images; **p257:** Semmick Photo/Shutterstock; **p291:** Buzz Pictures/Alamy Stock Photo; **p306:** Sue Smith/Shutterstock.

Artwork by QBS Media Services Inc

Every effort has been made to contact copyright holders of material reproduced in this book. Any omissions will be rectified in subsequent printings if notice is given to the publisher.

Links to third party websites are provided by Oxford in good faith and for information only. Oxford disclaims any responsibility for the materials contained in any third party website referenced in this work.

Contents

How to use this book

This book fully covers the syllabus for the OxfordAQA International AS Level Business course (9625). Experienced examiners and teachers have been involved in all aspects of the book, including detailed planning to ensure that the content adheres to the syllabus as closely as possible.

Using this book will ensure that you are well prepared for the assessment at this level, and gives a solid foundation for further study at university level and beyond. The features below are designed to make learning as interesting and effective as possible.

Activities

These are exercises to do which relate to the chapter content. They can be done in class or as part of individual study.

Progress questions

These are questions through the book to check that you understand the content as you learn. Answers are available in the back of the book.

Key terms

These are the most important vocabulary which students need to learn the definitions of. They are also compiled at the end of the book in a glossary.

Get it right

These are helpful tips and hints to give you the best chance of success.

Link

These are links to other parts of the book for students to find relevant information.

Case study

Subject

These are real-life examples to illustrate the subject matter in the chapters, and are accompanied by questions to test your understanding.

Exam-style questions

These questions are at the end of each chapter section. They use the same command words, structure and marks assignment as the OxfordAQA exams. Answers are available in the back of the book.

The questions, example answers, marks awarded and/or comments that appear in this book were written by the authors. In examinations, the way marks would be awarded to answers like these may be different.

At the end of the book, you will find a glossary of the key terms highlighted in bold in the text.

Business and markets

1 What is business?

This section will develop your knowledge and understanding of:

→ Key business terms and concepts

→ Why businesses exist

→ Entrepreneurs

→ Why business is important to an economy and society.

▲ **Figure 1.1.1**: Business is all around us: a bustling town in Zanzibar

Activities

1. Set up a folder for keeping cuttings from newspapers, advertisements and notes on what is going on in the business world around you. To begin with collect anything that seems interesting; later on you can be more selective.

2. Choose a well-known business in your country. Create a second folder in which to keep any information that you can find on that business. Keep the folder up to date.

Business activity is around us, everywhere. We pass shops on our way to school, we see lorries delivering products, we see advertisements on TV and in newspapers, and we see people going off to work.

All of these activities involve decision-making by owners, managers of businesses, customers and governments.

In this book, we will look at the decisions that need to be made, the factors that influence these decisions and how the decisions are made.

The best way to understand the contents of this book – and the subject – is to take a keen interest in the business world around you. The shops you pass, the people you know who work, and the products and services you buy can all tell you something about business behaviour. Newspapers and television programmes can be sources of ideas and understanding.

Unlike most other subjects, Business has two key features:

• Understanding can be found in the world around you.

• The subject is highly interdependent. This means, for example, that what you learn about finance can have an impact on marketing decisions and other areas of a business.

Key business terms and concepts

There are many terms and concepts that you will come across during your business course. You should understand the meanings of these terms.

When we eat a bar of chocolate we take many things for granted. We expect the shop to stock the chocolate and to accept our cash when we pay for it. We expect the chocolate to taste nice and be in a proper wrapper. We expect it to be sold at a price we can afford.

Case study

Sadie's new business

Sadie has worked in a printing business for a number of years. Although she enjoys her job and has developed many specialist printing skills, she really wants to work for herself. She is attracted by the idea of having the freedom to do what she wants and being her own boss. Sadie has some savings. She has seen a small printing business advertised for sale at a price she can afford. She believes she has the right contacts to get customers and the determination to make sure that their demands are met. She thinks she will be able to do this at a cheaper price than the business where she currently works, but she has not done her sums yet.

1. Why does Sadie want to set up her own business?
2. What potential problems might Sadie face in starting her business?
3. Why will careful planning be important for Sadie?

If we analyse the situation we can see the huge range of businesses that are involved in getting that bar of chocolate to us. These include:

- The farmer who grew the cocoa beans
- The farmer who grew the sugar
- The farmer who supplied the milk
- The businesses that supplied the other ingredients
- The transport companies and shipping agents involved in transporting the cocoa, sugar, milk and other ingredients to the factory; this may have involved lorries, ships and aeroplanes
- The insurance companies that insured the shipments
- The business that owns the chocolate factory
- The businesses that supplied the machinery to the chocolate factory
- The businesses that supplied other products and services to the chocolate factory, including telephones, gas, electricity, water, etc.
- The businesses that marketed the chocolate
- The television stations, magazines and newspapers that carried advertisements for the chocolate
- The wholesale businesses that supplied the shops
- The businesses that transported the chocolate to the shops
- The shop where we bought the chocolate
- The banks that provided finance and other services to all of the businesses mentioned above.

And all of this for one bar of chocolate!

Inputs and the transformation process

Any business that offers either **goods** or **services** would use a variety of **inputs** and resources to create their **outputs**. Businesses require, in broad terms, **capital** (finance or equipment); **land** (including resources); **labour** (the workforce); and **enterprise** (the individual with the determination, ideas and vision to make the business happen).

▲ **Figure 1.1.2:** The transformation process

Businesses aim to use these inputs and resources as efficiently as possible to produce the final product or service to be offered to the consumer. The example of a chocolate bar illustrates the **transformation process**, showing how inputs are transformed into outputs, and the many resources and businesses that are likely to be involved.

Key terms

Goods: items that you buy, such as food, books, toys, clothes and make-up.

Services: actions such as haircuts, parcel delivery, car repair and teaching.

Input: something that contributes to the production of a product or service.

Output: something that occurs as a result of the transformation of business inputs.

Capital: the finance needed to run a business as well as the equipment used in production, such as computers, factories, offices and vehicles.

Land: not just the land itself, but also all of the renewable and non-renewable natural resources on that land, such as coal, crude oil and timber.

Labour: the workforce of the business, made up of manual and skilled labour.

Enterprise: a person with enterprise has determination, ideas and vision and is willing to take risks in order to make the business happen.

Transformation process: the process of transforming "inputs" into "outputs".

Activity

See if you can think of any other businesses involved in getting the bar of chocolate to us!

So, what does a business do?

If you examine all of the examples above, the businesses carry out a wide range of tasks. However, one thing is common to all of them:

They all use resources of one sort or another to meet the needs and wants of customers.

These customers could be other businesses (the chocolate manufacturer buys cocoa from the farmer or wholesaler) or end customers (consumers) like you or me who actually eat (consume) the chocolate.

Businesses identify what their customers need and then set about meeting their customers' needs with the resources they have available.

> **Key term**
>
> Customer: the person/organisation that buys products or services. The final person/organisation in a chain is also known as the consumer.

Outputs: goods and services

Most of what happens involves businesses buying from other businesses. What the businesses buy includes, in this instance, raw materials (cocoa), finished products (bars of chocolate) and services (such as insurance and banking). Customers can buy from one business and then supply to another business, or they can come in at the last stage and buy the finished product.

To make the products or supply the services, businesses need resources. The resources available to a business need to be identified. Each of the businesses mentioned above need the following to function:

- **Goods and services**: The farmer needs fuel for the tractor, the chocolate factory needs cocoa to make the chocolate and the retailer (shop) needs chocolate bars to sell.
- **Machinery, equipment, land or premises**: The farmer needs a tractor and land, the chocolate manufacturer needs a factory and chocolate-making equipment, the shop needs premises, counters and displays.
- **People**: The farmer needs someone to drive the tractor, the factory needs people to work in the factory, the shop needs someone to serve you and, finally, the shop needs an end customer.
- **Enterprise**: The farm, the chocolate factory and the shop each need owners who take all the risks and make all the decisions.

Another essential item that each of these businesses need is money:

- To pay for the raw materials and other inputs such as wages
- To buy the necessary machinery, property and so on
- To make all of the risk-taking and decision-making worthwhile for the owner
- As a reward for all the work done.

Case study

Lee's restaurant

Lee owns a small restaurant. He has calculated that the food ingredients of a meal that is popular with customers cost him about $1.50. The price that the restaurant charges customers for the meal is $6. He thinks that the price is too low and should be a bit higher.

1   Why do you think that the price of the meal is $6 when the food ingredients cost only $1.50?

2   For what reasons do you think Lee might want to increase the price of the meal?

3   Review your answer to Question 1 when you have studied the concept of adding value (next page).

Progress questions

1 Give some examples of capital items in a farm growing melons.
2 What is the output from an office cleaning business?

Transformation – adding value

Continuing with the chocolate case study, the transformation from cocoa bean to chocolate bar involves many stages and many businesses, all helping to convert the cocoa bean into chocolate.

You might buy a bar of chocolate for $3 but you would not buy a cocoa bean for $3. Why not?

The bar of chocolate is something you would like to buy and you think is worth $3, but the cocoa bean has little value to you because you want chocolate.

However, if the farmer did not grow the cocoa bean you would not have the chocolate bar.

The simplified process is shown in Figure 1.1.3.

▲ Figure 1.1.3: Stages in producing a chocolate bar

Each stage of the process takes the product closer to what is required for the "end product", the product that the end customer wants: in this case, a bar of chocolate. This is known as adding value, because the work done at each stage adds value to the inputs of that stage, so at each stage the product is worth more. The value added is measured by comparing the value of the inputs to a good or service with the value of the good or service itself.

So, for example, the chocolate factory takes cocoa concentrate as an input which, together with other inputs, produces chocolate bars. The work done by the chocolate factory creates value. Created value/value added is measured by taking the value of the inputs to a process away from the value of the output.

Activities

1. Investigate three products you use every day. Describe the stages involved in getting these products to you, the consumer.
2. Identify the various stages in making a car. What value added is created at the retail stage?

Link

See section "Why businesses exist" for more on setting business objectives.

Key terms

Objectives: business objectives are the stated, measurable targets that provide the means to achieve business aims.

Strategy: a plan of action designed to achieve a long-term objective.

Tactic: a short-term course of action for the day-to-day management of a business or for trying to meet part of an overall strategy.

Profit: the difference between revenues and costs. Revenues and costs do not always happen at the same time as cash receipts and cash payments.

Profit is the money left after total costs are deducted from total income.

Progress questions

3. How does a transport business create value for a packet of tea?
4. How is "value added" measured?

Setting business objectives

A business should have objectives, something that its owners want to achieve. One objective might be to make money for its owners, but there may be other business objectives too. For example, an objective of a farmer running a chicken farm might be to double the number of chickens within three years and to sell eggs and chicken meat to customers in a wider geographical area.

Strategy and tactics

Setting objectives gives a business a sense of purpose and direction. However, these do not guarantee success. Objectives have to be developed into actual courses of action known as strategies and tactics.

A strategy is a plan setting out how a business as a whole will achieve its overall long-term objectives. A business objective of a car manufacturer could be: "To manufacture 5 million cars by 2020". The strategy could involve, for example:

- Building a new factory
- Increasing efficiency
- Improve productivity
- Designing new models of car.

Each of these could help the business achieve its objective of manufacturing 5 million cars by 2020.

A tactic is a short-term plan for the day-to-day operations of a business, with the aim of contributing towards the overall strategy. For example, in order to achieve productivity improvements the workforce might get prizes for the teams that make the biggest improvements to productivity.

Profit

Profit is what is left over for the owners of a business after its operating costs have been paid out of its revenues. Profit can be thought of as a reward for entrepreneurship. If revenues are not sufficient to cover operating costs, there is a loss, not a profit. It may seem strange, but there are different ways of measuring profit. However, a business cannot survive over the long term unless it can make a profit.

Case study

Stella's taxis

Stella runs a taxi business. She operates three taxis, with three drivers. During one month, the wages of the drivers were $3,000 in total, fuel costs were $2,000, and the costs of other items, such as repairs and maintenance for the taxis, office rental charge, phone and electricity charges, and so on, came to $2,500. Stella also takes the view that there should be a charge for the cost of the taxis themselves, which she has estimated at $1,000 per month. Revenues from taxi fares during the month were $11,000.

1   What would be the profit for the month if the total revenue from taxi fares is $11,000?

2   What would be the profit or loss if revenues are just $8,000?

Economic activity, the issue of choice and opportunity cost

Businesses can only survive and flourish if they meet customers' needs and wants. **Needs** are the products and services that are essential to our well-being whereas **wants** are those products and services that we desire but are not essential to us. A business should focus on how to meet customer needs and wants, but should know that it cannot meet every customer's needs or wants. A car manufacturer cannot possibly make cars for everyone in the world.

From the customer's perspective, the customer's own wants can never be fully met, either at an individual level or on a global level. There simply are not enough resources in the world for everyone to have a new car, a new yacht and a new iPhone. Not only are there insufficient resources to make everything that everyone wants, many people do not have the financial resources to buy what they need. Many poor people cannot afford the basic requirements of life: clean water, adequate food and shelter.

Because all our wants and needs cannot be met, we all have to make choices. We as customers have to prioritise what we buy, and businesses have to choose what products or services they will provide.

The process of businesses producing and customers buying is known as economic activity. The economic activity of a country is the process of suppliers (businesses) and customers (other businesses and end customers) interrelating to match needs and wants with available resources. In wealthy economies most needs and many wants can be met; in poorer economies the focus is likely to be on more basic needs and wants.

Link

Needs are covered in more detail in Chapter 2 Marketing.

The key point is that all participants in an economy have to make economic choices:

- Businesses have to make decisions about what they will make or what services they will provide. They also have to make choices about the inputs they will buy and use.
- Customers have to decide what products and services they will buy with their limited resources.
- Governments have to decide which services they will provide and what the role of government is in managing the economy.

In economic terms, choice is often an "either/or" decision: if I decide to buy the latest iPhone I will not have the money to buy a new pair of trainers; if I buy a new car I will have to go on a cheaper holiday; if a business decides on an expensive marketing campaign it may have to reduce spending elsewhere.

This aspect of choice introduces the concept of opportunity cost, an idea that you will meet throughout your study of Business. In making a decision, other opportunities have been foregone (given up). For example, if a government decides to build a new hospital rather than a new school, because it cannot afford to do both, it gains the benefit of improved healthcare but loses (foregoes) the benefit of better education facilities for some children. The benefit foregone from the next "best" alternative opportunity is known as the opportunity cost.

So, for example, if I spend money on an expensive meal rather than a new textbook, the opportunity cost is the lost benefit that I would have gained from the book. Of course, balanced against this I do have the benefit of enjoying an expensive meal! The opportunity cost of the government spending money on pensions may be that there is less to spend on defence. The opportunity cost of a business deciding to build a new factory is the income that would have been generated had the money spent on the factory been put to some other productive use.

> **Key term**
>
> Opportunity cost: the value of the next best opportunity that is lost by taking a particular decision.

> **Get it right**
>
> It is often useful to think what the opportunity cost of a particular decision is. But remember, opportunity cost is a concept rather than an actual cost incurred.

> **Progress questions**
>
> 5   Define opportunity cost.
> 6   Identify a decision you have made recently. What was its opportunity cost?

Efficiency

Business operations' efficiency measures the amount of resources that production uses relative to its output. A business will be more efficient if it uses fewer resources to produce a given output and this will also reduce costs.

Competitiveness

Most businesses operate in a competitive environment, where rival businesses sell similar products or services to the same target customers. The most successful businesses – those making the most

> **Key term**
>
> Efficiency: measures the amount of resources that production uses. Lower resource use for a given output is more efficient and less costly.

Case study

Angelo's shirts

Angelo has a business making and selling shirts at a shop in a city where there are a large number of shirt makers and there is keen rivalry between them. Most customers are tourists visiting the city.

1 In what ways might Angelo's business be competitive in the market for shirts in the city?

sales and earning the biggest profits – will be those that are the most competitive. A business can be competitive by operating at lower costs and selling products or services at lower prices. Alternatively, a business can compete in a different way, by offering a product or service that appeals to customers in a particular way, perhaps because of its quality or design, or the speed of service, or the location of the business, or convenience for the customer.

Businesses that are not competitive will struggle to sell their products.

Risk

We all take risks in life and it is just the same in business. Every day people take a risk when leaving their homes to go to work or school. When parents send their children off to school they are also taking a risk, expecting the school will educate them well and keep them safe. We all accept a certain level of risk; if not we would not set off to work or go about our daily business. It is the same with businesses. When an individual or group decide to start a new business, they are taking a risk that they will succeed. They will try to minimise that risk by doing research about their potential market and how acceptable their product/service will be to that market. They will research all of the costs involved and the expected price that they would need to charge, as well as the price that customers would be willing to pay. They will find out as much as they can about their possible competitors. They will decide whether or not they wish to concentrate on a specific part of the market.

An established business also takes risks when it decides to introduce a new product: will it be accepted by their current customers. If a business decides to move to another location, there is a risk that some stakeholders will object and will cause conflict.

Taking some financial decisions creates an element of risk. For example, if a business owner decides to increase the price of their product/service there is a risk that customers will reduce the amount they buy or will switch to another business.

The ways in which businesses deal with risk will appear in many places in this book.

Decision-making

A decision means that a choice has to be made, and when a choice is made, there is a risk. The risk is that the choice that is made may, in retrospect, prove to have been the wrong one, or not the best one

Key term

Risk: a situation involving exposure to danger, harm or loss.

that could have been taken. When a decision to do something (or not do something) is taken by a business, it is making a choice between two or more possible options. Unless the choice is obvious, there will be some uncertainty about which option is the best one to take. This is because, for each option, there might be different possible outcomes.

Constructing a simple decision tree

Decisions, and the possible consequences of decisions, can be illustrated in diagram form. Such a diagram takes a systematic approach to decision-making and is referred to as a **decision tree**. Drawn from left to right or from top to bottom, a decision tree uses probability and predicted outcomes in profits or sales to show the decision options and the possible outcomes from each of them. This technique can make it easier to understand the possible consequences of a decision because the options and possible outcomes are shown visually, rather than in lengthy text. Figure 1.1.4 shows an example of the structure of a decision tree. In this example, a factory is about to undergo a health and safety inspection by government officials, and if the factory fails the test it will be forced to close down. The management of the factory face a choice between spending money before the inspection to improve conditions in the factory, or to do nothing. Study the decision tree, and see whether you can follow its structure and logic. Estimates of the probability of each outcome can be added, to make the decision options more clear.

> **Key term**
>
> **Decision tree**: a quantitative technique that can be used to distinguish the likely outcomes of different decisions.

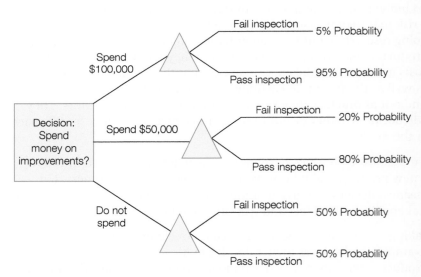

▲ **Figure 1.1.4**: The structure of a decision tree

Progress question

7   Draw a decision tree for the following situation.

The owner of a new retail shop in a town centre is deciding whether the shop should open five, six or seven days a week. If the shop opens for seven days a week, there is a 70% probability that weekly sales will be $80,000 and a 30% probability that sales will be $60,000. If the shop opens for six days a week, there is an 80% probability that weekly sales will be $72,000 and a 20% probability that sales will be $55,000. If the shop opens for five days a week, there is a 90% probability that weekly sales will be $60,000 and a 10% probability that sales will be $45,000. The costs of operating the shop would be $16,000 per week if it opens on seven days, $14,000 if it opens on six days and $12,000 if it opens on five days.

Ethical influences on decisions

Ethics are a moral code that guide the actions of businesses and people. This can relate to the way in which the owners and managers of a business treat their employees, or the materials they choose to use in their business. For example, a business that knowingly uses a substance that is harmful to the environment knowing that there is a less harmful alternative could be viewed as being unethical. However, it might be that the less harmful substance is unavailable in their country and that the business would be happy to change if it was available. Ethics are linked to social responsibility and the importance of these concepts has grown considerably in recent years as consumers are now becoming more aware of the businesses that are judged to be unethical in their practices. Some unethical businesses will be avoided by many consumers and by other businesses. Being ethical is increasingly being used as a marketing tool to increase the public image of a business, with the overall intention being to increase sales and profit. Governments might also look more favourably on businesses wanting to locate in their country if they are sure that their activities would be based on ethical decisions.

Owners and managers

The owners of a business are the people (or organisations) that are entitled to the profits that the business makes. The managers of a business are individuals who are in charge of the business operations and who make decisions about what the business should do. Managers are often employees of the business, receiving a salary for the work they do. In many businesses, especially small businesses, the business owner is also its senior manager.

Business functions

When a business grows above a certain size, it is usual for its operations to be divided into specialist areas. For example, in a manufacturing company, operations may be divided into manufacturing activities, sales and marketing activities, and office administration. The different areas of activity within a business are referred to as functions of the business or business functions.

Key terms

Owners of a business: the people who are entitled to the profits that the business makes.

Managers of a business: the people in charge of the business operations.

Business functions: the different areas of activity within a business.

The role of managers

The role of managers in a business is to provide leadership. They decide what the business should be doing and they monitor progress to check that actual results are in line with what is expected. Managers make plans about what should be done and organise work; they communicate the plans to the people involved in putting them into practice and co-ordinate their efforts; and they monitor actual performance and take control measures when this is not as good as it should be. Managers are sometime called 'the bosses' of an organisation, but in a large organisation there can be many levels of management, from the person at the top (who may be called a chief executive officer or CEO) down to junior managers.

Business plans

A business plan is a document that sets out in practical terms what a business is about. It will contain objectives, strategic and tactical plans, information about the market and financial forecasts. It is like a roadmap, setting out the way forward to reach objectives. Unlike strategic management plans that are designed to be used internally, the business plan has an external audience. The business will use this plan to obtain backing and finance when starting up or when changing its operations, for example, expanding, or entering new markets. The audience for a business plan will include banks, suppliers of venture capital, grant awarders, and potential purchasers or business partners. These people will be very interested in how the business is intended to develop, the timescale and how finance will be handled. Their focus is on whether money invested in the business will be returned and/or what level of return, or profit, is likely. A business plan can be any length, from the back of an envelope to a 100-page document. Most are several pages long.

The elements of a business plan

There is no set layout or wording for a business plan, though banks and government provide forms which give specific guidance. However it is set out, a plan should contain these elements, even if different headings are used.

Executive summary or basic information: This is short and contains the business name, a brief history, the legal structure, the product or service being sold, the resources needed and where these will come from, and a quick statement about hopes for the future. It will contain a brief statement of the purpose and the objectives of the business.

Product or service: A detailed outline of what will be sold and what market it will be placed in. The focus should be on how the product/service meets a market need and how this is different from any competition. It might include any patents, copyrights or trademarks.

Market analysis: An account of the market that might include details of the size, the competition, the target customer, market trends and future developments. Some indication of market research might be present.

Marketing plan: This is often an account of the marketing mix the business will use. This will tell interested people where the product/

Key term

Business plan: a document setting out the objectives of a business and exactly how the business intends to achieve them in practical terms. It contains objectives, strategic and tactical plans, market information and budgets.

service will be positioned in the market. It will include detail about the price, the promotion methods to be used, the way the product/service will be distributed to the target customer and what selling methods will be used. This section will focus on how the business will meet the needs of its customers.

Production plan: This section will tell readers how the product/service will be produced. It will include any patents held, the premises and equipment needed, details of suppliers and how quality will be maintained.

Organisational plan: This section deals with the people in the business. It might include names, abilities and experience. It will show how people will be organised and managed and include training arrangements. There might be an organisation structure diagram.

Financial plan: The key part of this section will be a monthly cash flow forecast for one to two years, using information drawn from all the other areas of the plan. There will also be a profit and loss forecast. This will enable the financing needs to be clearly identified.

Conclusion: This will summarise all the above and give some idea of the longer-term plan for the business.

The value of business plans

Business plans have a value for all kinds of business, whether large or small, established or about to start. For all types of business, a plan will set out the detail needed to implement strategic choices because it contains a detailed listing of how the resources of the business must be organised in order to meet objectives.

A business plan is particularly valuable for businesses starting up as it provides a focus for all the activities needed to operate and makes a business consider all the details involved, especially as the plan is often used to get finance from hard-headed banks or venture capitalists who need to be convinced that the business is financially sound.

For established larger businesses, a business plan is valuable for setting out how to implement a new project, including obtaining finance. This will also apply to a change of direction. Larger or well-established businesses have a tendency to just carry on with the same procedures year after year, so a business plan will make sure that the business reviews what it is doing at regular intervals.

A business plan may apply to the whole business or part of it.

A business plan should enable a business to:

- Successfully apply for a loan, a grant or other finance as the plan clearly sets out how the money will be used and repaid.
- Examine the business idea and future prospects in detail and in realistic practical terms. This will highlight any potential problems and make it difficult for managers to dismiss threats.
- Fully examine whether a particular idea is commercially viable. The research required for the plan will discover whether the market will be suitable for the product or whether the proposed investment in equipment will really generate enough cost savings.

Get it right

A good business plan answers four simple questions:

1 Why does your business exist? (Purpose or mission statement)
2 Where do you want to take it? (Objectives)
3 How will it get there? (Strategy)
4 What will it cost? (Budget)

- Have a sense of direction matched by a practical plan. This will give focus and enable problems to be identified early and action taken to overcome these.
- Determine whether the business has enough internal resources (money, expertise, equipment) for what is planned.
- Continually review progress in the areas set out in the plan. This is a working document so can be updated and changed as you use it. However, there is a cost to a business plan. It takes time and involves forecasts that may turn out to be inaccurate. It might be very difficult to be precise about future developments. The plan may be rigid and inflexible and employees may follow it even though conditions have changed. A business may come to rely on the plan rather than communicate with suppliers, customers and staff.

Progress questions

8 Outline the elements of a business plan.

9 Explain three advantages of a business plan for:

a A new business about to start up

b A well-established large business.

Case study

At Home Store

Ria and Tom Thenin had always wanted to run a business. An opportunity arose when a long-established furniture store went bankrupt. They were able to obtain the lease on the store building but they had to start with no furniture to sell. In order to start up they had to borrow some money from a bank. The bank required a business plan. The Thenins saw this as being a waste of time; after all they had a business to get going. It was only when they were writing it that they realised the process had made them think of all sorts of things they would have ignored.

"We thought the business plan was for the benefit of the bank and was paperwork we had to do to get the loan. However, it made us think about what we really wanted from the business and exactly how we were going to manage money, advertising and employing staff in the store. It made us research the market in our town and it showed us that people had more money for furniture and home products than we thought. This influenced our whole approach to what we sold. It even made us focus on the name for the business. Having a longer-term view meant we called it At Home, rather than just restricting the name to furniture.

"The business plan set out all the things we wanted to achieve – our objectives – and made us think not only about the next month but into the future. We stuck to it in the first year and kept referring to it. Things had gone so well we decided to continue with the plan and rewrote it for the second year and we still do this every year.

"This is one of the reasons we have started a household consultancy business, which runs alongside the store. We advise customers on how to make their houses attractive, and arrange for painters, builders and joiners to do the work. We are able to supply furniture and a whole range of electrical products as well. We wrote another business plan for this expansion and are on track to reach the objectives we set. The bank loan is nearly paid back and we are looking for new ventures. A business plan is a must for us."

1 Explain why the Thenins felt making a business plan was not a good use of their time.

2 Analyse the reasons why they came to see the benefits of drawing up business plan.

3 Discuss why they are continuing with business planning.

Key performance indicators

Business managers can monitor whether business plans are successful and whether the business is achieving its objectives and targets. They do this by measuring business performance. Some measure of performance, known as **key performance indicators** or KPIs, is considered by management to be an important guide as to how well (or badly) the business is doing. Examples of KPIs might be the rate of growth in annual sales or profits, productivity (such as the amount of production output per hour) or levels of environmental pollution from the manufacturing operations of the business.

Why businesses exist

Some businesses are created to fulfil a desire by an individual or group of individuals to provide a product or service that they believe customers will demand. The aim of the businesses will be to provide the goods and services demanded by **consumers**, hopefully in a way that yields a profit for the business. The **customers** of a business can be the final consumer (members of the public like you and me) or they can be other businesses. Some businesses produce for both markets. For example, a chair can be produced for use in the home of the final consumer or it could be a chair specifically produced for use in the offices of a business. In this case, we have examples of business-to-consumer and business-to-business transactions.

One of the main reasons for businesses to exist is to make a profit on their activities, but as we will see later there are other objectives that are pursued by businesses. Not all businesses aim for profit. Some exist to provide an essential good or service and will reinvest any profit into the business or into the society they serve.

Key terms

Key performance indicators (KPIs): measures of business performance that are considered by management to be an important guide as to how well the company is doing.

Consumers: people who buy goods or services for personal use or personal consumption.

Customers: people or organisations that buy goods or services.

Case study

Volkswagen

Volkswagen is one of the world's largest car manufacturers. It has stated that it aims to be "the most successful and sustainable automaker in the world".

Like all other car manufacturers, Volkswagen has been affected by important technological advances in the industry, and the development of electric cars, increasingly powerful batteries for electric cars and "autonomous driving technology" (self-drive cars).

Volkswagen responded to these changes by announcing a change of strategy in 2016, with a new set of business objectives for achievement by 2025, relating to electric cars and self-drive cars.

▲ **Figure 1.1.5:** Self-drive cars

1   What do you think the business objectives of Volkswagen might be with regard to electric cars and self-drive cars?

2   What KPIs might it use to measure its progress towards achievement of these objectives?

3   How might Volkswagen seek to maintain its competitiveness and leading position in the car industry, in the face of competition from rivals such as Toyota?

Why businesses set objectives

Whatever we do in life it always helps to have something to aim for. If, for example, we aim to improve our performance in our examinations we stand a better chance of achieving a higher grade. Businesses have aims too. A business's aim is where the business wants to go in the future; it is a statement of purpose. Setting these aims enables companies to develop strategies to achieve those aims, improving the chances of success.

Business owners and managers need to have a clear sense of purpose to help them focus on what needs to be achieved. This will help to direct and control business activity and to make decisions.

Examples of private-sector business aims could be:

- To be the largest car manufacturer in Asia
- To be the best-known brand name
- To lead the world in technology.

Examples of public-sector aims could be:

- To provide the best health service in the world
- To provide an unbiased TV and radio service
- To provide everyone with a reliable and healthy water supply.

On their own these aims give a business a sense of purpose, but there also needs to be some idea as to how these broad statements of direction can be translated into actual courses of action that might achieve the aims. This is where business objectives have a role. Objectives use measurable targets as a way to achieve aims. Benefits of objectives include:

- A sense of direction
- Focus for individuals and departments
- Framework for decision-making
- Motivation tool at an individual level and for teamwork
- A means of assessing progress and performance.

Common business objectives

Objectives provide the means to translate aims into achievable targets. Table 1.1.1 illustrates the difference between aims and objectives.

▼ **Table 1.1.1:** Aims and objectives

Aim	Possible objective
To be the largest car maker in Asia	To manufacture 5 million cars by 2025
To be the best-known brand name	To have a brand recognised by 20% of the population by 2022
To lead the world in car technology	To have the most fuel-efficient car by 2025

Experience and common sense tell us that:

> **The better the objective, the better the outcome.**

That is why the concept of SMART objectives has been developed. Experience has shown that SMART objectives achieve good results. The aims and objectives in Table 1.1.1 are all at the corporate level (in other words, they apply to the organisation as whole). Objectives can apply to any level of a business or organisation. These can be developed from the overall corporate objective (see Figure 1.1.7).

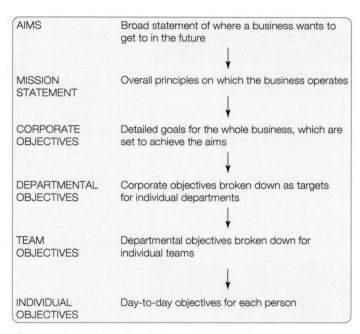

Specific	Objectives should focus on the business and its aims and be easily understood
Measurable	It should be possible to measure if and when objectives have been achieved
Achievable	There is no point setting objectives that cannot be achieved. Unachievable objectives are likely to have a negative rather than positive impact
Realistic/ Relevant	Objectives should be useful in their context to the overall achievement of an aim
Time specific	Objectives should have a time frame within which they should have been achieved

▲ **Figure 1.1.6**: SMART objectives

AIMS	Broad statement of where a business wants to get to in the future
MISSION STATEMENT	Overall principles on which the business operates
CORPORATE OBJECTIVES	Detailed goals for the whole business, which are set to achieve the aims
DEPARTMENTAL OBJECTIVES	Corporate objectives broken down as targets for individual departments
TEAM OBJECTIVES	Departmental objectives broken down for individual teams
INDIVIDUAL OBJECTIVES	Day-to-day objectives for each person

▲ **Figure 1.1.7**: Developing business objectives

Typical business objectives relate to the concepts of:

- **Profit:** Businesses need to make profits. It might be said that commercial companies are in the business of making profits. Profits are needed to reward the business owners; and unless they can make profits, commercial businesses are unlikely to survive.
- **Growth:** Many businesses measure their success by the rate of growth they achieve – typically the rate of growth in their sales revenues and profits.
- **Survival:** Some businesses may struggle, and suffer from falling sales and profits (or even losses). In this situation, their main objective might simply be survival, and this could involve reducing the scale of its operations. For example, a loss-making chain of retail stores might seek to survive by closing down some of its unprofitable stores.
- **Cash flow:** It might seem strange, but when a business makes a profit, it does not necessarily add to its cash. A profitable business might even be spending more cash on its operations than it is receiving from sales. One reason for this is that customers do not always pay for goods or services when they receive them, and payment is delayed. Another reason is that businesses have to spend money first, on materials and wages for employees, before

Get it right

Do not spend time *explaining* the SMART principles – show that you understand the principles by *using* the ideas. The identification of SMART objectives can sometimes help you demonstrate evaluation skills – if you can assess the extent to which a recommendation will meet objectives then that is evaluation in itself.

Activities

1 Think of an overall objective for your school/college.
2 What objective might you set for the Business department to achieve that overall objective?
3 Think of a suitable objective for your Business teacher.

they can make sales. A business objective, separate from the objective of making a profit, might therefore be to have a positive operational cash flow, receiving more from its sales than it spends on input resources.

- **Personal objectives:** People who work for a business will have their own personal objectives from the work they do, for example to earn a reasonable income or to get enjoyment from the work they do. Occasionally, a business owner may set personal objectives for the business. For example, the US business tycoons Elon Musk and Jeff Bezos both have a personal objective of developing space rockets for commercial travel in space, and have companies for which this is the prime business objective.

- **Social objectives:** Companies sometimes have objectives aimed at benefiting society, as well as making a profit. One major international company whose products include soaps and cleaning products has an objective of developing cleaning products that use less water, which will benefit societies in countries where water is in short supply.

- **Ethical objectives:** Businesses may also have ethical objectives, such as an aim to be a good employer, providing good wages and working conditions for all its employees.

Entrepreneurs

Motivation to set up a business

Some businesses are set up because a person or group of people believes that they can provide a product or service that customers will want. It might be that they have developed a totally new product that consumers are not even aware of yet. It might be that they have seen a gap in the market that is being ignored by existing businesses. There can occasionally be part of the market that large businesses do not consider to be worthwhile and therefore this provides an opportunity to a smaller business to satisfy that segment of the market. Sometimes a person who has lost their job decides that they will be in control of their own working life in the future and so they start up a business rather than get a job working for someone else.

▲ **Figure 1.1.8:** Bill Gates founded Microsoft in 1975, which went on to become the biggest PC software company in the world

What might motivate people to set up a business?

- To fill a gap in the market that is not currently served.
- To develop a new product or service.
- To be in control of their own working life.
- To benefit from the profits of a business.
- To meet a social need.
- To achieve a desire to be self-employed and to be in control of the business activities.

Many of the difficulties faced by new businesses and entrepreneurs are also the reasons why a lot of new businesses fail. This can vary from not having sufficient business skills and knowledge to a misjudged demand for the product or service.

Characteristics of an entrepreneur

All businesses started with an idea and, usually, with one person or a small number of people prepared to put the effort in to get the business started. These people are known as entrepreneurs, and they have shown the skills of entrepreneurship, which include:

- Having an original idea
- Developing the idea into a feasible business proposition
- Providing finance using their own savings and capital and/or, possibly, persuading others to do so
- Accepting the responsibility of owning the business
- Recognising the risks involved including the possible risk of failure
- Taking the risk.

TV stations around the world have TV programmes that put new entrepreneurs to the test, including *Dragons' Den* (which is called *Tu Oportunidad* in Spain, *Money Tigers* in Japan, *Leijonan luola* in Finland) and *The Apprentice* (known as *The Apprentice Africa*, *The Apprentice Asia*, *Big Boss* in Germany and *O Aprendiz* in Brazil), which are broadcast widely around the world in various forms. These provide an excellent insight into the business decision-making processes and the skills needed to succeed in business. These skills include:

- **Innovation:** the ability to come up with new ideas, and to see their potential value
- **Persistence:** the ability to keep trying even when there are problems and a project looks as if it might fail
- **Leadership:** taking decisions and persuading others of their merit
- **Assessing and taking risks:** most businesses start up with uncertainties so there is always a degree of risk involved.

Identifying a business opportunity

There are many ways in which new business opportunities are identified:

- Sometimes the business opportunity develops out of the work that the entrepreneur has been doing as an employee for someone else. He/she believes that they can prosper by setting up in business and providing the product or service better.

Case study

Sir Richard Branson

Some successful entrepreneurs gain notoriety within their country, and sometimes internationally, for the successes they have achieved in business. In the UK, Sir Richard Branson is well known for establishing a number of businesses over the years under the Virgin brand name, such as Virgin Music, Virgin Airways, Virgin Media and Virgin Money. Like other well-known entrepreneurs, stories about his success have emerged over the years and have remained in the public consciousness. As just one example, Branson developed a series of compilation music albums called *Now That's What I Call Music*, beginning with the first edition in 1983 and achieving its 100th edition in 2018.

1 Are you aware of any similar business tycoon in your own country?

2 What do you think has made this individual successful in business?

- Alternatively, sometimes the new business idea is developed from a hobby or passion that the person has. For example, a person who has always enjoyed designing and making clothes might decide to begin a business that produces garments that are individually designed for each customer.

- A gap in the market is identified. Perhaps a small segment of a market that is not currently served.

- The entrepreneur is a user of a product/service that they believe can be improved.

- They spot a need for a product/service that no one else provides. For example, a few years ago Mark Zuckerberg saw a use for a means of social communication; initially implemented on a small scale, Facebook is now used globally.

- They look for changes in lifestyle or attitudes that might lead to a new business idea. The increase in travel and a desire for a cheaper alternative to hotels lead to Airbnb being founded in 2008 by Joe Gebbia, Brian Chesky and Nathan Blecharczyk and only nine years later it is a global business. Based on the simple idea that people could earn some money by renting out their home or a room to visitors and meet the accommodation needs of travellers.

Difficulties of being an entrepreneur and starting up a business

Looking at successful entrepreneurs might make it appear as though starting a new business is easy to do. Some entrepreneurs are fortunate and do not experience many difficulties when starting out on their new venture. However, for the majority there are many difficulties to be overcome:

- Having sufficient finance to be able to put the idea into practice. Many good ideas are never pursued due to a lack of finance. Some entrepreneurs are refused finance many times before finally finding someone willing to help to finance their venture.

- Convincing people that your idea is a good one. This links to the finance issue above.

- If the idea is very innovative it can sometimes be difficult to find employees with the appropriate experience or skills.

- Customers need convincing that they need this product or service. An innovative product might be rejected by many people at first. Not all people are willing to try new things.

- Frequently, the first business idea fails, therefore the entrepreneur might have to rethink what they are offering.

How the business environment in a country influences the success of entrepreneurs and start-ups

The business environment can determine the potential of an entrepreneur or business start-up to succeed in many ways. The business environment means all of the internal and external factors that affect how the company functions. This includes employees, customers, managers, supply and demand, and regulations.

Key term

Start-up: a newly established business.

Success can depend on:

- The level of economic development in the country. If the country relies on natural resources to provide for basic needs, such as through hunting, gathering and agriculture (called a subsistence-based economy), there are fewer opportunities for new businesses to survive.

- The purchasing power of the population. If the majority of the population are on low incomes this reduces the possibility of selling new products/services to them.

- The attitude or willingness of banks or other financial institutions to provide finance. There are times when banks are confident in the state of the economy and are then more likely to lend to new businesses.

- The availability of appropriate raw materials and labour.

- Whether the economy of the country is experiencing a period of fast growth with higher demand for goods and services and increasing employment (called a boom) or a period of negative growth and decrease in employment, income and profit (called a recession). It is much harder for an entrepreneur to start a new business or launch a new product/service when a country is in recession. The population usually have less certainty about their earning potential and therefore their purchasing power.

- The government attitude to businesses. Are they supportive and willing to help new business?

▲ **Figure 1.1.9**: Some entrepreneurs are fortunate and do not have many difficulties when starting their new business

Why and how governments might support entrepreneurs and business start-ups

Why

- To create work for the population. This has a double benefit because as people start to earn an income they will pay tax to the government, meaning that not only does an individual have more money to spend but so does the government. The extra money allows individuals to enjoy a higher standard of living and as they demand more goods, the need for more people to be employed to provide those goods might also increase. This then also avoids the need to support those who are unemployed.

- To gain tax revenue. The extra tax revenue gained by the government can be used to provide better infrastructure (roads and communications), better education facilities and healthcare.

- To develop skills within their economy and to use these employees' skills to attract new businesses to the country.

How

- By giving loans to the business. Often, governments offer a lower rate of interest than a bank loaning the same amount. Also, governments will often provide loans to new businesses that banks might not be prepared to lend to.

- Making grants and subsidies available to new and existing businesses. These help to reduce the costs of a business and are much cheaper than a bank loan. Grants do not need to be repaid; subsidies might be in the form of lower business rates or reduced taxes in the early years of the business.

- Providing an initial period of low tax payments. In some cases, if the business is required to pay a local business tax for the premises, this can be deferred for the first year or two to allow the business to become financially more stable before adding an extra financial burden.

- Helping and supporting with business knowledge. Often a person starts up a business because they have a particular skill but they do not always have the business knowledge that is required to run a successful business. For example, they might be an excellent engineer but not have any accounting skills and therefore would need help to ensure that they are able to keep accurate financial records.

- Making land available for business development. This also helps local authorities who want to attract businesses to set up in their area. Some governments will allocate certain areas within their country where they want to attract business activity.

- Providing training schemes to help to develop the skills of potential employees. This type of help often encourages businesses to start up in areas where that extra support is available because this reduces the costs of training to the business.

Case study

Jumpstart Our Business Startups (JOBS) Act

The United States Federal Government has introduced laws to help new businesses to start up and to make finance more readily available to small businesses to help them grow more rapidly. Banks tend to prefer lending money to large, well-established businesses rather than small, new businesses. The government argues that small businesses are essential to the US economy and necessary to reduce unemployment in the country. Before the laws it was too difficult for small businesses to raise finance through the sale of shares.

These laws will:

- Increase the number of shareholders a company may have before full regulation by the stock exchange

- Allow greater advertising of the sale of shares for small businesses

- Make it easier for small businesses to offer new shares

- Make it easier for very small investments to be made in share purchases.

1 Why would banks prefer to lend to large, well-established businesses?

2 How could the new laws help reduce unemployment in the US?

3 Why would small businesses find it difficult to grow if they cannot raise finance through the sale of shares?

4 If your business exported electronic components to the US, how might you react to the announcement of these laws?

Factors influencing the number and type of start-ups in an economy

The state of the economy: boom or recession?

- During a boom period in an economy, consumer confidence tends to be high, which can also boost the confidence of someone who wants to start their own business. During a boom period, spending levels also tend to be higher, reassuring the new business owner that the goods or service being offered will be purchased. A highly confident and high-spending economy cannot guarantee the success of a new business though. Sufficient and accurate market research must also be carried out. The product or service needs to be one that the consumers want.

- A period of economic recession might deter a start-up due to expected lower levels of consumer confidence and lower levels of spending. However, if the product being offered is a necessity, is suitably priced and is aimed at the correct target market, then such a business might succeed despite the recession.

- When unemployment levels are high, people who are made redundant might feel there is little hope of finding another job and consider setting up their own business. It is not unusual for those with a skill, such as a plumber or electrician, to decide to start up their own business.

- A strong economy and high employment levels might also encourage new businesses to start up due to the level of confidence and spending in the economy.

Competition

- A high number of competitors in a market might deter start-ups. However, this might depend on whether or not the new product or service is offering something different from the existing businesses. If it is, then the new business might be able to succeed even in the presence of a large number of established businesses.

- The market power of existing businesses might prevent a new business from competing for consumers. A powerful, established business might be able to take steps to prevent a new business from gaining consumers. For example, the established business might undertake an aggressive marketing campaign or might reduce the price of its products below the price of the new business's products. Fear of this type of action might discourage start-ups.

Perceived gaps in the market

- Even with the threats outlined above, a new business might be aiming to fill a gap in the market. Perhaps there is a segment of the market that the larger businesses have not targeted. This presents an opportunity to a new business if they can successfully target their product or service at that specific market segment.

Ease of access to finance

- Banks are not always willing to lend money to businesses. In the UK, following the banking crisis of 2008, many new businesses have found it more difficult to obtain a bank loan to help finance their business start-up.

- It might be that the person wanting to start a business does not have savings or any collateral that they can offer as security for a loan.

- Loans may be available, but there are times when the rate of interest to be paid in return for the borrowed money is too high. High rates of interest increase the loan repayments and may mean the business idea is no longer feasible.

Government policy

Governments will often encourage start-ups in the hope that they will create more employment opportunities. The existence of government assistance might be a key factor in deciding whether or not to start a new business.

The encouragement might be in the form of help and advice on many of the issues involved in starting and managing a business. This is often provided free of charge – if the business is successful, jobs might be created and the government will then benefit from tax receipts from the business and its employees. In turn, the new business gains expertise that they might have lacked.

There are many factors that might influence the number of business start-ups, involving some or all of the factors outlined above. Equally, the type of business may also be influenced. For example, if finance is readily available and the business idea is unique, then the scale of the new business could be increased accordingly.

Why many start-ups fail

Later chapters discuss in detail the various issues in managing businesses. However, it is useful to give a broad idea of why many business ideas do not develop into flourishing concerns.

Many start-ups fail, often in their first year of operation. Some of the reasons may be within the business's control; other reasons may be beyond its control.

Some examples of problems that could contribute to failure and that are within the control of the business include:

- Weak business idea
- Lack of managerial skills
- Lack of suitable employees
- Lack of sufficient finance
- Lack of entrepreneurial skills
- Poor initial research
- Over-ambitious ideas
- Poor decisions.

Some examples of problems outside the control of the business include:

- Anticipated customers do not materialise
- Changes in the business environment affect customers
- Unexpected competition, or changes in the competitors' behaviour.

These are only typical suggestions at this stage. As you go through your Business course there will be many opportunities to reflect on the reasons why some businesses succeed while many others fail early on.

Why business is important to an economy and society

The impact of business on stakeholders

Traditionally, corporate business decisions have been made with the reaction only of the owners of the business at the front of the minds of those making the decisions. Gradually, the idea has developed that it is important to recognise that:

- It is not only the owners/shareholders who could be affected by a decision

Activity

Identify a business that has failed in your country. Find out what the main causes were. Were they internal or external?

- Others connected with a business in some way or other will be affected
- The views of other interested groups are important inputs into major business decisions.

Any individual or group of individuals that has an interest in the outcome of a business's decisions is known as a stakeholder.

Stakeholder groups involved in a business

Figure 1.1.9 shows the different stakeholders in a business and Table 1.1.2 shows the different types of stakeholders and their roles.

▼ Table 1.1.2: Stakeholders and their roles

Stakeholder	Role
Customers	Buy products/services, use after-sales services
Employees	Provide labour services to the business
The community	Provides local services, workforce, infrastructure
The government	Possible support/advice/grants, impose taxes (local/national, etc.), makes laws, regulations
Suppliers	Provide products and services, often on credit

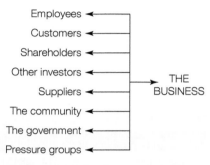

▲ Figure 1.1.9: Business stakeholders

Impact of decisions/actions on stakeholders and their reactions

Some decisions will affect many stakeholders, others will affect few. Some decisions will have an enormous impact, others a small impact. It is important to consider a decision and think through its likely consequences. For example, let us suppose a chain of coffee shops decides on a new marketing campaign:

- The immediate impact is likely to be more work for the employees in the marketing department as they put the campaign together.

Case study

Condor Copper

Condor Copper (CC) is considering opening a new copper mine in a part of your country that has high unemployment. The project will involve building new roads as well as housing for the new workforce. Building the mine and roads will be dirty and involve moving large amounts of soil and rock. There will be a lot of disruption for the town in the first two years of construction. After that there should be large profits to be made and the area will benefit from new infrastructure. CC plans to get grants from the government to help towards the construction costs.

1   Identify three stakeholders in CC.
2   Explain their interest in the copper mine project.
3   What role might each stakeholder have in the decision-making process?

▲ Figure 1.1.10: Mining can impact on the wider community

Link

See section 1.2 Types of business ownership for more on shareholders.

- This will probably mean more contracts for external suppliers of services such as advertising agencies.
- Once the campaign has been prepared, media companies could be involved through TV, newspaper and magazine advertisements.
- Eventually there will be an impact on customers, who, hopefully, will be persuaded to visit the coffee shops. This would have an impact on competitors who may in turn try to attract customers away from the business.
- It will probably take some time before the marketing campaign has an impact on the business's profits (and hence shareholders) and the wider operations of the business (and hence employees).

Table 1.1.3 illustrates the various ways that each of the stakeholder groups might be influenced by different business decisions.

▼ **Table 1.1.3:** Some ways a business might influence stakeholders

Stakeholder	Possible impact
Shareholders	• Change in levels of profits and dividends. *An increase may lead to a higher share price.* • Improved/decreased business prospects affecting share price. *A decreased share price may lead to investors selling.* • Bad/good publicity that affects share price. *Bad publicity is likely to reduce interest from shareholders and potential investors.*
Employees	• Changes in operations that can lead to possible redundancies. *Employees will not like redundancies.* • Changes of working practices that can affect jobs. *Employees will want to be consulted about changes.* • Developments that can lead to new job opportunities. *Employees may be pleased.* • Training schemes introduced by the business. *Employees may like the opportunity for more training.*
Customers	• The development of new products/services. *This might attract customers or increase sales to existing customers.* • New marketing initiatives. *This might have a similar impact as above.* • Developments affecting safety issues. *Bad publicity could lose customers.*
The government	• Changed levels of profit and taxes. *Government will welcome increased profits.* • Environmental, legal developments. *Government will not want adverse publicity.*
Community	• Developments leading to increased job opportunities. *This may help the local community.* • Issues affecting the environment. *The local community will want to stop any developments that damage the local and wider environment.* • Contributions from the business, e.g. sponsorship. *The community will benefit from sponsorship.*
Suppliers	• Changes by a company in the specifications for its products may result in changes in the types of material or component that the company purchases from its suppliers. *Suppliers might be either favourably or adversely affected, depending on whether the changes result in the company buying more or less from its existing suppliers.*

The impact of business on an economy and society

We have identified several stakeholder groups that might be affected by business decisions or activity. Businesses also have an impact on the economy (the system used to organise the money, industry, and trade of a country or region) in general. For example, when a new business starts up there are often new job opportunities that become available; this increases the total employment within an economy. As a business starts for the first time or grows, more goods and services become available, all of which add to the total value of goods and services offered in that economy. This is therefore adding to the overall wealth of the economy. The benefits of business activity can be felt by people who do not know of a business's existence. For example, because businesses contribute to the tax revenue of the country it might be possible for the government to spend more money on health and/or education. In this way benefits are gained that cannot be attributed to one specific business. Due to business activity, the general standard of living might be improved because the government can afford to provide more public services paid for by the income tax of employees and the tax on profits paid by businesses.

▲ Figure 1.1.11: Unemployment is a problem

Exam-style questions

1   How might efficiency be measured in a business that manufactures and installs windows for houses?

   A Profitability

   B Changes in the cost of glass

   C Sales growth

   D Sales revenue per employee   (1 mark)

2   Which one of the following comes first in a business planning process?

   A The business plan

   B Deciding business strategy

   C Deciding business objectives

   D Deciding business tactics   (1 mark)

3   What risk is involved in decision-making by a business? (3 marks)

4   What are the functions of a business manager? (3 marks)

5   Discuss the problems that a new clothes shop might face in its first year of trading. (12 marks)

6   "An entrepreneur is only interested in making a profit." Discuss the relevance of this statement to someone about to launch a new business. (12 marks)

7   Why might the need for an entrepreneur in a new business last for only a short time? (12 marks)

8   Explain the benefits that new business start-ups can bring to your country. (8 marks)

This section will develop your knowledge and understanding of:

→ Reasons for choosing different types of business and for changing business type

→ The nature of and influences on the business population in a country

→ Shareholders.

Reasons for choosing different types of business and for changing business type

Different types of business

There are many different types of business, both in their nature and their size. It is important to be able to recognise the various types of business in order to understand how they might have different objectives and how they might behave differently. It is easy to understand that a very large multinational business, such as Coca-Cola, Ericsson or Tata Motors, might behave differently from a small family business, but it is not so easy to see why a government-owned airline might behave differently from a privately owned airline. This chapter explores different types of business, where they fit in a country's economy and how they are owned.

Different types of private sector businesses

It is important to understand the different ways in which businesses are owned and the impact that this has on legal structure.

In local businesses there are differences not only in the size and type of businesses but also in the way the businesses are owned. Some examples include family-owned businesses (often shops or restaurants) but also examples of businesses whose owners are unknown or unseen (such as supermarkets, petrol stations and fast-food outlets). Often the owners of these businesses live in other countries.

There are reasons for these differences in ownership. The choice of how a business is owned has implications for the way it is treated legally – its legal structure.

The different forms of business also have various implications for the objectives set, how and where finance can be obtained, the distribution of profits and the impact of having either limited or unlimited liability. All of these issues will be discussed with reference to each form of business ownership.

The simplest form of business is a sole trader. However, before we can study any form of business ownership, we need to understand the concept of unlimited/limited liability.

Risk, ownership and limited liability

One of the important reasons why businesses choose different ownership types (legal structures) arises from the consideration of business *risk* and the consequences of things going wrong.

One of the roles of the entrepreneur is to take risks, for example:

- Business ideas may not work in practice
- Unforeseen events may disrupt plans
- Money (investments) can be lost. In some circumstances entrepreneurs can lose more than their original investment.

Imagine you own a window-cleaning business. Your investment would be a bucket, a ladder and some other small items. Let us suppose you accidentally drop a bucket on a famous person's head! If they sued you for damages you would stand to lose far more than your investment and far more than you could afford, even if you sold everything you had – if you owned a house you would probably have to sell that.

This is the concept of **unlimited liability** – whatever goes wrong is the liability of the owner of the business, which could be disastrous. One of the major weaknesses of this type of business is the fact that the law does not distinguish between the business and the owner of the business – "the person is the business and the business is the person". While it may be possible to get some kind of insurance to cover accidental problems like dropping a bucket, no insurance company would insure you for making the wrong decisions. The way to solve this problem is through the concept of incorporated businesses and limited liability.

For many centuries businesses survived and grew as sole traders. These are examples of what is known as "unincorporated businesses" meaning they are private sector businesses that have not been registered as companies. However, as business enterprise became larger, and the risks often became too great for individuals or small groups to take, the idea of limited liability was developed and became part of the business world.

Problem: The **unincorporated** business and its owner(s) are legally the same thing. The owner is liable for the debts of the business and the business is responsible for the debts of the owner.

Solution: Provide a mechanism to separate the legal identities of the business and the owners and so separate the liability. The owner gets the benefit of **limited liability**.

The solution is known as incorporation, in other words, going through a legal process to create a legal entity for the business that is independent of the owner(s). The business then becomes known as a limited company and the owners of the business can only lose the money they put in (or have agreed to put in) to the business: their share of the ownership. In return for this opportunity, incorporated businesses have to meet particular standards and abide by rules and regulations.

Limited liability enables businesses to grow without placing too much risk on the owners. In incorporated businesses the owners are the **shareholders**.

Key terms

Unlimited liability: a situation in which an individual or group of individuals are totally liable for the consequences of a course of action. For example, if a sole trader's business runs into trouble, the sole trader is personally responsible for paying all of the business's debts and could be forced to sell their personal possessions to pay their business's debts.

Unincorporated: a private sector business that has not been registered as a company. Sole traders and partnerships are unincorporated.

Limited liability: a situation in which the owners of a business can only lose the money they have put into the business and not their own personal wealth.

Shareholders: the owners of a limited company and other incorporated businesses.

Sole trader

Often when businesses start up, one single entrepreneur comes up with the original idea and owns and controls the business after it has started operating. This type of owner is called a **sole trader**. This is the simplest type of business organisation and it has no formal legal structure as it is, legally, no different from its owner. It is easy to set up and manage. It is important to remember that although there is only one owner, that owner can employ other people. This type of business has the advantage of the owner being in charge of everything, and he or she can make decisions without having to consult anyone else. However, there are three major drawbacks of being a sole trader:

- Any finance (money) required to start up the business or to expand it will be limited to whatever the sole trader can get hold of.

- The sole trader may have insufficient skills. Although he or she can buy in additional skills by employing people, the sole trader may not want to trust employees with responsibilities such as making decisions about running the business and its financial matters.

- A sole trader has unlimited liability: that is, if the business gets into debt the owner is liable for those debts and may have to use all his or her assets to pay them.

▲ **Figure 1.2.1:** Window cleaners are often sole traders

Progress questions

1 Give two advantages of operating as a sole trader business.
2 Why could a sole trader business have more than one person working in it?
3 Why is unlimited liability a problem for a sole trader?
4 Explain why limited liability is important.
5 Give one disadvantage of becoming incorporated.

Private and public limited companies
Private limited companies

Often as smaller businesses grow, they will want to protect themselves from the increasing risks associated with larger businesses. They will protect their own wealth by going through the process of becoming incorporated. The usual first step is becoming a **private limited company**.

The owners of private limited companies, who are often friends, relatives or business associates, will go through the legal procedures to set up the company (these will differ from country to country). Owners invest money into the business by buying "shares", which gives them a share of the ownership in proportion to the number of shares that they own. Ownership is restricted to an agreed list of owners, which can only change if the other shareholders (owners) agree. This restriction is one distinction between private limited companies and public limited companies.

Being a private limited company means that:

- Owners (shareholders) are more likely to risk their money as they have limited liability

Get it right

It is easy to make the mistake of thinking that a sole trader business is a business with only one person. There is only one owner, but that owner can employ other people. Indeed there are some quite large sole trader businesses.

Get it right

The term "company" has a very specific meaning. It refers to a private sector business that has been incorporated. Avoid using the term when referring to unincorporated businesses such as sole traders.

Key terms

Sole trader: a business owned by one person. The owner controls the business, often manages it and has usually provided all of the finance. There are no legal formalities needed to start up as a sole trader.

Private limited company: an incorporated business in the private sector where share ownership is limited to specified people, institutions or businesses. Shares are not available to the general public.

- More capital (finance) can be raised than for sole traders because more shares can be sold to existing and new shareholders if and when the shareholders agree
- The business can continue even if one of the owners dies because it is a legally separate entity
- Profits have to be shared between a much larger number of owners
- Incorporated businesses have to produce publicly available financial accounts
- Sale of shares is restricted, which may restrict the amount of capital that can be raised.

Setting up an incorporated business takes time and money.

Public limited companies

To overcome some of the difficulties facing private limited companies – most notably the restrictions on the amount of capital available – a private limited company can, provided it meets certain strict criteria, become a public limited company. This widens the potential ownership of shares to the general public rather than the agreed restricted list of permitted shareholders that applies to a private limited company. The process of converting to a public limited company is known as flotation. Clearly, members of the public who buy shares in a public limited company cannot run the business on a day-to-day basis so, once a year, the shareholders elect a board of directors to manage the business within very broad guidelines agreed at the Annual General Meeting (AGM) and specified in the legal documents governing the business. An AGM is a yearly gathering of a company's interested shareholders, where the directors of the company present a report about the company's performance and strategy. In most countries, all incorporated companies are required by law to hold these annually.

Key term

Public limited company: a private sector incorporated business with the right to sell shares to the general public.

Get it right

Not all large businesses are public limited companies and some public limited companies are relatively small.

▼ **Table 1.2.1:** Advantages and disadvantages of being a public limited company compared to a private limited company

Advantages	Disadvantages
Potentially a great deal more capital can be raised because shares can be sold to the general public.	Forming a public limited company is a lengthy and very expensive process.
A higher public profile for the business as the shares can be traded on the stock market.	There is much greater scrutiny of business activities by the government authorities, the stock market and the public.
A better image because a public limited company has to meet strict criteria for governance and operation and should be under constant scrutiny.	Much more financial information about the company is available in the public domain.
	There is a separation between ownership (general public and other businesses/organisations) and control (board of directors).
	Since anyone can buy shares on the stock market there is an increased risk of a takeover.
	Shareholders might want short-term speculative gains that are not to the long-term benefit of the business.
	Directors might see re-election at the AGM as their priority rather than considering the interests of other stakeholders or the company.

Case study

Mobile phone apps

Miguel Ramos owns and manages a successful business producing software apps for mobile phones. He operates the business as a sole trader with two full-time employees, but he has plans for expansion and taking on more staff with IT and programming skills. He also intends to change the business to a private limited company. There are several reasons for this decision.

- He has concerns about the personal financial risks he will be taking as the business grows and is exposed to more risks. A sole trader is personally responsible for all the unpaid debts of the business, whereas in a company the potential liability of a company's owners for its debts is limited to the size of their investment in the business. So Miguel's personal wealth outside the business will be protected.

- He thinks that there might be some tax advantages in operating as a company instead of as a sole trader.

- If the business is successful, Miguel will need to attract and retain individuals with top-class IT and programming skills. He thinks that one way to do this will be to offer these skilled individuals an interest in the ownership of the business, by awarding them some shares. When employees also own shares in their company, they are likely to become much more interested in its long-term success.

1 What do you think might be the disadvantages of changing from a sole trader business to a private limited company?

2 Why will Miguel not want to change the business to a public limited company?

Activity

In your country, find examples of public limited companies. What distinguishes them from other types of business?

Case study

Facebook in 2012

Facebook Inc, the world's largest social networking site, had announced plans for a stock market flotation. It planned to raise $5 billion. Facebook was only eight years old, but it had 845 million users worldwide and made a profit of $1 billion in the most recent year. It was started by Mark Zuckerberg and other students at Harvard.

As a private company Facebook did not have to release much information about its operations. "That will all change," said one media commentator at the time of the flotation. "Releasing information about the company will become part of Facebook's duties as a publicly listed company. In addition, Facebook will be heavily influenced by shareholders' needs, whereas it is the users and employees who are currently determining its development."

Facebook wanted to expand into new markets and to produce new products. The flotation also rewarded the existing shareholders, who were largely the founders and employees, and realised value for its then owners, who were able to trade some of their shares but still retain overall control. The flotation only made a very small proportion of share capital publicly available – it is thought that the business was then worth at least 20 times the flotation amount. Facebook users did not notice much difference following the flotation.

1 What is meant by the term "flotation"?

2 Why might the owners of Facebook have been concerned that Facebook would have to be more open about the operations of the company?

3 Why might Facebook have wanted to float shares that only represent 5% of its value?

Progress questions

6 Why might a private limited company want to convert to a public limited company? Give three possible reasons.

7 Why might a new business not seek to be a public limited company from the outset?

Private sector and public sector organisations

Traditionally, economists have drawn a distinction between the public sector – those businesses and business activities owned by the government – and the private sector – those businesses owned by individuals or groups of individuals. There are many differences between private sector and public sector organisations, including the way in which they are financed and their organisational objectives.

The public sector has declined significantly in size and importance in most countries over recent years and is likely to continue to do so as governments around the world focus on increased competition and entrepreneurship. Despite this change, the public sector continues to make important contributions to most countries through businesses such as state-owned schools, universities and hospitals, which may not operate as effectively in the private sector. Useful examples of public sector businesses include the US railway company Amtrak, the US postal service USPS, the BBC in the UK, the Indian Oil Corporation and Pakistan International Airlines.

It is important to recognise the distinction between public and private sectors as it has an impact on business objectives and behaviour.

Problems relating to changing from one legal structure to another

As a business grows it is likely to need to change its legal structure, possibly to gain additional finance or to gain limited liability. The usual progression for change of legal structure is shown in Figure 1.2.2.

When any of these progressions take place the outcome is likely to be the loss of the advantages of the current ownership structure and the gain of the benefits of the new ownership structure.

In any given situation it is important to look at the present position of a business, in particular what the constraining factors are, and then look at the consequences of changing the legal structure, how the constraining factors change and whether any disadvantages have been introduced. In assessing the consequences of changes it will be important to consider a variety of stakeholders.

A particular issue is the cost involved in any transition. It is very expensive and time-consuming to convert from a private limited company to a public limited company.

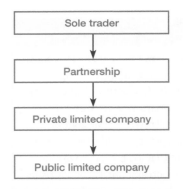

▲ **Figure 1.2.2:** Changing the legal structure of a business

Non-profit organisations such as social enterprises and charities

Non-profit organisations do not earn profits. The money earned by or donated to a non-profit organisation is used to reach the organisation's objectives. Typically, such organisations are charities or social enterprises.

Social enterprises

There are many different types of business and business objectives. Most of the businesses you will meet in these chapters were started by entrepreneurs who are often motivated by profit. It is therefore useful to look at the social entrepreneur, who has the same drive and determination to start a new business but whose overriding objective is social rather than financial. A business started by a social entrepreneur is known as a social enterprise.

The objectives of a social enterprise might include:

- **People (social):** to provide opportunities for disadvantaged communities or for local people
- **Planet (environmental):** to operate the business in an environmentally sustainable way
- **Profit (economic):** to provide a return for the owners, but not necessarily as the overriding priority.

> **Key term**
>
> Social enterprise: a business venture whose main aim is helping people and/or the environment as opposed to making a profit.

> **Progress questions**
>
> 10 Define the term "social enterprise".
> 11 Explain how a social enterprise differs from other business ventures.

> **Activity**
>
> Find out about a social enterprise in your country. In what ways does it benefit the community?

Charities

Charities are non-profit or not-for-profit organisations that aim to provide a contribution to the social well-being of individuals or groups of people. One well-known international charity is the Red Cross, which aims to provide emergency help for people in need in countries around the world. The organisation relies on donations from people who wish to support the work of the Red Cross in order to acquire any necessary materials and equipment. There are many charities worldwide. Some aim to protect and help animals whose existence is threatened. Others exist to protect and/or help specific groups in society, for example people who require help due to a physical disability such as blindness.

> **Key term**
>
> Charity: a non-profit or not-for-profit organisation that aims to provide a contribution to the social well-being of individuals or groups of people.

> **Case study**
>
> **Social enterprises in Africa and South Asia**
>
> Alive & Kicking (A&K) is an example of African social enterprise. By manufacturing sports balls, A&K creates jobs for adults and promotes health education through sport. It states its vision as being of "an Africa where every child can play with a real ball, where thousands of jobs are sustained in the production of balls, and where sport contributes to the eradication of deadly disease." A&K operates in Kenya and Zambia.
>
> Another example of social enterprise is the growing microcredit market in South Asia, particularly in Bangladesh. With technology becoming steadily cheaper and more widely available, it is becoming economically efficient to lend tiny amounts of money to people with even tinier assets. This is known as micro-finance, which aims to help the poor while allowing banks to increase their business.
>
> Some microcredit markets are aimed particularly at helping women, who usually find it much more difficult to borrow from traditional banks. The Grameen Bank in Bangladesh is particularly well known as a social banking enterprise.
>
> 1 Why might A&K have to make a profit?
> 2 In what ways is A&K concerned about the well-being of its stakeholders?

How do charities differ from business organisations?

- Producing a profit to return to shareholders is not a charity's primary objective. Some charity organisations sell merchandise but then use any profit made to support the work of the organisation.
- Charities rely on donations from individuals or from fundraising.
- Some charities are set up to help with a one-off specific issue or event, such as the earthquake in Nepal or flooding in Bangladesh. When the need for help no longer exists, the charity would also cease to exist.

Co-operatives

Co-operatives are organisations that are owned by their members. Membership can be achieved in several ways:

- In a consumer co-operative the members will be the customers. Some retail outlets are run as co-operatives.
- In worker co-operatives the members are the employees.
- In agricultural co-operatives the members are the farmers.

By working together, members hope to achieve greater power in the market through:

- Being able to buy bigger quantities (for example, seeds for farmers, products for shops) than if they operated on their own.
- Influencing business decisions. For example, employees may want to take strategic decisions themselves, and they can do that in a worker co-operative.
- Negotiating as a group in markets rather than operating individually. For example, farmers joining forces to sell their produce to buyers will have more power to negotiate with customers such as large supermarket chains and multinational food manufacturers.

Co-operatives have proved quite successful in some circumstances, preventing, for example, the exploitation of poor farmers. However, their use is not widespread and their usefulness is limited by:

- Access to finance: money from members is likely to be limited compared with a public limited company
- A lack of business expertise of members
- The potential complexity of decision-making if all members have to be consulted.

Good examples of co-operatives can be found in the banking sector. For example, the Co-operative Bank in New Zealand gained a very high customer satisfaction rating of 96%. It was also named the inaugural winner of the 2011 Canstar Blue Customer Satisfaction Award in banking, obtaining the maximum five-star rating in every category.

Key term

Co-operative: a business owned by its members, who could be employees, customers or groups such as local farmers.

Issues with types of business
Differing objectives
The objectives of a business are likely to change as the business becomes larger or when it is more established in the market.

For most business start-ups, the primary objective is "survival". As the business gains a place in the market this objective might change to increasing market share and/or profit maximisation.

New businesses or sole traders need to survive before they can begin to make a profit.

Once a sole trader has become profitable the owner of the business can decide to make a compromise between the level of profit desired and the amount of work that they wish to do. Many sole traders might decide to "satisfice", which means to make enough profit to satisfy and support their desired lifestyle rather than to chase higher profit, perhaps at the expense of their personal life.

Contrast that with private limited companies and public limited companies, which will strive to survive but will also need to make enough profit to meet the needs of shareholders. To do this, such businesses will often strive to achieve market domination and, as a result, profit maximisation.

Other than having diverse objectives, different types of business will also have alternative ways of raising finance, distributing any profits and operating with limited or unlimited liability. These issues are outlined in Table 1.2.2.

▼ **Table 1.2.2**: Comparison of different types of business

Business type	Objectives	Sources of finance	Distribution of profits	Unlimited or limited liability
Sole trader	Survival Profit Independence	Owner's savings, bank loan, family and friends Profits retained in the business	Owner owns all profits Profits are either withdrawn or retained in the business	Unlimited liability
Private limited company	Survival Profit Market share	Owner's savings, bank loan, sale of shares to family and friends Profits retained in the business	Profits are retained in the business or paid out as dividends. Dividends are shared according to the number of shares held	Limited liability
Public limited company	Revenue/Profit maximisation Market share Market domination Minimise costs	Bank loans, debentures, sale of shares on the stock exchange Profits retained in the business	Profits are retained in the business or paid out as dividends. Dividends are shared according to the number of shares held	Limited liability
Public sector organisations	Provision of merit goods Assist social well-being	Local or central government finance	Profits revert to the government or are reinvested into the business	Guaranteed by government

continued overleaf ⟶

continued from previous page ⟶

Business type	Objectives	Sources of finance	Distribution of profits	Unlimited or limited liability
Social enterprises	Survival Promote social good	Owner's savings, venture capital, shares and bonds	Some returned to the owner(s) and some reinvested into the business	Limited liability
Charities	Promote social good or a specific goal, e.g. fight poverty or starvation	Donations from organisations or members of the public	Reinvest or use to provide given service	Limited liability: limited by guarantee
Co-operatives	Meet the needs of the members	Money from the members	Divided between the members	Limited liability

The nature of and influences on the business population in a country

Primary, secondary and tertiary sector businesses

The economy can be divided into three categories:

- **Primary sector**: this sector consists of all those businesses directly related to the extraction and exploitation of natural resources. Primary sector industries include farming, fishing and extracting minerals such as oil, copper and iron ore. The products of these industries are sometimes sold to final consumers but are often sold to customers in the secondary sector to be processed.

- **Secondary sector**: businesses in this sector manufacture products. They convert a variety of inputs (often including products from the primary sector, labour and products from other secondary sector businesses) into products that are sold to customers. These customers may be final consumers or other businesses.

- **Tertiary sector**: these businesses are not involved with natural resources or manufacturing. They provide services. These services might be provided to final consumers (for example, a train service or a retail outlet) or to other businesses (for example, writing computer software for a large insurance company), or both.

Key terms

Primary sector: businesses that extract raw materials from the natural environment, for example, farming, mining, fishing, oil production, etc.

Secondary sector: businesses that manufacture and process raw materials, including those from the primary sector, for example, producing electricity from coal, producing petrol and diesel from refining oil, the car manufacturing industry, cotton making, etc.

Tertiary sector: businesses that provide services, such as banking, retail, transport, tourism, etc.

Activity

Identify as many different types of business as you can in your area. List what they do and who owns them. Do the businesses manufacture products or provide services, or both? Who are their customers? Which do you think are successful?

Get it right

Businesses in case studies are likely to come from any of these sectors. It is important to recognise who their suppliers are likely to be and who their customers are.

Historically, it has been the case that as countries grow they progress from being predominantly agricultural economies (primary sector), through to manufacturing economies (secondary sector) to principally service economies (tertiary sector). A good example of this is the UK, which, prior to the Industrial Revolution, was agricultural and is now predominantly service-led, with businesses clustered around banking, finance, media, etc. Many countries in western Europe have similar economies.

The advantages and disadvantages of family businesses

Many small businesses are also family businesses. Family businesses are often private limited companies in which all of the owners are related members of one family. Perhaps surprisingly, family-owned or family-controlled businesses account for over 80% of all businesses in the US, approximately 80% of employment within Pakistan is generated by family businesses, and about 85% of private sector businesses in China are family-owned.

Not all family businesses are small. Some very famous international businesses have developed from being owned by families, including Ford in the US, Samsung in Korea, Tata Motors in India, Waterstones in the UK, Kuok Brothers in Malaysia and the Fecto Group in Pakistan.

The success of family businesses is often related to the culture of the country in which the business is based. Some cultures emphasise individualism, whereas others encourage family bonds.

> **Key term**
>
> **Family business**: a business in which all of the owners are members of one family.

▼ Table 1.2.3: Advantages and disadvantages of family businesses

Advantages	Disadvantages
Employees and owners have a more obvious personal stake in a business through family ties.	Family disagreements, which can damage a business.
A better sense of direction when strategy has been agreed by family members.	Lack of access to capital, particularly early on.
A common sense of purpose.	Division of tasks may create conflict, friction and a less clear sense of direction.
They are generally able to take a longer-term view, in contrast to most shareholders who often want quick returns.	Nepotism can lead to inappropriate appointments to key positions.
Family members will work hard to avoid problems that might, in some cultures, lead to "shame on the family".	Contributions by professional managers from outside the family can be held back.
Trust, which can be of benefit to a business, may be easier for family members than for groups of unrelated people.	It may be easier to misappropriate profits, resources, etc.
	Family loyalties may cause problems to be "covered up".

> **Activity**
>
> Identify a family-owned business in your area. Talk to the owner. What does the owner like about being a family business? What problems does the owner identify with being a family business?

Case study

The Gazania Organization

The Gazania Organization is a limited liability company based in Mauritius. The organisation owns and operates holiday resorts in Mauritius as well as owning several hotels in Europe. The organisation is owned and managed by the Medici family with Donald Medici as its major shareholder and managing director. The three children – Djamel Medici, Aureli Medici and Eric Medici – serve as directors within the organisation and are the other shareholders. Djamel manages the overall running of the business, Aureli manages accounts and Eric manages the European properties.

The three adult children have forged a formidable team, leading development and acquisitions of new hotels for the Gazania Organization. Djamel was the first to join his father's company in 2001, followed by Aureli in 2005 and Eric in 2006. All three are working together to expand the company's real estate, retail, commercial and hotel interests internationally. The children are expected to continue with efforts to achieve Donald's growth objectives.

With thoughts of one day inheriting the business, the children work very hard to achieve those objectives. Djamel is regarded by everyone as the senior of the three children but there are signs that Aureli would like a bigger say.

Donald Medici is known for his eccentricity and unconventional businesses practices. He exhibits an unconventional leadership style, which has many

▲ Figure 1.2.3: Holiday resort in Mauritius

characteristics. One of those is the need for power. This is exhibited on every piece of real estate Mr Medici owns. Every casino, building or golf course has his name on it. He is eccentric and powerful, yet he makes very smart business decisions. He is also a risk-taker.

1   Identify factors leading to the continued success of the Gazania Organization.

2   Donald Medici's personality seems to have worked in this family business. Why might his approach have created problems in other organisations?

3   The children have joined the business in stages. Why might this have avoided some of the problems associated with family businesses? What additional problems could have arisen?

Small and medium-sized enterprises

The definition of a small and medium-sized enterprise (SME) varies from country to country. A business employing fewer than 15 people is classed as a small business in Australia, and a medium-sized business can have up to 199 employees. In the US, however, a business with up to 500 employees can be classed as small. In the European Union, a small business is defined as one that has fewer than 50 employees and a medium-sized business as one that has fewer than 250 employees. SMEs create a large proportion of the jobs in their economy.

▼ Table 1.2.4: Advantages and disadvantages of SMEs

Advantages	Disadvantages
Create jobs contributing to the overall level of employment in the economy.	Are often not as stable as a larger business as they do not have the same amount of resources as a large business.
Generate competition for larger businesses, which is good for consumers.	Might have to charge higher prices than large businesses.
Might supply a part of the market that has been ignored by large businesses.	It can be difficult for the smaller businesses to obtain finance for new projects or for expansion.
Can often respond faster to changes in the market than large businesses.	Can be a limited range of expertise in the smaller business that might limit the activities or efficiency of the business.
The service provided by small businesses is usually more personalised.	
Can service the needs of large businesses.	

Large businesses

The definition of a **large business** can vary between countries. In the US a business is classed as being large if it employs more than 500 workers, whereas in the UK a business employing more than 250 people is classed as a large business. Many large businesses employ many times more than those figures. For example, as at December 2016 Facebook had more than 17,000 employees and Toyota had 348,877 worldwide.

▼ Table 1.2.5: Advantages and disadvantages of large businesses

Advantages	Disadvantages
Can attract large numbers of investors.	Can be inflexible and, therefore, take a long time to react to market changes.
Have more resources.	
More established and recognised by consumers.	May experience diseconomies of scale, such as difficulties in communicating with large numbers of employees or inefficiencies caused by the duplication of efforts.
Brand recognition leads to customer loyalty.	
Larger staff base and the ability to employ specialists.	
Can negotiate discounts with suppliers for bulk buying and can often obtain loans on lower interest rates than smaller businesses.	
Potential for larger profits due to higher levels of production leading to more sales.	

Key term

Large business: a business that has a large number of employees, assets and turnover.

Activities

1   Identify three large businesses operating in your economy.
2   Identify the brands associated with them. Try to find out how many people they employ.

Progress questions

12 Identify two advantages to a country of a large number of SMEs in the economy.
13 Explain one disadvantage of being a large business.

Shareholders

Shareholders are the owners of limited companies and other incorporated businesses. They have bought a "share" of the ownership of the business by buying shares.

Ordinary share capital (equity)

Ordinary share capital, also known as equity, is obtained through the sale of ordinary shares in the business. Shares entitle the holder/owner of the shares to some ownership of the business.

There are other types of shares that a business can issue but the Oxford International AQA AS syllabus focuses on ordinary share capital.

Shareholders can buy shares in private limited companies and public limited companies. Shares in private limited companies can only be sold to new shareholders if all of the existing shareholders agree. The sales in a public limited company can be sold to the general public and can be bought by new or existing shareholders.

The role of shareholders and why they invest

Shareholders provide finance to businesses by buying shares of that business. Shareholders have the right to participate in the AGM of any business for which they have bought shares. They have the right to vote for the senior directors of the business.

Why do shareholders invest in businesses? By buying shares, shareholders are investing in the future of that business and must believe that it has a strong possibility of making profits. The primary reason for buying shares is to obtain a share of any profit made. Another reason is to make capital gains through rising share prices; if the business increases in value then this is reflected in an increase in the share price. If the shareholder then sells their shares at this higher price, they make a "capital gain". However, there is no guarantee that a shareholding will increase in value – it could also decrease if the business is not doing very well.

Dividends

Dividends are the return paid from the profit made by a company to shareholders for each share that they hold. At the AGM of a company, the dividend to be paid per share will be agreed. Dividend per share is the amount of profit that it has been agreed should be paid out to shareholders divided by the number of shares issued by the business.

Many companies pay dividends twice a year, one mid-way through the year and once after the AGM. When this occurs, dividends are usually measured as dividends paid in the previous 12 months.

Dividends are paid out of the accumulated distributable profits of the company and, when a dividend is paid, these distributable profits fall by the amount of the dividend paid.

> **Key term**
>
> Ordinary share capital (equity): the money raised by selling shares to shareholders.

> **Key terms**
>
> Dividend: the reward paid to shareholders from the profits of a limited company.
>
> Dividend per share: the reward per share that is paid to shareholders of a limited company.

To calculate dividend per share, you divide the total dividends that the company has paid by the number of ordinary shares that the company has issued:

$$\text{Dividend per share (\$)} = \frac{\text{Total dividends paid}}{\text{Number of ordinary shares in issue}}$$

For example, suppose a company has paid out $250,000 in dividends and they have 200,000 ordinary shares issued. The dividend per share would then be $\frac{\$250,000}{200,000} = \$1.25$.

Shareholders frequently calculate the dividend yield on shares they hold. The decision to buy shares in a particular company is sometimes based on the dividend yield of those shares. Dividend yield is the rate of return a holder of ordinary shares receives for each share held.

It is calculated by:

$$\text{Dividend yield} = \frac{\text{Dividend per share}}{\text{Market price per share}} \times 100\%$$

The market price per share (also known as the share price) is the price at which a specific share is valued at on the stock exchange at any given time.

> **Key term**
>
> **Dividend yield:** the rate of return that a holder of ordinary shares receives based on the market price of each share held. A dividend yield can be calculated only for companies whose shares have a market price; these are public companies whose shares are traded on a stock market. The dividend yield is calculated on dividends paid in the previous 12 months.

Activities

A company has just paid a dividend for the year of $6 million on its 40 million shares. The current share price is $4.00.

1 What is the dividend per share?
2 What is the dividend yield?

Influences on share prices

A share price is the price of one single share. Shares prices can vary day-to-day and even within a day. The share price can be affected by:

> **Key term**
>
> **Share price:** the price of one single share.

- Changes in the general economy. Economic events that might lead to a recession might cause the prices of shares to fall due to the expected difficult economic conditions. Such economic impacts can be in the domestic economy or internationally.

- News about the specific business. For example, if a company announces a change of its chief executive the share price can rise or fall as a result of the news. A change in the board of directors can also change investors, view of the company as well as their willingness to hold shares in that company.

- The arrival of a competitor. This can reduce the potential to make the same amount of profit, which can affect the return to shareholders.

- A business issuing more shares (the share price can fall).

- Falling company profits or unexpected increases in profits or dividends.

- The development of an innovative product or process.
- The performance of the sector of the economy that the company is in. For example, if the business operates in the mining sector and the other businesses in that sector are performing better, the share price of a lower-performing company is likely to fall.
- Supply of shares. If shareholders sell large numbers of shares in a company the price is likely to fall due to the larger number of shares now available for sale.
- An international financial crisis, such as the banking crisis of 2008. The banking crisis of 2008 caused a recession, considered by many to have been the worst financial crisis in recent times.

Share prices in general are measured by a stock market index, which measures movements up or down in the market prices of all shares within the index. It is not unusual for an index to rise or fall by as much as 1% or 2% in a day, as investors respond to new information about company prospects and profits, or a changing economic or political outlook, but index movements are usually less than this. The market price of shares in an individual company, however, can rise or fall by a much greater amount in a short time, as new information comes in about the company, its profitability and new developments that affect the company's future prospects.

Activity

In small groups select a small number of public limited companies and monitor any changes in the quoted price of their shares. At the same time follow any news stories about those businesses either in newspapers, on the companies' websites or on the internet in general. Discuss how the activities of the business might have influenced the share price on the stock exchange.

The significance of share price changes

A change in the share price of a company **does not** affect the amount of money or finance that a company has. If the share price of a company rises, it does not mean that they have more money available.

The money that a company gains from the sale of shares is the amount that it receives when the shares are first issued and sold. After that time, any sale or purchase of existing shares are financial transactions between buyers and sellers and do not affect the money in the company.

One significant effect of a falling share price is that the shares then become cheaper to purchase and could enable a rival business to buy part of the ownership of a company at a lower cost and attempt to take control of it.

A rising share price can make potential investors believe that they could make a profit if they buy shares now and then sell them later at a higher price.

Similarly, a falling share price can also be an invitation to potential investors to buy if they believe that the fall is temporary and that the share price will rise in the future.

A key significance of share price changes is how this affects the confidence of existing and potential shareholders. A loss of confidence in a company is likely to have wide implications and might even affect the willingness of customers to deal with it. This impact can depend on the size of the business and how well known it is.

The change of share price also has an impact on the market capitalisation of a company.

Market capitalisation

Market capitalisation is the valuation of a business by using the total value of the business's shares (share price multiplied by the number of issued shares).

In December 2016 Exxon had a market capitalisation of more than $373 billion; at the same time, Microsoft had a market capitalisation of more than $400 billion. The Chinese IT group Alibaba had a market capitalisation of about $490 billion in July 2018 and over 2.5 billion shares in issue.

Many companies are much smaller. For example, in July 2018 the giant international shipping group Maersk had a market capitalisation of about $26 billion and about 21 billion shares in issue. Many public companies are much smaller still.

A fall or rise in the price of shares will affect the market capitalisation of a business. If a business announces a fall in profit, many shareholders might decide to sell their shares in that business because they expect their dividend to fall due to the business having a smaller amount of profit. If a lot of shares are then made available on the stock exchange, there could be more shares available than are being demanded by investors. This is likely to cause the price of each share to fall. As the market capitalisation is calculated by the total number of shares issues multiplied by the market price of the shares, the total market value of the business (market capitalisation) would also fall. The reverse can also happen if something occurs that causes the market price of the shares in a business to increase.

Changes in the market capitalisation of a business are sometimes outside the control of the business. For example, if the country is heading towards a recession then the confidence of investors might fall, which could cause a fall in share prices. A change in government can also affect business and investor confidence, causing share prices to rise or fall. The recent vote in the UK to leave the European Union was expected to cause a fall in share prices but, surprisingly to many analysts, the share prices generally increased.

Shares prices can change suddenly and sometimes surprisingly, which affects the market value of businesses whose shares are quoted on the stock exchange.

> **Key term**
>
> **Market capitalisation**: the total value of all the shares issued by a limited company at the current market price for the shares.

Exam-style questions

1 Which one of the following companies operates in the tertiary sector of the economy?

   A A copper mining company

   B An airline

   C A producer of seats for cars

   D A manufacturer of mobile phones   (1 mark)

2 At the beginning of the year, a company had 300 million shares in issue and the share price was $2.20. The company is now planning a new issue of 60 million shares. The current share price is $2.15. What is the company's market capitalisation?

   A $620 million

   B $660 million

   C $774 million

   D $792 million   (1 mark)

3 What is the meaning of limited liability?   (3 marks)

4 A company has 32 million shares in issues. Its market capitalisation is $240 million. The dividend yield is 4%. What is the dividend per share?   (3 marks)

5 What are the main ways in which a charity differs from a commercial limited company?   (8 marks)

6 What might be the main objectives and characteristics of a farming co-operative of 20 farmers growing olives in a local region?   (8 marks)

7 Why might it be difficult for a small company to compete successfully against a much bigger rival company?   (8 marks)

This section will develop your knowledge and understanding of:

→ Market conditions and how they can affect demand, business decisions and profits

→ How changes in the external environment can affect costs, demand, business decisions and profits.

Link

Analysis of competition will also be covered using Porter's five forces model in *Oxford International AQA Business Studies A2* in Chapter 3 'Analysing the industry environment'. Knowledge of this theory will not be required for AS examinations.

There are many factors that can have an impact on the decisions and potential for success of a business. Some factors are within the control of the business while others are external to the business and are out of its control. However, there are actions that can be taken that can minimise the impact of those factors on the business. These will be examined in the following section.

Market conditions and how they can affect demand, business decisions and profits

The degree of competition

Businesses usually operate with some degree of competition. It is extremely rare for a business to be the only one offering a product or service unless it is the inventor of a totally new product.

Competition can take different forms:

- **The number of competitor businesses in a market.** A large number of businesses offering the same or similar products/ services can make it difficult for any business to gain or maintain a competitive advantage. A high level of competition can result in businesses being forced into action, such as lowering the price of their products.

- **The size of competitor businesses.** If a business identifies its main competitor(s) as being much larger businesses then it can be difficult to compete. Smaller businesses to do not enjoy the same benefits – they tend to lack the purchasing power of their large rivals and might also find it more difficult to secure access to the best outlets for their goods.

- **The length of time in the market.** A well-established business is likely to have a competitive advantage over a newer business due to the customer loyalty that might have developed over the years. Customers are often hesitant to try new products if they have used the same brand for a number of years. Consumers often feel more certain about quality when buying a known brand.

Barriers to entry

Barriers to entry are obstacles that make it difficult for a new competitor to enter a specific market. These obstacles may include government regulation, start-up costs, or patents and licensing requirements. It is important for new businesses to understand the potential barriers to entry in a specific market before entering it, as this increases their chance of survival.

Key term

Barriers to entry: obstacles that make it difficult to enter a specific market.

▲ **Figure 1.3.1:** Competitor pricing can be an issue if you are a small, new entrant into a market of already established larger businesses

What might be barriers to entry into a market?

- **Competitor pricing** can be a barrier. When entering a market with several large established businesses, a new business can expect to face a competitive response, often in the form of price reductions. As the larger businesses are already established they have more resources to draw on to support reductions in price. They might even be willing to accept lower profits for a short time, or even a loss, until the new business withdraws from the market because it is losing money. The new business might choose to enter the market with lower prices than their competitor but this often causes even lower prices to be offered from those already in the market. If a new business is starting out on a large scale they might be better able to compete. However, not all new businesses are large scale, for example, someone deciding to open a small general grocery store when there is a large supermarket already in the area.

- **Economies of scale.** Economies of scale exist when a large business is able to reduce the costs of its products by making them on a large scale. Costs are spread over a large number of units produced. With lower costs, a business can compete against smaller rivals – such as a new market entrant – by selling products at lower prices.

- **Customer loyalty** can be a large obstacle to any new business. It can take many years to build up a strong reputation and customer loyalty and a new business might have to compete with several well-established businesses and consumer brands. Incentives might have to be offered to encourage customers to try the products of the new business. These could include loyalty cards or money off future purchases. An example might be soft drinks, where major companies such as Coca-Cola have a global brand for their product to which many consumers are loyal. New entrants to the soft drinks market might struggle to win customers for their untried brand.

- **Start-up costs** can be small or large, depending on the type of business being started. Start-up costs might include the costs of investment in premises and equipment and the cost of hiring employees. Some businesses require substantial amounts of expensive equipment, which can be a huge barrier to many new businesses unless they are able to secure significant financial backing.

- **Government restrictions and regulations** also apply to some types of business. For example, a business cannot simply decide to set up a zoo or a theme park as such enterprises are regulated and require a licence in order to operate. In some countries, the construction of new buildings requires government permission. The government decides whether or not permission should be granted for a building to be constructed in a given location.

- **Trademarks or patents** that have been registered by existing businesses prevent other businesses from producing exactly the same product or from using the same trademark, brand or logo. Some companies invest heavily in research and development so that they can "stay ahead of the game" and deter new entrants to the market.

However, there are a number of well-known examples where technology has enabled new entrants to disrupt an existing market and establish their own position of market strength. Spotify and Netflix have entered the entertainment market successfully by offering online streaming of music and film services, Airbnb is challenging the traditional hotels market, and Uber and similar companies have taken a huge market share from traditional taxi companies and even public transport businesses.

Impact on business decisions and profits

When faced with a high degree of competition a business might decide that they must sell their product at a lower price than their competitors. This can allow them to gain or maintain a foothold in the market and to gain some customer loyalty. However, this means that their profit margin (the difference between price of the goods and the cost paid for them by the business) will be reduced. This can be sustainable in the short term but businesses need to have profit in the longer term to allow for growth and reinvestment.

When a business cannot compete on price then other options will have to be explored. For example, the business can develop a unique selling proposition/point (USP) – something that will differentiate their product from all others on the market. Early mobile (cell) phones were differentiated by the addition of a camera and then by the quality of the camera. A business that can stand out from its competitors increases its chances of success. A business might have to spend additional money to research and develop a differentiated product or a totally new product to introduce to the market.

A business might have to decide to find a new market or niche for its products or services. Customers might have to be found in another country, for example. This option adds further complications when trading internationally. For example, the laws of the other countries will have to be followed and there are also variations in the exchange rate to consider.

Many businesses accept that demand for their product or service will be low when the business is first launched, and growth in demand can often take several years to grow to the desired level. New businesses must investigate their potential market thoroughly and must be prepared to make changes to their decisions to their original plans if necessary. For example, a business that had an intention to aim for the mass market might find that competition is too strong and that it must find a niche market if it is to be successful.

> ## Link
>
> Exchange rates are covered in more detail on page 56.

> ## Progress questions
>
> 1 Explain two barriers to entry to an industry or market.
> 2 Explain how a business might overcome one barrier to entry.

Market size, growth and decline

Some of the decisions made by a business will depend on the size of the market they are entering. Decisions will also be affected by whether the market is growing or declining.

Market size

Market size is the measurement of all the sales by all of the businesses that are supplying to that market. This may be expressed in terms of size by value – the total amount spent by customers on products in that market. This will be equal to the total sales revenue received by all of the supplying businesses. It may also be expressed in terms of size by volume – the total quantity of products or services sold in terms of tonnes, litres or numbers of units.

For example, if looking at the size of the takeaway coffee market in Russia, the market size expressed by value is the total amount spent on takeaway coffees, in rubles.

For the same market but expressing it in size by volume, it is the number of cups of coffee sold.

Market size indicates what is happening to the market as well as being a starting point for calculating the performance of businesses in the market.

> ## Key term
>
> Market size: the total sales revenue or volume in the market.

Market growth

Market growth is the absolute or percentage increase in the size of a market. Calculating it will enable a market trend to be seen, helping businesses to plan ahead. A growing market indicates opportunities but may also mean more competition as businesses are attracted in. A declining market may indicate that a wise action would be to withdraw the product or stop advertising, but it may mean that competition will be falling as competitors leave. On the other hand, competition may increase as businesses try to get their share of falling sales.

Market growth is usually measured as a percentage amount from one year to the next. Using percentages makes comparisons easier between different markets. To calculate market growth as a percentage amount, you should use the following formula:

$$\frac{\text{Market size this period}}{\text{Market size last period}} - 1 \times 100\%$$

For example, suppose that the value of seaborne freight traffic in container ships rose from $11.8 trillion in 2017 to $12.35 trillion in 2018.

The rate of market growth in 2018 is:

$$\frac{12.35 - 11.8}{11.8} - 1 = 0.0466, \text{ multiplied by } 100 \text{ to get } 4.66\%.$$

Market growth shows that the size of the market is increasing, but it is also useful to compare the actual rate of growth achieved with the rate of growth that was expected at the beginning of the year by industry experts. In this example, a growth rate of 4.66% might be lower or higher than expected.

In this example, market size has been measured by total revenues in the industry. There might be other ways of measuring market size and market growth, such as the overall capacity of container ships worldwide.

Market decline

Market decline is the decrease in the size of the market, in either absolute or percentage terms. It is calculated in the same way as market growth, and is a negative figure. If a market is declining it could mean that some competitors will withdraw but it could also mean that it is not viable to keep producing and selling in that market. It is also possible that competition becomes more intense as those remaining in the market fight for the falling number of customers. It is also possible that while a mass market can be in decline, a niche market can remain strong.

Concentration ratio

Another factor affecting business is the amount of a market that is dominated by a small number of large businesses.

Concentration ratio is a calculation of the percentage of the total market held by a small number of businesses, typically three, four or five businesses. The concentration ratio ranges from 0% to 100%, and an industry's concentration ratio indicates the degree of competition in the industry. A five-company concentration ratio of 0% would mean that there are many, many businesses in the

> **Key term**
>
> **Market growth:** the absolute or percentage increase in the size of a market.

> **Key term**
>
> **Market decline:** the absolute or percentage decline in the size of a market.

> **Activity**
>
> 1 Total revenue of companies in the commercial aviation industry reached $754 billion in 2017, up from $709 billion in 2016. What was:
>
>   a the size of the commercial aviation market in 2017?
>
>   b the rate of market growth in the commercial aviation market in 2017?
>
> 2 Total revenue from ebook sales in the UK were $53.8 million in 2017, down from $54 million in 2016.
>
>   What was the rate of decline in the UK market for ebooks in 2017?

> **Key term**
>
> **Concentration ratio:** the ratio of the combined market shares of a given number of companies to the whole market size.

industry and none of them hold a larger share of the market than others. If the one-company concentration ratio of an industry is equal to 100%, this indicates that the industry is just one company. If the concentration is low, it simply means that the top few companies are not influencing the market production and the industry is thought to be highly competitive. On the other hand, if the concentration is high, it means that just a few companies influence the products or services provided in the market.

For example, we can calculate the concentration ratio of the three largest businesses in an industry.

If:

- Business Alana has 36% share of the market
- Business Betrand has 26% share of the market
- Business Cecile has 18% share of the market.

Then the three-company concentration ratio for that market is 36 + 26 + 18 = 80%.

There can be many businesses in a market but the concentration ratio shows how much of the market is *concentrated* in the control of a small number of businesses; in this case three. Such a high concentration ratio can make it difficult for smaller businesses to compete due to the market power of the dominant businesses in the market. Examples of industries with high concentration include sugar, gas distribution, coal extraction and tobacco products. Those with low concentration include construction and wholesale distribution.

Case study

Concentration ratio

Suppose that the market for buttons is dominated by three or four companies, and annual sales for the most recent year (Year 3) and the two previous years are shown in Table 1.3.1.

▼ Table 1.3.1: Sales in the industry for Years 1, 2 and 3

Sales	Year 1 $m	Year 2 $m	Year 3 $m
Total sales of three biggest companies in the industry	460	484	520
Total sales of four biggest companies in the industry	520	616	720
Total industry sales	800	880	1000

The three-company concentration ratio for each year and the four-company concentration ratio for each year are shown in Table 1.3.2.

▼ Table 1.3.2: The three-company and four-company concentration ratios for each year

Three-company concentration ratio			Four-company concentration ratio		
Year 1	Year 2	Year 3	Year 1	Year 2	Year 3
460/800	484/880	520/1000	520/800	616/880	720/1000
57.5%	55%	52%	65%	70%	72%

1 What do these figures show about the market share of the three biggest companies?
2 What do these figures show about the market share of the four biggest companies?
3 What do these figures show about the market share of the fourth-biggest company?

Progress question

3   In an industry with hundreds of small businesses in operation, there are four large businesses that dominate the industry. The four large businesses have the following market shares: Business A has 24%; Business B has 20%; Business C has 12% and Business D has 10%. Calculate the concentration ratio for this industry.

How changes in the external environment can affect costs, demand, business decisions and profits

There can be frequent changes in the business environment and we will explore six of them in this section. These will be discussed in terms of their possible effect on business costs, the demand for the business's goods or services, the profit of a business and the decisions made by businesses.

Incomes

The incomes of the population can either increase or decrease and both movements will impact on businesses.

Income levels can vary according to whether the economy of a country is experiencing a boom or a recession. During a boom period there is upward pressure on wages, while in a recession there is less pressure to increase wages due to the fear of job losses that can often occur at this time.

The level of incomes can have both a direct and an indirect effect on the costs of businesses. The direct effect is due to the need to pay higher wages to employees. The indirect effect is that, if suppliers to a business increase the wages of their employees, there can be an increase in the price of the goods that it supplies to other businesses.

However, there are possible benefits to be gained by some businesses of an increase in incomes and by others due to a fall in incomes. Businesses providing luxury goods or services are likely to see an increase in demand when incomes are rising while the providers of basic goods and services are likely to see a decrease in demand. For example, demand for expensive furniture might rise if incomes rise while demand for more basic goods, such as bread and cereals, falls. However, if the reverse happens and income levels are falling then the producers of luxury items might see a decrease in demand and producers of cheaper items might experience an increase in demand. When incomes fall, people do not necessarily buy fewer items but might switch to lower-priced options, causing demand for them to increase.

What should businesses do when faced with a change in the level of income?

Costs

An increase in incomes might be due to an increase in wages paid to employees, which will increase costs to those businesses paying the higher rate. If the wages of employees of the suppliers are increasing, this increase in wage costs might be added to the price of materials supplied to other businesses.

Demand

When incomes increase, customers have more spending power (assuming that prices do not rise at the same rate as incomes) and demand for many goods is likely to increase. Luxury goods might see an increase in demand but some basic goods might not see any increase at all. Some products such as salt and bread might not see any increase as incomes increase, but consumers might buy more expensive versions of that type of product when they have more income.

Decreases in income can result in a decrease in demand for luxury goods as consumers focus their spending on essential goods and services.

Business decisions
Product-related decisions

When incomes decrease, producers and retailers of luxury goods might decide that they will need to compete on something other than price if they do not want to decrease the price of their product to maintain sales. It might be decided that actions must be taken to make sure that their product is a "must have" product so that, even when incomes decrease, consumers will feel that they must still buy it. Branded goods usually have strong customer loyalty and, therefore, consumers will still try to purchase the products.

Businesses might also consider increasing or decreasing output depending on whether incomes have increased or decreased.

Employee-related decisions

An increase in incomes might encourage businesses to increase their prices to enjoy a higher profit and/or to compensate for any higher wages that the business is now paying.

If an increase in incomes is substantial, a business might consider replacing employees with machinery. Although this would cause an increase in expenditure in the short term, the reduction in wage costs might make it beneficial in the longer term.

If any decrease in incomes reduces demand significantly, businesses might have to consider reducing the number of employees required.

Profit

An increase in incomes might lead to a fall in the total profit earned by a business if their wage and salary costs have risen. The impact might depend on the business's ability to compensate for the increase in wage costs by increasing prices.

However, an increase in incomes might lead to increased spending by consumers and, therefore, an increase in total profit.

Businesses might also feel that any increase in incomes in the economy will allow them to increase prices, which can increase profit. This will depend on how consumers react to any price increase. If the new price is felt to be too high then demand for those products might fall, which could leave the business with reduced profit. This depends on how much demand falls. Consumers are likely to respond to changes in price of products differently, depending on the type of product involved. If the product or service is essential, such as water, then demand is unlikely to change much if at all when prices increase or decrease. This would result in an increase in profit.

However, if the product is a type of meat then demand might experience a large fall because consumers can switch to other meats or to vegetarian options. There are many substitutes available, so why should consumers pay the higher price? This situation would be likely to reduce profit.

A decrease in incomes often leads to a general decrease in the level of demand within an economy. Basic goods, such as water, are unlikely to see any change in demand because this is an essential good. Similar to the increase in price, a decrease in incomes is likely to lead to a decrease in demand for some products or a switching to cheaper alternatives. For example, when incomes fall people generally still want to buy the same amount of food but they might now look for cheaper alternatives. This move can lead to a decrease in demand and profit for those businesses providing more expensive foods and an increase in demand and profit for those providing the cheaper alternatives.

Activity

In small groups, make lists of the following goods/services in common use in most households:

- Items that you think are essential
- Items you feel are not necessary at all
- Items that you believe could be substituted for a suitable alternative.

Discuss how demand for each of the goods/services listed might be affected by an increase and a decrease in incomes.

Interest rates

Interest rates are the cost of borrowing, for example, bank loans or mortgages. They are also the reward paid to savers for putting their money into savings accounts.

Changes in interest rates can affect businesses in various ways.

Costs

Many businesses finance their new investments by borrowing. A change in interest rates will increase or reduce borrowing costs, depending on whether interest rates go up or down.

If a business has used a bank loan to purchase new production equipment, an increase in interest rates will increase the repayments on the loan. This is an increase in costs to the business, which might have to be passed onto consumers in the form of higher prices. Otherwise the business must "absorb the higher cost", which will result in a lower total profit.

Key term

Interest rate: the cost of borrowing or the reward for saving.

Demand

The effect of a change in interest rates on customer demand is probably best understood by the effect on demand for consumer products. An increase in interest rates will affect individuals and households that have variable rate loans, such as loans taken out to buy a house. If interest rates go up, consumers will have to pay more in interest, leaving less money available for spending on other items or saving.

As a result, it is probable that total spending on consumer goods will fall. Consumers might buy fewer goods or services, or they might switch to buying cheaper alternative products.

Another possibility is that consumers will continue spending as before, but will increase their total borrowings to do so, for example by spending more on their credit cards.

Business decisions

An increase in interest rates might cause a business to postpone or cancel any planned investment in new equipment because of the higher cost of borrowing. If businesses do cut back on their planned investment, this could affect business decisions about developing and making new products, or increasing the scale of production.

Business managers might also think that one increase in interest rates might soon be followed by another increase, and concerns about rising costs of borrowing could affect their confidence and make them much more cautious in general about undertaking new investments.

Profit

Since changes in interest rates affect the costs of a company that borrows, they inevitably have an immediate effect on the company's profits.

If a change in interest rates affects decisions by a business about investing in new equipment, profits over the longer term will also be affected. This is because new investments are expected to increase revenues and profits over time. If interest rates go up and a business cuts back on investments, its profits over the longer term will probably not be as high as they might have been.

Exchange rates

Exchange rates are the value of one country's currency relative to the currency of another country. For example, the value of the pound sterling to the euro, or the value of the Japanese yen to the US dollar.

The impact on a business of any change in the value of the currency will depend on whether the business is an importer or an exporter.

Let's take the example of the US dollar ($) in relation to the pound sterling (£). If the value of the dollar increases against the pound then each dollar will buy more UK pounds. If a business in the UK is buying either components or finished goods from the US, the UK business will have to spend more pounds to pay for the goods in dollars.

For example: a UK business buys (imports) computer chips from the US. Each batch of 1,000 chips costs $1,500.

> **Key term**
>
> Exchange rate: the value of one country's currency relative to the currency of another country.

To convert dollars into pounds, it is necessary to divide the dollar value by the exchange rate. So, if £1 equals $1.2 the UK business will have to pay:

$$\frac{1,500}{1.2} = 1,250$$

Therefore, the cost in UK pounds will be £1,250.

However, if the UK pound strengthens and is then worth $1.3 then the cost of the purchase will be:

$$\frac{1,500}{1.3} = 1,153.85 \text{ in other words, £1,153.85 (a saving of £96.15)}$$

However, if the US dollar strengthens against the UK pound then the cost in terms of UK pounds will increase. For example, £1 = $1.1.

$$\frac{1,500}{1.1} = 1,363.64 \text{ in other words, £1,363.64 (an increase in cost}$$

of £113.64)

However, if the business is an exporter and goods and/or services are being sold to the US then the impact is somewhat reversed. For example, a UK business sells furniture to the US. If the total value of one shipment of furniture is sold for $20,000 and the current exchange rate is £1 = $1.2. The value of the furniture in UK pounds is:

$$\frac{20,000}{1.2} = 16,666.67 \text{ in other words, £16,666.67 will be received}$$

If the UK pound strengthens against the US dollar to mean that £1 = $1.3 then the amount received in UK pounds will be:

$$\frac{20,000}{1.3} = 15,384.62$$

In this case, when converting the US dollars back into UK pounds it has taken $1.3 to purchase each £1 and fewer pounds have been gained in income by the UK business.

The business could decide to increase the price of the furniture to maintain its income level but this could be met by a decrease in demand for its products. This might depend on the uniqueness of the furniture and whether there are many suitable substitutes that consumers might purchase instead.

However, when the US dollar strengthens against the UK pound to, say, £1 = $1.1 then the income gained by the UK business will be:

$$\frac{20,000}{1.1} = 18,181.82$$

In this case, fewer dollars are required to buy each UK pound, meaning that income is increased.

However, when a business exports its goods they are often sold to another business, which will then use them as part of its manufacturing process or it will sell the imports to consumers, for example, the furniture case.

When a currency weakens against another one, the cost of purchasing those goods increases and, therefore, adds to the costs of the business. The business must then decide whether it is able or wise to increase prices to compensate for the increase in costs or whether the increase should be absorbed into the profit margin.

Table 1.3.3 shows the effects that movements in an exchange rate have on the importer and on the exporter.

An adverse change in an exchange rate could possibly wipe out the expected profits for an exporter or importer, and a favourable exchange rate movement could result in unexpected higher profits.

▼ **Table 1.3.3**: Summary: effect of movements in an exchange rate

	Impact on an importer in the euro area, paying for imports in US dollars	Impact on an exporter in the euro area, who charges foreign customers in US dollars for the goods that it sells
US dollar strengthens against the euro	The business will need to pay more in euros to acquire the US dollars it needs to pay for goods priced in US dollars.	The business will convert the dollar income it receives into euros, and a stronger dollar means that it will obtain more euros from the US dollars it receives.
US dollar weakens against the euro	The business will pay less in euros to acquire the dollars it needs to pay for the goods priced in dollars.	The business will convert the dollar income it receives into euros, and a weaker dollar means that it will obtain fewer euros from the US dollars it receives.

Activity

Find the value of three different currencies relative to your own currency or to the US dollar. Try making slight changes to the exchange rates and calculate whether the cost of a particular transaction would be better or worse for a business in your country. You can use a transaction value of your own choosing. Then discuss what steps you feel a business might take to improve the outcome.

Cost of inputs

As we have seen, movement in the exchange rate, incomes and interest rates can all have an impact on the cost of inputs of a business. These costs might increase or decrease as described above.

Case study

Exchange rates

Exchange rates can fluctuate by fairly large amounts over a short period of time. For example, the exchange rate between the US dollar and the pound sterling (dollars per pound) was 1.3579 at the beginning of January 2018, 1.4221 at the end of January 2018 and 1.3203 at the end of June 2018.

This means that:

- Between the beginning and end of January 2018, the dollar weakened against sterling by about 4.7%

$$\frac{1.4221 - 1.3579}{1.3579} \times 100\%$$

- Between the end of January 2018 and the end of June 2018, the dollar strengthened against sterling by about 7.2%

$$\frac{1.3203 - 1.4221}{1.4221} \times 100\%$$

1 During July 2018, the exchange rate between the US dollar and sterling (dollars per pound) moved to 1.3150. What does this indicate about changes in the value of sterling during July?

2 Some concern was expressed in the financial markets about a large fall in the value of the Chinese currency (called both the renminbi and the yuan) during 2018. Why do you think this might be a matter of some concern?

Progress questions

4   A UK business imports car components from Germany. At the time of the transaction the UK pound (£) is worth 1.15 euros (€). The German business expects to be paid in euros. The total value of the components is €25,000. What is the total cost of the purchase in pounds (£) to the UK business?

5   What is the total value in pounds (£) if the exchange rate changes to £1 = €1.2?

6   Can you work out the effect of a movement in the exchange rate between the US dollar and the euro for a US importer who pays for imported goods in euros, and for a US exporter who prices goods sold in Europe in euros?

Cost of inputs can also change if a supplier decides to increase or decrease their prices to the business. This is outside the control of the business – although a business might decide to search for a cheaper supplier if prices have been increased too much.

There are other influences on the costs of inputs that a business can have, at least, some control over. A decrease in the amount produced by each employee each day will increase the overall cost of the production of that product. If the employees are paid for each hour worked then the cost of wages will have increased if less is produced in each time period. However, many businesses pay their employees per item produced, in which case it is in the interests of the employee to produce as many items as possible. There can be an additional cost incurred in the use of this method if the quality of the items produced falls due to employees rushing to complete as many items as possible. Some businesses combine payment according to the number and quality of items produced. For example, any rejected items would be deducted from the total number of items produced before payment is calculated. This can reduce any costs associated with wastage.

If the cost of inputs decreases, businesses might decide to decrease the price of their goods to consumers. However, price might not be adjusted at all and any decrease in input cost could lead to an increased profit being enjoyed. The reverse would be true of an increase in input costs, in other words, the amount of profit would probably fall as the increase in costs is absorbed by the profit margin.

Government policies

Government policies can influence business behaviour and success in many ways. This can be in the form of intervening in business activity for the good of the economy and/or consumers. Government policies might protect small businesses from being dominated by larger businesses or from unfair competition from overseas businesses.

The government also determines the legal framework governing employment.

The attitudes of governments vary from country to country, with some believing in more intervention than others. There is general agreement that governments need to help to encourage a healthy business sector so that the economy and population as a whole might benefit.

Many governments will take steps to encourage business but also to discourage harmful activity.

How might a government encourage businesses?

- By having a taxation system that encourages business investment and development.
- By providing information to help businesses that want to export or import. It is vital that such businesses understand any restrictions or difficulties when trading with certain countries.
- By giving grants and subsidies to develop new ideas and businesses and to support those businesses providing essential goods and services, as well as to encourage businesses to locate in areas of high unemployment.
- By offering financial incentives to businesses to employ and train young people or those people who have been unemployed.
- By giving contracts to businesses located in their own country instead of awarding contracts overseas.

In each of the cases listed above, it is likely that these could contribute to a decrease in the level of costs borne by the business because the government is offering some level of financial support. This might be by having lower taxes on new businesses or by giving grants to help businesses start up or expand.

Such measures can allow a business to be competitive on price by making it possible to reduce some of the costs involved in business. For example, training costs can be very high but can be offset by governments when a business employs young people or the long-term unemployed.

Help from governments might also make the difference between a business being started or not. For example, a start-up business might not go ahead if tax rates are very high. A lower rate of tax means that a business will keep more of their profit within the business and it can then be used to secure the future of the business. Profit is the reward for the risk taken by an entrepreneur, and if most of the profit has to pay for taxes, the entrepreneur might think it is not worth the risk to start or expand the business.

However, there are occasions when a government might act to constrain business activity.

How the state might intervene to constrain businesses

Governments recognise that although businesses are generally beneficial to a community and country, left to themselves businesses might not have full regard for the consequences of their actions on people in general.

Therefore, in the same way as there are rules and regulations governing our individual lives (what side of the road we drive on, what behaviour we regard as illegal, what age we can leave school, etc.), there need to be laws and regulations to govern businesses. A business may find its activities constrained if:

- Products and/or services provided by the business are, in some sense, regarded as harmful (such as tobacco products) or unsafe (for example, electrical products that can give an electric shock)

- It has processes that may damage the environment
- It does not treat its employees fairly
- It has become too powerful and exploits people
- It is involved in unfair practices, such as using bribery to get contracts, or agreeing with other businesses to fix prices
- Markets are not competitive or they fail
- It does not meet internationally agreed standards.

The greatest influence of the government on business activity results from its role in managing the economy.

Progress questions

7 Give three reasons for government to constrain the activities of a mining business.

8 Why is it not a good idea to allow education to be limited to only those who can afford it?

9 Explain why a failing in the harvest of a key source of food (such as wheat, maize or rice) might require intervention from the government.

Link

More development on how and why a government might intervene in business activity will be covered in *Oxford International AQA Business Studies A2* Chapter 4 "Analysing the external environment to assess opportunities and threats; political and legal change".

Competition

Competition can be from other businesses in the same country or, increasingly, from businesses in other countries. As the business world becomes more global, international competition has inevitably increased.

For example, the competition might be in terms of:
- Price
- Quality
- Design
- Innovation.

Competition is not always about price competition. The type of industry will often determine the nature of competition within it. For example, within the motorcar industry manufacturers are constantly trying to bring out newer and better models to entice consumers. Extra gadgets are added such as Wi-Fi and satellite navigation systems to differentiate one model from another. In such competitive industries it can be difficult to keep consumers interested without spending large amounts of time and money developing new ideas. A business in such an industry will frequently decide to spend a large proportion of its budget on research and development (R&D).

Although competition is not always about price, it often is. This is true, for example, when foreign competitors are able to produce rival goods more cheaply than a domestic producer, and sell them more cheaply. This is sometimes called "flooding the market" with cheaper products. Low-price competition may be able to win a substantial share of the market from domestic producers.

Demand

A new initiative by a competitor to win market share will affect customer demand for the products or services of other businesses in the industry. A competitor might reduce its prices, or it might introduce an upgraded model of its product, such as a smartphone with enhanced features but for the same price as the previous version.

Companies affected by a competitor's initiative have to decide what to do and how to respond. They might decide to do nothing, and suffer a fall in customer demand for its products. Alternatively, they might decide to respond and take an initiative of their own to attract customers (or at least retain their market share).

Costs

Competition can affect costs as well as revenues. To remain competitive, a business might need to improve the design of its products, or spend more on advertising in order to maintain (or improve) market share. Online retailers might decide to offer a free delivery service when before customers were required to pay for delivery. Competitive initiatives cost money. The success of any initiative will depend on whether the benefits from extra sales (or maintaining market share and sales) exceed the costs of the initiative.

Business decisions

Competition within an industry or market means that businesses must continually take new initiatives – **innovate** – to remain competitive. In many industries today, in high-technology industries such as telecommunications, robotics, pharmaceuticals/medicines, and in consumer industries such as travel and entertainment, businesses must continually offer new or improved products or services. If they do not then they risk losing market share, and their longer-term survival may even be at risk.

Competition in many industries is also global. The increased globalisation of business means, for example, that a business in Pakistan no longer competes just with other businesses in Pakistan but also with businesses in other countries such as Indonesia, China or Brazil.

When competition is global, cost and price can be critical factors for remaining competitive, and businesses might think about relocating manufacturing operations from their existing location to countries where costs, such as labour costs and costs of property, are much lower. So a manufacturer with a production site in Germany, for example, may decide to open up a production facility in China, where costs are lower, and a manufacturer in China might switch operations to Vietnam, where costs are lower still.

What might influence the competitiveness of overseas businesses?

- **Access to a cheaper labour force.** Wage rates in some countries are much lower than in others often due to the cheaper cost of living in that country.

- **Access to cheaper raw materials.** Some raw materials are found in specific geographical areas and the businesses located in those areas might be able to purchase the raw materials much cheaper than those businesses located in other countries.

- **Government protection from competition.** The government in some countries will impose tariffs and quotas on goods being imported from abroad. This will either limit the amount of goods that can be sold into that country or it will make the goods more expensive, which can make the goods uncompetitive compared to those produced in the home country.

- **Government grants or subsidies.** These reduce the costs of production for those businesses receiving them. This enables those businesses to reduce their overall costs and to possibly lower the price to the consumer.

Profit

Competition affects costs and demand, and businesses must often innovate to remain competitive. Businesses that compete successfully win market share and enjoy an increase in sales and profits. For businesses that are uncompetitive, the reverse is true: actions by competitors will damage their sales and profits.

Activity

In small groups or individually, identify up to ten different products; some that are produced in your own country and some that have been produced overseas. Compare each product with a competitor product, taking note of any difference in price, difference in quality, and/or any difference in design. Discuss how much such differences might influence consumers and why.

This activity can conclude with a presentation or a question and answer session between groups regarding the various products investigated.

Exam-style questions

1   The three-company market concentration ratio in a market has increased from 62% last year to 68% this year. What does this indicate?

   A   That the biggest three companies in the market suffered a fall in their combined total annual revenues this year.

   B   That the biggest three companies in the market suffered a fall in their combined market share this year.

   C   That the biggest three companies in the market increased their combined total annual revenues this year.

   D   That the biggest three companies in the market increased their combined market share this year. [1 mark]

2   The total size of the market for a particular product, measured in annual sales revenues, grew from $672 million in Year 1 to $712 million in Year 2 and $750 million in Year 3.

   What was the rate of market growth in Year 3, and was this higher or lower than the rate of market growth in Year 2? [3 marks]

3   Why would it be difficult for a new competitor to break into the market for passenger air transport? [9 marks]

4   Why might the demand for consumer goods increase when wages and salaries are rising at a faster rate than the rate of inflation? [9 marks]

5   Natasha has a retail business in Hong Kong selling Japanese products such as paintings and ornaments. She buys her goods for resale in Japan, paying for them in Japanese yen. She prices them in her shops for Hong Kong dollars.

   How might Natasha's sales and profits be affected by an increase in the value of the yen against the Hong Kong dollar? [9 marks]

Business and markets

2 Marketing

This section will develop your knowledge and understanding of:

→ The importance of marketing

→ Marketing objectives

→ The value of and influences on marketing plans and marketing budgets

→ External and internal influences on marketing planning, objectives and decisions.

▲ **Figure 2.1.1:** A marketing planning meeting

Activities

1 Businesses market their products in different ways. In what ways do you think that a company might try to persuade people to buy:
   - a mobile phone (or cell phone)
   - a chocolate bar
   - a ticket to watch a film at the cinema (movies)?

2 How do you think that a car manufacturer might be persuaded to buy windscreens for its cars from a particular windscreen manufacturer rather than from a competitor supplier?

Key terms

Marketing: activities that promote and sell products or services.

Competition: in business, a situation in which two or more business organisations seek to persuade the same customers to buy their products or services in preference to those of rival businesses.

Market leader: the biggest and most successful business in a specific sector.

The importance of marketing

How marketing decisions influence competitiveness

This chapter looks at the nature of marketing and marketing activities, and the role of marketing within business organisations.

Businesses make products and offer to provide services, but how do they get customers to buy them? How do they get customers to buy their products instead of choosing to buy rival products from competitors? The answer is that they market their products and persuade customers to buy them.

Marketing and competition

In most markets there are several businesses (in some areas there are increasing numbers of businesses) competing with each other to sell their products to the same customers. When there is competition, business organisations try to persuade the same customers to buy their goods or services in preference to those of their rivals, by offering them something with greater appeal to customers. Businesses often seek to be more successful than their rivals, for example by being the market leader.

- Marketing helps to make the products or services of a business more attractive to customers. Marketing activities can be used to make customers aware of a product, to make them interested in the product and what it has to offer, and then to make a decision to buy it.

- Marketing can also be used to learn more about customer preferences, so that products can be adapted to meet customers' needs better, or so that ideas for new products can be developed.

- Marketing can also be used to find out more about what customers will be prepared to pay for a product, and how they might react to a rise or a reduction in price.

Marketing decisions by a business will affect its competitiveness. How should products be marketed, and what methods of marketing should be used? How much should be spent on marketing? When should marketing activities be undertaken? It might be supposed that by spending more money on marketing, a business will succeed in selling more of its products. However, this is not necessarily true. Marketing activities should be planned and co-ordinated if they are to achieve their aims and objectives.

The terms "marketing" and "selling" are sometimes confused. Marketing activities consist of a range of issues, including aspects of product design, pricing, distribution, promotion and selling. Promotion consists of activities that that make people aware of a product or service, encourage them to like it, and persuade them to buy it. Selling activities are concerned with getting customers actually to buy a product or service. Selling is just one aspect of marketing.

Consumer goods and industrial goods

Consumers are people who buy products and services for personal use or consumption. Consumers are sometimes referred to as "households". Consumer goods: goods or services purchased by consumers.

You are probably aware of ways in which goods are marketed to consumers, because you are a consumer yourself and so you will regularly buy consumer goods. Typically, consumer goods are sold through shops and retail stores, or online.

However, some businesses make products or provide services to other businesses: for example, manufacturers of commercial aircraft sell their planes to airline companies, and manufacturers of robotic fork-lift trucks sell their products to other industrial companies. Some companies, such as manufacturers of laptop computers, sell their products to both consumers and to businesses. Industrial goods are goods that are produced for industrial and commercial buyers, and not for consumers, for example, factory machinery.

Methods of marketing products are different between consumer goods and industrial goods. Business-to-business (B2B) marketing is marketing by a business to other businesses, and business-to-consumer (B2C) marketing is marketing by businesses to consumers.

The interrelationship between marketing decisions and other functions

Marketing is just one function within a business, and marketing activities must be co-ordinated with the activities of other functions. Decisions about marketing must be consistent with what the other functions are doing, or are able to do.

▼ Table 2.1.1: Interrelationships with other functions

Function	Related marketing decisions
Operations: In a manufacturing company, what is the production capacity (output capacity) of the manufacturing function? When is the manufacturing function planning to make the product, and in what quantities?	In a manufacturing company, the maximum output capacity, the planned production quantities and the timing of production activities will affect marketing decisions about how much needs to be spent on marketing activities, and when these should take place.
In a service business, what is the capacity of the business to deliver services to customers with the resources at its disposal?	For a service organisation, marketing decisions will depend on the availability of resources to deliver the services, as well as the nature of the services themselves.

continued overleaf ⟶

continued from previous page ⟶

Function	Related marketing decisions
New product development: What are the special features of a new product under development?	The features of a product and its design will affect the "marketing message", and how the product should be promoted and sold to customers. A business may have a department or function dedicated to new product development. (It may be called the research and development or R&D department.) However, new product development is also an element of marketing.
Finance function: How much should be allocated to the marketing budget, for spending on marketing activities? There is a limit to what the business can afford.	Spending on marketing activities is restricted by the amount provided for in the marketing budget. The marketing function needs to work with the finance function to agree what the marketing budget should be. The finance function is also concerned with the costs of a product and the profits from selling it. Marketing decisions about pricing must seek to ensure that a product will be sold at a profit.
Human resources (HR) function: The HR function deals with recruiting and training employees.	Decisions about marketing will be affected by the number of people available to work in marketing. In a service business, marketing decisions are also affected by the numbers of people employed who can provide the service.

International marketing

Many businesses are global. Companies source their materials and manufacture goods in different countries around the world. They also sell them to customers in many different countries. The names of some "global" companies are recognised throughout the world, in industries such as oil, soft drinks and car manufacturing. There are also many global brands of consumer products and services, such as food products and fast-food chains. Information technology and telecommunications make it possible for companies in markets such as social media and financial services to market themselves and their services globally.

Global business opens up new markets for companies, but it also creates new challenges.

- In a global market, companies have more competitors and must compete with them to promote and sell their products.
- There are also many more potential customers, but consumer tastes often vary between different countries and regions of the world. Companies may therefore need to adapt their products and marketing activities to suit local conditions.

Case study

Zara

Zara is a fast-fashion company based in Spain but operating globally. It was founded in 1975, and Zara is the main brand of the Inditex group of companies. The company has been hugely successful in designing, producing and selling fashion products. It is "fast fashion" because it is able to produce and sell a large number of clothing collections each year, and it is therefore able to respond very quickly to changes in consumer tastes for fashion.

1 How must marketing decisions by Zara be co-ordinated with the activities of other functions in the company, particularly with product design, production and distribution?

Example

McDonald's operates a huge chain of fast-food outlets around the world. Food preferences vary between countries, and McDonald's adapts the products that it sells to meet local tastes. It does not sell identical products in every country where it operates.

Marketing objectives

Marketing activity by a business (and by not-for-profit organisations too) must have one or more objectives. **Marketing objectives** are a statement of what marketing activity is trying to achieve, and the success or failure of marketing can be judged according to whether the objectives have been achieved. There are various objectives that might be set.

Sales volume and sales value

A business might set an objective to achieve a certain amount of sales in a planning period, such as a year.

Sales volume: Sales can be measured by volume of units sold (sales volume), such as the quantities of petrol (gasoline), kilowatt hours of electricity or number of new cars. An objective to sell a certain number of units of a product can also be set for individual products, such as cartons of orange juice, tickets to a sporting event or the number of subscribers to a music streaming service. To set a sales objective in units, however, the product or service must be a standard item, so that every unit sold is more or less similar to all other units.

Sales value: It is more usual to measure sales by value (sales revenue earned is also known as sales value). This is the total revenue from sales, or total revenue from sales of a particular product. A company that makes and sells a range of different products may set an objective of achieving annual sales of a certain amount.

Many companies have a broader business objective of growing their business. If so, a sales objective may be to increase annual sales by a certain percentage amount compared to the previous year. In other words, companies may have a **sales growth objective**. Sales growth is measured as:

$$\frac{\text{Sales in Year 2}}{\text{Sales in Year 1}} - 1 \times 100\%$$

Activities

1 Select a consumer product.
2 Name at least three competitors in the market for this product.
3 Is the product you have selected marketed and sold globally?

Key terms

Marketing objectives: aims for achievement through marketing activities, which should contribute to the achievement of overall business goals. Examples might be to increase sales (volume or value), increase market share or expand into new international markets.

Sales volume: the amount of sales of an item in a given period of time, commonly measured in units of sales.

Sales value: the amount of revenue from sales in a given period of time. It is always expressed as a money value.

Alternatively:

$$\frac{\text{Sales in Year 2} - \text{Sales in Year 1}}{\text{Sales in Year 1}} \times 100\%$$

Market share

Another marketing objective may be for a business to **maintain or increase its** market share. For example, if sales of a company's product during a year are $50 million and total sales in the market for the product are $250 million, the company has achieved a 20% market share.

- When total sales in a market are the same from one year to the next, companies that increase their market share will do so at the expense of competitors.
- When a business's sales increase by 5% in a particular year but the total market has grown by 10%, the company will have lost market share. Market share can be more important than sales value or sales volume in a rapidly expanding market, such as markets for digital products.

A possible problem with setting market share as an objective is that the total size of a market is often difficult to measure or estimate accurately. For some products, there are fairly reliable figures for market size, such as the total number of new cars sold nationally, where regulations require that all new car sales must be registered. For many markets, the total market size may be estimated, but estimates can be unreliable. For example, how is it possible to measure total annual sales of cheese globally, or even nationally, when there are so many different producers of cheese?

Customer retention and repeat sales

In some markets, a marketing objective may be to achieve a certain customer retention rate. Customer retention is very important for any product or service where customers pay an annual subscription fee or membership fee. It is common for many subscribers to a service to cancel their subscription at the end of their subscription period, and a marketing objective may therefore be to minimise the number of subscribers who do not renew (known as the rate of "**churn**"). For example, if 20% of subscribers to a television service do not renew their subscription, the retention rate is 80%.

Companies selling subscription services will also want the rate of churn to be lower than the rate of growth in new subscribers.

> ### Key term
>
> **Market share:** the proportion of total sales in a market obtained by the products of a business over a given period of time.
>
> **Customer retention rate:** the proportion of customers who continue to buy the product or service of a business from one year to the next.

Case study

Sales objectives

Sales of a company's products were $12 million in Year 1 and $14 million in Year 2. The total size of the market for similar products is estimated to be $50 million in Year 1 and $60 million in Year 2. The company's marketing objectives for Year 2 were to increase sales by 15% and increase market share to 25%.

1 Was the company successful in achieving its marketing objectives?

Customer retention is also important for some companies that do not charge subscriptions, but whose advertising revenue is dependent on the number of its users, such as social media companies Facebook and Twitter.

A similar marketing objective may be to achieve a certain level of repeat sales by customers. A repeat sale is a sale to a customer who has already purchased the company's products or services before. For example, supermarket chains may give loyalty cards to customers and offer "special deals" such as discounted prices or money vouchers to cardholders. These help to persuade customers to continue buying from the supermarket (and the supermarket is able to monitor repeat sales through the use by customers of their loyalty cards).

Sales per product/employee/region/store/customer

Marketing objectives may be set for the amount of sales per period for each product, or the average amount of sales per employee, per geographical region, per store or per customer. These measures are also useful for comparing the sales performance of different products, regions and stores.

▼ Table 2.1.2: Possible marketing objectives for a given time period

Marketing objective	Method of measurement	Comment
Sales per product	Volume or value of sales	The marketing objective may be to increase a target level of sales (or sales growth) for individual products that the business sells.
Sales per employee	Value of sales/ Average number of employees in the period	The marketing objective may be to increase sales per employee. Since the number of employees is likely to vary over time, the average number of employees in a period should be used to calculate the average figure. Companies that employ sales representatives may set objectives for the average value of sales per sales representative.
Sales per region	Value of sales/ Number of regions OR Value of sales for each individual region	When a company organises its operations by geographical region (such as the Americas, Australasia, and Europe, the Middle East and Africa (EMEA)), it may set objectives for the average sales per region, or (more usually) the target value of sales for each individual region – since regions differ in size and characteristics.
Sales per store	Value of sales/ Number of stores	Average sales per store may be a marketing objective for a retail company that operates a number of stores. Alternatively, separate sales objectives may be set for each individual store – since stores differ from each other by size and location.

continued overleaf ⟶

Activity

The global market for carbonated soft drinks has been dominated for many years by a small number of global companies.

Carry out research to establish the identity of the leading companies in the market for carbonated soft drinks, and the share of the market that each of these companies holds.

Identify rival companies in the market for carbonated soft drinks, and look for any news reports or marketing initiatives by these companies to increase sales or gain market share for their products.

continued from previous page ⟶

Marketing objective	Method of measurement	Comment
Sales per customer	Value of sales/ Number of customers Average value per sales transaction (= Total sales/ Number of sales transactions)	A business may know how many customers it has: a company selling subscription services, for example, knows the (average) number of subscribers it has in a period. If a company does not know how many customers it has, a marketing objective may be the average sales value per sales transaction.

Example

A retail store achieved annual sales turnover of $400 million last year from its 52 stores. Marketing is organised on a regional basis, with four regions (North, South, East and West). The company has 11,200 employees at the beginning of the year and 10,800 employees at the end of the year. During the year, the 52 stores registered a total of 6 million sales transactions.

Its marketing objectives for the year included average sales per store of $8 million, average sales per employee of $35,000, average sales per region of $104 million, and average value per sales transaction of $65.

▼ **Table 2.1.3:** Did the retail store meet its marketing objectives?

Marketing objective	Measurement	Objective achieved?
Sales per store	$400 million/52 = $7.69 million	No
Sales per employee	Average number of employees = (11,200 + 10,800)/2 − 11,000 $400 million/11,000 = $36,364	Yes
Sales per region	$400 million/4 = $100 million	No
Average value per sales transaction	$400 million/6 million = $66.67	Yes

Get it right

It is tempting to think about marketing entirely in the context of business-to-consumer (B2C) marketing. However, it is important to remember that there is also business-to-businesses (B2B) marketing, for which marketing objectives, strategies and tactical plans may differ from consumer marketing.

Progress questions

1   Why is it often impracticable for a company to set a marketing objective in terms of total sales volume?

2   Why might it be difficult to set a marketing objective in terms of market share?

3   What is customer retention, and what type, or types, of business are most likely to set the customer retention rate as a marketing objective?

4   Why is it usually more appropriate to set a marketing objective in terms of sales revenue for each individual region rather than set a marketing objective of average sales per region?

Case study

Television subscriptions

A company sells subscription television services in three subscription packages: a general entertainment package, a sports channel package and a film channel package. Customers can subscribe to one, two or three packages.

The company operates in three different countries, and the contents of each package vary between each country.

Operating figures for the current year are shown in Table 2.1.4.

▼ Table 2.1.4: Operating figures for the three countries in which the company operates

	Country 1	Country 2	Country 3	Total
Package	Number of subscribers	Number of subscribers	Number of subscribers	Number of subscribers
	million	million	million	million
General entertainment	5.0	3.0	4.5	12.5
Sports	9.0	7.0	6.5	22.5
Film	7.5	6.0	7.0	20.5
	21.5	16.0	18.0	55.5
Subscription revenues	$5.2 billion	$4.5 billion	$4.5 billion	$14.2 billion

1 What marketing objectives might the company set for its subscription services?

Other marketing objectives

A business can have other marketing objectives, some of which might be difficult to measure quantitatively. Here are some examples:

- To build awareness of the company's brand name and brand image.
- To improve relationships with customers.
- To win new customers.
- To launch new products successfully.
- Sales per sales channel. For example, a company might have different objectives for the value of sales through retail stores and the value of online sales.

Value of and influences on marketing plans and budgets

Marketing should be planned. There are several reasons why plans are valuable in business.

- Planning gives an organisation a clear sense of direction and what it is trying to achieve. Plans should be communicated to everyone involved in putting the plans into action, so that they understand priorities and know what is expected of them.
- Good planning should give business managers an understanding of what achievements are realistically possible.
- Plans provide a benchmark for monitoring actual progress. Actual performance should be reviewed regularly against the plan. If comparison of actual results with the planning objective or target

shows that performance is falling behind or below target, management can decide whether control measures are needed to improve performance, or whether the plan needs to be reviewed and revised.

- Plans set a time frame for achievement. Plans are a statement not only of what the organisation is trying to achieve, but also when.

Marketing objectives, strategy and tactics

Marketing objectives have already been described, but we can make a distinction between broad and longer-term objectives, medium-term objectives and short-term objectives. Business planning in general, including marketing planning, often takes the form of a hierarchy of plans: objectives, strategies and tactics. Strategic plans are influenced by long-term broad objectives, and tactical planning is influenced by strategic plans.

Broad objectives are generally long term and general in nature. Long-term objectives may not be quantified, and are stated in general terms, although they often have a time frame for achievement. For example, the objectives of a business, as we have seen, may be to increase sales or increase market share. Quantitative targets may be included in long-term objectives. For example, the longer-term objective of a business and its marketing activities may be to:

- Double total sales within five years
- Increase its market share to over 40% within five years
- Achieve 60% of total sales online within four years.

Marketing strategies are plans for achieving the broad marketing objectives. For example, if a company's objective is to double sales within five years, how should it plan its marketing activities to make achievement of the objective possible?

Strategies may have a short-term time frame, but strategic planning generally covers a period of several years, and so may be described as medium-term planning.

Here are some strategies that a company might adopt to achieve its objective of increasing sales or market share:

- Expand internationally, and sell the company' s products in more countries
- Innovate and develop new products that make use of digital technology, robotics or artificial intelligence
- Increase the amount of money for marketing activities (in other words, increase the size of the annual marketing budget)
- Develop customer awareness of the company and its brand ("build the brand")
- Build a warehouse facility for handling and despatching online sales orders
- Reduce costs in order to become a low-cost competitor in the market and sell products at the cheapest prices
- Decide the positioning of the company's product in its market.

Strategies should have a time frame, and many strategies have a quantified target. For example, if a company decides on a strategy to concentrate more on international sales, the five-year strategy may be

Key term

Marketing strategy: a marketing plan for achieving marketing and business objectives.

Link

Market positioning is explained on page 105.

for the company to make 60% of its sales in other countries outside its domestic market. A car manufacturer may have a strategy of developing five new models of electric car within ten years, so that 50% of its total sales in ten years' time come from electric cars.

Marketing strategies need to be consistent with the other long-term business strategies and the activities of other functions within the business.

Tactical plans are detailed plans for achieving strategic objectives. They are short-term plans of actions that are intended to achieve the marketing objectives that have been set. Marketing tactics consist largely of activities within the so-called "marketing mix", such as sales promotions, advertising, direct selling, pricing products, methods of distribution to customers, face-to-face selling, telephone selling, public relations, business exhibitions (such as air shows and book exhibitions).

Example
A company sells food and products for garden birds, such as seed mixes, feeders and manufactured nests. All its sales are online. It is enjoying success with its business, as concerns for environmental issues have been increasing among the population generally. It has developed the following hierarchy of targets, including marketing strategies and tactics for the next financial year.

Business objective
Increase sales revenue by 20% in the next year

Marketing objectives
Increase the volume of traffic to the company's website by 50% compared with last year
Increase repeat purchases by 15% compared with last year
Increase the average order value from $90 to $100

Marketing strategy
Increase awareness of target consumers of the company and its products

Redesign website to make it more user-friendly and engaging for visitors

Encourage repeat sales from existing customers

Increase average order value through adjustments to product prices and special offers

Marketing tactics
Run a TV advertising campaign early in the year

Develop a Facebook advertising campaign to run through the year

Advertise on Google

Develop website content to improve display of products, and include "package deal" offers

Email existing customers with offers of cut-price deals

Reduce free home delivery threshold from $50 to $40

Appoint an individual to work full time on social media interaction (Facebook, Twitter, etc.).

Case study

Premier League

In the UK, The Football Association Premier League Ltd (Premier League) organises the country's top football league. Its shareholders are the 20 teams that make up the league. In addition to scheduling match fixtures, the Premier League also negotiates broadcasting rights for screening matches, with television companies and other entertainment companies. The substantial revenues from broadcasting rights are distributed among the League's members. Premier League matches are the most watched across the world.

Individual clubs receive money from the Premier League but are also able to obtain revenues from other sources, such as ticket sales for attendance at matches and sponsorship deals. With their huge income, from broadcasting rights in particular, clubs are able to recruit some of the world's top footballers.

Several Premier League clubs have established ladies' teams, but revenues from this source are currently small.

1 Suggest what might be the overall objectives and marketing strategies of the Premier League.
2 Suggest what might be the overall objectives, marketing strategies and tactical marketing plans of an individual club in the Premier League.

Marketing budget

A budget is a plan, usually expressed in financial terms. Many organisations, especially larger organisations, prepare a budget each year for the next financial year. The "master budget" is a financial plan for the organisation as a whole. This is built up from a number of functional or departmental budgets, including a marketing budget.

A **marketing budget** is a financial plan for marketing in the next financial year, stating how much should be (or can be) spent on marketing activities. In other words, a marketing budget is a marketing expenditure plan. Marketing management are expected to keep total spending within the amount stated in the budget, and are held responsible for any over-spending.

The budget may be simply a total amount of permitted expenditure on marketing. More likely, it will analyse the total expenditure into spending on different marketing and selling activities, such as TV advertising, internet advertising, telephone selling, sales promotions, and so on.

Budgets, including a marketing budget, have several different **purposes**.

- A marketing budget is a plan that fits in with the budgets for other functions in the organisation, such as production, logistics, accounting and finance, and human resources management. It is part of a co-ordinated annual plan for the organisation as a whole.
- It informs marketing management how much they are allowed to spend in the financial year. Tactical marketing plans for the financial year must be consistent with the spending limit in the financial plan (the budget).

> ### Key term
>
> **Marketing budget**: a financial plan, setting out the approved amount of expenditure on marketing activities for a financial year.

- A marketing budget enables a business to co-ordinate its planned marketing activities with the budgeted activities of other functions, such as production, procurement and recruitment.

- It provides a way for management to monitor actual spending as the financial year gets under way. Budget reports may be produced every month, or every three months, showing what actual spending has been in the year to date, and comparing this with expected spending, as specified in the budget. If actual spending differs substantially from the budget, management can investigate the cause or causes and take remedial action if this seems appropriate.

External and internal influences on marketing planning, objectives and decisions

Marketing plans and objectives, and marketing decisions in general, are influenced by a number of different factors. Some of these influences are internal and specific to the organisation itself. Other influences are external, and arise from the environment in which the organisation operates.

The main influences are summarised in Table 2.1.5.

▼ **Table 2.1.5:** Internal and external influences on marketing

Internal influences	External influences
Available money to spend on marketing.	Technology and communications for marketing.
Available staff with appropriate marketing skills.	Ethical influences (especially environmental influences).
Available know-how and experience of marketing management.	Market conditions and competition: domestic and international competition in the market.
Productive capacity (output capacity).	
Geographical spread of business activities.	

Resources

All organisations, even the largest, have limited resources. Objectives, plans and day-to-day decisions are constrained by the limits to what the organisation is capable of with its available resources.

There is a limit to the amount of money they have available to spend, and a limit to the number of employees (particularly skilled employees) available to do certain work. As a general rule, small organisations have fewer resources for marketing than larger organisations. There will be a limit to:

- The amount of money available for spending on activities such as advertising and sales promotions

- The availability of skilled employees, such as talented salesmen or IT specialists with a knowledge of digital marketing or analysing marketing data

- The availability of marketing managers with the knowledge and experience to make sound marketing decisions

- Productive capacity: marketing activities should not aim to achieve sales in excess of the organisation's output capacity
- The geographical spread of activities (except for large international companies).

Technology

Although organisations are limited by the resources they have available, developments in technology and communications have made it much easier for businesses to reach out to potential customers. Digital marketing communications can be:

- Instant
- Directed at particular individuals or groups of individuals
- Relatively inexpensive.

Digital marketing

Digital marketing is a general term for the marketing of products or services using digital channels such as the internet. Businesses use their website to advertise and sell their products and services. They also advertise on social media, on search engines such as Google, and using mobile apps. They send marketing emails to customers on an e-mailing list. For example, many companies that offer holiday packages regularly email previous customers with offers of new holidays at attractive prices.

Digital marketing does not always use the internet. For example, digital billboards are advertising screens in public places showing images, video and text, and delivered by computer software.

Social media marketing

A large proportion of advertising and sales promotion is now conducted through social media. Social media includes social networking sites such as Facebook, LinkedIn and Google+, microblogging sites such as Twitter, photo sharing (such as Instagram and Snapchat) and video sharing sites such as YouTube.

Social media sites are used by businesses both to deliver marketing messages, but also to engage with customers and potential customers. Consumers may be persuaded to buy products from a company whose social media page is responsive (with active and positive two-way communication), or offers promotions, educational content or interesting visuals.

Relationship marketing

Relationship marketing is a marketing activity that does not focus on making immediate sales. Instead, it seeks to develop long-term customer loyalty and interactive engagement with the business. The relationship is typically developed through social media, but it encourages ongoing two-way communication, for example through satisfaction surveys, instalment payment plans or extended product warranties. Through communication with individual customers, it is possible to build a customer profile and recognise an individual's buying patterns. These can then be used to offer promotions and encourage repeat buying. An example is a company selling cars to private buyers: having sold customers a new car, they will engage regularly via emails and direct mail to maintain a relationship, so that customers are encouraged to go back to the company for repairs and maintenance and, eventually, a repeat car purchase.

Dynamic pricing

Dynamic pricing is real-time pricing, where the price for an item is varied up or down in response to demand. It is a marketing technique that uses the internet.

Airlines use dynamic pricing to adjust the prices of flights. Typically, prices may be set at a low initial price to attract early customers, and depending on the strength of demand, prices are then raised gradually (as directed by a computer program) as the flight fills up. In this way, an airline can expect to fill all or most of the seats on its flights.

E-commerce

E-commerce is a term that describes conducting business over an electronic network, primarily the internet. It includes digital marketing, for both B2B and B2C marketing.

An example of e-commerce, not yet mentioned, is the use of e-catalogues and e-markets by businesses to sell their products to other businesses. A company may sell products out of an e-catalogue on its own website, but there are also e-markets where the products of several different suppliers are marketed to online buyers, most of them businesses.

There are also business-to-consumer e-markets, such as online selling by Amazon, and consumer-to-consumer (C2C) websites for selling products; eBay is perhaps the most well known of these.

M-commerce

M-commerce (short for mobile commerce) involves marketing products through wireless hand-held devices such as mobile phones, tablets and laptops.

Online selling

Online selling is a general term for selling products or services via the internet or a mobile app. Customers can usually buy products or services and pay for them online. Products may be delivered digitally (such as films, music and books) or delivered physically to the buyer.

Activity

Choose one or more methods of digital marketing and carry out research into how businesses use their websites, social media sites or search engines to market their products or services.

Study how the products and services are marketed, and write up notes on how effective or ineffective you think these methods of marketing seem to be.

Progress questions

5 What is dynamic pricing?

6 What is the purpose of digital relationship marketing?

7 Explain how social media might be used by a company to market its products.

Ethical influences on marketing

Many companies, particularly large companies, have ethical business objectives. Ethics in business relate to the way a business treats its suppliers and customers, the concerns that it shows for people in society, communities and the natural environment.

There are many examples of ethical business objectives and policies. Here are just a few examples:

- A company that sells fashion clothes may have a policy of using manufacturers who treat their workers well, providing them with clean and safe working conditions and paying reasonable wages
- A company that produces eyewear might donate products to disadvantaged children around the world who have problems with vision
- Food producers may have a policy of sustainable sourcing, buying raw materials and commodities only if they come from a renewable source
- Producers of cleaning products may have a programme for developing products that use limited amounts of water, for the benefit of consumers in countries with severe water shortages.

Businesses that have ethical objectives, ethical strategies and behave ethically will often use ethical marketing methods. Table 2.1.6 shows some examples.

▼ **Table 2.1.6**: Ethical marketing practice

Being truthful	Being fair	Protecting customers
Honest advertising Not making false claims for a product	Fair pricing for products and services	Protecting the privacy of personal data about customers, and not using it for personalised marketing without the individual's knowledge and consent

Key term

Ethical marketing: marketing that promotes ethical aspects of an organisation's products and activities. Ethics in business and marketing relate to issues such as environmental protection, social responsibility and employee welfare.

Companies may also use their ethical business practices to interest potential customers in their products and services. **Ethical marketing** might even be defined as generating customer interest or building a customer relationship by including social and environmental considerations in their products and promotions. Companies may, for example, publicise their environmentally friendly products or socially responsible employment practices and materials sourcing practices.

For example, if a company sells its consumer products in biodegradable packaging, it is being environmentally responsible and at the same time it is likely to advertise the fact that the packaging is biodegradable on the packaging itself because this may persuade some customers to buy the products.

Example

Xerox, the information technology company, was named in 2018 as one of the world's most ethical companies by the Ethisphere Institute, an organisation that promotes ethical business practices, for the twelfth year in succession.

Ethical standards were scored in five different categories: the company's ethics and compliance programme, its culture of ethics, its governance and leadership, innovation and reputation.

Market conditions and competition

Marketing decisions are affected by conditions in the market and by the nature of the competition and what competitors are doing. Here are a few examples of how market conditions can affect the marketing decisions that a business makes.

Product life cycle

Some products go through a "product life cycle", although the length of the cycle can vary substantially. A product begins its life when it is first developed and introduced to the market. If it is successful, demand for the product will grow, and the product will enter a strong growth phase. Eventually, demand will level out and the product enters a "mature" phase of its life. Eventually, demand begins to fall, and the product goes into a decline phase. Eventually, the product may be removed from the market entirely. You might be able to think of examples, such as black-and-white televisions. Demand for desk-top computers is much less than it used to be.

Marketing decisions will be influenced by the stage of its life that a product (or service) has reached. In the early stages of a product's life, the aim of marketing may be to make potential customers aware of its existence and to encourage early customers to buy it. During the growth phase of a product's life cycle, the aim of marketing might be to reach out to as many customers as possible and achieve strong sales growth, possibly internationally as well as domestically. In the mature phase, marketing might be directed at maintaining market share. As demand for the product declines, the decision might be to reduce the amount of marketing for the product, and switch resources to marketing other products.

Social habits and attitudes

Demographic change, and changing social habits and attitudes can also influence marketing decisions. Demographic change is change in the size or composition of a country's population. In some countries, a large proportion of the population is young, whereas other countries have an "ageing population". Changes in a population lead to changes in attitudes and social habits. For example, younger generations today are on the whole more familiar than older generations with technology, media and communications. Marketing activities need to adapt to widespread use of the internet and mobile technology.

There has been an increase in environmental awareness in recent years, and a substantial number of people are in favour of measures to protect and preserve the environment, reduce pollution, protect wildlife, and so on. Marketing decisions may be made with the aim of promoting the "green credentials" of the business, in order to appeal to environmentally conscious consumers.

> ### Key term
>
> **Product life cycle**: stages through which a product's market progresses, from introduction to the market to decline and withdrawal from the market.

▲ **Figure 2.1.2** Some countries, such as China, have an ageing population.

Competition

Businesses cannot ignore their competitors, and their actions may be strongly influenced by what competitors are doing. If they want to maintain or increase their market share, they must market their products or services as effectively – or more effectively – than competitors. Marketing decisions may be about whether to increase or reduce the price of product, and if so by how much. If competitors use new methods of selling and distributing their products, for example through online selling, businesses will respond.

Some global companies are able to market their product or products internationally, with much the same marketing methods in most countries: some soft drinks manufacturers and car manufacturers are examples. Some companies compete with just a few competitors in a global market, such as manufacturers of commercial aircraft. For many companies that operate internationally, however, marketing decisions may vary according to different market conditions and different competitors in each country. For example, companies might price their products and distribute them differently between national markets and product designs might vary to suit the tastes of consumers in each country.

Exam-style questions

1 A company has a stated aim of becoming the market leader in the domestic market for cleaning equipment. This is an example of:

    A   A marketing objective

    B   A marketing strategy

    C   A marketing tactic

    D   A marketing budget.   (1 mark)

2 During a one-year period, a company sold 10,000 units of a product. Of these 2,500 were repeat sales. This means that during the year:

    A   25% of customers bought the product for a second time

    B   25% of sales were to customers who had bought the product previously

    C   75% of customers buy the product just once

    D   only 25% of customers were satisfied with the product they bought.   (1 mark)

3 A company sells annual subscriptions to a music streaming service. At the beginning of the year it had 6 million subscribers and at the end of the year it had 6.2 million subscribers. During the year it gained 800,000 new subscribers, but 600,000 subscribers did not renew their annual subscription.

    What was the customer retention rate during the year?

    A   25%

    B   75%

    C   90%

    D   91.2%   (1 mark)

4 A company had 15,200 employees at the beginning of Year 1, 16,000 employees at the beginning of Year 2 and 16,600 employees at the end of Year 2. Company sales were $140 million in Year 1 and $150 million in Year 2.

    Calculate by how much sales per employee increased or fell during Year 2 compared with Year 1.   (4 marks)

5 The fishing industry is subject to internationally agreed rules on fishing rights and fishing quotas. Explain how a change in these rules might affect the marketing plans of a company that operates a small fleet of fishing vessels.   (4 marks)

6 Many companies prepare a marketing budget each year. Explain the benefits they can obtain from doing this.   (9 marks)

7 A medium-sized high-tech company currently designs and manufactures drones and sells them into its domestic market. It is now considering whether to expand its business into international markets.

    Assess the arguments for and against international market expansion in this case and make a judgement.   (12 marks)

The value of primary and secondary marketing research

What is marketing research?

Marketing research is research into aspects of marketing to obtain information that will be used to make a marketing decision or prepare a marketing plan. The term "market research" is often used instead of marketing research: market research involves obtaining information about a particular market.

What information is obtained? Marketing research aims to obtain information that will be relevant to a particular marketing decision or the preparation of a marketing plan. It might be information about consumer preferences, the amount of money that consumers spend on certain types of product, where customers buy their products, how many people watch advertisements on television, or respond to marketing initiatives on one or more social media websites. There are many other items of information that marketing researchers may want to obtain.

▲ **Figure 2.2.1**: Analysing marketing research data

Primary and secondary marketing research

There are two approaches to obtaining marketing data.

Primary market research involves obtaining information directly from its source. Typically this means obtaining information directly from consumers or customers. Methods of conducting primary research include face-to-face interviews, telephone surveys, and asking customers for feedback via digital media. Primary marketing research is undertaken by an organisation for its own specific purposes.

Secondary market research involves obtaining information from studies or other research that has been conducted by someone else, or from sources that already exist. There are four broad types of source for secondary market research: published government statistics, research published by a research organisation or trade association, published research by universities and other educational institutions, and company websites (which often contain extensive details about the company, its products and its markets).

Both types of marketing research have their benefits and limitations, as shown in Table 2.2.1.

▼ **Table 2.2.1**: Benefits and limitations of primary and secondary research

Primary marketing research	Secondary marketing research
Information obtained has direct relevance for a marketing decision or marketing plan.	Information can be obtained for a low cost or possibly free of charge.
Can be effective in obtaining the required information, especially from face-to-face interviews.	Can be used to obtain general information that has relevance to a market, such as the size and age distribution of regional populations, and average household incomes.
Researchers can ask structured pre-prepared questions (questionnaires).	Fairly easy and quick to obtain.
Information obtained is unique: no one else has it.	
BUT It can be expensive to carry out primary research, and primary research takes longer to plan and carry out than secondary research.	BUT Information obtained is not customised to the specific requirements of the organisation, and does not provide all the information required.

Qualitative and quantitative data

Marketing research obtains data, which is analysed to produce relevant information. Marketing data is either qualitative or quantitative:

Qualitative data is data about the quality or perceived quality of something: it is commonly expressed in the form of opinions or judgements. For example, a group of consumers may be asked for their views about the reasons they like or dislike a product or an advertisement.

Quantitative data is data in numerical form. How many times do you buy a certain product each month? When did you last buy this product? A large number of people might be asked a particular question – such as which country did you go to on holiday last summer – and answers can be quantified by the numbers of people who went to each country.

Researchers often prefer quantitative data to qualitative data, because quantitative data can be analysed more easily, and is "hard evidence". This is why marketing research questionnaires may ask respondents for numerical answers to questions about opinions.

Example

Market researchers may want to learn whether consumers are likely to buy a new product. In face-to-face interviews, researchers can use a questionnaire to ask questions such as:

	Not at all	Not much	No opinion either way	Slightly	Very much
How useful did you find the product					

	Certainly not	Probably not	Not sure	Probably	Definitely
Will you buy the product again?					

Answers give qualitative opinions but these can be quantified by giving scores of 1, 2, 3, 4 or 5 to the various answers, to obtain an average opinion (say, 2.4) and the proportions of respondents giving each different view.

Progress questions

1 What is the purpose of marketing research?
2 What are the main sources of secondary marketing data?
3 What methods might be used to obtain primary marketing data?

Case study

Video advertising

A company has prepared a short video advertising a chain of low-price hotels that it operates. Before it puts the advertisement out on to social media and possibly also television, the company wants to obtain views from members of the public about the advertisement and how effective it might be.

It wants to obtain both qualitative and quantitative data.

1 What type of market research should be used to obtain the required information. Explain the reason for you suggestion.

Market mapping

Market mapping uses a diagram or chart to "map" products in a particular market according to two characteristics, such as price and quality. For each characteristic there are two extreme measures, such as high price and low price, and poor quality and high quality. These are shown in the market map as two axes, a vertical and a horizontal axis.

Products or competitors in the market are then placed in the map according to how they rate for the two characteristics. An example is shown in Figure 2.2.2, which is a market map for restaurants in an area that rates each restaurant by price level and quality of food.

In this market map, there are only five local restaurants but in practice there would probably be many more.

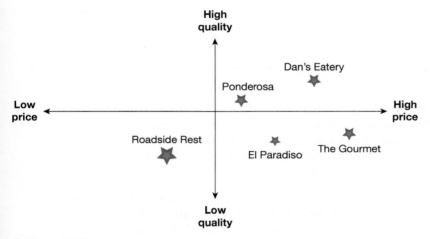

▲ **Figure 2.2.2:** A market map

A market map can be used to identify possible "gaps" in the market, where a newcomer to the market may be able to target successfully. In the example here, there are no restaurants offering good quality food at a fairly low price, so there may be a gap in the market here.

Market maps can be used to look for gaps in the market by looking at other product characteristics, such as:

- Necessity/luxury item
- Simple/complex
- Low-tech/high-tech.

Sales forecasts

An important reason for obtaining marketing research data is to prepare a sales forecast for a future period, such as the next year. Making accurate sales forecasts is extremely difficult, because what will happen in the future is not easy to predict. Companies can try to forecast sales on the basis of past experience (historical sales), what they expect to be different in the future, and their marketing objectives. Sales forecasts are a prediction, and they may also be used as a sales target: but they are unlikely to be "100% accurate".

Even so, sales forecasts are hugely important for business planning. The amount of sales ("sales demand") is the starting point for deciding on the scale of operations in the future period to which the forecast relates.

- A manufacturing company's plans for the quantities of product that it will make will depend on expected sales demand for the product. If sales demand is expected to grow, a decision must be made about how to make the additional quantities of product. Will more employees be needed? Or additional or better machinery?
- Similarly, the sales forecast for a service organisation will determine how many people the organisation needs to deliver its services.
- Forecasts of sales growth might trigger decisions about investing to increase operational capacity.

So when a company is preparing its "master budget" for the next financial year, the sales forecast is usually the starting point for planning.

The accuracy of sales forecasting

There are several ways of producing a sales forecast, but none of them are necessarily reliable.

One approach to sales forecasting is to **use historical data about sales demand** and apply a quantitative/mathematical technique to the data in order to prepare a sales forecast for the future. This approach is based on the view that future sales can be estimated mathematically from past sales.

Another approach to sales forecasting is to **obtain opinions or judgements from people whose views might be reliable**. For example, a sales forecast might be obtained by gathering the views of "experts", such as sales managers, and reaching a consensus view about future sales. Another method is to carry out a marketing research exercise (sampling) and asking a sample of potential customers about their buying intentions.

Sampling

The purpose of sampling in marketing research

When an organisation wants to obtain marketing data from customers or potential customers, it can carry out primary marketing research. It will need to decide what method of research it should use: face-to-face interviews, telephone interviews, requests for feedback, and so on.

However, unless the market is very small, it is impossible to obtain data from every customer and potential customer. Asking for detailed opinions from a large number of people will take a lot of time and effort, and so will cost a lot of money. Obtaining the views of a sufficient number of them should provide a reliable guide to what everyone thinks, and will take less time and cost less.

So for practical reasons, data will be obtained from a selected number of customers. Data is gathered from a sample of customers or potential customers, and it is assumed that the data obtained from the sample will be representative of the entire population of customers and potential customers.

> **Key term**
>
> Sampling: obtaining data from a small number of individuals in a population, in the expectation that the results from the sample will be representative of the population as a whole.

Case study

Motor boats

A manufacturer of small motor boats is preparing a sales forecast for the next year. Sales demand has been growing strongly in recent years, and in the current year sales growth (measured by sales revenue) is expected to exceed 20%. The company is now operating near capacity.

A number of different methods have been used to prepare the sales forecast, but the sales estimates produced by each method differ considerably.

What might the consequences for the company be in the following situations?

1 If actual sales prove to be much lower than forecast.
2 If actual sales demand proves to be much higher than forecast.

Choosing a sample: bias

A problem with sampling is that the data obtained from the sample might not be representative of the "population". There may be bias in the responses.

Example

The example here is not a marketing example, it may explain clearly how bias in sampling might occur. Suppose that a school is carrying out a survey into the number of hours each week that students do homework. It will take too much time and effort to obtain data from every student so it is decided to obtain responses from a sample of 50 students. The school has 1,800 students aged between 10 and 16, and class sizes are 50 students.

The data obtained from a sample will be biased in any of the following situations:

- The 50 students in the sample are all in the same class at school.
- The 50 students in the sample are all the same age.
- The school population consists of 50% boys and 50% girls, but the sample consists of 40 girls and 10 boys.

The sample may also be unreliable because the sample size is not large enough, and the responses of just 50 students chosen at random might not be representative of the school population as a whole.

Random sampling

The aim should be to obtain responses from a sample of respondents that are likely to represent with reasonable accuracy the views of everyone. In other words, the aim should be to eliminate bias as much as possible from the survey sample.

Random sampling is a method of sampling in which the sample is selected at random from the "population", so that everyone in the population has an equal chance of selection. For example, suppose that a manufacturer of shoes sells its products to 200 retailing companies. If it wants to obtain data about the buying intentions of these retailers in order to prepare a sales forecast, it might decide to obtain data from a sample of 40. A random sample would be taken, with each retailer having a 1 in 5 chance of being selected for the sample.

Key term

Random sampling: sampling in which every individual within a population has an equal chance of being selected for the sample. A sampling frame (a list of everyone in the population) is necessary for random sampling.

Random sampling has its problems.

In order to take a random sample, it is necessary to know about everyone in the entire population. This is often impossible. For example, a random sample of consumers in the market for mobile phones cannot be obtained, because it is impossible to identify individually all the many millions of consumers in the market.

To obtain a random sample, it is necessary to prepare a sampling frame from which the sample can be taken. A sampling frame is a list of everyone in the population from which the sample will be taken.

When obtaining a random sample, it is assumed that everyone in the population is similar to everyone else. This may be true in some cases, but it is not true in many others. To obtain a representative sample from a population, it may be necessary first of all to divide the population into different types or categories, known as strata.

Stratified sampling

Stratified sampling will result in a sample that is more representative of the population as a whole when the population is divided into different types of people. With stratified sampling:

- Two or more different categories or strata are identified within the population a whole
- A sampling frame is prepared for each of them individually
- A random sample is taken from each of the strata
- The size of the sample for each of the strata should reflect the proportion of the total population that each of them represents.

Example

A car manufacturer is preparing a sales forecast for car sales to its business customers next year. It knows the full extent of its customer base, which consists of 200 customers, and it intends to use random sampling to obtain data about buying intentions from a sample of 40 customers.

Its customers differ in size and the amount of their purchases. Ten customers are large international companies that purchase cars regularly and in large quantities. Fifty companies are medium-sized international companies that also purchase fairly frequently, but in smaller quantities. The remaining 140 customers are smaller companies that buy cars less frequently and in smaller quantities.

If a random sample of 40 is taken from the population as a whole, regardless of the different types of customer within the population of 200, the selected sample may not be properly representative of all the different strata within the population. For example, medium-sized companies may be under- or over-represented in the sample. With stratified sampling, a random sample would be taken from each of the strata. Assuming that the sampling is based on numbers of customers in each category (rather than the amount of spending on cars by each category), a random stratified sample would contain 2 large companies (5% of the sample), 10 medium-sized companies (25%) and 28 small companies (70%), with customers from each category selected at random.

Key term

Stratified sampling: sampling in which a population is divided into categories or strata, and a sample is taken from each of the strata. Stratified samples should ideally be selected randomly.

Quota sampling

A problem with random stratified sampling, as with random sampling in general, is that it is only possible when every member of the population can be identified individually, so that a sampling frame can be prepared. In practice, especially when taking samples of consumers from a consumer market, this is not possible.

Quota sampling is non-random stratified sampling.

- The entire population is divided into strata.
- An estimate is made of the proportion of the total population belonging to each of the strata.
- When the total sample size is decided, a sample is obtained from each of the strata, and the sample size for each is decided according to the proportion of the total population that it represents. However, the samples cannot be selected randomly.

Strata commonly used in quota sampling for a consumer market are age, gender, socioeconomic status, nationality and educational attainment.

The value of sampling

Since sample results may contain bias so that they are not representative, it is reasonable to ask why it is worth obtaining samples. However, sampling can be valuable.

- Sample results are often reasonably representative of the population as a whole, and help businesses to improve their knowledge of their market.
- Marketing research is carried out to help with marketing decisions and marketing planning. Sampling is one method of obtaining marketing research data.
- Data obtained from sampling is probably better than having no data at all.

> **Key term**
>
> Quota sampling: non-random stratified sampling. This is used when the total population is divided into different categories or strata, but a sampling frame for the population is not available.

Case study

Developing a new biscuit

A biscuit manufacturer has developed a new biscuit product, targeted at adult customers, and it wants to obtain data about the likely demand for the biscuit. It believes that sales demand is likely to differ between adult consumers according to their age, and it has decided to hire an agency to conduct quota sampling on its behalf in two large towns, one in the north and one in the south of the country. Government statistics, obtained from secondary marketing research, show that 50% of the adult population is aged between 18 and 25, 20% are aged over 25 and up to 50, and 30% are aged over 50.

The total sample size will be 300. Responses will be obtained by researchers using questionnaires and face-to-face interviews with people in the street in the centres of the two towns.

1. How would a quota sample be structured?
2. How might the population be stratified other than by age?
3. A quota sample is not a random sample. What might the researchers do to reduce the risk of bias in the sample that is taken?

However, there is a trade-off between the value of the information obtained from a sample and the sample size. The results from a large sample are likely to be more reliable than the results from a much smaller sample, but the cost of obtaining the sample might be much higher. If so, the value of more reliable information should be weighed against the additional cost of obtaining it.

Progress questions

4 Why are sales forecasts important?

5 Why is it often necessary to use sampling to obtain marketing research data?

6 What is the purpose of a sampling frame?

7 Why is it not possible to use random sampling to obtain a quota sample?

Influences on choosing a form of marketing research

How does an organisation decide which form of marketing research it should use to obtain marketing information? The main considerations are set out in Table 2.2.2.

▼ **Table 2.2.2**: Influences on choosing a form of marketing research

Influence	Comment
What is the purpose of the research?	Research is carried out to obtain information to assist with marketing decisions or prepare marketing plans. If general information is required about market conditions, secondary marketing research may be sufficient. A market map might be used to look for gaps in a market.
How much will it cost?	Some methods of marketing research are much less costly than others. Obtaining customer feedback via social media or email is inexpensive. The use of researchers for face-to-face interviews or telephone interviews is much more expensive, and so unlikely to be worthwhile unless the marketing data obtained is considered to be worth the cost.
How long will it take to obtain the information?	Market research using questionnaires can be a lengthy process. It takes time to design a suitable questionnaire and to plan a face-to-face interview or telephone interview programme. When questionnaires are sent by post or email to respondents, they must be given a sufficient amount of time to respond. Feedback from social media can be continuous.
The reliability of the research findings	It seems that face-to-face interviews are probably the most reliable way of obtaining data from customers or potential customers, although there may be a risk of bias in the results obtained. With planned interviews, questions can be prepared carefully in advance. Research findings may also be much less reliable when individuals do not respond when asked to provide data, or when only a small proportion of customers provide their views in feedback (and most do not).

The interpretation and use of marketing data in marketing decision-making and planning

Marketing research produces data. Data is of limited value unless it is used to provide information that is of value for marketing decision-making and planning. Business managers (marketing managers) need to understand what the marketing data appears to be telling them.

- There are various ways in which marketing data can be used to provide marketing information. Data about the buying intentions of a sample of consumers can be used to prepare sales forecasts, or predict sales growth. Marketing research data can also be used to obtain information about customer preferences and buying habits, and how these are changing.

- Historical sales data can be used to detect changes in customer buying habits, for example an increase in online buying by consumers and businesses, and an increase in online selling by manufacturers direct to consumers.

- Marketing data might be interpreted using statistical analysis. Two methods of statistical analysis are correlation and measurement of confidence levels.

Correlation

Correlation analysis is a statistical technique that is used to measure the strength of the relationship between two variables. A simple example is the relationship between a person's height and weight. As a general rule, we would expect taller people to be heavier than shorter people. This is by no means true in all cases: there are tall people who weigh very little and short people who are very heavy. But as a general rule, we expect to see correlation – a relationship – between height and weight.

Correlation may be positive or negative

Correlation is **positive** when the value of one variable increases when the value of the other variable increases, and falls when the value of the other variable falls.

Correlation is **negative** when the value of one variable falls when the value of the other variable increases, and increases when the value of the other variable falls.

Examples of positive and negative correlation are show in Figure 2.2.3.

> ## Key term
>
> **Correlation**: relationship between the values of two variables, and how changes in the value of one variable relate to changes in the value of the other variable. Correlation may be positive, negative or non-existent.

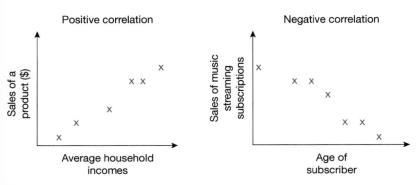

▲ **Figure 2.2.3**: Positive and negative correlation

In these examples:

There is positive correlation between average household incomes and sales of a product, and negative correlation between the number of subscriptions to a streaming service and the age of subscribers.

Lines of best fit

It might be assumed that there is a linear relationship between the variables in each case, and that we can draw a "line of best fit" through the data. There is a statistical technique for doing this, called linear regression analysis. Using linear regression analysis, we can calculate lines of best fit for our two examples, which might be the lines shown in Figure 2.2.4.

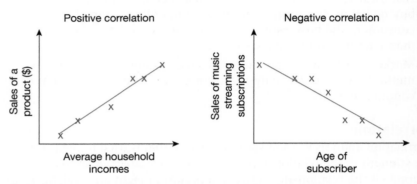

▲ **Figure 2.2.4**: Correlation and regression analysis: lines of best fit

We can use a line of best fit to make estimates. For example, if we think we know what average household income will be next year, we can make an estimate of what sales of the product are likely to be.

Correlation coefficient

But how reliable is an assumption of correlation between two variables? Correlation is not just positive or negative, but it is also either weak or strong. When historical data is used to measure correlation between two variables, we can calculate a statistical measure known as a **correlation coefficient**, which measures the closeness or strength of correlation between the two variables. This can have any value between +1 and −1. The closer the correlation coefficient is to +1 or to −1, the stronger is the correlation between the two variables.

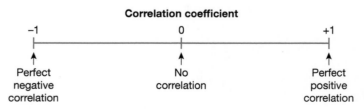

▲ **Figure 2.2.5**: Correlation coefficients

Case study

Ice cream

An ice cream manufacturer has investigated the correlation between daily sales of its products within a region of the country and air temperatures at midday in the region's main city. It has obtained data about air temperatures from secondary research into government statistics, and data about ice cream sales from its own records. Analysis has shown that the correlation coefficient between daily temperature and ice cream sales is +0.83.

1 How might this correlation coefficient be interpreted?
2 How might this information be used by the ice cream manufacturer to make a marketing decision?

Correlation is not causation

Strong correlation means that there is a close relationship between the value of two variables. However, it does not necessarily mean that changes in the value of one variable cause changes in the value of another. It is often convenient to assume that there is a causal relationship, but measurements of correlation are not proof of this.

For example, there may be strong positive correlation between levels of air pollution in a big city and sales of face masks, with a correlation coefficient of +0.89 based on historical records of face mask sales and pollution levels. It might be tempting to conclude that changes in pollution levels are the main cause of changes in the volume of face mask sales. However, such a causal relationship is not "proved" by the high positive correlation coefficient, even if it might be assumed that causation exists.

Activity

Correlation between two variables can be measured using historical data, but in marketing it might not be easy to identify situations where correlation exists.

Draw up a list of relationships between two variables in marketing where you think there might be strong correlation between the variables. For each of these relationships you have identified, suggest how you would obtain historical data for measuring the extent of the correlation between them.

Hint: One of the variables in a relationship could be a marketing activity.

Confidence levels

A confidence level is measured as a probability and is the probability (or an estimate of the probability) that something will happen, or will not happen. For example, a company might estimate that there is an 80% probability that by refreshing its social media pages daily, sales of its products will increase. This also means that there is an estimated 20% probability that sales would not increase.

A film company might estimate on the basis of past experience that if it spends money on advertising a new blockbuster movie, there is a 75% probability that audiences for the film will be at least 10% higher.

Estimates of probability, or confidence levels, can often help with marketing decisions about whether or not to undertake a marketing activity.

Key term

Confidence level: the probability that an outcome will occur

But where do the estimates of probabilities and confidence levels come from? Past experience? Expert judgement? Guesswork? Confidence levels are only useful for decision-making in marketing if they are reasonably reliable.

In some situations, a level of confidence can be measured statistically, from historical records or from marketing research data. For example, it might be possible to measure the probability, at a given level of confidence, that:

- Car buyers will replace their car with a new one within one to five years of purchase
- 18–20-year-olds will spend between $10 and $15 each week on sweets (candy)
- Mobile phone (cell phone) users will spend on average between 30 minutes and two hours each day sending and receiving text messages.

Distribution of probabilities

It is often possible to show the results of historical data or marketing research data as a probability distribution. This is a graph or chart showing the variations in the data values obtained and the frequency of each data value in the results, expressed as a percentage of the total. It has been found from experience that a probability distribution often takes the form of a bell-shaped curve, known as a **normal distribution**.

Figure 2.2.6 illustrates how marketing research data about the amount of time city centre workers spend travelling to and from work each week can be summarised in a probability distribution.

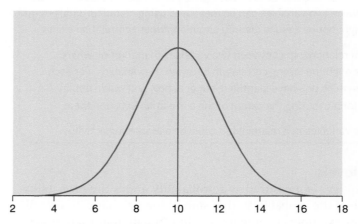

▲ **Figure 2.2.6**: Normal distribution

The graph in Figure 2.2.6 shows the responses from all the individuals in a marketing research sample. This shows that responses ranged from about one hour to about 17 hours per week, and that the spread of results is evenly balanced above and below 10 hours a week. The average time for the entire sample, known as the **mean** of the distribution, is 10 hours.

Analysing a probability distribution

The data used to prepare this probability distribution can also be used to obtain a measure of the variations in values around the mean (average) of 10 hours, and to establish, at a given level of confidence, the range within which the travelling times of individuals are likely to occur.

Looking at the graph of the probability distribution, you might also agree that it shows that most individuals spend somewhere between about 6 hours and 14 hours a week travelling to and from work. Using statistical analysis it might be possible to make the following conclusion.

"At the 95% confidence level, weekly travelling times are between 6 hours and 14 hours."

Another way of saying this is that at a 95% confidence level, the **confidence limits** are 6 hours and 14 hours. It means that 95% of workers spend between 6 hours and 14 hours each week travelling to and from work. And it also means that if you were to select any individual worker, there is a 95% probability that he or she will spend between 6 hours and 14 hours each week travelling.

The value of confidence levels and confidence limits for market research

Confidence levels and confidence limits are important in market research because they quantify the probabilities of what might occur. They recognise that variations in values exist, but that most values lie within a measurable (quantifiable) range.

Example

Market research into shopping by customers at a supermarket has found that the average (mean) amount of spending by customers at each visit is $35, and:

- At the 95% confidence level, spending per visit is between $15.40 and $54.60
- At the 99% confidence level, spending per visit is between $9.20 and $60.80.

This means that 95% of customers spend between $15.40 and $54.60 when they visit the supermarket, so that if you select any individual customer, there is a 95% probability that he or she will spend an amount between $15.40 and $54.60.

Similarly, it means that 99% of customers spend between $9.20 and $60.80 when they visit the supermarket, so that if you select any individual customer, there is a 99% probability that he or she will spend an amount between $9.20 and $60.80.

In statistical analysis of probabilities, the confidence level most commonly used is 95%.

Example

Confidence levels can be used to express confidence limits in different ways, as the following example illustrates.

Marketing research by a company that uses m-commerce to sell its products has found that, in a sample of 2,000 individuals between the ages of 18 and 21, the average time a person spends on a smartphone is 3.5 hours per day. The research also found that:

- At a 95% confidence level, individuals spend between 2.4 hours and 4.6 hours per day on their smartphone
- Also at a 95% confidence level individuals spend more than 2.78 hours per day on their smartphone
- Also at a 95% confidence level individuals do not spend more than 4.22 hours per day on their smartphone.

Big data and data mining

The analysis of marketing data has become much more sophisticated with the use of digital technology such as machine learning and artificial intelligence. Marketing researchers are able to gather vast amounts of data about individuals and their buying habits, and analyse this data to prepare targeted personalised marketing.

Example

Netflix is currently the world's leading provider of streamed entertainment services. Customers pay the company for access to watching films and tv shows. Netflix is able to build up data about the viewing preferences of individual customers, and by analysing this data, is able to personalise marketing initiatives, sending messages to individuals about other films that they might like to watch.

Big data

Big data is accumulated over time by organisations. For example, companies that operate supermarkets are able to use customer loyalty cards to accumulate data about what their customers buy and how much they spend, and they can use this data to send personalised sales promotions to individual customers, such as money off purchases of certain products.

The practice of accumulating data about customers and using this to prepare targeted marketing initiatives is not new, but big data has taken the practice to new levels of sophistication. The term "data warehouse" is used to describe the vast databases in which the data is stored. Companies might gather data about individuals from many different sources, and will often pay to obtain databases of personal information (subject to what is permitted by the law).

Features of data mining

Computers and complex programs are used to mine big data. Data mining techniques mean that big data can be analysed in many different ways, to obtain insights about customers or consumers that have not previously been recognised or understood. The purpose of data mining in marketing research is therefore to help companies decide how they should market their products or services to groups of customers/consumers, or to individuals.

Successful data mining uncovers facts that were not previously known, and that are not obtained from "traditional" marketing research methods.

> ## Key terms
>
> **Big data**: very large databases holding vast amounts of data.
>
> **Data mining**: analysing big data, typically using techniques such as machine learning and artificial intelligence, to obtain new information.

Exam-style questions

1   From market research data, it has been established that the correlation coefficient between annual purchases of new footwear by an individual and the individual's income is +0.3. This means that:

   A   correlation is positive, but to a fairly limited extent

   B   correlation is strongly positive

   C   correlation is non-existent

   D   high-income earners are 30% more likely to buy footwear than low-income earners.   (1 mark)

2   Explain which method of primary marketing research is usually the most costly to carry out, and why.   (3 marks)

3   Statistical analysis is often used in market research and the findings from market research are often expressed in terms of confidence level and confidence limits (or confidence interval). Explain the meaning of a 95% confidence level.   (3 marks)

4   Market mapping might be used to identify gaps in a market. Explain with an example how this is done.   (4 marks)

5   Many retailers of consumer goods are increasingly using data mining for marketing research in addition to using the more traditional methods of obtaining marketing research data. Explain why.   (9 marks)

6   A television company wants to carry out research into the amount of time spent by individuals aged 16 and over watching television each week. It suspects that younger people up to the age of 25 watch much less than older people, and that viewing patterns differ significantly between people in the north and people in the south of the country. It decides to obtain marketing data using face-to-face interviews by researchers.

   Explain why the researchers should use quota sampling to obtain the relevant information they need.   (9 marks)

7   Rufus is the marketing manager for a company that manufactures a range of watches and clocks. He is responsible for preparing sales forecasts, and revising forecasts when this seems necessary. On many occasions, the forecast that he produces turns out to be inaccurate.

   Do you think that it is a good idea for companies to prepare sales forecasts? Assess the advantages and difficulties, and make a judgement.   (12 marks)

This section will develop your knowledge and understanding of:

→ The process and value of segmentation, targeting and positioning
→ Influences on choosing a target market and positioning
→ Segmentation, targeting and positioning in international markets.

The process and value of segmentation, targeting and positioning

An important aspect of marketing strategy is to decide what products to sell, who to sell them to, where to sell them, and at what price. This might seem obvious. For example, you might suppose that a car manufacturer will want to sell cars to anyone who wants to buy them. However, it is not so simple. Customers or potential customers for cars can vary widely in their views about what type of car they want, and how much they are willing to pay.

It is unusual for all customers in a market to want the same things from a product, and they may respond in differing ways to attempts by a business to get them to buy it.

So an important task in marketing is to identify different types of customer for a product or service, who share similar attitudes about what they want, and who are likely to respond to marketing initiatives in a similar way.

Market segments and market segmentation

A market segment is a group of people who share one or more common characteristics, and who might be expected to want the same things from a product and react to marketing initiatives in a similar way. Customers in each segment can be expected to want different things from a product than customers in different segments.

Companies should identify segments within their market. This is called market segmentation. They should then use their analysis of segments in the market and decide which segments they should target for selling their products or services.

For example, the market for cars might be segmented by manufacturers according to family size (people carriers), lifestyle (sports cars for individuals who enjoy speed, and small cars for individuals who use cars only for short local journeys), or income (expensive and cheaper cars).

Similarly, the market for air travel may be segmented according to income or social class (different classes of seats) or lifestyle (frequency of travelling).

Methods of segmenting a market

A market may be segmented in different ways. A challenge for businesses is to choose a method of segmentation for their products

Key terms

Market segment: a part of a market that is distinctive in some way from the rest of the market.

Market segmentation: analysing a market and either dividing the market into segments for the purpose of marketing, or identifying attractive/distinctive sections within the overall market.

or services that is likely to be the most effective for developing a marketing strategy and achieving their marketing objectives.

The most common methods of segmenting markets for consumer goods or services are:

- Demographic
- Geographic
- Income
- Behavioural
- Psychographic.

Demographic segmentation

"Demographics" is a term for the statistical analysis of a population in a geographical area, and what the population consists of. One aspect of demographics is the total size of the population, but a population can be analysed in any of the following ways (or in combinations of the following ways):

- Age
- Gender
- Race
- Religion
- Family size
- Education.

If a market is divided into segments based on demographic factors, it means that the business believes that consumers of their product or service will react in different ways according to that factor or those factors.

For example, a company that publishes newspapers might take the view that members of the population differ in their attitudes to what they want to read in the papers they buy. If so, it might segment the market for newspapers according to social class or educational background.

Geographic segmentation

A market can be segmented on the basis of differences between different areas, regions or countries. If a business uses geographical segmentation, this means that it sees big differences in consumer habits and preferences between geographical areas.

For example, a manufacturer of pre-cooked meals might consider that demand for different types of pre-cooked meals and attitudes to buying pre-cooked meals differ between regions of the country. If so, it can segment the national market according to region, and consider its marketing strategy for each region separately.

Income segmentation

A market can be segmented on the basis of differences between the income of individuals or households. This would mean that customers in the market make decisions about what to buy, and react to marketing initiatives differently, according to their income.

For example, a manufacturer of coats might consider that customers make their decisions to buy a new coat, and respond to marketing initiatives to persuade them to buy coats, on the basis of their income. The company may design different types of coat, and sell them at different prices and through different channels, for each of the segments it has identified.

Behavioural segmentation

Behavioural segmentation means segmenting the market according to the ways in which different groups of customers act (behave) when they make their buying decisions. There are different ways of looking at customer behaviour.

- **Purchasing habits**: Customers may put a lot of thought and energy into making a buying decision, or may not think much before they buy. For example, a company that sells cars may find that some customers take a long time in deciding what type of car to buy, a BMW or a Mercedes, and want to obtain a lot of information before making their choice. Other customers may decide to buy a BMW because they bought a Mercedes the last time and so want to try something different. Other customers might buy a BMW or a Mercedes without too much thought, because this is the brand they have bought in the past.

- **Usage rate**: A market might be segmented between regular users, middle-level users and occasional users of a product or service.

- **User status**: Consumers may be segmented between non-users of a product or service, prospective users (who might buy, but have not bought yet), first-time buyers, regular buyers and ex-customers who have switched to a competitor's product.

- **Benefits sought**: A market might be segmented according to the benefits that customers expect from the products they buy. For example, customers in a supermarket may be segmented according to those who look for the lowest price or best bargain; those who want particular types of product, such as vegetarian food and environmentally friendly household products; and those who want convenience, so that they can buy what they want and get out of the supermarket as quickly as possible.

Psychographic segmentation

Psychographic segmentation is a method of segmenting a market according to the shared personality traits, beliefs, values, attitudes, interests, or lifestyles of consumers.

- **Personality**: When a market is segmented according to personality, the business considers that people make their buying decisions on the basis of their personality (or the personality they think they have). However, there are many different aspects of personality, and it is probably easier to identify one segment in the market – such as customers who are outward-going and sociable – rather than to segment the entire market into different personality types.

- **Lifestyle**: Again, it may be difficult to segment an entire market according to the differing lifestyles of consumers, but it may be possible to identify one or two distinctive segments, such as people who lead an active or sporty life, and consumers who enjoy home cooking. For example, a company that makes tennis balls will focus on consumers who are likely to play sports and ignore those that do not.

- **Social class**: It might also be possible to segment a market along the lines of social class, when a business believes that buying decisions by consumers relate to the social class to which they belong.

Again, psychographic segmentation may be used to identify specific segments of a market, without trying to segment the market as a whole. For example, a private school might identify senior professional people as a segment of the market that is likely to respond to its efforts to attract pupils.

Activity

Spend some time watching advertisements, on television, at the cinema, in social media, or in newspapers or magazines.

Can you identify whether the advertisements appear to be targeting a segment of the market for the product or service it is advertising? If so, can you identify the method of segmentation that has been used?

Case study

Travel company

Anywhere Holidays and Travel is a company that sells a wide range of different types of holiday. It is well aware that customers want many different types of holiday, from cheap holiday packages in the sun, to adventure holidays in the Himalayas or the Andes, luxury cruises, weekend breaks, and so on. It is considering ways of segmenting the market for holidays, in order to plan its marketing activities.

1 How might you segment the market for holidays according to the following methods?
- Demographic
- Geographic
- Income
- Behavioural
- Psychographic.

Influences on choosing a target market

The purpose of segmenting a market is to make strategic marketing decisions about how the business should try to market its products or services. In order to do this, it should select one or more target markets.

A target market is a segment of the market in which the business tries to sell its products or services.

- A business may not segment its market at all, because it considers all its customers to share the same characteristics and buying habits. It therefore sells exactly the same product to all its customers and uses the same or similar marketing methods for all of them. This is called mass marketing.

- A business may segment its market with the intention of selling its products or services to every segment. However, it uses different marketing methods for customers in each different segment.

- A business may decide to focus on just one, or possibly a few, market segments, but not on all of them. This is called target marketing. The business develops products and uses marketing methods to attract customers in its chosen segments.

Why is target marketing necessary?

A business may decide to target one segment of a market (or a small number of segments) for any of the following reasons:

- It does not have the resources to compete in the entire market, especially if it is a small business.

Key terms

Mass marketing: marketing a product to the entire market, without segmenting the market.

Target marketing: focusing business activity (including marketing) on one or more segments of the total market.

Case study

Perfumes

A cosmetics manufacturer makes a small range of perfumes that it sells globally under its widely known brand name. The company has been in business for many years, and is in competition with a number of other international brands.

1 Suggest how the company might segment the market for perfumes.

2 Suggest how it might select target market segments for most of its marketing activities.

- It cannot compete with the biggest companies in the market, which are able to produce and sell their products more cheaply, and have more resources.
- Its products or services have some unique features that will appeal to customers in one segment of the market, but not in others. For example, a company producing energy drinks might target a group of consumers who are physically active and play sports.
- The marketing objectives of a company might mean that it will focus its activities on just one segment of the market. For example, a company that makes and sells records under a record label may have an objective of being the leading company in the market for classical music.
- It may decide that focusing on one segment of the market is likely to be profitable, whereas marketing to other segments would not be.
- A company may want to enter the market for the first time, and may decide to begin by targeting just one segment of the market to begin with, and expand into other segments perhaps if it is successful.
- In order to achieve sales growth, a company might decide to move into another market segment, instead of trying to grow sales in the segment where it currently operates. For example, a company may seek to grow its business by expanding its operations into another country.

Niche markets

A niche market is a very small segment of a larger market. It might be described as a segment of a market segment. A company might identify a business opportunity for selling a product or service to a small part of the market, and targeting it with its marketing initiatives. This is known as niche marketing or micromarketing.

The business logic in micromarketing is that a company can be "a big fish in a small pond" rather than a small competitor in a larger segment of the market.

For niche marketing to be successful, the chosen niche market must be sufficiently large to earn a profit for the company or companies operating in it to make a profit.

A niche market may be restricted to a small geographical area, and a business targeting it would operate only in that small area. For

Key terms

Niche market: a very small section of the total market.

Niche marketing: targeting business activity (including marketing) on a small, specialised market.

example, a small company in the travel business might specialise in providing guided tours to museums and art galleries in Madrid.

In the past, a business has been successful in producing and selling left-handed scissors, which at the time represented a niche market.

There are also niche markets for business products. For example, a company might specialise in making lighting systems for submarines.

Product differentiation

Some companies have an objective of being the biggest in their market – the market leader – or at least as big as their main rivals. Market leaders are often able to maintain their leadership by selling a popular product at a low price.

However, not every company can be a market leader. The challenge for companies is to find a way of being successful in their market, and making a profit, without being the biggest. For example, how can a company that makes sheets of paper for computer printers succeed against larger competitors? How does a manufacturer of toothpaste or covers for smartphones distinguish their products from those of competitors?

In competitive markets, businesses seek to differentiate their products from those of competitors. Product differentiation involves marketing products that are similar to others in the market, but that have some unique minor variations in the design of the product or differences in the way a product is sold, or differences in price.

For example, a car manufacturer selling hatchback family saloon cars might seek to differentiate their car models from those of other car manufacturers by including additional product features (for example, satellite navigation) in their cars or highlighting their fuel efficiency or comfort. The idea behind product differentiation is to try to make a product seem different, or even unique, to potential customers.

In addition to differentiating products by variations in design, a company can use marketing activities such as advertising and branding to create an attractive product image.

Market positioning

Within a market or a market segment, companies decide how to "position" their product or service by differentiating it from those of competitors. If we use the term "product quality" to mean features of a product (or service) design or image, we can define product positioning as choosing a combination of price and quality within a market or market segment in a way that distinguishes the product from those of competitors.

The previous example of a market map (Figure 2.2.2) showing how businesses can be differentiated by price and quality, applies to product positioning. This is reproduced in Figure 2.3.1.

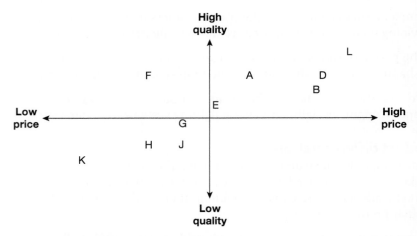

▲ Figure 2.3.1: Product positioning on a market map
(Individual products are shown as letters on the map)

Case study

Travel suitcases

Travel suitcases and bags are sold both through retail stores and online. They are sold throughout the year, but sales volumes peak during the summer and winter holiday periods.

1 Suggest how the companies that manufacture travel suitcases and bags might position their products, either in the market as a whole or within particular targeted segments of the market.

Companies can select a target position for their products so as to differentiate themselves from competitors, for example by offering a better-quality product, but perhaps at a higher price, or by selling an "economy" product that differentiates itself from competitors in the same market segment by differences in design (quality) and price. The products of all competitors in the market can be mapped in the market by differences in price and quality, and companies can decide where they want to position themselves in the market.

International markets

Some global companies sell their products and services around the world. Other companies may base their operations in one country, but sell their products in both their domestic market and in selected other countries.

Opportunities

The main benefit of selling to international markets is that they are bigger than domestic markets, and so there is greater opportunity for sales and profit growth. For example, it makes sense for a company in the Netherlands selling tulip bulbs to sell their product to buyers in nearby countries, such as Germany, Belgium and the UK, as well as selling them in the Netherlands. Some companies, such as car manufacturers, need to compete internationally in order to succeed against foreign competitors in their domestic markets, because the market for cars is global.

In some markets, for example the market for luxury watches and jewellery, there are particular centres around the world where a large proportion of the selling and buying takes place, and manufacturers of luxury watches and jewellery will target these international centres.

Amazon is a company that began its operations in just one country, the USA, and has grown into one of the world's largest companies through expanding its warehousing and distribution systems throughout the world. It could not have achieved its current size and profitability without expanding internationally.

Difficulties

Many markets for consumer products can be segmented geographically, because consumer tastes, preferences and buying behaviour vary between countries. Customers in different countries might also react differently to marketing initiatives.

A difficulty with selling to segmented international markets is that if each national market differs in its characteristics, different marketing approaches will be needed in each country, and adapted to the language of the country. Companies will need to learn and understand the market characteristics in each country. If international operations grow beyond a certain size, companies might need to consider setting up marketing operations in its larger foreign markets.

Another problem is that if a company operates from its own country, it might need to use agents to sell its products in other countries. If it uses agents and foreign distributors, it is unlikely to have full control over how its products are marketed.

Exam-style questions

1   A business believes that there are interesting marketing opportunities from segmenting its market by means of differing lifestyles of consumers. This means that the method of market segmentation the company is using is:

   A   Behavioural

   B   Psychographic

   C   Income

   D   Demographic   [1 mark]

2   Explain why it is easier to sell digital services internationally than physical products.   [4 marks]

3   Some travel companies arrange specialised package adventure holidays, such as trekking in the Himalayas or cycling through Vietnam and Cambodia. Their marketing strategy is to position themselves in a niche market within the overall holidays and travel market.

   Explain the difficulties with niche marketing.   [9 marks]

This section will develop your knowledge and understanding of:

→ The elements of the marketing mix (7Ps)

→ Product as an element of the marketing mix

→ Influences on pricing in the marketing mix

→ Influences on the promotional mix

→ Influences on distribution (place) in the marketing mix

→ Influences on people, process and physical environment in the marketing mix.

Elements of the marketing mix (7Ps)

The **marketing mix** is a term for all the ways that an organisation uses to market its products or services to customers. A combination of marketing elements is used, hence the term "mix".

> **Key term**
>
> Marketing mix: combination of policies and activities for achieving marketing objectives and targets.

The 4Ps

Originally, the marketing mix was described as the 4Ps: product, price, place and promotion. In marketing their products or services, businesses choose elements from each to prepare a marketing plan.

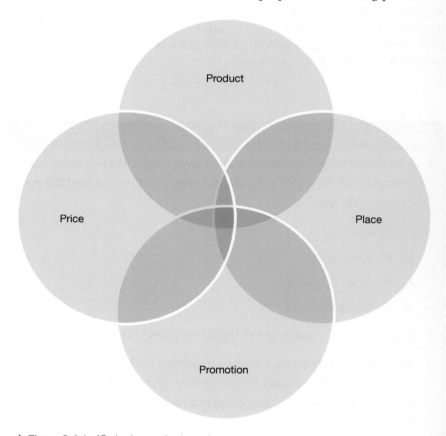

▲ **Figure 2.4.1**: 4Ps in the marketing mix

▼ Table 2.4.1: The marketing decisions for the 4Ps

	Explanation	Marketing decisions
Product	"Product" is the item that is being marketed: the term refers to both goods and services. The product must be able to offer something that customers want or need. Businesses can market their products by making them more attractive to customers, and satisfying their needs.	• The design of the product: product features, what the product does — its features and benefits, its technology • Packaging of the product: how packaging protects the product, or makes the product convenient to use, carry or store • Related services, such as after-sales service and sales returns • Guarantees or warranties
Price	"Price" is the amount that customers pay for the product. As a general rule, more customers will buy a product (or will buy more of a product) at a lower price. But businesses need to set prices at a level to earn them a profit. Businesses can market their products by selling them at a price that customers will pay for the benefits they receive.	• Setting "normal" prices • Price discounts • Special offers • Credit terms (giving customers time to pay) • Setting prices to compete with prices offered by competitors for similar products • Setting prices for new products
Place	"Place" refers to the methods or channels for delivering the product to customers. Businesses can market their products by selling them at a place or through a channel that is convenient for them to use.	• Decisions about how to distribute the product: through a large network of distributors/retailers or through a limited/exclusive distribution network. • Online selling: "place" may be a website or a social media page • Printed catalogues for customers to buy from their home • Where to sell: how much geographical area to cover • Decisions about transport, warehousing and logistics (delivery)
Promotion	"Promotion" refers to all aspects of communicating information about a product to actual or potential customers. It includes activities such as advertising (in all its forms), sales promotions, direct marketing/direct selling, and public relations (PR)	• Choosing a suitable mix of promotion methods • Deciding on the "message" that is communicated by the promotion • Deciding on the frequency of promotions

The 7Ps

The concept of the 4Ps applies to physical products, but does not cover all the elements of marketing activity for services. In the 1980s the marketing mix was redefined as the 7Ps, to include three additional elements relevant to the marketing of services.

▼ **Table 2.4.2**: The additional three elements in the 7Ps

	Explanation	Marketing decisions
Physical evidence	"Physical evidence" refers to the physical environment in which a service is delivered. The nature of the physical surroundings can be used to impress customers with the reliability or quality of the service to be delivered.	• Physical evidence: furniture, room layout, equipment • Functionality: ensuring the physical space is set out to deliver the service • Interior design: decorations • Room temperature, air quality
People	"People" refers to the individuals who deliver the service to customers. Customers' perceptions of a service are influenced by the people they interact with. In some industries the people themselves are the product (e.g. live entertainment, professional services).	• Recruitment and training of staff • Uniforms • Waiting times; queuing systems • Complaints handling • Social atmosphere
Process	"Process" refers to the way in which a service is delivered and the processes that take place in delivering the service. For example, "process" in a restaurant refers to the way in which customers are greeted on arrival and then served, up to the point of their departure.	• Designing the process to satisfy customers • Deciding whether processes should be standardised or whether they should be customised to meet individual customer requirements • Use of industry best practice • Making sure that there are enough people to deliver the service to the standard required

Activity

Choose some products or services that you buy. The products can be anything that you buy in a shop, at a market stall or online. Services can be anything you buy that is not a physical product, such as a visit to the hairdresser or a bus ride.

For each of the products that you have chosen, make a note of the features of the 4Ps in the marketing mix for the product that you were aware of when you made your purchase, and your reasons for buying the product.

Similarly, for each of the services that you have chosen, make a note of the features of the 7Ps in the marketing mix for the service that you were aware of when you made your purchase, and your reasons for buying the service.

Then make a note of how effective you think the marketing mix has been for each of the products and services, in persuading you to buy it.

Case study

Fitness centres

A company operates a number of fitness centres around the country. These are located in town or city centres, often close to the main railway station or bus station. Customers pay an annual membership subscription to join one of the centres, and can use all the facilities provided in their chosen centre.

There are two competitors, both operating their own fitness centres in the same locations. The company is preparing a marketing plan, within its available marketing budget, with the objective of increasing its market share.

1 Select any three of the 7Ps in the marketing mix for the fitness centres, and for each "P" that you have selected, suggest marketing measures that the company might take to persuade existing customers to renew their membership subscriptions and potential customers to join.

Progress questions

1 What is a marketing mix?
2 In planning the marketing mix for a product, what types of marketing decision relate to "place" in the mix?
3 In planning the marketing mix for a service, what types of marketing decision relate to "physical environment" in the mix?

Industrial goods and consumer goods: B2B and B2C marketing

Most of the examples in this chapter have been examples of consumer markets and consumer products. Companies that sell products to other businesses, rather than to consumers, must also market their products and select what they consider to be the most suitable marketing mix for doing this.

For physical products, the same 4Ps apply to the marketing mix as for consumer goods, but the make-up of the marketing mix will be different.

- Business customers buy some consumer goods, but most of their spending is on industrial materials and components. Product quality, and whether products are made to specific industry standards, is often an important factor in buying decisions by businesses.

- Business customers are often much more price-conscious than consumers. They will pay a fair price for goods of the quality that they want, but they will often negotiate, to try to get a reduction in price, for example a discount for buying in bulk. Credit terms can also be important. Businesses do not pay by credit card for most of the goods they buy, but they do want to be given time to pay.

- Business customers specify where goods that they buy should be delivered. Elements in the marketing mix for "place" might be delivery times, the method of transport used to deliver the goods, and who pays for delivery costs (which would also be an aspect of "price" in the marketing "mix").

Case study

Farm equipment

A company manufactures farming equipment, such as tractors and harvesters. It sells its products worldwide. It is preparing a plan for marketing its equipment.

Another company manufactures television sets, which are sold mainly to the consumer market.

1 Explain how the 4Ps of the marketing mix might differ in the marketing plans for these two companies.

- Promotions for industrial goods are very different from promotions for consumer goods. Businesses rely much more on face-to-face selling and supplier-buyer relationships. Some products are advertised in trade journals or company websites, but in some industries, exhibitions, business fairs and road shows are also part of the promotions mix.

The marketing mix for consumer goods will also differ according to the nature of the product, for example between:

- Luxury items and essential items
- Occasionally purchased items and regularly purchased items.

The marketing mix for national and international markets

In many respects, elements in the marketing mix for a product may be the same in different countries, and a company that sells its product in international markets may use a marketing mix similar to the one used in its domestic market. The product design and other product features may satisfy the same needs of customers worldwide. TV advertisements and advertising videos for a consumer product, such as an electric razor or a washing machine, may be the same in different countries, except for the language used.

But there are also likely to be differences between countries that affect the marketing mix in each country. Here are some examples.

- The choice of methods to promote a product is likely to differ between countries. For example, where access to the internet use is limited, it will be difficult for a company to use digital marketing methods.
- Where a large proportion of consumers in a country are environmentally aware, a company might need to promote its 'green' products more heavily in order to win market share.
- When a product requires after-sales service (such as cars) the provision of after-sales service in other countries becomes an important feature of "product" in the marketing mix, and an exporting company must have an after-sales network in place in every country that it sells to.

▼ Table 2.4.3: Digital elements in a marketing mix

Digital elements in a marketing mix	
Digital products	**Digital marketing methods**
It might be a digital product that is marketed and sold. A digital product is defined here as any product that is delivered to the customer in digital form, via the internet, such as software apps, downloads of music or films, and digital books.	Businesses might use digital methods to market any type of product or service. These include: • Email advertising • Use of website for advertising • Use of social media pages for advertising.
For digital products, product design and product features are crucial elements in the marketing mix. Some digital products are delivered free, with the product provider seeking to obtain revenues through advertising. With other digital products, the company makes a charge of some kind, such as a subscription charge on a price for add-ons to an app.	In addition: • Big data and data mining are enabling companies to target personalised marketing at individuals • Networks of individuals on social media can spread publicity about a company and its products, especially when an item 'goes viral'.

Here are features of digital marketing that should be considered within the 4Ps of a digital marketing mix.

- **Design**: The layout, navigation and general look of web pages will influence the impressions and opinions of visitors to the website.
- **User experience**: Visitors to a website or social media page must have a positive experience from using it. For example, a customer must be able without difficulty to buy something on a website and pay for it.
- **Content**: As a general rule, videos are more appealing to users of a website than images, and images are more appealing than text.
- **Search**: Potential customers must be able to find a company's website easily using a search engine.
- **Email**: Companies should be aware of the effectiveness of email in communicating with individuals on its opt-in subscriber list.
- **Social media**: The success of social media as a marketing channel depends on good-quality content that drives people to the company's social media page.

An integrated marketing mix

A marketing mix is an integrated combination of different marketing decisions and activities, which together can be described as a mix of elements within the 4Ps for products and the 7Ps for services. Businesses have different marketing mixes, according to conditions within their market. Businesses that plan their marketing mix with the aim of achieving clear marketing objectives are much more likely to be successful with their marketing than businesses that have an unplanned – and so probably disorganised – marketing mix.

Product within the marketing mix

The product (or service) itself is an important element within the marketing mix. It must have features that are attractive to customers and that customers want to buy. The design features of a product may include its:

- Quality (what it is made out of, and in the case of food products, taste and calorie content)
- Functions (what it does)
- Design features (what it looks like, ease of use)
- Reliability
- Prestige from ownership (such as branded goods).

Influences on product within the marketing mix

Products within a market, especially a competitive market, change continually. There are several reasons for this:

- **Technological advance**: Advances in technology drive changes in products and the development of new products. To mention just a few: electric cars, self-drive cars, new medicines, drones. Businesses also improve the design of existing products, to increase their appeal and value to customers. To remain competitive, businesses must keep up with their rivals, and if they cannot match what competitors are doing, they will lose market share.
- **Life cycle**: Some products have a limited life cycle. A notable example is protected medicines and drugs. When a pharmaceuticals company develops a new drug, it is able to obtain patent protection for a number of years. Patent protection makes it illegal for any other company to make and sell a similar drug during that time. However, when the patent runs out, other drugs companies can start to make it, and its price should fall drastically due to the competition. So pharmaceutical companies try to continue developing new medicines and drugs, for which it can obtain patent protection, and sustain its revenues.
- **Revenue**: Some companies introduce updated versions of their basic product in order to boost sales revenues. Smartphone makers, for example, expect a large increase in sales when they bring a new model to the market (probably annually).
- **Growing the market**: Some companies develop new products in order to attract new customers.

Product life cycle and the marketing mix

The marketing mix for a product will often depend on the stage it has reached in its life cycle, and the expected length of the life cycle. The "classical" life cycle of a product has four phases: introduction, when the product first comes to market; growth, when sales of the product increase as it gains market acceptance; maturity, when the sales for the product stop growing and the market has reached its maximum size; and decline (followed by eventual withdrawal from the market). This is illustrated in Figure 2.4.2.

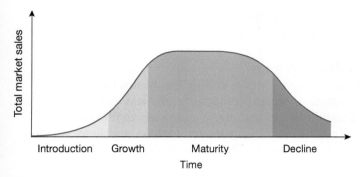

▲ **Figure 2.4.2:** Classical product life cycle

During the introductory phase, marketing is directed towards creating awareness of the product, and getting the first customers to buy it. During the growth phase, marketing focuses on achieving as much growth in sales as possible, making the product available to many more customers. When the product reaches its mature phase and total sales level out, companies compete with each other for market share, and marketing activity focuses on this. Finally, when the product goes into its decline phase (and eventual withdrawal from the market), and sales and profits begin to fall, companies switch their marketing efforts to other products that are in earlier stages of their life cycle.

Some products have a much shorter life cycle than others. With advances in technology, digital products in particular might have a fairly short life cycle, before they are replaced by something that is more technologically advanced. This is particularly true for specific models of a product: for example, smartphones have a much longer market life cycle than a particular make and model of smartphone. On the other hand, some products have very long life cycles, such as brands of chocolate bar.

The life cycle of a product may not follow the "classical" pattern. During the maturity phase of a life cycle, or even when a life cycle appears to be going into decline, it might be possible for companies in the market to find ways of extending the product's life, through a new marketing initiative, referred to as an **extension strategy**.

Extension strategies can include:

- Adding new features to a product
- Upgrading a product
- New packaging to make the product more convenient to handle or user-friendly
- Identifying new markets for the product (for example, international markets), or
- Re-branding an item.

It may be argued, for example, that the development of digital radio (a new product feature) has extended the life of radios as a product. Changes in consumer tastes have also helped the revival in some countries of the market for vinyl records.

Activity

Select a product or service that you are familiar with, preferably a product that has been purchased in the past by someone you know or by yourself. For example, you might choose an e-reader as your product, a digital app, a mobile phone, sunglasses, or visits to a theme park.

For the product or service you have chosen, make notes about the phases in its life cycle that you think the product has gone through (and is currently going through), and how the product appears to have been marketed during its life.

Key term

Extension strategy: marketing strategy to extend the profitable stages of a product's life (growth and maturity).

An extension strategy should have the effect of increasing or maintaining a company's sales and profits.

New product development

Since products do not have a never-ending life, businesses need to develop new products to remain competitive and stay in business. New products should offer something to customers that existing products do not provide, so that customers want to buy them. Apple for example, has aimed at producing a new model of its smartphone each year, with each new model providing additional features compared with the previous model.

With recent advances in digital technology, many manufacturers are incorporating digital features into their products. For example, many items of household equipment now include computing/digital devices which enable their owners to control them from a remote location via the internet. (These products are referred to in general as the Internet of Things (IoT).)

Competitors continually seek to change product features or develop new products in order to gain a competitive edge over rivals. In many industries, companies that do not continually develop new products or new models of existing products will 'lose out' to competitors that innovate.

Product portfolios: the Boston Matrix

When they plan their marketing strategies and tactics, companies should consider their product portfolio. This is the collection of products they make and sell, taken together. Most companies do not sell just one product, they sell a number of different products. Individual products within the portfolio are likely to be at different stages of their life cycle, and some are likely to be more successful than others.

The long-term success of a company may well depend on having a combination of products, some in the mature phase of their life cycle, some new to the market or in their growth phase and some in decline. Some products will need cash for investment, and other established products will earn profits and generate cash for the business. New products are needed in the portfolio as eventual replacements for those that go into decline, so products needing cash can be financed by those that are generating cash.

The Boston Matrix (also known as the Boston Group Consulting Matrix) is a model for examining the make-up of a company's product portfolio, to decide whether it is a good combination of products at different stages of their commercial development, or whether there might be a worrying gap.

The Boston Matrix is a 2 × 2 matrix, with four quadrants. The matrix shows, for each product in the portfolio:

- The rate of growth in the market for the product
- The market share that is enjoyed by the company's product.

Each product within a company's portfolio can be placed in one of the quadrants of the matrix, with their importance (in terms of sales) illustrated perhaps by the size of the shape representing them. The format of a Boston Matrix is shown in Figure 2.4.3, and an example of how the Matrix might be used to analyse a product portfolio is shown in Figure 2.4.4.

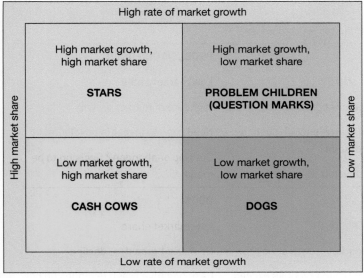

▲ **Figure 2.4.3**: Format of the Boston Matrix

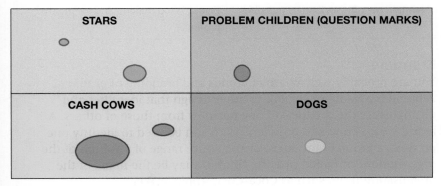

▲ **Figure 2.4.4**: Boston Matrix example

- **Stars** are products with a high share of the market in a high growth market. At the moment, they are likely to be "cash neutral", not bringing cash into the business but not using up cash either. These products need sustained marketing effort to maintain growth and market share, and eventually become cash cows.

- **Cash cows** are products with a high market share in a mature market where there is now no growth or little growth. They are profitable and earn cash for the business. Marketing efforts should be directed at sustaining the life and market share of cash cows.

- **Problem children**, also known as question marks, are products with a low market share in a strong growth market. They have potential to become cash cows, but only if the company invests more heavily in them to win a bigger market share. The question is: Should the company invest in its problem children, and if so, which ones?

- **Dogs** are products with a low market share in a low-growth market. They may be earning enough cash to cover the expenditure incurred on them, but usually they are sold off or closed down.

The features of each category of product are summarised in Table 2.4.4.

▼ **Table 2.4.4**: Boston Matrix summary

STARS	PROBLEM CHILDREN
High market share	Low market share
High rate of market growth	High rate of market growth
Cash neutral (earns enough cash to cover expenditures)	Need cash to invest in development
Continue to develop	Develop or abandon? Decision to be made
CASH COWS	**DOGS**
High market share	Low market share
Low rate of market growth or no growth	No market growth or decline
Cash positive (cash revenues exceed expenditures)	Cash negative (cash revenues do not cover expenditures)
Maintain benefits as long as possible	Divest (stop making and selling the product)

Branding

You are probably well aware of brands and branding of products. A brand is a name or symbol or other design that identifies and distinguishes the products of one business from those of others. A brand is also known as a trademark. It can be used to identify one product, a group of products, or the entire range of products of the organisation (in which case the "brand" may be the name of the organisation itself, such as Coca-Cola, Apple or Ikea).

Brands can be an important aspect of "product" in the marketing mix, especially for consumer products.

Benefits of branding

- Branding makes it easier for customers and potential customers recognise the product. When a product has "brand recognition", customers are familiar with what it is.
- Recognised brands can motivate customers to buy the product. Customers may prefer to buy a branded product than a non-branded product, or a product with a brand they do not recognise.
- Brands can help to create customer loyalty. Having purchased one brand of products (and with suitable marketing by the company) customers will often stick to the brand and buy it again.

- Brand marketing can be expensive, but companies are usually able to charge a higher price for a branded product, especially a product with a "quality" brand name.
- When a company has an established brand for a range of products, it can use the brand to extend its product range to achieve sales growth – by adding the new product to the branded product range.
- Brand names can also help consumers who are searching for a company's products and website on the internet, and so assist with online selling.

Many of these benefits of branding apply to "own label" brands. Own label brands are brands marketed under the name of a retailer, typically a supermarket group. Own label products are usually sold at a lower price than similar products with different brand names, but they create recognition and loyalty among customers, who trust the retailer to provide reasonable quality for the price charged. Own label brands can also be applied to a wide variety of different consumer products.

Pricing within the marketing mix

Price is an important element of the marketing mix. The price charged for a product will affect the demand from customers to buy it.

- Organisations may be a market leader. Depending on the extent of their dominance in the market, they may be able to act as "price maker", setting prices in the market that smaller competitors will respond to.
- Organisations may be "price takers", in the sense that the prices they charge will be influenced strongly by the prices charged by competitors for their products.
- Pricing decisions may be temporary or for the longer term. For example, a company may run a short promotion offering a price discount to customers who buy a minimum quantity of a product, or who buy before a closing date for the offer. Promotions of this sort aim to achieve a short-term boost in sales.
- When companies sell a range of products under the same brand name, the level of prices for all the products in the range should be consistent with the "brand image".

New product pricing: market skimming and market penetration pricing policies

When a company is about to launch a new product, for which there is (as yet) no rival on the market, it has a choice of pricing policy for the product. Two alternative policies, both of which recognise that sales demand for the new product will depend on the price charged, are market skimming and market penetration pricing. (Penetration pricing can also be used for new products that are launched in a market where rival products already exist.)

Activity

Select a brand name that you are familiar with, and make notes about the following items.

Does the brand name apply to one product, a group of products, or the company as a whole?

What are your views or opinions about the brand – in terms of product price, quality or any other features you are aware of?

How is the brand marketed, in terms of the 4Ps (or 7Ps)?

Price skimming is a pricing policy in which the company sets a high initial price for the product. This should not be so high that it deters all potential customers, but it will be sufficiently high that only a relatively small number of customers will buy it at that price. The price is then reduced a little, to attract a few more customers. Gradual price reductions continue until the price is reduced to a longer-term level. By gradually reducing the price from an initial high level, the company is "skimming the market". Examples of successful price skimming can be found in the markets for technical products such as the Apple iPhone. A price skimming strategy is more likely to be effective when the product has a strong brand name or a unique selling point (USP) that make customers want to buy it even at a fairly high price.

Price penetration is a pricing policy in which the company sets a low initial price for the product. The aim is to obtain as many customers for the product as is reasonably possible in a short period of time. When the product is expected to enter a strong growth phase of its life cycle, penetration pricing is a way of gaining a big share of the growing market. When the new product is launched into a market where there are already rival products, the aim is to win a target share of the market. After an initial period, the market price may be raised to a longer-term level. An example of price penetration in UK retailing has been the success of low-price supermarket chains Aldi and Lidl. A price penetration strategy is most likely to be effective when demand for the product is sensitive to price.

Price discrimination

Price discrimination is a policy of charging different prices for the same product to different segments of the market. A higher price is charged to some customers and a lower price is charged to others – for exactly the same product. There are several ways of applying a price discrimination policy.

- Lower prices may be charged to individuals above or below a certain age, for example prices for children below a certain age. This type of pricing policy might be applied, for example, to customers for cinema tickets, or tickets to a museum or art gallery.
- Price discrimination may be based on time of day or season of the year. For example, a travel company may charge lower fares for travelling outside certain "peak times" of the day.
- Students may pay lower prices for educational material, such as books.

Price discrimination is easier to apply in practice to services rather than to goods. This is because if there is price discrimination for goods, it may be possible for some customers to buy the product at a lower price and sell it on at a higher price to customers who might otherwise have bought it from the company at the "normal" higher price.

It may be necessary to ask customers to show an ID card as proof of their age or student status.

Price discrimination and price differentiation

Price discrimination and price differentiation might sound much the same, but they are different concepts in pricing and marketing.

- Price discrimination involves charging different prices for exactly the same product to different segments of the market.
- Price differentiation involves charging different prices for different versions or designs of a product to different segments of the market.

For example, when an airline charges different prices for first class, business and economy seats for a flight, this is price differentiation, because customers get a different level of service according to the class of ticket they buy. Charging customers different prices for exactly the same type of seats on similar flights, according to the time of day of the flight, would be price discrimination.

Price elasticity of demand

Price elasticity is a term, used in economics, for the relationship between changes in the price of a product and demand for the product. Price elasticity measures the responsiveness of demand for a product or service to a change in its price. It can be measured for both pricing and demand for the product of an individual company, or for price and demand in the market as a whole.

Price elasticity of demand can be measured as:

$$\frac{\text{Percentage change in demand for a product}}{\text{Percentage change in price}}$$

If the price of a product is increased, demand will (usually) fall. If the price of a product is reduced, demand will (usually) increase. Price elasticity of demand is therefore a negative value, although the minus sign is often ignored.

If any change in the price of a product results in no change whatsoever in demand, the price elasticity of demand is 0. For example, if the price of an item is doubled but there is no change in sales demand, price elasticity of demand is 0. This is rare in practice.

Inelastic demand

If a percentage change in the price of a product results in a smaller percentage change in demand, price elasticity of demand is said to be **inelastic**. For example, if the price of an item is increased by 5% and sales demand falls as a result by 3%, demand is inelastic at this price level. So if the price elasticity of demand is between 0 and 1 (ignoring the minus sign), demand is inelastic.

Example

A company sells 30,000 units of a product each month at its current selling price of $10 per unit. It estimates that if it raises the selling price to $11 per unit, demand for the product will fall to 28,000 units per month.

The change in demand per month would be $\dfrac{2,000}{30,000} = -6.67\%$

The change in price would be $\dfrac{1}{10} = 10\%$

The price elasticity of demand is inelastic, because the percentage change in demand would be less than the percentage change in price. (And if the price is increased, monthly revenue from sales of the product would rise from $300,000 to $308,000.)

> **Key term**
>
> **Price elasticity of demand:** a measure that compares the (percentage) change in demand for a product when there is a (percentage) change in the price. Price elasticity is usually either inelastic or elastic.

Elastic demand

If a percentage change in the price of a product results in a larger percentage change in demand, price elasticity of demand is said to be **elastic**. For example, if the price of an item is reduced by 5% and demand increases as a result by 10%, demand is elastic at this price level.

Example

A company sells 12,000 units of a product each month at its current selling price of $20 per unit. It estimates that if it raises the selling price to $21 per unit, demand for the product will fall to 11,000 units per month.

The change in demand per month would be $\dfrac{1,000}{12,000} = -8.33\%$

The change in price would be $\dfrac{1}{20} = 5\%$

The price elasticity of demand is elastic, because the percentage change in demand would be greater than the percentage change in price. (And if the price is increased, monthly revenue from sales of the product would fall from $252,000 to $231,000.)

Measuring the amount of the increase or fall in revenue

The change in sales revenue from a change in sales price can be calculated as a factor:

$$(1 +/- P\%) \times (1 +/- D\%)$$

Where P% is the percentage change in price and D% is the percentage change in demand.

So if an increase in price by 10% is expected to result in a fall in demand by 20%, the change in sales revenue is measured as a factor: $1.10 \times 0.80 = 0.88$.

This indicates that total sales revenue would fall by 12% $(0.88 - 1 = -0.12)$.

Price elasticity of demand and price differentiation

A price differentiation policy is effective when the price elasticity of demand is elastic in the segment of the market where a lower price is applied, but fairly inelastic in the main segment of the market.

Case study

Increasing prices

A company sells two products, Product A and Product B. It is considering whether to increase the unit price of each product by 5%. If it does so, demand for Product A is likely to fall by 3% and demand for Product B is likely to fall by 8%.

1 At the existing price level, is the price elasticity of demand for Product A elastic or inelastic? What about Product B?

2 What will happen to total sales revenue from Product A if the price is increased by 5%?

3 What will happen to total sales revenue from Product B if the price is increased by 5%?

4 What conclusions can you draw about the effect on sales revenue for a product, in response to a change in its price, depending on whether price elasticity of demand is inelastic or elastic?

5 Can you draw any conclusions about the effect on profit of a change in price?

Example

Suppose that a sports venue is considering whether or not to reduce prices charged to children aged 12 or under by 25%, instead of charging the same price to all customers, regardless of age. It estimates that for children's tickets the price elasticity of demand is 2.4. Reducing the price for children is not expected to have any effect on demand from customers aged over 12.

There will be no change in sales revenue from customers aged over 12. For children aged 12 and under, total revenue will change by a factor of:

$(1 - 0.25) \times (2.40) = 1.80.$

In other words, total revenue from sales to children aged 12 and under will increase by 80% (= $(1.8 - 1) \times 100\%$).

The value of the concept of price elasticity to business

Price elasticity of demand can be used to measure changes in sales revenue from a product, in response to changes in its price. However:

- It measures estimated changes in sales revenue, but not changes in profit, which is often a matter of greater concern to business than revenue.
- Unless there is reliable marketing research data about the likely effect of price changes on demand, estimates of changes in demand might be unreliable. Price elasticity might also change in response to other factors in the market, such as a price increase or price reduction by a major competitor.

Progress questions

4 What are the four stages in a typical product life cycle, and how are these relevant to marketing?

5 What is an extension strategy?

6 What is the Boston Matrix and how might it be relevant to marketing?

7 What is the value of branding for consumer products?

8 What is price skimming and when might it be applied as a pricing policy?

9 What is the difference between price differentiation and price discrimination?

The promotional mix (promotion as an element of the marketing mix)

The promotional mix can include anything within the marketing mix that is categorised as a promotion activity. So the promotional mix includes advertising, sales promotions, selling by a sales force, exhibitions and trade fairs and public relations.

Key term

Promotional mix: a specific combination of promotion policies and activities within the "promotion" element of the marketing mix. The promotional mix includes advertising, sales promotions and face-to-face selling.

▼ **Table 2.4.5:** Methods of sales promotion

Promotion method	Examples
Advertising	Advertising (perhaps as a campaign for a limited period of time) via TV, radio, magazines, newspapers, trade journals, on billboards, in social media and search engines.
Sales promotions	Activities designed to stimulate quick sales, such as in-store displays, competitions, two-for-one offers, free gifts with every purchase.
Selling	Face-to-face selling by sales representatives, telephone selling, direct mail, selling by email.
Exhibitions and trade fairs	Exhibitions where manufacturers display and market their products to commercial and industrial customers, such as agricultural exhibitions and book trade fairs.
Public relations (PR)	Obtaining free publicity in the media for a company and its products. Companies often hire specialist PR firms for this work.

The most suitable selection of promotion activities will depend to a large extent on the type of product that is being marketed, and the type of customer – business or consumer. An analysis of the differences is shown in Figure 2.4.5.

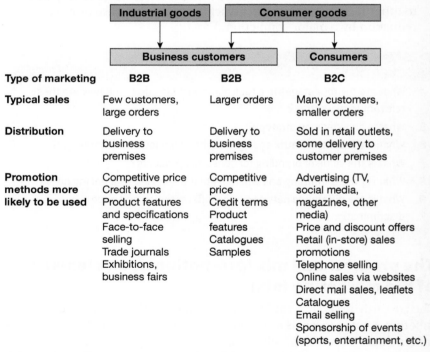

	Industrial goods	Consumer goods	
	Business customers		Consumers
Type of marketing	B2B	B2B	B2C
Typical sales	Few customers, large orders	Larger orders	Many customers, smaller orders
Distribution	Delivery to business premises	Delivery to business premises	Sold in retail outlets, some delivery to customer premises
Promotion methods more likely to be used	Competitive price Credit terms Product features and specifications Face-to-face selling Trade journals Exhibitions, business fairs	Competitive price Credit terms Product features Catalogues Samples	Advertising (TV, social media, magazines, other media) Price and discount offers Retail (in-store) sales promotions Telephone selling Online sales via websites Direct mail sales, leaflets Catalogues Email selling Sponsorship of events (sports, entertainment, etc.)

▲ **Figure 2.4.5:** The promotional mix, products and customers

The promotions mix for products and target customers may be a combination of the promotions shown in the table above, but businesses will choose a mix that suits the nature of the products they sell and the customers they sell to.

Some methods of promotion will not be suitable for some products and some customers. For example, the offer of a 10% discount on the next purchase of a product might be effective in boosting sales of snacks such as crisps but is much less likely to persuade an industrial buyer of a new factory robot.

Public relations (PR)

Public relations, or PR, is concerned with communications to the general public about an organisation or its products. Many large companies hire external companies to manage their PR.

At one time, communications with the general public meant trying to get favourable coverage (or respond to unfavourable coverage) in TV news, newspapers or journals. PR is now also very much concerned with communications in social media, such as creating or responding to the spread of messages and stories ('fake news' or otherwise).

PR is different from other forms of promotion, and to the extent that it is included in a planned promotions mix, the main question for marketing planners is to decide how much money to allocate to PR in the marketing budget.

Choosing a suitable promotional mix

Marketing and sales promotion have undergone enormous changes since the advent of the internet, social media, and smartphone and mobile phone technology. Here are just a few of the issues that marketing executives now need to consider.

- **Advertising**: At one time, the most effective form of advertising for consumer products was TV advertising, together with advertising in magazines and newspapers (depending on the nature of the product advertised). Today, TV viewer numbers and circulation numbers for printed newspapers and journals are falling in many countries. To a large extent, spending by companies on advertising has switched to search engines such as Google and social media such as Facebook and Twitter, but it may not yet be clear just how effective these forms of advertising are.

- **Social media**: Social media are used worldwide by huge numbers of individuals, and promotions through social media can reach customers and potential customers anywhere, at any time and for relatively little cost. However social media have their problems too, because of interactive communications and participation by individuals. Businesses cannot always control what is being said about their products in social media: bad publicity may counter the efforts of advertising. Some companies need to employ full-time social media managers to respond rapidly to feedback they receive from individuals. It is possibly too early to judge yet whether social media are effective for advertising, and growth in user numbers may be slowing down, especially in countries with developed economies.

- **Face-to-face selling**: Face-to-face selling is expensive. A sales force has to be paid salaries, and travelling and subsistence costs can be high. The strength of face-to-face selling is that when sales representatives are good at their job, they are often effective at getting customers to buy. However, sales orders usually need to be large enough or frequent enough to justify the use of sales staff.

- **Telephone sales**: In theory, telephone selling can be effective; however telephone selling to consumers has acquired a bad reputation due to unethical (and often illegal) selling practices.

- **Loyalty cards**: Loyalty cards issued by retail companies such as supermarkets to customers can persuade customers to remain loyal to the card issuer, and make repeat purchases through the offer of special deals and price discounts on their next purchase. Loyalty cards have the added benefit of enabling the cards issuer to build a database of the buying habits of individual card holders, so that personalised promotional offers can be put together for individuals.

Case study

Promoting new products

Two companies are planning to launch a new product.

A company that owns a chain of fast-food outlets is adding a new "healthy" meal to its menu of meals for customers. By promoting this new healthy meal, the company also thinks that it can also promote its chain of stores more generally.

A manufacturer of office equipment is adding a new desk-top computer to its product range. This will replace an existing desk-top model, which will be withdrawn from the market. A key feature of the new model is that it can be controlled remotely from a hand-held mobile device.

1 Suggest what you consider to be a suitable promotions mix for each of these companies, to promote their new product.

What is the aim of promotions?

The objective of promotional activities is not necessarily to persuade customers to buy a product or service. In some cases, the marketing objective might be to raise customer awareness of a product or service; in other words, to get customers to realise that the product exists. Having raised customer awareness, the next step might be to strengthen customer interest in the product, and get them to think about it a bit more. Having built up customer interest, the final step might then be to use sales promotion activities to get customers to buy the product.

Sponsorship is an example of raising awareness of a company or its products. Sponsoring a sports event, for example, will not persuade many customers to buy the sponsor's products, but it may enhance the reputation of the sponsor and make customers more aware.

Place (distribution) in the marketing mix

Place (more commonly referred to as distribution) in the marketing mix is concerned with how and where a product is bought by customers. For example:

- Consumer products may be sold through retail outlets such as department stores, supermarkets, shops, street kiosks, vending machines, and so on. Or they may be purchased online. Digital purchasing is also called **e-commerce**.

- Industrial products may be sold after negotiations between a supplier and a business customer (leading to a purchase order and sales contract) with the goods delivered to the buyer's premises.

Key term

E-commerce: the conducting of business by digital means.

A strategy for "place" in the marketing mix is known as a **distribution strategy**.

Here are some questions that a business needs to answer when developing a distribution strategy.

- Where do customers look for the product (or, in the case of industrial goods, where do they look for suppliers of a product)?
- For consumer products with physical sales outlets, where do customers buy them – at retail stores, department stores, kiosks at railway stations or bus stations, airport terminals?
- What proportion of sales will be online? How will the product be delivered to customers when they are sold/bought online?
- Does the company have access to all the physical outlets it would like?

When products are sold through physical outlets, such as retail stores, there must be a distribution strategy for:

- Market coverage: how much of the market (in geographical terms) will the product be distributed to? A local area only? The domestic/national market? Internationally?
- What distributors should be used.

Intensive, selective and exclusive distribution

- With an **intensive distribution policy**, the aim is to sell the product through as many outlets in as many locations and markets as possible. Intensive distribution is often appropriate for regularly purchased and relatively low-price items, such as sweets (candy), headache tablets, and cans of soft drink.
- With a **selective distribution policy**, a business chooses distributors for its products who are consistent with the image of the product that it is trying to promote. For example, a manufacturer of perfumes may choose to distribute its products only through department stores and retail specialists that have a "reputation" for selling high-quality products. Companies may also choose distribution outlets that have some technical knowledge of the product and specialise in selling particular types of product: for example, a manufacturer of bicycles might have a policy of distributing its products through retailers who have some knowledge and understanding of bicycles.
- With an **exclusive distribution policy**, a business gives a retailer the exclusive right to sell its products. These exclusive rights are often restricted to a geographical area: for example, there may be exclusive car dealerships, giving a distributor the sole right within a specified area to sell new cars of a particular car manufacturer. Exclusive distribution is likely to be suitable only for high-value products.

A multi-channel distribution policy is one that uses more than one "channel" for selling and distributing products to customers, such as a mix of online sales with deliveries to the customer address, online sales with the customer who then collects the purchase from a specified location ("click and collect") and selling through retail stores. A company operating a fast-food chain of stores might use both its own outlets and franchises to sell its products. A company may use selective distribution in one country and exclusive distribution in another.

Key terms

Intensive distribution policy: policy of selling as much of a product as possible, in as many markets and as many locations as possible.

Selective distribution policy: policy of distributing a product through selected outlets/distributors.

Exclusive distribution policy: policy of giving a distributor the exclusive right to distribute a product, typically within a specified geographical area.

▲ **Figure 2.4.6**: An exclusive distribution policy is usually best suited to selling high-price products

The aim of distribution policy is to sell the company's products (typically, as much as possible) in a way that is consistent with the company's overall marketing objectives and strategies.

Other elements in the marketing mix

The remaining three items in the 7Ps in the marketing mix for services are people, process and physical environment. Like the 4Ps of product, place, promotion and price, these aspects of the marketing mix should be planned in a way that will help the business to achieve its marketing objectives.

People

Services are delivered by the employees of a business, and what the employees do is part of the "product" that the business sells and the customer buys – people are the "product". Good standards of service can improve the relationship between a business and its customers, and enhance the company's reputation.

The aim of "people policy" in the marketing mix should be to ensure that people deliver the service to customers in a way that is consistent with the overall marketing policy. Influences on "people policy" include:

* The nature of the service provided: Is it a physical service and the main "product" for customers, such as legal advice or a medical service? Or is it a support service, such as a customer help desk, a technical support service, or a complaints handling team?
* What skills are required to deliver the service?
* Does the service involve direct interaction with the customer, such as waiter/waitress service in a restaurant or a doctor's services for a patient? Or is there no direct interaction with the customer, for example the writing of software by a programming specialist?
* How should the organisation ensure that it has a sufficient number of people able to deliver the service to the required standard? This has implications for recruitment policy and employee training policies.
* Will the use of uniforms help to improve the perception of customers about the quality of service they are receiving? (A uniform can mean a business suit, rather than casual dress.)

Process

Process refers to the procedures or actions, often carried out in sequence, that are required to deliver a service to a customer. Customers have expectations of what they should receive from a service, and the aim of a policy for process in the marketing mix should be to ensure that these expectations are met, or exceeded.

Example

You may have been out to dinner in a restaurant. If so, you may be aware of the process in delivering a meal to customers. The stages in the process will normally include (although this list is not comprehensive):

- Greeting the customers at the door and taking them to seats at a table, after coats and hats have been taken from them and put in a cloakroom

- Giving each of the customers a menu, or providing a menu for each seat at the table

- Asking them whether they would like a drink, and taking orders for drink

- Giving them time to decide what they would like to order, for starters and main course

- Taking the orders for starter and main course, and orders for further drinks

- Serving the starter after a reasonable waiting time

- Giving customers time to eat the starter at their leisure

- Repeat this process for the main course

- Asking customers whether they would like anything further – a dessert or coffee for example, and serving these within a reasonable time

- Providing an invoice when a customer asks for it, and taking payment after the customer has had time to check the bill

- Assisting customers to get ready to leave, and giving farewell greetings when they leave.

▲ **Figure 2.4.7**: Eating dinner in a restaurant

This process may seem straightforward, but the quality of the service can be damaged if any of the steps in the process are omitted or are not done properly (such as making customers wait too long for their food or drinks).

So a marketing plan should consider all the steps required to deliver a service to customers to the required standard, and they should ensure that their people are trained in how to deliver it properly. Influences on service include:

- The nature of the service and the steps required to deliver the service

- Marketing objectives: the quality of the service required

- Customer expectations

- The speed with which a service can be delivered: delivery time. For example, an ambulance service might have a target for the maximum time to reach a patient after a call for assistance has been made to the service.

Process is an important element in the marketing mix for online selling. The success of online selling depends largely on the ease of navigation through a company's website, and the ease with which customers can view the company's products and purchase and pay for them.

Physical environment

There should also be a marketing policy for the physical environment in which customers receive a service. The physical environment should be consistent with the image that the business wishes to present.

Influences on decisions about the physical environment will therefore include:

- The marketing strategy of the business – product and price. What standard of service does the business wish to provide? For example, a top-class hotel should provide facilities in guests' rooms to a high standard, for example with regard to furniture, lighting, bathroom equipment and so on. A hotel whose policy is to provide a lower standard of service to a lower price will provide fewer or cheaper facilities.

- What customers expect from the physical environment of a service. A key marketing objective is to meet customer expectations.

- Refurbishment. A physical environment deteriorates over time, with use and age. A business should have a refurbishment policy and should refresh its physical environment on a planned and regular basis.

Case study

Marketing a small shop

Diana has just opened a small shop near a railway station, for the sale of sandwiches, snacks and drinks. Most of her sales are made early in the morning and during the evening, to commuters travelling to and from work by rail, and also at lunchtimes, to people working in the area. She has some money to spend on marketing. Her business and marketing objective is to win a sufficient number of customers for the shop so that her business will become profitable in the shortest possible time.

1 Suggest what you think might be a suitable marketing mix for Diana's shop that will help to achieve her objective.

Exam-style questions

1 Which one of the following is generally regarded as an element of "product" in the marketing mix for a business?

   A Online selling

   B Selective distribution

   C Extension strategy

   D Price skimming   (1 mark)

2 Which one of the following elements in the promotional mix for a product might be used for promoting products to both consumers and business customers?

   A Website catalogue

   B Trade fair

   C TV advertising

   D Loyalty cards   (1 mark)

3 It has been estimated by a company that if the price of its product is increased by 3%, demand will fall by 1%.

   State whether the price elasticity of demand for the product at its current price is elastic or inelastic, and by how much total sales revenue will change if the price increase goes ahead.   (3 marks)

4 Explain the advantages of a price penetration strategy, and when this policy might be used in a company's marketing mix.   (4 marks)

5 The sales and profits of some companies might be increased through a policy of price discrimination.

   Explain the nature of price discrimination, giving an example, and why the price elasticity of demand for a product or service might be relevant for the success of a price discrimination policy.   (9 marks)

6 The marketing mix for an industrial product will differ from the marketing mix for a consumer product.

   Analyse how the marketing mix for an industrial product such as an office robot might differ from the marketing mix for a consumer product such as a mobile phone.   (9 marks)

7 McDonald's is a global company that operates a worldwide chain of fast-food outlets. It invests heavily in marketing, but its marketing mix might vary between countries.

   Analyse, for an operator of a chain of fast-food outlets, how its promotional mix might differ between countries.   (9 marks)

8 A company has recently been established to manufacture high-quality perfumes and cosmetics. It must make a decision about how to distribute their products, by means of intensive, selective or exclusive distribution.

   Explain the advantages and disadvantages of each method of distribution, and make a judgement.   (12 marks)

Managing operations, human resources and finance

3 Operational performance

3.1 Operations management

This section will develop your knowledge and understanding of:

- → The importance of operations management in business
- → The nature and value of operational objectives
- → The external and internal influences on operational objectives, plans and decisions.

The importance of operations management in business

The operations function is the part of an organisation that produces goods or services and delivers them to customers. Operations management is the activity of managing the resources of the operations function. For example, a railway company operates train services, a pharmaceuticals company produces drugs and medicines, a film company in Hollywood produces films, and so on. Every business organisation has an operations function, which is at the centre of what the organisation does and why it exists. Operations management is the activity of managing the resources of the operations function.

Key term

Operations function: the part of an organisation that produces goods or services and delivers them to customers.

Organisations refer to their operations function in different ways, according to the nature of what they do. In a company that makes goods, operations managers might be called production managers and logistics managers; in a supermarket, the operations manager is the store manager; and in a private hospital, the operations manager might be called the administration manager.

Operations management is a crucial part of business management, because success in business depends on delivering goods or services that customers want to buy, in a cost-efficient and an effective way.

The nature and value of operational objectives

Operational decisions and other business functions

The activities of the operations function, and the decisions that operations managers make, affect all other functions within the organisation. Decisions made by the other functions can also affect operations. The relationship between the operations function and the other main functions in most businesses is shown in Figure 3.1.1.

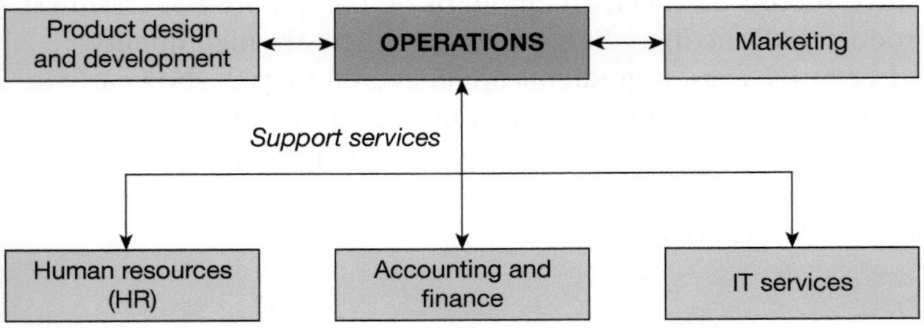

▲ **Figure 3.1.1**: The relationship between operations and other business functions

Case study

Entertainment company

An entertainment company is planning to hold a music festival. The operational requirements for holding the festival include renting a site, building stages for the performing artists, installing sound and filming equipment, and erecting stalls and other facilities for visitors to the festival.

1 How do you think that decisions by the operations function for the festival might affect the activities of the other functions in the entertainment company?
2 How might decisions by other functions in the company affect decisions that are made by the operation function?

Product design and development: The design and development of new products depends on the ability of the operations function to make them, and decisions by operations management about resources and capacity.

Marketing: Prices for products depend largely on the costs of producing them, and the distribution of products to customers depends on where they are made, and in what quantities.

Human resources (HR): The HR function is a support function, and is required to recruit and train the individuals that operations management want to employ, and the skills they should have.

Accounting and finance: The accounting and finance function needs to provide the finance that operations management require for investing in new equipment. It also measures the costs of operations.

IT services: The information technology systems within an organisation must provide the information the operations function needs for conducting and managing its activities.

Procurement (materials purchasing): Many companies have a procurement function, responsible for purchasing raw materials, components and services on behalf of the organisation. Procurement activities (in other words, buying) are determined by the materials that the operations function requires for making products or delivering services.

Operations and business competitiveness

The operations function can affect business competitiveness in several ways. See Table 3.1.1.

Example

The company Pret A Manger operates a number of shops around the world, selling sandwiches, salads and baguettes. A reason for its competitive success has been an emphasis on the quality and freshness of its products. All the ingredients for its products are high quality, such as free range eggs. Ingredients are delivered to each shop early in the morning, and the products are freshly prepared in a kitchen that is in or very close to the shop. All products sold are prepared the same day, and there are no "sell by" labels. Unsold items at the end of each day are offered to charity.

▼ **Table 3.1.1**: Operations and business competitiveness

How operations can affect business competitiveness	
Operating costs	The costs of operations are a major proportion of the costs of most products and services. By producing goods or services at a cost lower than the costs of competitors, an organisation can sell them at a lower price (and so increase demand from customers), or it can sell them at the same price as competitors and earn a bigger profit margin. Operating efficiently is an important way of managing cost.
Quality	The attractiveness of products to customers depends on a combination of price and quality. Quality may be in the product itself, or in the way it is made available (speed of delivery or convenience of purchase). Some companies compete successfully by focusing on product quality in comparison to the competition, even if this means selling the product at a higher price.
Green products	Some companies compete successfully by making products that have some appeal to customers who are environmentally aware. For example, a company might offer products that can be recycled after they have been used.

The transformation process

The contribution of operations to business competitiveness can also be explained by the transformation process. In every business, input resources are transformed into outputs (products and services) that are sold to customers. See Figure 3.1.2.

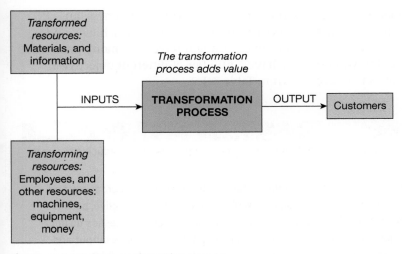

▲ **Figure 3.1.2**: The transformation process

The transformation process takes external resources such as materials and information, and uses its own internal resources such as employees and equipment to transform them into goods or services for selling to customers. Operations are at the centre of the transformation process.

This process should add value, because the selling price for the output goods or services should be higher than the cost of producing them.

Businesses succeed competitively by adding value through their operations and marketing. Value is added by reducing the costs of the inputs or increasing the value of the outputs.

Operations management and global business

The challenges for operations management are similar for businesses that operate internationally to those whose activities are restricted to a domestic market. However the scale and diversity of operations is greater with a global business.

Companies that operate on a global scale have opportunities to sell more goods and make bigger profits. They are competitive by:

- Reducing costs, for example by locating operations in countries where labour and other production costs are cheaper
- Achieving growth in operations and sales by selling to a bigger (global) market.

A company that operates internationally has greater logistical challenges to manage, since goods have to be distributed from the places they are made to the markets around the world where they are sold, often over long distances. International companies might also have production centres in different countries, close to their markets, and may source components from different sources. For example, some car manufacturers with production facilities in the USA source their car engines from Europe and many components from Mexico.

Operational objectives

Since operations are important for business competitiveness, an organisation should set objectives for its operations to achieve, and targets for each of these objectives. It might have one main operational objective, but will probably have a number of different objectives. Typical objectives are shown in Table 3.1.2.

▼ **Table 3.1.2**: Operational objectives

Objective	Comment
Costs: total costs and costs per unit	An organisation might set objectives for limiting total operating costs, or for reducing the cost per unit produced.
	A business might set itself the objective of limiting total operating costs. If it produces and sells the same amount of output every year, this would be a reasonable objective, because reducing total costs should result in higher profit. However, since most businesses do not produce a constant volume of output (for example, they might try to increase output and sales, and grow the business), a more appropriate cost objective would be to limit or reduce the cost per unit produced (or the cost per item of service delivered).
	Major companies in an industry may have an objective of being the least-cost producer (in other words, producer of items at the lowest cost per unit), so that they can sell at lower prices than competitors or earn bigger profits. The purpose of setting objectives for cost is to be competitive, and to ensure that profit targets are achieved. There might also be an objective for capacity utilisation (explained below) as a way of controlling costs per unit.

Objective	Comment
Quality	Customers make many of their buying decisions on the basis of both price and product quality. Businesses should have a clear idea of the quality of product or service they wish to provide and should set objectives (e.g. to improve quality) and targets. Aspects of quality include design quality, reliability and functionality (what the product does and how it is used).
Speed of response	For some products or services, speed of response may be an important operational objective. For example, with online selling, customers will often expect to receive delivery of their purchases quickly.
Flexibility	When an organisation operates in an uncertain or complex area, flexibility in operations may be a necessary objective. Flexibility means being able to respond to unexpected events, or deal with complex customer requirements. For example, a manufacturing company (for example, a producer of fashion goods) might need the ability to respond quickly to changes in demand. A provider of a service might need the flexibility to tailor the service to the specific requirements of individual customers.
Environmental objectives	Many companies have environmental objectives, in addition to commercial objectives. Environmental policies are aimed at helping to achieve sustainable development for the world's economy, and are concerned with protecting the Earth's natural resources from excessive use and pollution. Environmental objectives may include the aim to use energy efficiently, use raw materials from a renewable source, reduce levels of pollution and waste, recycle, and reduce the amount of waste sent to landfill. Companies might also have a more general objective of complying with the environmental legislation in the countries where they operate.
Customer satisfaction	The aim of every business should be to satisfy customers by providing goods or services that they need and want. An organisation may set objectives and targets for customer satisfaction, such as reducing the number of complaints or increasing the proportion of customers who buy the organisation's goods or services again.

Example
D S Smith is an international company that produces packaging material from paper and plastics. In 2018 it announced its objective of manufacturing its products using 100% recycled paper and plastics by 2025. In 2017 it had already succeeded in sourcing 37% of the plastics it used (24,000 tonnes) from recyclable sources.

Case study

Hermès

Hermès is a French company producing luxury goods such as handbags and silk scarves. Its handbags are made by skilled staff, and since the company hires just 250 new craftsmen each year, output and supply is restricted. Demand for Hermès handbags is strong, and many customers are willing to wait several years to obtain one. Most of them sell for $4,000 or more.

1 On the basis of this information, what do you think are the objectives of operational management at Hermès? Explain your reasons.

Activity

HCA Healthcare is a UK company operating a number of award-winning hospitals and clinics. They treat patients no matter what their condition is or becomes during treatment. Their consultants and critical care nurses are available on a one-to-one basis 24/7. 90% of the company's hospitals have been rated outstanding or good by an independent regulator.

Task

Use the internet to find details of HCA Healthcare, or any other company operating private hospitals. Make notes of what you consider to be their main operational objectives, explaining your reasons. Can you identify any conflict between the objectives you have identified, so that the company has to make a trade-off between them?

Trade-off between operational objectives

Some operational objectives might not be fully compatible with each other. For example:

- It is probably not possible to be the least-cost producer in an industry and at the same time respond quickly, and in a flexible way, to demand that occurs. Speed of response and flexibility in operations usually come at some cost.
- A trade-off is also usually required between cost and quality. Better quality usually comes at a higher cost.
- Environmental objectives may also be incompatible with least-cost production, because manufacturers might need to spend more money on reducing levels of pollution and disposing of waste, or might have to pay higher prices to buy raw materials from environmentally sustainable sources.

Objectives and targets may therefore differ between businesses, depending on their circumstances and the conditions in which they operate.

External and internal influences on operational objectives, plans and decisions

In settings their operational objectives and targets, and making their operational plans, businesses are subject to a range of influences. Some of these are internal to the business itself, and others are external, arising from the environment in which they operate. See Tables 3.1.3 and 3.1.4.

▼ **Table 3.1.3**: Internal influences on operational objectives, plans and decisions

Internal influences	Comment
Resources: material, labour, capital equipment	Operations are restricted by the availability of resources, such as: the amount of labour (especially skilled labour); the availability of scarce raw materials; the amount of machinery, equipment and other capital assets in use; and space for accommodating operational activities. Businesses cannot achieve ambitious operational objectives with insufficient resources for doing so.
Business objectives	Operational objectives are subordinate to objectives for the business as a whole. Business objectives may therefore strongly influence operational objectives, for example in terms of price and quality, international operations and environmental policies.
Finance	When a business wants to expand its operations, or make them more efficient, it will usually need additional finance to pay for more machinery, equipment and other resources. However, operational objectives and plans are constrained by the amount of finance available for investment.
Marketing issues	Decisions driven by marketing considerations might affect operational plans. For example, the marketing function may identify changes to a product design that are needed to meet customer demand better; or a business may need to reduce it prices (and so reduce its operating costs) to remain competitive.
Product concerns	Vey occasionally, a company might experience problems with product quality. For example, a car manufacturer had to recall over 300,000 cars due to concerns about an electrical fault in some of its models. The product recall on such a large scale called for a response from the operations function, to handle the recalled cars, inspect and repair them and return them to customers. There might also have been a requirement to change operational processes to reduce the risk of a similar fault occurring again in the future.

▼ **Table 3.1.4**: External influences on operational objectives, plans and decisions

External influence	Comment
Technological change	Changes in technology, particularly digital technology, can have a profound impact on the design of products that the operations function is required to make, or the production methods (or service delivery technology) that they use. An example is the change in operations required for online selling by retailers: companies have changed their operating methods by establishing large warehouses and delivery systems for goods sold online.
Market conditions and competition	Operational plans and decisions are influenced by changes in market conditions, such as an unexpected increase or fall in demand, or initiatives by a competitor. Businesses must respond and adapt to changes that occur, for example by copying a new initiative by a major competitor (such as a change in product design or delivery methods) in order to remain competitive.
	The need to be aware of competitors, what they are doing and the initiatives they are taking applies to both domestic and international competition.
	Market conditions can be affected by events or incidents other than changes in demand or competitor activity. For example, a budget airline had to adjust its operational plans (flight schedules) and short-term operational decisions in response to strike action in France by air traffic controllers.
Ethical and environmental influences	Operational objectives may be influenced by ethical and environmental issues, particularly in companies that have sustainability policies and policies for corporate social responsibility. For example, a company may have a policy of sourcing its raw materials only from renewable sources, and refusing to buy from suppliers who do not respect human rights or employment rights of their employees.
Legal and regulatory change	New legislation, such as regulations allowing or banning the use of certain materials or production methods, can result in a change in operating plans. For example, concerns about the possibility of legislation (e.g. in the EU) against some of their business activities may influence the operational objectives and plans of search engine companies such as Google.

Example

Shortages of resources can affect long-term planning, but may also disrupt short-term plans and operational decisions.

In 2018, a temporary shortage of carbon dioxide (CO_2) disrupted the plans and decisions of several companies in the UK. CO_2 is used in food packaging, in the production process for soft drinks and to stun animals for slaughter. When the shortage occurred, companies such as Coca-Cola reported shortages of some products, meat processors reported a halt or slowdown in production, and bakery company Warburtons halted production of crumpets at two factories because it did not have CO_2 for packaging.

Progress questions

1. What is the transformation process in business operations? How does it add value for a business?
2. Identify four operational objectives that a business might have.
3. What is flexibility in operations?
4. What is meant by a trade-off between operational objectives?

Exam-style questions

1 A restaurant has 40 tables, catering for up to 160 customers. It opens five days each week and operates in an area where there are a number of competitors.

   Explain two operational objectives that this restaurant might have to compete successfully. (4 marks)

2 A transport company operates a fleet of barges for transporting goods up and down a major river. It operates throughout the year, and competes for business with other barge operators, as well as with road transport companies. Road haulage is an alternative to transporting goods by river.

   Analyse how the operations of the transport company might help it to compete successfully with its rival transport companies. (9 marks)

3 Manufacturers of household appliances such as central heating boilers, washing machines and ovens are responding to advances in digital technology by producing a new generation of products that include a digital device that responds to commands from a remote user via the internet. This new generation of products is known collectively as the Internet of Things (IoT).

   Analyse how the operations function in these manufacturing companies must adjust to these advances in digital technology by co-operating with the following functions in the business: research and development, marketing, and accounting and finance. (9 marks)

3.2 Operations planning and data

This section will develop your knowledge and understanding of:

→ The purpose and use of operational plans and budgets
→ Operations data for measuring productivity and other aspects of operational performance
→ The interpretation of operational data.

Operational objectives, plans and budgets

The previous section suggested what the operational objectives of a business organisation might be. Once a business has identified its operational objectives, these should be developed into formal detailed plans with targets for achievement. Formal planning has the advantages of:

- Establishing clear targets for achievement within the period covered by the plan
- Comparing actual performance with the plan as the period progresses, and taking remedial measures when actual performance is not as good as required
- Communicating plans to everyone concerned so that they understand requirements
- Co-ordinating the efforts of everyone involved in the preparation and implementation of the plan.

An operational budget is a financial plan for operations, setting out what the planned operations are expected to cost during the period. The operations budget is a plan that links operational plans and targets to the overall financial objectives of the business.

Operational plans in a manufacturing company should cover five broad aspects of operations, in addition to cost. See Figure 3.2.1.

> **Key term**
>
> Operational budget: plan for operations expressed in money terms.

Product	Plant	Processes
Make products that customers need and want: performance, quality reliability, aesthetics	Machines and equipment required: consider future demand for products, equipment reliability, factory layout, maintenance, heath and safety	Choose appropriate operating process: consider available capacity, labour skills, production methods, maintenance requirements

Programmes	People	Costs
Schedule operations: dates and times for deliveries to customers and from suppliers, availability of storage, transportation	Planning to have a sufficient number of employees with the required skills to perform operations	Keeping costs within budget, meeting (or beating) cost targets

▲ **Figure 3.2.1**: Aspects of operations management

▼ **Table 3.2.1**: Operational targets

Aspect of operations	Examples of targets
Costs and output volume	Output per week or per employee per week Costs per unit produced Unit profit/unit contribution
Quality	Rates of scrap/rejected items Reliability Customer complaints (number) Customer loyalty (repeat business) Customer satisfaction (feedback of ratings)
Efficiency and flexibility	Labour productivity Machine productivity Order lead times from suppliers Capacity utilisation
Environment	Use of energy % of materials from recycled sources % of materials purchased from sustainable sources Compliance with environmental legislation

Operating targets

Within operational plans, there should be targets for achievement. These targets should ideally be quantifiable, so that actual performance can be compared more easily with the planning targets. Targets are also set as averages. Table 3.2.1 shows targets that might be set by operations management.

Example

All types of business can identify environmental targets. For example HSBC, the international bank, set the following targets for 2020, compared to a baseline year of 2011:

- Cut annual carbon emissions per full-time employee to 2.0 tonnes from the baseline of 3.5 tonnes in 2011
- Source 40% of electricity from renewables
- Reduce waste from offices by 75%
- Reduce paper use by 66%
- Reduce water consumption by 50%.

Operations data for measuring productivity and other aspects of operational performance

Labour productivity

Productivity is another word for efficiency. Labour productivity is concerned with the amount of time it takes workers to do their job or to perform a task. Another way of thinking about labour productivity is that it is the amount of output that workers can produce in a given period.

Key terms

Efficiency: the rate at which a task is performed or output is produced.

Productivity: efficiency; often used in relation to labour efficiency.

Output: the quantity of products manufactured or services provided.

Labour productivity can be measured as:

$$\frac{\text{Quantity of output produced in a period of time}}{\text{Average number of employees in the period}}$$

Alternatively:

$$\frac{\text{Quantity of output produced in a period of time}}{\text{Number of hours worked in the period}}$$

Example

A manufacturing company produced 900 tonnes of output during a particular week, during which the average number of employees was 750. The total number of hours worked during the week was 30,000.

Labour productivity can be measured in any of the following ways.

Output per employee per week:	Output per hour worked:	Time to produce 1 tonne:
900 tonnes/750 employees = 1.20 tonnes	900 tonnes/30,000 hours = 0.03 tonnes per hour	30,000 hours/900 tonnes = 33.33 hours (= 33 hours 20 minutes)

If the company has an operational target of improving labour productivity by 10% (compared to this week and using the same number of employees), its aim will be to increase output per employee per week to 1.32 tonnes (= 1.20 tonnes × 1.10).

Productivity and labour costs per unit

Labour productivity affects the labour cost of an operation. Improvements in productivity reduce the labour cost per unit produced, and lower productivity results in higher labour costs per unit. For example, suppose that employees are paid $30 per hour and that it currently takes 20 minutes to make a unit of output. The labour cost per unit is $10 (= $30 × 20/60). Now suppose that the time to produce a unit is reduced from 20 minutes to 18 minutes: following this improvement in productivity the labour cost per unit falls to $9 (= $30 × 18/60).

This is why, in businesses where labour costs are a high proportion of operational costs, targets for improving labour productivity are often included in operational plans and budgets.

Improving labour productivity

When data shows labour productivity has fallen, and needs to be improved, it is necessary to learn the cause of the poor performance in order to consider the best way of dealing with the problem. See Table 3.2.2.

Capital productivity

Businesses that invest capital by acquiring fixed assets such as machines, equipment, motor vehicles and buildings expect a return on their investment. Productivity can be improved by using machines, and organisational targets for the productivity of their fixed assets.

The productivity of machinery or equipment can be measured in a way that is similar to measuring labour productivity.

Capital productivity (the productivity of any type of machine or equipment) can be measured as:

$$\frac{\text{Quantity of output produced in a period of time}}{\text{Number of machines in the period}}$$

Alternatively:

$$\frac{\text{Quantity of output produced in a period of time}}{\text{Number of machine hours operated in the period}}$$

▼ Table 3.2.2: Improving labour productivity

Reason for poor labour productivity	Comment: dealing with the cause of poor productivity
Employees insufficiently skilled	Providing training for employees should improve their skill or knowledge, and make them more efficient in the work they do.
Too much idle time	If employees on a fixed weekly wage or monthly salary have nothing to do, they are still being paid. Improving the organisation of operations might achieve a reduction in idle time, so that productivity improves.
Poor planning or organising of operations	Improvements in the way that operations are organised might result in productivity improvements.
Poor employee motivation	A well-motivated workforce is likely to be more efficient than a dissatisfied workforce or a workforce operating in unpleasant conditions. So improving employee motivation should improve productivity. The problem is that improving motivation is not necessarily easy to achieve.
Out-of-date or ageing equipment	Investing in capital – machines and other equipment – can help to improve labour productivity. In many cases, using equipment and machines might enable an organisation to reduce the number of people it employs. However, investing in capital equipment can be expensive, and the benefits from improving labour productivity should be weighed against the costs of the equipment.

Example

A manufacturing company produced 4,500 units of output during a particular week, using two machines. The total number of hours operated during the week was 80 hours on one machine and 70 hours on the other.

The productivity of the machines can be measured in any of the following ways.

Output per machine per week:	Output per machine hour:	Machine time to produce 1 unit
4,500 units/2 machines = 2,250 units per machine	4,500 units/(80 + 70) hours = 30 units per hour	150 hours/4,500 units = 0.033 hours = (0.033 × 60 =) 2 minutes

Improving capital productivity

When data shows that capital productivity is getting worse, it is necessary to discover the reason why this has happened, and consider ways of dealing with the problem. There are various reasons for poor capital productivity. See Table 3.2.3.

▼ Table 3.2.3: Improving capital productivity

Reason for poor capital productivity	Comment: dealing with the cause of poor productivity
Machines/equipment have been under-used	Operating machines for more hours per day will increase the total output per machine per day. However it will not improve the output per machine hour or the machine time required to make one unit.
Machine downtime is too high	Reducing the number of hours that machines are not operating will also increase the total output per machine per period of time. It will not increase the output per machine hour worked, but it will increase the output per available machine hour (the hours when machines are either in operation or available for operation but not in use). Downtime for machines might be reduced by ensuring that machines are well maintained, so that breakdowns are less frequent and shorter in duration when they do occur.
Machines are inefficient because they are too small for the output they are required to produce	Efficiency can often be improved by replacing existing machines with larger or more technically efficient machines. Investing in capital – machines and other equipment – can help to improve labour productivity. In many cases, using equipment and machines might enable an organisation to reduce the number of people it employs. However, investing in capital equipment can be expensive, and the benefits from improving labour productivity should be weighed against the costs of the equipment.

Land productivity

In some industries, operational targets might be set (and performance measured) for productivity in the use of land. The most obvious example is farming, where land productivity is measured by:

- The quantities of crops produced in a year (or growing season) per acre or hectare of land farmed, or
- The number of livestock (cows, sheep, goats, etc.) per acre or hectare of land farmed.

The productivity of farmland might be improved with the use of pesticides and other chemicals, but these can have a damaging effect on the environment, by making land uninhabitable for wildlife or by polluting ground and rivers.

Another way of improving productivity is to make use of better equipment for sowing and harvesting produce, in order to increase the quantity of produce from the land each year.

Sales performance

In some businesses, operational performance might be measured in terms of sales. This might occur, for example, when output consists of many different items, or non-standard items. When output is not measurable in standard units, an alternative measure of operational performance is sales revenue per employee per period.

$$\text{Sales revenue per employee per period} = \frac{\text{Total sales revenue in the period}}{\text{Average number of employees}}$$

In retail businesses, performance might be measured instead in terms of sales revenue per square metre of floor space.

$$\text{Retail performance} = \frac{\text{Total sales revenue in the period}}{\text{Square metres of floor space in the store}}$$

Example

A store had annual sales turnover of $700,000. It employed on average ten people full time during the year. Its floor space is 250 square metres.

Sales revenue per employee per year = $700,000/10 = $70,000 per employee.

Sales per year per square metre = $700,000/250 = $2,800.

Interpretation of sales revenue per employee

Changes in the sales revenue per employee in a company can help management to assess whether its performance is improving over time. For example, if sales revenue per employee increased from $500,000 per year to $700,000 per year, the company's performance is improving and the company may be able to pay its employees a bit more. However, it is not easy to compare the sales per employee of different companies, because they might have different production systems: for example one producer of washing machines might manufacture all its components internally, whereas a competitor might outsource a large proportion of component manufacture. The company doing everything internally will have lower sales revenue per employee, because it will employ more people.

For example, in a recent year, Samsung employed about 93,000 people and annual revenue per employee was $1.9 million. This compared with Hewlett Packard, which employed 49,000 people and achieved annual sales per employee of $1.0 million, and IBM which employed 380,000 people and had annual sales per employee of just $210,000. All three companies are in the IT industry, but their results are not properly comparable.

Unit costs (average)

Operational targets and operational performance can be expressed in terms of the average cost per unit of output produced. For the purpose of operational management, costs mean operational costs (and not marketing costs or costs of support services such as HR and accounting).

$$\text{Average unit cost} = \frac{\text{Total operating costs in the period}}{\text{Units of output in the period}}$$

In a manufacturing company producing a standard product, output can be measured as the number of units produced, and units might be expressed in tonnes, litres, units of product, and so on. For an energy generating company, output may be measured in terms of kilowatt hours (kWh).

Key term

Average unit cost: total cost in a period divided by the number of units produced.

Get it right

Do not confuse total costs and average costs per unit. When an operation increases its volume of output, total operating costs will rise, but the average cost per unit might fall. For example, if it costs $100 to make one unit of a product and $180 to make two units, the total cost increases by $80 when the second unit is made, but the average cost per unit falls from $100 to $90.

Case study

Operating cost of a bus company

A bus company operates a fleet of 20 buses, travelling non-stop between two towns. During one particular week, the buses travelled an average of 600 miles each, and the average number of passengers was 35 per journey. Total operating costs for the week were $168,000.

1. What was the operating cost per unit during the week, if units of output are measured as passenger miles travelled?

In some industries, output measurements are slightly more complicated.

Example

A road haulage company transports goods by road. It has ten trucks, and in one particular week, the trucks travelled on average 2,400 miles each carrying goods. The average size of transport load varied but on average was 1.5 tonnes per journey. Operating costs for the week were $108,000.

So how do we measure the unit cost of operations? As a cost per truck per week? Or as a cost per mile travelled? Since costs are likely to depend not just on distance travelled, but on the weight of goods carried, it is usual to measure unit costs of haulage as a cost per tonne per mile, or cost per tonne/mile.

In this example, the total number of tonne/miles carried = Number of trucks × Average distance travelled × Average load per journey. Here this is 10 × 2,400 × 1.5 = 36,000 tonne/miles.

The cost per tonne/mile carried was $108,000/36,000 = $3.

Reducing unit costs

Unit costs of output can be reduced in either of two ways (or a combination of both). See Table 3.2.4.

▼ Table 3.2.4: Ways of reducing the operating cost per unit

Method	
Reduce total operating costs, without reducing the quantity produced	Operating costs can be reduced by improving productivity or by reducing spend on unnecessary items, or buying things more cheaply.
Increase the volume of output per period	When output volume increases, total operating costs will also increase to some extent, but in spite of the increase in total expenditure, the average cost per unit may fall.
	Output volume can be increased if there is spare capacity.

Key terms

Capacity (operating capacity or output capacity): the maximum output that operations can produce in a period, given its existing resources and normal methods of operating.

Capacity utilisation: the percentage of operating capacity that is used in a period of time.

Progress questions

1 What are the main aspects of operations management in a manufacturing company?
2 How might labour productivity be measured?
3 How might labour productivity be improved?
4 What is land productivity?
5 How might sales revenue be used to set targets for operating performance?

Capacity and capacity utilisation

Operating capacity (also referred to sometimes as output capacity) is the maximum amount of output that operations could produce in a period of time, given its existing resources (employees and equipment) and normal methods of operating.

Estimating capacity

Capacity can be estimated from the average output per labour hour or machine operating hour, and the number of available hours during normal working time in a period.

For example, suppose that the current productivity level at a factory is five units per machine hour, there are six identical machines making the item, and each machine is expected to operate for 40 hours each week. Weekly capacity would be calculated as 1,200 units (= 6 machines × 40 hours × 5 units per hour).

Capacity utilisation

Capacity utilisation is the percentage of operating capacity that is used in a period of time. Actual capacity utilisation is often less than 100%, due to low demand, or machine breakdowns.

$$\text{Capacity utilisation} = \frac{\text{Actual or planned output}}{\text{Maximum output}} \times 100\%$$

Example

A factory has capacity to produce 100,000 units of a product per month. Due to low demand for the product, the budgeted capacity utilisation is 85%. During May, actual output was 88,400 units.

100% capacity = 100,000 units per month

Budgeted capacity utilisation per month = 80% × 100,000 = 80,000 units

Actual capacity utilisation in May = (88,400/10,000) × 100% = 88.4%.

Measuring capacity utilisation in different industries

Capacity utilisation measures the extent to which the resources or assets of a business are being used, but measurements of capacity can vary between different types of business. For example:

- In the passenger airline industry, capacity utilisation is measured by the percentage of seats that are filled on flights. Capacity utilisation can also be measured for flights to different locations or flights in different sizes of aircraft.

- In the hotels industry, capacity utilisation is measured by the proportion of hotel rooms that are occupied by guests. For example, a hotel with 40 rooms which operates for 365 days each year has a capacity of 14,600 room nights per year. Capacity utilisation is measured as the number of "room nights" that were actually occupied during the year, as a percentage of 14,600.

- Capacity utilisation in a restaurant is more difficult to measure, because the same table might be occupied by several different customers during the same day, so what is 100% capacity?

Interpreting capacity utilisation

Capacity utilisation in any industry is likely to be less than 100%. The extent to which it is below 100% may be an indicator of the sales revenue (and profit) that the business is losing by not operating at a higher capacity.

For example, suppose that a hotel charges $200 dollars per night for a room and has a maximum capacity of 14,600 room nights per year. If capacity utilisation is, say, 70%, this means that there are 4,380 room nights per year when rooms are unoccupied. If the hotel were able to operate at 100% capacity, its annual revenue would be $876,000 higher (4380 × $200).

Capacity utilisation above and below 100%

Capacity utilisation is often less than 100%, and occasionally for short periods of time, capacity may be above 100%. See Table 3.2.5.

Operating at above 100% capacity is only temporary; otherwise the higher level of capacity will become a new normal 100% capacity level.

Capacity can be managed in a way that reduces the unit costs of output.

Other measures of operating performance

Objectives and targets can be set for any different aspect of operating activities. The choice of suitable targets will depend on the nature of

▼ **Table 3.2.5**: Operating at below or above 100% capacity utilisation

Possible reasons	
Operating below 100% capacity utilisation	**Operating above 100% capacity utilisation**
Lack of demand from customers. Low demand due to seasonal factors (e.g. ice cream in winter, ski boots in summer)	Increasing overtime working
Inefficient operations: poor operations management	Putting on an extra shift
Machine breakdowns	Hiring temporary labour
Higher than expected labour turnover: temporary shortage of employees	Subcontracting some work to outside suppliers
	Reducing the amount of time spent on scheduled machine maintenance

Key term

Labour turnover: the number of employees leaving a business in a given time period. It is usually expressed as a labour turnover percentage rate.

the operations. For example, when an operating objective is customer satisfaction, a key target and measure of performance might be waiting times, such as:

- Waiting times before a service is provided, such as call waiting times at a customer service centre, and passenger waiting times for a train or bus service
- Waiting times for delivery of a product.

And for a transport company such as an airline, a bus company or a passenger rail company, measures of performance might include total passenger numbers and the average seat capacity in journeys.

Operational performance measurements differ between businesses because of the different nature of their business activities.

Interpreting operations data

Operations data is produced in order to help with the management of activities and resources. Data is used to set targets for performance, and to report actual performance. Data about actual performance should be interpreted in order to decide whether any measures should be taken to improve operations. Figure 3.2.2 gives a useful approach to interpreting operations data.

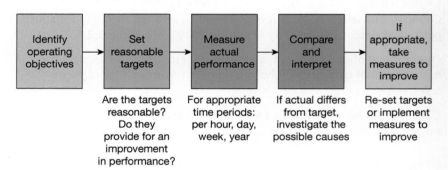

▲ **Figure 3.2.2**: Interpreting operations data

Case study

Operations performance in call centres

A research team for a television programme about customer service levels made 100 telephone calls, over a three-day period and at different times of the day, to the customer service centres of five different companies. The team recorded the response times, from the moment the caller stopped dialling to the moment that they heard a live human voice answering the call. The team found that, on average, the average time to answer for all five companies was less than three and half minutes. The fastest average for an individual company was just one minute 39 seconds. The quickest response time for a single call was 50 seconds.

Two companies had much worse response times than the other three. The longest waiting time for a response for one of these companies was 24 minutes 47 seconds. For the other, the longest wait was 29 minutes 33 seconds, when the call was then cut off.

Companies with customer call centres should set targets for average and maximum waiting times for calls to be answered.

1 What do you think might be the causes of lengthy call waiting times?

2 What methods do you think operations management might use to reduce call waiting times at their customer call centre?

Exam-style questions

1   A factory employed 20 people, each working 40 hours per week. During one week the factory produced 2,800 units of output. What was the average output per person per week, and what was the average time to produce one unit of output?   (2 marks)

2   A factory estimates that its weekly output capacity is 24,000 units of product. During July it produced 18,600 units.

   Calculate the capacity utilisation of the factory in July.   (2 marks)

3   The income of crop farmers depends largely on the amount of produce they grow each year.

   Explain two possible reasons for poor productivity by farmers in the use of their farmland.   (4 marks)

4   The operations manager of a manufacturing company has set a target of increasing labour productivity among operating staff by 5% over the next two years. The manager considers that the current low level of productivity is attributable to high rates of labour turnover and absenteeism from work.

   Analyse how reducing the rates of labour turnover and absenteeism should result in an increase in labour productivity.   (9 marks)

5   A factory is operating at 100% capacity, but current demand exceeds capacity. The factory management have been asked to take measures to increase output to meet the unexpected level of demand.

   Analyse the short-term measures that the factory management might take to increase output capacity above 100%.   (9 marks)

Measurement and importance of capacity and capacity utilisation

Capacity

As explained previously capacity is usually defined in terms of the output of products or services that could be provided in a given time period using the current resources available. This is a relatively simple concept in some situations:

- The capacity of a football ground or theatre is usually governed by regulations and refers to the number of people allowed into the stadium
- A piece of machinery is often designed to be capable of producing a predetermined amount per hour
- A bank will have a given amount of queuing space, staff and service points.

However, in some circumstances the idea of capacity is less clear.

What would be the capacity of a restaurant? In normal circumstances it would be determined by the number of chairs and tables available for customers and the number of employees there are to prepare the food and serve it. However, for a special occasion a restaurant can often find space to fit in extra people.

What is the capacity of a supermarket? It would normally be determined by the number of staff available, the checkouts available and the size of the car park. However, at peak times (festivals, etc.) throughput of customers can be increased beyond the normal capacity by taking special measures, for example by opening longer hours, employing temporary staff and helping customers pack their bags.

It is usual, particularly for the service industries, to consider capacity to be the maximum possible output in "normal circumstances".

▲ **Figure 3.3.1**: Building that took place in Rio for the 2016 Olympics illustrates the perceived need for an increase in capacity

Case study

Olympics 2020

Getting the planning right for an enormous event like the 2020 Summer Olympics and Paralympics in Tokyo, Japan always attracts a great deal of media attention. When a city holds an event like this, there is great discussion over whether the infrastructure will be ready in time – for example the stadia, swimming pools and cycling tracks.

Just as important are details such as:

- Will transport systems cope with the extra traffic?
- Will there be sufficient hotel accommodation?
- Will immigration systems be able to cope with large numbers of people arriving in a short time period?

Each of these details raises the question: "Is there enough capacity to cope with the large increase?"

If, for example, new hotel accommodation is provided just for the Games period there could be far too much capacity both before and after the Games. If extra capacity is not provided there could be chaos when the Games are taking place. However, providing extra roads, trains and so on, can be extremely expensive, particularly for a short period of time.

An alternative to providing additional trains may be to find ways to use the existing capacity more effectively. Managers must determine to what extent trains and the railway network are being used. Perhaps not all trains are full, perhaps some services are not important, perhaps the tracks could be used more, perhaps there are times when insufficient employees are available. Looking at the level of use of existing capacity – the level of capacity utilisation – managers can identify ways of accommodating large increases in passengers without having to go to the huge expense of new trains, track and staff.

1 Explain why it is likely that railway systems are not currently always operating at full capacity.
2 Explain two ways that the rail network could increase capacity without buying new trains.

Capacity utilisation

Businesses need to know how effectively they are using the resources available to them. If a hotel is regularly less than half-full then a lot of its rooms will be unused and this is a waste of resources. If demand for a restaurant is so high that customers have to wait half an hour for a table, it cannot provide the best service to all of its customers. If a car manufacturer is producing significantly below the maximum possible level then expensive equipment is idle.

If capacity utilisation is at 100% then the business is producing as much as it possibly can with its existing resources and method of working.

Progress questions

1 Why is it difficult to measure capacity utilisation in a hospital ward?

Implications of operating under or close to maximum capacity

Common sense probably tells us that the higher the level of capacity utilisation, the better.

- Greater utilisation means greater production. This means there is potential for more sales which will, if the price is right, mean more profits.
- Greater utilisation means that valuable resources do not stay unused – if they are unused that would be incurring unnecessary costs.
- Greater utilisation means spreading fixed costs out over a larger volume of production.

Example

Suppose a machine has fixed costs of $500 per day. If the machine can produce 1,000 units per day at maximum capacity then:

- The average fixed cost at maximum capacity is $0.50 per item ($500/1,000)
- The average fixed cost if only 250 items are produced is $2.00 per item ($500/250).

If the higher level of production is achieved it would be easier for the business to make a larger profit.

What reasons are there for ensuring capacity utilisation does not go too high?

- When people and machines are working as hard as they possibly can, and for long periods of time, there is a greater risk of things going wrong. Machines break down, people make mistakes, systems go wrong.
- There will be no possibility of increasing output to meet any special orders – perhaps from a highly valued customer. The order will have to be turned down and the customer might take their business elsewhere.
- Employees, including managers, may feel under pressure and become demotivated or leave.

What if there is too much capacity?

A business may find itself facing declining demand for its products. Although it may continue production at current levels (and therefore maintain capacity utilisation) inventories will increase, causing increased costs and possibly increased wastage. The business could also decide to cut back production, which means working well below capacity either from time to time or for long periods. In either case, there is too much capacity at a point in time. There can be a variety of reasons for declining demand including responding to fluctuating demand patterns (perhaps due to seasons) or overcapacity in an industry – the worldwide steel industry and the car industry both suffer from having the capacity to produce far more than is demanded.

Operating at below 100% capacity has implications for cost. When the utilised capacity of an operation is less than 100%, this means that there are idle resources that are being paid for but which are not producing anything. Employees are being paid to do nothing, or they can take more time to finish their work. Expensive machinery and other equipment will be idle. Operating at 80% capacity does not mean that operating costs fall to 80% of their level at 100% capacity.

Example: seasonal demand and capacity

When there is seasonal demand for a product, it might be possible to reduce operating costs by limiting output capacity. For example, the demand for skis for a company making cold-weather products might be 60,000 pairs in one half of the year and 150,000 pairs in the other half. At the moment, the company's output capacity is 150,000 pairs per half year (25,000 pairs per month).

If the company could use the quiet period of the year to make an extra 45,000 pairs of skis it could build up inventory, so that in the busy period it can produce just 105,000 pairs of skis and have sufficient to meet the high seasonal demand. By reducing capacity to 105,000 pairs of skis per six months (17,500 pairs per month) the company can reduce the resources it needs to make the skis (with fewer employees and less machinery) and so improve productivity and reduce costs.

The importance of efficiency and productivity

Business operations' efficiency measures the amount of resources that production uses relative to its output. A business will be more efficient if it uses fewer resources to produce a given output and this will also reduce costs.

If productivity increases, the ratio of outputs to inputs rises and average cost of the output will fall. This explains why productivity is such an important concept for business.

Example

The owner of a hairdressing salon pays staff $10 per hour for a basic haircutting service. At the moment staff deal with four haircuts in an hour, at a labour cost of $2.50 per cut.

If productivity can be increased so that each employee can deal with five haircuts in an hour instead of four, the average labour cost will fall to $2 per haircut, a reduction of $0.50. The business could then

> **Key term**
>
> **Efficiency:** measures the amount of resources that production uses relative to its output. Lower resource use for a given output is more efficient and less costly.

reduce its price by \$0.50 and maintain its profit margin, keep the price the same and increase its profit margin by \$0.50, or reduce its price by less than \$0.50 and also increase its profit per haircut.

The same is true for improvements in efficiency in the use of equipment or materials. If more efficient use can be made of these, costs will fall and the business will be in a position to decide whether to reduce price, which is likely to increase sales at the same profit margin, or to keep price the same and gain increased profits through increased profit margin.

Ways and difficulties of increasing efficiency and productivity

Productivity
There are a number of ways to increase productivity.

Invest capital
Spending money on more efficient modern machinery and equipment should lower unit costs in the medium to long term. However, spending on new capital equipment may be expensive, so that the improvements in productivity might be offset by the high cost of the new equipment. An alternative method of using equipment to improve productivity might be to increase the output from the existing equipment by better maintenance and more careful use.

Train employees
A skilled workforce is more likely to make fewer mistakes and finish their tasks more quickly. They might resolve problems more quickly and will not need to ask someone else for guidance, thus saving time. However, training may be expensive and disrupt existing production, and must be targeted on the right people and the right tasks. Arguably, however, businesses do not train their employees enough, and so miss the opportunity for big improvements in productivity.

Improve employee motivation
There is an opinion that better motivation of employees should lead to higher productivity, because they will be more interested in their work and will try to perform tasks better. However, there is no conclusive evidence of a link between motivation and productivity, and opinions on the subject remain divided. Motivated employees may enjoy their work, but if they do, they might take longer to complete it because they want to do the job well.

Change the organisation's culture
Employees will function more efficiently if the organisation structures and culture are changed to increase the efficiency of the procedures and working practices. An example of this is the use of lean production techniques in some manufacturing companies.

Efficiency and unit costs
As we have seen, efficiency relates to the amount of resources used relative to output, or the amount of output per unit of resource used. For example, by increasing labour productivity, the amount of

Key term

Productivity: a measure of efficiency, not simply a change in output. It is often expressed as a measure of how efficient labour is at production in a given time.

Get it right

Productivity is a measure of efficiency, not simply a change in output. It is often expressed as a measure of how efficient labour is at production in a given time using the formula output divided by number of employees in that time. Productivity can also refer to the land or capital. Higher productivity will result in lower costs per unit of output as more is being produced using the same inputs.

Link

Lean production is explained on page 158.

labour time per unit produced is reduced. However, improvements in efficiency do not necessarily result in a lower cost per unit. The cost of improving productivity and efficiency needs to be balanced against the benefit gained.

- For example, training improves the skills of workers, who should be able to work more efficiently and with a lower level of wastage: this achieves a saving of resources. However, training has a cost and skilled workers might want higher pay: this means that there might also be some increase in costs in spite of the improvement in productivity.
- Changing structures and systems within a business may result in greater productivity; but making big changes may be a costly exercise that adds to overall costs in the short term.

Increasing productivity is a valuable activity – it often reduces average unit costs. However, this does not mean that any change to increase productivity should necessarily be adopted. There are likely to be costs that might include the cost of new equipment, training and an increase in wages to match increasing skill levels, a lack of sufficient demand or the cost of reforming organisation structures and operating systems. In addition the estimates of increased productivity might be inaccurate. A business should take each of these issues into account when deciding whether to go ahead with a change to increase productivity.

Flexibility and speed of operations

An ability to adapt in a flexible way to changes or variations in demand, and an ability to respond quickly to customers, can be important elements in operational efficiency and effectiveness. It might be argued that in a large business whose activities cover a wide geographical area (for example, internationally), or a wide range of products or services, giving local managers the authority to make decisions ("decentralisation of management authority") might help to improve effectiveness and efficiency. The advantages and disadvantages of decentralisation are set out in Table 3.3.1.

▼ **Table 3.3.1**: Decentralisation to improve effectiveness and efficiency

Advantages	Comment
Knowledge of customers	Local managers have a better understanding of what customers want, and so are able to provide better customer service.
Knowledge of local conditions	Local managers also have a better understanding of local conditions (such as the availability of casual labour in the area), and can adapt with flexibility to meet variations as local conditions change.
Faster decision-making	If decision-making is decentralised and delegated to local managers, it is possible that decisions will be taken more quickly, because they do not have to be referred up to senior management at a remote head office.
Disadvantages	**Comment**
Some loss of central management control	Decentralisation of management authority inevitably involves some loss of control by head office management.
Loss of standardisations	When local management are able to adapt operations to meet local conditions, there could be some loss of standardisation in the products or services that the business delivers.

Case study

Habasit

Habasit is a company in India that manufactures conveyor belts for use in food-processing industries. Conveyor belts in this industry are vital as they transport food products from one process to the next. If the belt breaks, production is disrupted. If the belt is dirty or unhygienic the food will be contaminated and made worthless. The belts are made of a strong flexible material. They are covered with several coatings which provide protection against infective bacteria, make cleaning easy and importantly provide a non-slip surface so less food material sticks to the belt. The belts last longer than previous models. One pastry manufacturer was able to reduce flour consumption by 30% as less stuck to the surface. The Indian food-processing industry is worth $135 billion and is estimated to grow at an annual rate of 10% to reach $200 billion by 2020. The Indian government is actively trying to make this happen with the long-term view of making the country a world leader by 2055.

1 How will the use of conveyor belts like the ones manufactured by Habasit increase productivity?
2 Why might improvements in productivity from the installation of conveyor belts fail to result in a reduction in the unit costs of food products?

Lean production

The nature and importance of lean production

Lean production is a "way of life" rather than a set of processes.

The idea behind lean production is that a business takes a systematic approach to ensuring that the whole process of producing and supplying products and services works to provide the customer with the highest possible appropriate quality with the minimum waste. A business achieves this by examining all of its activities and processes and finding ways in which to improve on the methods employed.

By employing the ideas behind lean production a business can expect to:

- Have systems that are more responsive to rapidly changing markets
- Meet the demands of customers through prompt delivery and appropriate quality
- Reduce costs through elimination of all types of waste.

Adding value and avoiding waste

An underlying principle of lean production is that every operating activity should add value. This means that the benefits from performing the activity should exceed the costs of doing it. There are many activities that do not add value: these are wasteful and should be eliminated as far as possible, so that operations are lean and without unnecessary elements.

So what creates waste? The so-called **seven wastes in production** are set out in Table 3.3.2.

Key term

Lean production: in manufacturing businesses, using resources as efficiently as possible by minimising waste and eliminating activities that do not add value, while ensuring quality.

▼ **Table 3.3.2**: Examples of waste in manufacturing operations

Cause of waste Reduce or eliminate to become more lean	Comment
Over-production	Over-production means producing more output than is needed to meet current demand. When this happens, the excess production is added to inventory, waiting to be sold. Inventory is a cost but it is also an idle resource.
Inventory	For the above reason, inventory levels should be kept as low as possible, and items should be produced as close as possible to the time the goods are needed. This is the concept of just-in-time or JIT, which you will learn more about later in this chapter.
Waiting time	Waiting time occurs when machines or employees are doing nothing, waiting for something to happen before they can do anything themselves. Waiting time, such as hold-ups in production, are a waste and an unnecessary cost: employees are still paid, even though they are doing nothing, and expensive equipment is producing nothing.
Inappropriate processing	Sometimes a task can be performed by simpler, less expensive machines or equipment, when more expensive items are used instead to do the work.
Transporting items	When goods are being moved from one place to another, nothing of value is happening. Transport should be kept to a minimum.
Motion	Similarly, when people are moving from one place to another, they do not add value. Minimising the movement of employees within the production area reduces waste.
Defective units	Producing defective units in the production process is also wasteful, because the defects are either scrapped or must be re-worked to correct the defect. When there are defects in production, there is waste and costs are higher than they would otherwise be. An ideal objective should be to "get things right first time".

Case study

GSEP Limited

GSEP limited is a business in India manufacturing rubber and plastic parts for cars, such as windscreen seals. In a very competitive market GSEP needed to reduce costs. A thorough investigation into all aspects of the business's operations revealed:

- Considerable areas of unused space
- High levels of machine breakdown time
- A long time spent maintaining machines and resetting them
- Large amounts of waste material
- Quality problems.

Application of lean production ideas enabled GSEP to change the thinking in the business. The "culture of blame" has become a "culture of continuous improvement"

with employees wanting to play a positive role in the development of the business. Employees are empowered to make decisions. Redesigning the production system, increased training and improved operating procedures have eliminated a lot of the waste. Quality has improved and productivity increased dramatically.

These changes are all part of the lean production programme at GSEP.

1. Why is a "culture of blame" a problem?
2. What benefits and disadvantages can there be from empowering the employees?
3. Why has increased training had a key role in the changes at GSEP?
4. What do you think "lean production" means in this context?

Lean production techniques

Lean production involves exploring the entire operations of the business, looking for ways to make improvements. The improvements that can be made in any operation are likely to be highly specific to the nature of the operation. So there are no universal answers to becoming a lean manufacturer.

Lean production examines processes which include avoiding over-production and a build-up of inventories, reducing or avoiding waiting times, reducing movements of product items and people, and eliminating defects in production.

A general approach to lean production involves:

- Doing simple things well
- Doing these simple things better
- Involving all employees in a process of continuous improvement
- And in doing so, reduce or avoid waste.

These together with a review of all aspects of a business should lead to a leaner, more efficient enterprise.

Benefits of lean production

Lean production can help a business to remove the following problems:

- Quantities of defects – products or services that do not meet customer expectations
- Excessive inventory holding of raw materials, finished products, work-in-progress or, in the case of services, the means to supply the service
- Requiring employees to perform complex tasks
- Excessive movement of people, components, products in the process of providing the product or service to the customer
- Producing or supplying a greater quantity than is needed
- Over-complicated designs and production processes
- Wasted time
- Wasted resources.

Lean production methods

Although ways of achieving lean production will differ between businesses and their operations, there are some common approaches that may be used to make improvements and eliminate waste. These include:

- Kaizen – this is a Japanese term that means that a business should seek continuous improvements
- Simultaneous engineering
- Just-in-time (JIT) operations.

However, not all these methods tools will apply in particular circumstances and there may be other ways of cutting down on waste and inefficiencies.

Activity

What examples of waste can you identify at your school or college?

Kaizen in the context of lean production

Kaizen is a Japanese word meaning "change for the better", but it is commonly assumed to mean "continuous improvement". The concept became prominent when Toyota introduced it into its car manufacturing production system. The basic idea is that the employees of an organisation are the best people to know how a task should be undertaken. The Kaizen idea is that employees should be given the responsibility of working out how their jobs can be changed so that efficiency and quality can be improved.

This contrasts with the traditional view that "the manager knows best".

Implicit in this idea is the concept that a series of small improvements suggested by the workforce can produce results that are just as good as massive new investments, hence the notion of "continuous improvement".

It is closely associated with the lean production philosophy.

- It involves making small but frequent changes in operating activities in order to make small improvements.
- Changes are frequent, so improvement is continuous.
- Changes are small, so improvements are incremental, building up over time. Individually they are small, but cumulatively they become large.
- Most changes involve individuals or small work teams, not large work groups or entire departments.
- Improvements come from the knowledge and experience of employees and do not require consultants or people with specialist knowledge.

The 5S process as part of Kaizen

One aspect of Kaizen is a so-called "5S" approach to organising the workplace, and a requirement for visual order, organisation, cleanliness and standardisation in order to achieve incremental improvements in efficiency and safety. The five elements of a 5S process are set out in Table 3.3.3.

Key term

Kaizen: processes to achieve continuous improvement.

Activity

Lean manufacturing originated in Japan with the car manufacturer, Toyota, and its Toyota Production System (TPS). The main aim of the TPS was to eliminate the seven wastes (see Table 3.3.2). It has also focused on simplifying or eliminating complex tasks, for example by replacing people with robots to improve efficiency. The system also harnesses the knowledge of its entire workforce, by involving them in identifying and recommending ways to improve activities in the workplace. Many of the improvements are small, but they are continuous.

Find out what you can about lean production at Toyota.

Get it right

Lean production should apply to all aspects of operations and operating activities.

▼ **Table 3.3.3**: The 5S approach to Kaizen

1	Sort	Get rid of unnecessary items in the workplace, and leave only those needed for the work to be performed. Remove all tools and materials that are not required to do the work.
2	Set in order, or Simplify	Next, arrange all the remaining items so that they are arranged in an efficient way, and can be easily and quickly found. The most frequently used components should be placed nearest to where the work is done (reducing the need for motion and transport)
3	Shine	Continually clean the work area and the tools, machines and other equipment in it, so that everything is returned to a nearly new status, reducing the likelihood of faults and defects.
4	Standardise	This is the process of ensuring that what has been done in the first three stages of 5S become standardised practice, so that there are common standards and ways of working.
5	Sustain	Maintain any changes that are introduced. Repeat the 5S process to identify areas for further improvement.

You do not need to learn the 5S process in detail, but it is a useful illustration of the Kaizen concept.

For Kaizen to work, it must have the full understanding and support of management and all employees.

Kaizen will not work if:

- There is a lack of management commitment
- Employees do not understand what is required or the principles of lean production
- Employees are unwilling to take on responsibilities to look for and make changes
- Management are not prepared to provide the necessary resources or give employees time to discuss ideas for improvements among themselves
- The whole organisation does not subscribe to the ideas of Kaizen.

Simultaneous engineering

One of the key features of lean production is improved responsiveness to customers' needs. To an extent that can be met with flexible production, but that will not work when a product has become obsolete. What is needed in this situation is a new product. If the time taken to launch a new product can be reduced then the business will be more responsive to customer needs. This can happen using **simultaneous engineering** – managing the process for launching a new product in such a way that some of the development processes can take place at the same time.

Traditionally, the process for a new product is as shown in Figure 3.3.2.

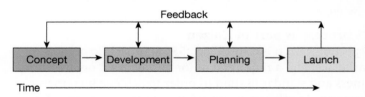

▲ **Figure 3.3.2**: Traditional approach to product development

If some of these activities can be undertaken simultaneously then the length of time from conception to launch can be significantly reduced, improving the likelihood that the product is successful in launch.

A better approach would be as shown in Figure 3.3.3.

An approach to simultaneous engineering

So how is simultaneous engineering achieved in practice for new product development, so that the time to market for a new product idea is minimised? Typically, a multi-disciplinary design team is established with representatives from all the business functions with an interest in the new product: technical/engineering, the production department(s), and marketing. It may also be important to involve suppliers of the raw materials and components that will be required to make the product, so the design team may also include a representative from the procurement (buying) function.

> ## Key term
>
> **Simultaneous engineering**: managing the processes for launching a new product so that various stages in development can take place at the same time instead of sequentially.

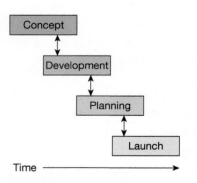

▲ **Figure 3.3.3**: Simultaneous approach to product development

Working as a team, people from the different functions can discuss the new product requirements from their own perspective, and reach agreement about how the new product should be designed and manufactured. This process will take much less time than if each function is asked to give their views about the new product separately (often one after another), and spend time resolving their disagreements.

The benefits from a team approach to new product design are:

- Reducing development time and time to market for the new product
- Getting new products to the market before similar new products from competitors
- By being first in the market, winning a competitive advantage over rivals
- By taking less time to develop a new product, and so improving development efficiency and reducing costs.

The benefits of simultaneous engineering also come from discovering faults early on in the product design process, so that the design can be amended before too much wasted time and effort has been spent, for example in developing and testing complex models (prototypes) for the new product. Simultaneous engineering, by creating a system for product development where the objective is to get the design right first time, is consistent with lean production principles.

Just-in-time (JIT) in the context of lean production

Just-in-time (JIT) is an approach to operations that aims at removing the need for inventory. This is achieved by ensuring that items are available for operations when they are needed, but not before. Two aspects of JIT, JIT production and JIT purchasing, are explained in Table 3.3.4.

▼ **Table 3.3.4**: JIT production and purchasing

JIT production (JIT manufacturing)	Finished output is produced just in time to meet demand, and not before. This removes the need to hold finished goods inventory. When a manufacturing process consists of several stages, JIT production also means having the part-finished work-in-progress ready for each stage in production when it is needed, and not before. This reduces the amount of work-in-progress held in the production process.
JIT purchasing (JIT procurement)	Raw materials and components are delivered by suppliers at exactly the time they are needed for production, and not before. This removes the need to hold inventories of raw materials and components. JIT purchasing requires co-operation with ordering and delivery arrangements from suppliers.

Key term

Just-in-time: managing the flow of raw materials, work-in-progress, finished products in a production system so that items are available exactly when they are needed for production and not before.

As an example, Honda has a large production facility in the UK, which makes full use of JIT purchasing. Deliveries from many suppliers take between five and 24 hours from ordering to delivery, so that deliveries can be scheduled to arrive when they are needed. Deliveries of car seats from local manufacturers take just 75 minutes.

An effective lean production system will minimise inventories and flows throughout the process by ensuring purchases, production and deliveries to customers have as much co-ordination of flows as possible.

Case study

Jaguar

The car manufacturer Jaguar introduced lean production methods into its factory in Birmingham in the UK. Before the changeover to lean production, the company produced a car model on a production line with 30 workers and a supervisor. With the introduction of lean production, the workers were divided into smaller teams of seven, each with a group leader. Each team worked in its cell and was responsible for its own work. A form of JIT system operated: when a team wanted more items to work on, it sent out a signal and the required items were delivered just in time.

If a worker encountered a difficulty and needed help, the group leader tried to solve the problem quickly. If the group leader could not solve the problem, help was requested and the entire production line was halted until the problem was resolved.

A real-time notice board kept each group informed about their target output for the day and their progress towards achieving the target. They were also kept aware of any bottlenecks in the production process.

The teams were encouraged to discuss work issues together, and identify ways of reducing or eliminating activities that did not add value.

1 In what ways do you think that this new system of production might have improved efficiency in the factory?

2 In what ways do you think that this new system of production might have improved the quality of output?

Case study

Lean production and health service resource use

Health services around the world are facing the same pressures:

- Medicines and treatments are becoming more widely available but more complex and expensive
- People are living longer and need more heath care
- Costs are generally increasing
- People are becoming more aware and demanding about health issues.

Health services rely mainly on people to provide services – doctors, nurses, administration staff – and on suppliers to provide medicines and equipment.

The costs of treating people need to be reduced. It is not realistic to reduce wages, nor would it be acceptable to reduce the treatment given to ill patients. What is needed is an increase in the efficiency of the use of resources that the health service has available.

A recent survey of nurses in a hospital showed that they were concerned about:

- Excessive paperwork
- High levels of waste
- Storage rooms full of unwanted items but shortages of essential items
- Duplication of some tasks such as interviewing new patients
- Having to repeat patient details to the various different doctors
- Not knowing what to expect next
- Some wards over-full, others nearly empty
- Hospital facilities only available for short times each day.

1 Why is it important to improve efficiency in health services?

2 How could ideas about lean operations help reduce costs in hospitals?

It might not be possible to eliminate the need for inventories entirely, but when operated successfully, JIT achieves substantial reductions in inventory.

If it is not operated successfully, JIT might result in items not being ready when they are needed for production or sale. When this happens, delays occur, resulting in waiting time and waste.

Implications and justification of adopting a JIT approach

A consequence of JIT production means that inventory levels of raw materials, components, work-in-progress and finished products can be kept to a minimum. It also means carefully planned scheduling and flow of resources through the production process. Modern manufacturing businesses use sophisticated production scheduling software to plan production for each period of time, which includes ordering the correct inventory. Flows of information between customer and business, and between parts of the business, are critical. This need for information flows is closely related to process innovation.

Supplies are delivered right to the production line only when they are needed. For example, a supermarket might receive exactly the right number and type of bananas for one day's sales, and the supplier would be expected to deliver them to the correct loading bay in the supermarket's stores department within a very narrow time slot.

▼ **Table 3.3.5**: Advantages and disadvantages of JIT production

Advantages	Disadvantages
• Lower inventories of all types means a reduction in storage space, which saves rent and insurance costs.	• There is little room for mistakes as minimal inventory is kept for reworking faulty products.
• As inventory is only obtained when it is needed, less working capital is tied up in inventory.	• Production is very reliant on doing things on time, and if there are any delays, the entire production process can be brought to a halt.
• There is less likelihood of products or inventory becoming obsolete or out of date.	• JIT procurement depends on having reliable suppliers who are willing to enter a JIT purchasing arrangement.
• Avoids the build-up of unsold finished product that can occur with sudden changes in demand.	• There is no spare finished product available to meet unexpected orders, because all product is made to meet actual orders – however, JIT is a very responsive method of production.

Progress questions

2 Why might improvements in productivity (efficiency) fail to result in a reduction in unit costs of output from operations?

3 What are the seven wastes in lean manufacturing?

4 Define Kaizen.

5 What is JIT purchasing?

Get it right

JIT operations do not only apply to the manufacture of products, but it can also be used effectively for the provision of services, where the service makes use of inventories of supplies, or where the service is provided in a sequence of several different stages.

The value of customer service

Customer service is experienced by customers every time they have contact with a business. This can be from the moment they make an enquiry about a product or service through to dealing with any issues after the purchase has taken place. The way in which a customer is treated by the business is likely to have an impact on how they view the business and whether or not they are likely to buy from that business again.

Many customers first experience customer service once a purchase has been made. The way in which any complaint or query is dealt with is likely to have a strong effect on future potential purchases by that customer.

There is a strongly held belief that a dissatisfied customer will tell many more people about their negative experience than they will tell about a positive experience. This alone indicates that good customer service is essential if a business is to retain its credibility with customers.

The aims and benefits of customer service include:

- Giving customers what they want and expect. Customers value the service they receive, and are often willing to pay more for better service.
- Quality. Good service enhances the quality of what the business provides to its customers.
- Maintaining customer loyalty. If a customer has a complaint that is dealt with to their satisfaction they are more likely to make repeat purchases from the business. If they receive poor service, they are likely to go to somewhere else when they buy again.
- Maintaining or reinforcing the reputation of the business. If the business has portrayed itself as being one that cares about its customers then delivering good customer service can reinforce that image.
- A reputation for good customer service can give a business a competitive advantage, and help it to sell more and make more profit.
- Being alerted to a problem with a product or service that the business was not aware of. Sometimes a customer might be the first one to experience a problem. By having contact with the customer, the business can investigate to ensure that the problem does not occur again.
- A possible decrease in costs. A business might be self-promoting through its excellent customer service and this might save on marketing costs. Word-of-mouth-advertising by satisfied customers can be the most effective marketing a business can have.

Key term

Customer service: the process of providing a service to customers, before, during and after a purchase. The aim should be to deliver customer satisfaction.

How to improve customer service

Remember that customer service is not restricted to after-sales service but that good customer service should be experienced throughout all contact with a business. This can begin with an initial enquiry about a product or service.

Customer service can be improved in the following ways:

- Have a dedicated customer service department. A team of people within the business who specialise in customer service. This can help to ensure that all issues are dealt with in the same way, particularly when dealing with after-sales issues. It can cause a fall in customer loyalty if two people complain about the same fault on the same product and one is offered a replacement while the other is offered a repair. If this becomes known then customers might view that as unequal treatment and therefore lose confidence in the customer service offered by that business.

- Staff training. Some staff might benefit from training in how to deal with customers before and after-sales have been made. The training must be appropriate to the role of the employee in the business. For example, staff involved in selling technical items, such as computers, should be fully trained to use the items and be able to explain the differences between different models of computers. They should be fully aware of all of the functions and capabilities of each computer they are selling. Failure to be trained in this way could lead to the selling of a computer that is not appropriate for a specific customer. This can lead to dissatisfaction and distrust of the business.

- Take time with customers. This is true whether it is time to help them to make a purchase or time to listen to and deal with a complaint after purchase.

- Listen to customers. The business might believe their product is the best but if a customer is sold a version that is not suitable for what they need then the business should accept that perhaps their sales staff made a mistake. It might be costly in the short term to replace an item but the benefits in the longer term can be higher due to a satisfied customer and word of mouth.

- Investigate complaints. Even if the complaint has not been raised before it should be investigated. A minor issue in production might be identified which, if rectified, can prevent future complaints.

- Use complaints as an opportunity to improve the business.

- Listen to internal customers. Employees or departments within a business are the internal customers of that business and they should also be listened to so that improvements can be made both to the product or service or to customer service.

Example

Portakabin is a manufacturer of modular buildings, which it sells or hires out to customers. The company prides itself on the quality of its customer service, from the selling process (dealing with customer enquiries, providing price quotations and drawing up contracts), through to delivery of the buildings and after-sales service.

▲ **Figure 3.3.4**: Customer service is an important part of business

The company's customer service standards include providing a service response or a visit to the customer within 24 hours, and answering the phone to customer enquiries (by a person, not an automated system) within four rings.

The company aims to complete delivery of its buildings within the promised time (and at the quoted price). For late delivery to buyers, the company provides an extended six-month warranty on its buildings, and customers who hire buildings receive one week's free hire for every day that delivery is late.

The company states that a major reason for its customer service standards is that most of its profits come from repeat business, and in a competitive market, poor service will mean the loss of repeat business to competitors.

The benefits and disadvantages of different mixes of resources

Capital, labour and enterprise are the three inputs needed for production. Capital and labour are often substitutes for each other. For instance, a field can be ploughed by one person and a tractor (capital intensive) or by 20 people using hand ploughs (labour intensive). It is the relative proportions and costs of each input that are important. Capital-intensive processes require a relatively high level of capital investment and are likely to be automated to produce on a large scale for a long time. Labour-intensive processes require a relatively high level of labour and are likely to produce individual customised products or on a small scale over a short time.

Businesses have to decide on the proportions of labour and capital to use in their production process. This decision will be influenced by:

- The method of production. Mass production like car manufacturing is likely to be capital intensive; skilled one-off production like making bespoke fitted furniture is likely to be much more labour intensive.

- How personal the product is. Personal services like hairdressing are likely to be labour intensive; an oil refinery is capital intensive.

- The relative costs of labour and capital. Businesses in high-income developed countries like the USA are more likely to be capital intensive compared to businesses in low-income countries where labour is relatively cheap.

- The size of the business. Small businesses are more likely to be labour intensive compared to large businesses that can afford the initial investment in capital.

- Customer's preference. Businesses in markets where personal service is valued are more likely to be labour intensive.

▼ **Table 3.3.6**: Benefits and limitations of capital- and labour-intensive production

	Benefit	Limitation
Capital intensive	<ul><li>Ability to produce output on a large scale using repetitive automated tasks, e.g. assembly processes; machinery can deliver this much more quickly than labour</li><li>Usually lower unit costs when production is in large quantities, compared to using labour</li><li>Enables economies of scale</li><li>Increased labour productivity</li></ul>	<ul><li>Difficult to produce a range of varied one-off or very short-run products</li><li>Difficult to deliver personal services</li><li>High start-up costs: cost of capital may be too high for a business to buy machinery</li><li>Unreliable machinery can be very costly</li><li>Employees may be bored and become disruptive</li><li>Difficult and expensive to vary amount of capital in short run</li></ul>
Labour intensive	<ul><li>Can produce one-off unique products</li><li>Well suited to deliver personal services; people often prefer service from another person, not a machine</li><li>Where labour is relatively cheap lower unit costs are available, especially where mechanised operations are difficult</li><li>Relatively easy to vary labour force — recruit or retrench</li><li>Low start-up costs</li></ul>	<ul><li>Cannot produce large-scale output quickly</li><li>Limited economies of scale</li><li>Production is dependent upon skills, which means employees can disrupt production easily by industrial action or absences</li><li>Legal constraints may make it difficult to vary labour force</li></ul>

The use of capital or labour also depends on what the customer wants. For example, individuals going on holiday might be satisfied with buying a holiday online. Others might be happy to pay more for a personal and labour-intensive service in planning and obtaining a tailor-made holiday.

Progress questions

6   You are a consultant advising a number of businesses on starting up. The managers of these businesses ask for your advice on how to set up their production processes. Advise them in relation to the relative amounts of capital or labour they should use. Include in your responses any factors they need to think about.

Businesses seeking advice:

a   A board games manufacturer

b   A sports car manufacturer producing kit cars

c   A personal sports coach

d   An accountant specialising in farm accounts

e   A bottle manufacturer.

7   Explain the meaning of the following terms:

a   capital intensive

b   labour intensive.

Quality

To a large extent, quality is something in the eye of the beholder. People have different perceptions about quality, what makes one product or service superior in quality to another, or what is acceptable quality and unacceptable quality. Some people associate quality with a premium price, or an exclusive brand. Others look more closely at whether the product is well designed or well made, and whether it does everything the user wants from it. Other aspects of product quality might be ease of use and after-sales service.

Differences in the perception of quality also apply to services. For example, people eating in restaurants are likely to judge the quality of their meal by their enjoyment of the food, the time they have to wait for service, and whether they receive the standard of service they expect.

For consumers, quality relates not only to the technical specifications of a product, but also to the whole range of benefits that the customer is purchasing, such as ease of use, after-sales service, and short delivery lead times.

▼ **Table 3.3.7**: How to measure quality

Quality feature	Comment
Excellence	The standard of excellence in a product; the design quality, and the workmanship and attention to detail put into making it.
Comparative excellence	Whether the product compares favourably with rival products (or services) that are available.
Fitness for purpose or use	The extent to which a product does what it is designed and expected to do; or the extent to which it meets the customer's needs.
Lack of defects	Quality also depends on the quality of the processes used by the manufacturer or service provider.
Acceptable quality and value for money	Quality also depends on the quality of the processes used by the manufacturer or service provider.

"Quality" will mean something different for a consumer buying clothes than it will for an industrial buyer of clothing material – or industrial safety wear, say. Quality will mean something different for the purchase of computer equipment, engineering components, building materials, cleaning supplies, accountancy services or catering services.

Actual or perceived quality is an important feature of a product or service. A business must provide a level of quality that satisfies its customers at a price they pay to obtain it. If it does not, customers will not buy.

The importance of quality

As we have seen, quality is defined by the customer. However, it is in the interests of all businesses to know the quality levels that customers expect and to have systems in place to deliver the quality that customers expect and minimise the risk of customers being dissatisfied with the quality that they receive.

Many businesses use a combination of quality control and quality assurance to manage quality. Some businesses go much further, and apply a system of total quality management (TQM).

A clear focus on quality for even the smallest of businesses can save money, attract customers and may even be the route to growth.

The benefits and difficulties of improving quality

Although it must be remembered that quality is a relative feature of a product or service, whatever level of quality is chosen there will be a trade-off between the benefits of improving quality and the costs of achieving a higher level of quality. The costs will be largely dependent on which system of improving quality is chosen; however, in most situations the costs and benefits shown in Table 3.3.8 are likely to apply.

▼ **Table 3.3.8**: Benefits and costs of improved quality

Benefits of improved quality	Possible costs involved in improving quality
Improved customer satisfaction	Market research needed to establish customer expectations.
Improved reputation	Inspection may be expensive in a quality control system.
Important part in developing brand	Rejected items will either be waste or will need to be corrected.
New products can benefit from reputation of brand name	Production may need to be stopped to trace and correct faults.
Reduced costs of putting things right	Training expenses particularly for TQM.
May allow for higher prices to be charged	Better-quality materials will cost more.
Gives a new dimension to competing	Suppliers may charge more for improving their quality standards.

Difficulties of improving quality

Once it has been accepted that there is a problem with the quality of products being produced a business must decide how to remove the problem. This can have consequences for the whole of the workforce and to the costs of the business.

For example:

- Employees might feel that there is some blame being attached to them and their work, causing negative feelings towards the business and management.
- Introducing a system such as TQM might be viewed negatively by some employees and for this system to work, all employees need to be engaged in it. This can be particularly difficult if there has previously been a blame culture in the organisation. Time will be

> ## Key term
>
> **Total quality management (TQM):** a structured approach to managing the quality of an organisation's products and services, involving the principles of "right first time" and continuous improvement, and involving all employees within the organisation.

needed to explain the benefits of TQM to the employees if they are to accept this method of improving quality.

- Using TQM can be seen as giving more responsibility to employees, who might feel that this should mean an increase in pay. Alternatively, some employees might not feel comfortable with the extra responsibility. There is a positive side to this argument, however, in that some employees will feel more involved in the whole process and will be more motivated in their work.

- Employees asked to undertake training might perceive this as a criticism when it is only a recognition that they have not been given sufficient training and the intention is to correct that. It must be made clear to employees that this is not due to their errors but to an oversight of management or a proposed change in working practices. This is an added cost to a business and might have to be passed on in the price to consumers.

- It can also be costly to introduce a quality control system both in terms of administration, labour and also possibly testing equipment.

- Some quality issues are difficult to identify and the problem might not be inside the business but might lie with suppliers of materials or components. This can be difficult to deal with if the business has a long-standing relationship with the supplier. For the sake of the reputation of the business, new suppliers might have to be found.

The first difficulty might be getting employees to agree that there is a problem. It might be that a competitor has started to produce a similar product of much higher quality and therefore, in order to compete, the business will have to improve the quality of its own products. There can also be a change in consumer perception of what level of quality they expect. Businesses must meet those changed expectations if they are to succeed. The product might have been acceptable in the past but it is not acceptable now.

The consequence of poor quality

When a business fails to appreciate the importance of measuring, improving and maintaining quality there are several consequences that can be experienced:

- Levels of wastage can be high as goods are either rejected at the end of production or by customers. This is costly both in terms of wasted materials, cost of reworking or lost customers.

- The reputation of the business can be harmed, which can be particularly damaging if the business had built a reputation on quality. A good reputation built over many years can be lost overnight if a faulty product is discovered. It might be that the product does not perform as expected or is found to be dangerous or to have caused damage or injury.

- Marketing costs might increase significantly if the business has to undertake a campaign to regain its reputation

- Sales will almost certainly fall if there is a perception that the product does not match customer expectations regarding quality.

- Due to lost sales and increased costs there is likely to be a negative impact on profit. This can affect the future of a business

Case study

Starlight Fireworks

The managing director of Starlight Fireworks (SF), Sue, is having an angry discussion with the production manager, Steve. "Half the fireworks at the New Year display failed to go off and our customers want their money back. Our reputation has been badly damaged," she said. "Our competitors always get it right, why not us?"

"Well it was raining that day and I was short of staff," said Steve. "It's not my fault. I checked everything myself before the fireworks were sent out, and they looked all right. I can't set them off to see if they work," he said angrily.

"We spend a lot of money on quality control, why isn't it working?" said Sue.

"We only test about 1 per cent of our production so a lot of faults get through especially now we're using a new cheaper supplier of raw materials," said Steve. "Some of our machines are very old, and the workforce don't help, always complaining about having too much to do."

1   What are the shortcomings of the quality checking techniques used at SF?
2   Why do quality procedures need to be improved?
3   Why should Sue be concerned that Steve blames things outside his control for what goes wrong?

because there will be less money to invest in future research and development or marketing.

- If a product is produced, which is known to be of poor quality the price will have to be low enough to tempt people to buy it. In order to achieve a desired level of profit, the amount sold will have to be high due to the lower profit per item sold.

If a business has a concern about the quality of its final product, an inspection team might need to be employed which adds further cost to the production process.

Methods of quality control

Quality control is a traditional method of working towards a desired level of quality. It is based on inspection (through testing and random sampling) of a product or service before it is provided to the customer. It may involve the workforce (employees) through quality control inspectors and quality control departments, often at the end of the production process, but generally it does not involve all of the employees.

Key term

Quality control: inspecting goods received from suppliers or inspecting items during the production process to check for defects, normally using sampling. The term may also be applied to inspecting finished goods from the manufacturing process, to check for defects before they are sold to customers.

▲ **Figure 3.3.5**: Quality control in action

There are usually three stages of quality assurance and quality control:

- **Prevention:** When a product is designed the designers should take into account the customers' quality requirements. Processes (such as manufacturing, providing a service) should be designed to achieve this level of quality. Measures to achieve a required level of quality is referred to as quality assurance.

- **Inspection:** Products are regularly inspected/tested to see if quality standards have been met. In a production process this could be undertaking random sampling, for a service it could be using a mystery shopper or something similar. Inspecting and testing is referred to as quality control.

- **Correction and improvement:** Once the product/service has been found to be significantly unsatisfactory, faulty products/ services need to be corrected and design or processes adjusted to ensure that the problem is not repeated.

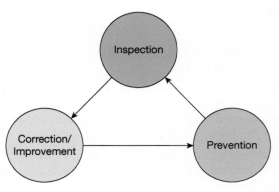

▲ **Figure 3.3.6:** Prevention, inspection and correction or improvement

Quality control suffers from the disadvantage that it finds problems only after they have happened. Also, because it only identifies the problem *after* it has happened, it may be difficult to identify what stage of the process is causing the problems, and, in turn, which employees are responsible for the problem. It is also an "add on" to the production process rather than part of the whole process. The quality control process relies on the skills of those involved in the inspection process – a job that may be tedious and demotivating – rather than relying on all employees.

The importance of quality assurance

Quality assurance refers to ensuring a process meets agreed standards. It refers to a range of measures, beginning with finding out what customers want and expect, and designing products and services accordingly. It also includes approaches to the design of methods for making products or delivering services to achieve the required quality standards. Quality assurance may involve the workforce more than quality control, as it can involve the delivery of quality throughout the production process.

- The total cost of managing quality is the cost of quality assurance measures plus the cost of quality control (inspection and correction).

- Investing more in quality assurance should reduce the need for quality control, or should at least reduce the frequency of defects, and so reduce the costs of quality control.

- Without adequate quality assurance measures, the costs of quality control and correcting defects could be high.

Quality assurance works on the principle of "right first time". This can be achieved by looking at the processes, from beginning to end, of getting the product, or service, from design to the customer.

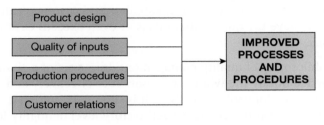

▲ **Figure 3.3.7**: Quality assurance

The benefits of quality assurance are:

- Problems should be identified before the end of the process thereby saving costs of putting things right

- There is little need for final inspection thus saving the costs of an inspectorate

- When there are problems it should be easier to trace back to where the fault is occurring in the processes, saving future costs or problems

- The responsibility for quality at various stages can be identified, improving accountability

- There are greater opportunities for employees to take pride in their work thus improving motivation.

In some circumstances quality assurance procedures will enable claims to be made about the business and its products. So, for example,

Case study

Managing quality of shirts

A company manufactures shirts. There are broadly two ranges of shirt that it makes: an expensive range of shirts made from high-quality cotton, and a cheaper range of casual shirts. The company has systems in place for design quality, quality assurance and quality control.

1   How would you distinguish between quality design, quality assurance and quality control for the shirts that this company makes?

Get it right

Quality assurance guarantees that the processes should meet planned standards of product design or service delivery, but it does not necessarily guarantee the outcome – processes can go wrong.

the ISO 9000 award is given to businesses that demonstrate quality assurance procedures that meet particular standards. Other examples include industry and government awards – certificates of safety and other levels of quality such as the organic nature of a product, sometimes known as "kite marks" – which can be used in marketing when particular standards are achieved.

Aims and effectiveness of TQM

TQM takes the ideas of managing quality a stage further. TQM is an integrative philosophy for ensuring the continuous improvement of products, processes and services. It makes everyone in a process responsible for the quality of their own part within the processes. This means that management, workforce, suppliers and customers all work together to achieve the quality that meets or even exceeds customers' expectations.

TQM is a philosophy of quality management. It is a set of activities that are carried out by the whole organisation to effectively and efficiently achieve company objectives. It is systematic so that it provides services or products with a satisfactory level of quality for customers, and it does so at the appropriate time and price.

Quality values are applied in order to seek continuous improvement and excellence in all aspects of performance. The search for better quality never ends.

Quality improvements can be achieved by introducing better ways of organising work, to improve the quality, speed, flexibility or the reliability of a product, service or process, or to reduce cost. It is a culture of sustained continuous improvement focusing on eliminating waste in all processes.

Although TQM originated in US businesses, managers in Japan took on the ideas of TQM more enthusiastically from the 1940s. Through information and feedback, committed leadership, planning, employee involvement and training processes companies such as Toyota were able to raise quality standards to levels never before thought achievable.

Key aspects of TQM are:

- **Getting it right first time**: Quality should be designed into products, services and processes, with the aim of achieving zero defects, or getting as close as possible to zero defects.
- **Quality chains**: The quality chain extends from suppliers through to consumers, including the internal supply chain between units or functions within the organisation. The quality of work in each link of this chain impacts on the next one, and will eventually affect the quality provided to the consumer. So in a company that manufactures food products, the team that purchases the food items from farmers and growers is a supplier to the team that prepares the food in the manufacturing process, and this team is a supplier to the team that packages the food, which is a supplier to the team that distributes the food to retailers and the team that markets the food products. So the process chain consists of the groups shown in Figure 3.3.8.

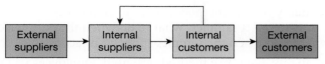

▲ **Figure 3.3.8**: A quality chain

- **The internal customer**: Businesses are set up as if each stage of a process is a new "customer", providing checks and balances in the process. So, very simplistically, if a person stacking shelves in a supermarket notices damaged tins of food, they will behave just like a customer, and complain to the warehouse people who provided the tins to the stacker. The concept of the internal customer is an extension of the concept of the quality chain.

- **Continuous improvement**: Quality improvement is not seen as a one-off exercise. By seeking to improve continuously, organisations stay open to new opportunities and approaches, and encourage learning and flexibility at all levels. In this respect, TQM includes a Kaizen approach to quality improvement.

- **Quality circles:** Small groups of employees are created to meet regularly and discuss ways in which they can improve the quality of their work and cut out waste. Ideally these groups are empowered to put their ideas into practice, making improvements at their stage in the quality chain.

Quality assurance is an important aspect of TQM. It is important to identify the costs of quality, or the lack of quality and quality failures, to prove that financially prevention is better than cure. This involves shifting the focus of quality management from quality control (inspecting output and rejecting or re-working defects) to establishing an effective system for quality assurance.

TQM differs from quality assurance in one key way: TQM is about a culture of improving the whole process, including external suppliers, whereas quality assurance is about improving procedures.

Progress questions

8 What is the difference between quality control and quality assurance?

9 Why does a TQM approach to quality emphasise quality assurance rather than quality control?

10 Explain why the involvement of employees is key to implementing total quality management systems.

The potential for Kaizen in TQM

Although the origins of Kaizen are in improving production processes to achieve greater efficiency, it can clearly be applied to a product or service to focus on quality. Indeed the best uses of Kaizen will aim to improve both the processes and quality at the same time.

The link between quality and training

All of the methods for improving quality will involve the need for managers and employees to be able to undertake tasks effectively:

Get it right

Remember, in your answers to questions relating to TQM you should refer to the strategic nature of TQM. TQM is not so much a solution as a way of thinking that can lead to solutions. It is an integral part of the lean production philosophy.

- When quality control methods are used, employees will need to know how to select samples, what to do when they are selected, and what to do when the samples show up unacceptable errors.
- Where quality assurance methods are used, employees will need to know the standards of assurance and the methods used to achieve the desired standards. They will also need to know how to react when standards do not meet assured levels.
- To implement TQM, a business will need to train employees so that they know how concepts like the internal customer and quality circles work. They will also need to know how quality circles work. They will need to understand and be able to implement Kaizen. Managers will need to adopt new management techniques. In addition, the whole culture of the organisation will need to change and adapt.

For all of these methods it will be essential for managers and employees to be trained effectively. TQM, particularly, will need major training programmes to facilitate the thorough change in attitudes and working methods that will be needed. Indeed, TQM cannot be successful without appropriate training of all employees and managers.

▼ **Table 3.3.9**: Advantages and criticisms of TQM

Benefits of TQM	Criticisms of TQM
• Better quality products and services • Greater customer satisfaction • Less waste • Lower inventory levels • Improved productivity • Shorter new product development cycles • Improved delivery times • Better use of human resources (since less time spent dealing with quality control problems and defects)	• Too much focus on quality. An organisation should consider other matters too, such as changes in demand for products and services. • Too much bureaucracy: too many quality committees and too much quality documentation. • TQM can be a time-consuming activity. The potential benefits need to justify the time and effort required.

Progress questions

11 Explain why relying on sampling products can still lead to customer complaints.
12 Explain why different groups of customers may have different ideas about quality standards.
13 Give three benefits of quality assurance.
14 How can "internal customers" improve quality?
15 What is the main difference between TQM and quality assurance?

Ways and value of improving flexibility and speed of response

Flexibility is the ability to change or adapt something easily in response to changes in conditions or circumstances.

Operational flexibility is the ease with which a productive system can adapt to a changing market environment, and when demand differs from expectation. In particular this means being able to vary the quantities produced, the time of delivery to the customer or the exact specification details of the product or service. The specification can be a design that the producer intends to sell or a description of what the customer is looking for. Flexibility is very important in today's rapidly changing business environment. It enables a quick response to a market change or a buyer's different demand. It allows businesses to exploit new opportunities.

The need for flexible volumes

Volume flexibility is the ability to operate efficiently, effectively and profitably over a range of output. Demand can change quickly or more slowly over a longer time period. Volume flexibility is needed to guard against uncertain demand for a product.

One way of responding flexibly in the short term to unexpected high demand is to arrange for employees to work overtime, or by adding an extra operating shift.

Some manufacturing companies have a flexible manufacturing system. A flexible manufacturing system (FMS) is a way of arranging production systems so that the company can react quickly to changes in the type or quantity of product being manufactured. Machines and computerised production systems are set up so that they are able to manufacture different parts and handle varying levels of production.

Long-term volume flexibility

There should also be sufficient flexibility to enable a business to respond to unexpected demand for a product at different stages of the product life cycle. As the product begins to sell in the introduction stage the demand will be for small quantities and this demand will increase as the product moves through the growth and maturity stages before declining, though there may be increased demand from a successful extension strategy. The time span involved could be from a few months in the case of a novelty toy to many years in the case of a breakfast cereal. A business must be able to vary its volume of production to deal with the changes over time.

This will involve preparation and planning. If there is no flexibility the business will be unable to meet demand as this increases and eventually it may find that it is producing products that are not selling.

Short-term volume flexibility

A business receives orders from customers. It never knows exactly when these orders will come in so it must be prepared to produce products for a range of volumes. Some orders may be for particular quantities over a period of time, for example, "please supply 200 items

> **Key term**
>
> Operational flexibility: the ease with which a productive system can adapt to a changing market environment.

> **Link**
>
> The product life cycle model is discussed in Chapter 2 Marketing.

per week for the next two years". But even an order like this might change as perhaps the customer finds it needs to change the order for some reason.

Other orders may be for a single time or for varying quantities, such as "please supply ten items this week. We hope to continue ordering from you in the future". These orders demand the ability to be flexible as failure to meet an order may result in the loss of any future contracts. This applies particularly where a business is supplying another business that is using a JIT production system where materials are ordered just in time to use them for production immediately. Businesses must therefore have the ability to be flexible about the quantities they can produce. This flexibility must include being able to supply at a quality and price the customer is happy with.

The need for flexible delivery times

Products which are ordered have to be delivered. This can apply to services as well as physical products. Education and training is a good example. Colleges offer flexible learning experiences which suit the demands of their learners. This can be done through the use of the internet, offering part-time courses or by agreeing times for lectures and seminars with the customers. In a competitive market this kind of flexibility can be an important factor in winning customers. In the domestic consumer market many customers are demanding flexible delivery times for products they have ordered. Increasingly businesses are finding that offering to deliver at a time that suits the customer is an important reason for getting a sale. The Knowhow case study illustrates the way that businesses are emphasising flexible delivery as a selling point.

Case study

KNOWHOW delivery services

We'll deliver your product at a time to suit you on behalf of Currys and PC World.

The key to our delivery service is flexibility; you can choose your delivery in the morning or the evening and even over the weekend – just select an option to suit you. Our first delivery is made at 7 a.m. and last at 8 p.m. and we will always phone you 30 mins before we are due to arrive.

Great news! KNOWHOW offers you the choice of 4-hour time slots for your delivery to ensure that your large product arrives when you want it to, as an alternative to our standard free all-day delivery. Simply choose at the checkout which slot suits you best, giving you greater control over your delivery time.

Subject to availability, you can select from:

7 a.m.–11 a.m. 9 a.m.–1 p.m.

11 a.m.–3 p.m. 1 p.m.–5 p.m.

3 p.m.–7 p.m.

This flexible delivery slot leaves you free to carry on with what's important to you and relax with the KNOWHOW that we'll deliver to you between those times.

1 Explain the advantages to the customer of flexible delivery times.

2 What problems might flexible delivery cause for Currys?

Taken from https://trackit.teamknowhow.com/uk/deliver-and-install

The need for flexible specifications

Consumer expectations are growing in line with the developments of technology. In many countries, people who buy new cars want them built to their own specification, with a bewildering choice of engine sizes, colours, accessories and so on. People buying laptops want to choose many of the features such as processor, hard disc, memory, operating system and software. Services, such as insurance and banking services, are expected to be "tailor-made". In response, many manufacturers and providers of services want to offer as much flexibility as possible. Their production systems need to be able to respond to this wide range in specification demanded by customers.

In markets where businesses supply other businesses with materials or components the increasing use of JIT manufacturing systems, where businesses order materials just in time to use them for production immediately, means that flexible delivery times are essential for obtaining an order.

Exam-style questions

1   Explain the difference between quality control and quality assurance.   (3 marks)

2   A small company has developed a new water purifying system that, in its view, demonstrates better quality than similar products on the market. Demand for the company's system is growing in its domestic market, but management now thinks that it is time to expand production and marketing operations internationally.

    Analyse two opportunities and two challenges that the company would face from expanding its operations internationally.   (9 marks)

3   A company uses drones to deliver goods to consumers, and advertises that they will deliver products to the customer's chosen address within 48 hours of receiving an order. This is considered a fast response time.

    Analyse how the objective of speed of delivery may either compromise or be consistent with objectives for total cost, quality and customer satisfaction.   (9 marks)

4   Daniel is the managing director of a company that manufactures household furniture. The company obtains its raw materials from a number of different suppliers and sells its finished products to department stores and specialist retailers, with a few additional online sales. Demand is growing for the company's products and the company's factory is nearing its floor space capacity.

    Daniel believes that production efficiency will be improved by introducing just-in-time (JIT) purchasing and production methods into the factory's operations.

    Assess the arguments in favour of and those against the introduction of JIT methods.   (12 marks)

5   Lisa is the managing director of a company that manufactures soap products and detergents. She is impressed by improvements in quality that have been achieved by some competitors in the industry and she has plans to introduce systems within her own company for Kaizen or continuous improvement.

Her colleagues have advised her that there may be difficulties in adapting the company's production systems for Kaizen methods.

Assess the benefits and difficulties of implementing systems for continuous improvement within the company. (12 marks)

6 Good Feet is a company that manufactures boots and walking shoes. The company's factory operations are labour intensive because labour costs in the country are relatively low compared to costs of capital equipment. The company has experienced some problems with the quality of its production systems and output, with a high rate of rejected items in quality control inspections.

The company's management believe that since the company's objective is to deliver low-priced boots and shoes to customers, some problems with quality are inevitable.

Analyse measures that the company might take to improve the quality of output whilst still delivering low-cost boots and shoes to the market. (12 marks)

This section will develop your knowledge and understanding of:

→ Managing supply to match demand and the value of doing so

→ Influences on the amount of inventory held

→ Influences on the choice of suppliers

→ The importance of managing the supply chain effectively

→ The importance of logistics.

Managing supply to match demand and the value of doing so

Matching the supply of a product or service to demand can be difficult to achieve. Many products or services have variable demand, sometimes due to seasonal factors, but also due to changes in other market conditions, such as initiatives by competitors. For example, in the eyewear market, demand for a company's spectacles (glasses) might be affected by an unforeseen shift in customer preferences from spectacles to contact lenses, or by an aggressive marketing campaign by a major competitor.

A successful business must be able to have an as accurate as possible idea of the level of demand for its products or services. At times of high demand, it is not always possible to increase supply and therefore a business might decide to influence the level of demand. This can be done by increasing the price of the product or service being offered. In this way the demand is likely to reduce slightly. The remaining customers will pay a higher price, increasing the revenue of the business. One example of this is the price of holiday flights and accommodation in peak holiday times. During the most popular holiday times such as school holidays, travel companies increase the price of flights and accommodation. Customers who have to take their holidays within that period will have to pay the increased price. Those who can delay will pay less but travel at a less popular time.

Sometimes a business can be taken by surprise by the high level of demand for its product or services and might decide to work to increase its supply to match the demand.

However, there can be times when the demand increases suddenly and businesses can struggle to supply their customers within a reasonable time. Demand for some products is seasonal and demand can vary significantly at different times of the year.

In many cases, businesses choose to limit their normal output capacity, and then deal with unexpected or seasonal increases in demand by finding ways of temporarily increasing capacity. They consider this preferable to having higher normal output capacity but operating with unused resources for large times of the year.

Each business must decide how to handle fluctuations in demand.

- A business might be able to produce goods to order. This is usually necessary when products or services are customised to exact customer specifications.
- Businesses might choose to outsource some of the production to other businesses.
- Alternatively, a business might manage the employment of its employees in a way that increases their flexibility and availability to the business.

Ways of managing supply to match demand
Producing goods to order

One method used by some businesses is to produce goods only once they have been ordered by a customer.

The suitability of this method of matching supply with demand depends on the type of products involved. If the goods involved are fairly low-priced and easily obtained elsewhere, everyday clothing for example, customers might not be willing to wait for their new coat or trousers, unless items are being made to meet the specific needs and demands of the individual customer. People buying clothes usually expect them to be available immediately. However, if the item is a high-cost item that has a long production process, such as a private aeroplane, then it is more usual for the producer to wait until the order has been placed before buying in all of the materials required to complete the order. In this case the materials and components are expensive and specialised, and it would therefore probably not be practical or sensible to hold inventory just in case an order is placed.

This avoids the need to hold inventory of finished goods, possibly for long periods. There are advantages and disadvantages to producing to order. See Table 3.4.1.

▼ **Table 3.4.1**: Disadvantages and advantages of producing to order

Disadvantages of producing to order	Advantages of producing to order
The time delay between receiving the order and delivering the product to the customer might be too long, leading customers to purchase elsewhere.	The amount of inventory held can be reduced: this reduces the associated costs of warehousing and investment in inventory.
It is difficult to know just how many resources are needed at any particular time. Labour and machinery might lie idle for some time.	The reduction in inventory also reduces the chances of inventory becoming out-dated or spoilt while in storage.
Capacity utilisation might be low. This is an inefficient use of resources.	The products can be customised to meet the needs of each individual customer. This gives the products a unique selling point (USP), and is a major advantage of producing to order in some industries.
Suppliers might not be able to respond satisfactorily to the irregular demand for fresh supplies that might result from this approach.	

Outsourcing

Outsourcing is the business practice of arranging for an external supplier to manufacture goods or perform services that are traditionally performed in-house by the company's own employees and production systems.

It can be thought of as a form of subcontracting. The difference between subcontracting and outsourcing is rather subtle:

- Subcontracting involves arranging for external suppliers to perform certain tasks or make certain components or products on a regular basis. For example, subcontracting is common in the building construction industry, where construction companies regularly subcontract some tasks, such as the production and installation of doors and windows, the installation of electricity and plumbing, and decoration to specialist subcontractors.

- Outsourcing involves either employing external suppliers to perform regular business functions on a permanent basis that would traditionally be done in-house such as office cleaning, vehicle fleet management or accountancy services, or using an external supplier to perform some functions to help the business cope with temporary increases in demand.

So a builder might subcontract the task of installing the electrical components in a house to a specialist firm of electricians, and outsource all of the accounting functions to a firm of accountants.

Difficult economic conditions, globalisation and increased competition, particularly in the 1990s, forced businesses to re-examine their operations and seek cheaper ways of operating. Sometimes small, specialist businesses can carry out some functions previously carried out by large businesses, and they can do it a lot more efficiently and cheaper. As a result many large businesses outsource most of their non-core activities, such as human resources (HR), accounting, IT, training and so on. Outsourcing is also used as a means of indirect privatisation when public service organisations outsource to private sector businesses.

It is not only large businesses that outsource. Often small businesses will outsource functions in which they have little expertise. For example, a small business may outsource its HR and accounting functions to businesses specialising in those activities. This type of outsourcing services is sometimes known as business-process outsourcing.

Before undertaking outsourcing, a business needs to weigh up the situation.

> **Key term**
>
> **Outsourcing:** using another business (third party) to undertake some of the functions of a business (the host business).

▼ Table 3.4.2: Potential advantages and disadvantages of outsourcing

Potential advantages	Potential disadvantages
Enables the business to focus on its core.	Functions and jobs will be lost in the outsourcing business.
Increases opportunities for flexibility – outsourced contracts can be renegotiated, or even ended.	Quality may be more difficult to manage.
Greater scope for growth without high capital investment.	Issues to do with different cultures and languages.
Possibility of reduced operating costs.	Outsourcing functions involving sensitive information (e.g. accounts, HR) may create greater security risks.
Third party may do job better.	Could be difficult and expensive to reverse the process if circumstances change.
Short-term outsourcing enables a business to meet short-term increases in demand above its available internal capacity.	

Case study

Outsourcing at Newtown Hospital

Newtown Hospital is in a country where there are both state-run hospitals and also privately owned and managed hospitals. Newtown Hospital is a state-funded hospital. In recent years, it has faced increasing demands from patients for medical investigations and treatment. It is looking for ways to address this, but the demand for some forms of treatment is variable and difficult to predict. Two private-funded hospitals in the area appear to have spare capacity, but demand for their services is restrained by the high prices they charge for treatment.

An external company specialising in treatment for some forms of eye condition, such as glaucoma, has been approached by the hospital's management, to find out whether it would be willing to take on the task of investigating patients' eye conditions, somewhere on the hospital premises.

The hospital has also been experimenting with forms of artificial intelligence and digital equipment to connect patients to hospital monitoring systems from their homes.

1   What measures might the hospital take to improve its imbalance between the demand for its services and its available resources and financial budget resources to meet them?
2   What are the practical difficulties with the proposals you suggest?

Key term

Temporary contract: a contract usually specifying a short-term period of employment, for example, nine months, or until the completion of a project or order.

Flexible labour

There are times when a business needs to have as much flexibility as possible regarding the size or productive capacity of the workforce, so the approach to HR would then need to focus on flexibility too.

There are several forms of flexible labour:

- Temporary contracts
- Zero-hours contracts
- Agency workers.

Temporary contracts are contracts of employment that are for a short-term, and may have a fixed time until they end. When demand fluctuates, and there are times when it is low (for example, during a recession) a business might prefer to employ workers on temporary contracts rather than full-time permanent contracts, giving the business the opportunity to reduce its workforce, if necessary, without incurring redundancy costs.

Some businesses employ workers on a zero-hours contract. This means although the employees are expected to be available for work, they will only be paid for the hours that they are actually required to work. If, for example, a shirt manufacturer employs staff on zero-hours contracts then the employees will only be paid for the hours they are actually producing shirts. If one order for shirts is met at 11 a.m. and the next order cannot be started until 4 p.m. then the business will not pay the employees for the five hours which they were not required to work. Workers employed in a restaurant will be expected to be available for work, but if there are not many customers and the employees are not required to wait on tables or to cook then they will not be paid. However, if later on the restaurant becomes busy then they will be expected to work and will be paid for that time only.

Similarly some businesses prefer to employ workers on part-time contracts rather than full-time contracts. This can be because the part-time employees might be willing to be flexible about which hours they work thus allowing the business to use them at the time that is most beneficial to the business. Full-time employees will attend work for the required number of hours each day and will have to be paid regardless of whether there is work for them to do or not.

Agency employees are workers who have a contract of employment with an external agency that specialises in supplying businesses with short-term staff to cover a temporary shortfall in the number of full-time workers. Agency working is fairly common in some areas, such as hospitals. When a hospital is short of nurses for treating patients, it might obtain some on a temporary basis from a nursing agency. The contract is between the business obtaining the agency staff and the agency: agency workers have their contract of employment with the agency.

Advantages of temporary or flexible contracts

Temporary contracts can be used when the business does not have a need for additional permanent staff but does need extra employees at a particular time. One example of this can be when a business has seasonal demand which can require different numbers of employees at various times of the year. Flexible contracts can be used to allow a business and/or its employees to vary the number of hours worked. Variations might be based on guaranteed minimum hours of employment which can be averaged out weekly, monthly, quarterly or annually depending on the contractual agreement between employer and the employee.

Key terms

Permanent contract: a contract of employment that does not specify a time period or have a termination date.

Zero-hours contract: a contract of employment where the employee does not have any guaranteed hours of work. Employees are only paid for the hours they are actually required to work, which might be zero in any given time period.

Part-time contract: a contract of employment for a specified number of hours that is less than the number of hours worked by full-time employees.

Full-time contract: a contract for a permanent job.

Agency employees: individuals who are employed by an agency. Businesses can hire workers from an agency to make up a shortfall in their own internal staff.

Flexible contracts: these allow the hours and days of work to be varied by agreement between employers and employees according to the needs of the business and/or the individual employee. These can include an agreement to allow flexible working hours within agreed parameters.

- In the case of temporary contracts, the relationship between the business and the employee can be ended more easily than if the employee was employed on a permanent basis. The employee understands that the contract might only be for a short time.
- The business does not need to pay any redundancy pay to the employee if the work they are employed to do is no longer required.
- In the case of flexible contracts, the hours worked can be increased or decreased by the business depending on how many hours of work they need from each employee.
- When part-time contracts are issued rather than full-time contracts, the business has the opportunity to ask part-time employees to vary the number of hours worked and to work the required hours at different times of the week. It might be easier to get a part-time employee to work some extra hours if the business situation requires it.
- The main advantage to a business is that of financial saving. Zero-hours contracts only require payment to workers for the hours they actually work; temporary contracts enable a business to end the contract as soon as the employee is no longer required. Part-time contracts allow a business to reduce its wage bill by employing workers for a limited number of hours each week but perhaps giving them the opportunity to ask such employees to work extra hours if needed.
- The main advantage of flexible contracts for workers is that it gives them more flexibility and control over how they spend their life.

Disadvantages of temporary or flexible contracts
- Employees on a temporary contract, a flexible contract or a part-time contract might not feel as much loyalty towards the business as those employed on a permanent full-time contract.
- Employees might not have sufficient motivation with their work to put in as much effort as a full-time employee might. Employees do not have any security of employment and therefore income. This might lead them to look for employment elsewhere if more permanent employment can be found.

Case study

Delicaroma

Delicaroma is a chain of coffee shops that prides itself on using the best ingredients and providing an outstanding service to its customers. However, a recent article in a national newspaper has accused the business of exploiting its employees through the use of zero-hours employment contracts. The article claims to have interviewed one of the employees of Delicaroma and states that employees are expected to be available for work from 7 a.m. until 10 p.m. for six days a week but that they are not guaranteed any hours of work at all. The contract also prevents them from taking any work with another business. The result of this is that the employees are contractually bound to Delicaroma but might not be able to earn enough money to support themselves and their families.

Recently there has also been an increase in the number of customer complaints in several of the branches of Delicaroma.

1 Briefly explain any advantages that Delicaroma might gain from the use of zero-hours contracts.
2 Suggest an employment contract that might be more beneficial to the employees of Delicaroma.
3 Explain why a change in the contract of employment might lead to higher levels of customer service.

Problems of failing to match supply to demand

The main problems of failing to match supply and demand are summarised in Table 3.4.3.

▼ **Table 3.4.3**: Problems with failing to match supply to demand

Supply or capacity exceeds demand	Demand temporarily exceeds supply/normal capacity
If the business produces output in excess of demand, there will be unused finished goods inventory and the business will incur some costs (e.g. on materials and inventory insurance) before it is necessary.	There is unsatisfied demand unless measures are taken to increase supply temporarily. Customers may switch to buying rival products from competitors.
If the business reduces output to match demand, there will be (expensive) unused resources, such as equipment and full-time labour.	Temporary staff may be employed to increase output, but they are likely to be less skilled and less efficient than full-time staff.
There will be problems with managing the excess inventory, with risks of obsolescence, deterioration and damage.	The business may lack sufficient flexibility to adjust its output temporarily to a high level of demand.
Unsold inventory may eventually have to be scrapped or sold at a heavily discounted price.	

Influences on the amount of inventory held

Purpose of inventory

The inventory of a business is the raw materials, partly made products (work-in-progress) or finished products held as needed to supply customer demand. These are all part of the operations function. The raw materials are an input, work-in-progress is part of transformation from inputs to output, and finished products are output. Each of them is essential.

- **Raw materials** form a vital input for manufacturing businesses. Without them no transformation to output is possible. A business making products must have raw materials to be combined with other inputs, so some will be held in the business so that production can take place when required. Inventory is also held so that a sudden increase in orders can be supplied without having to wait for new raw materials to be delivered.

- **Work-in-progress** consists of products in the process of being made (semi-finished products) and are an inevitable part of manufacturing operations. Some products remain work-in-progress for a long time. For example, hard cheeses require maturing over a long period. While they are maturing they are work-in-progress.

- **Finished products** are the output that will be sold and supplied to customers. Before they are dispatched they will be held as inventory. Many businesses sell products from inventory so they must have them ready for when an order arrives. A retail store or wholesaler has to hold inventory for this purpose.

Holding inventory has benefits and costs and an efficient business will hold enough inventory to meet its needs but not more than is necessary for production or to meet demand. Inventory that is held as raw materials acts as a buffer between sudden unexpected increases in production and the ability to produce. Finished products act as a buffer between customer demand and the ability to meet it.

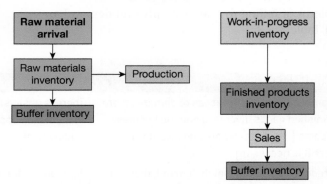

Raw materials and finished products can both act as buffer inventory.

▲ **Figure 3.4.1:** Types of inventory

Progress questions

4   Outline two reasons for holding inventory.

5   How does work-in-progress differ from finished products?

Costs and benefits of holding inventory

Costs of holding inventory

All types of inventory are a cost to a business. This is because they represent resources that are not actually generating revenue. Money will have been spent on producing inventory and this money could be used in other ways. This is an opportunity cost. Other reasons for the costs of holding inventory include:

- Rent for the space where inventory is held

- Employees, machinery, cost maintaining appropriate storage facilities for keeping inventory

- Insurance and security

- Any interest due on money borrowed to pay for storage and inventory

- Products may become obsolete (out of date or replaced by superior products) and cannot be sold for a price that covers the cost of production

- Products may get damaged, stolen or perish in storage

- In addition inventory ties up space which could be used for other purposes and it may slow down a business's response to change.

There are also inventory costs due to the process of ordering and these include:

- Administration costs in monitoring and tracking inventory
- Inspection and returning low-quality items
- Transport and handling costs.

▲ **Figure 3.4.2**: High and low inventory businesses

Benefits of holding inventory
Keeping up with demand
Holding high inventory levels means that the chances of selling out of finished products and missing revenue are less.

There will be enough inventory to meet expected demand. If demand for a product varies, holding some inventory will be essential to supply the increases in demand that occur. Uncertainty will be reduced.

Preventing shortages that halt operations
Holding raw-material inventory is an insurance against unexpected shortages of supplies. It will enable production to continue even if raw materials cannot be obtained for a period of time. This continuity may be valuable and enable a quick response to a change in the market.

Obtaining discounts
Suppliers often offer a lower price for materials bought in bulk (purchasing economies of scale). Unit costs can be reduced by taking advantage of this and holding the raw materials as inventory. Ordering and transport costs may also be reduced by a single large order. The reduction in costs must be balanced against the cost of holding the inventory.

Guarding against the effects of inflation

If commodity prices are rising it may be cost effective to buy large amounts of raw materials before their price rises thereby gaining protection from the effects of inflation or gaining greater revenue by holding finished products for sale later at a higher price.

Holding too much inventory is an additional unnecessary expense, holding too little can result in lost production and sales revenue. Many businesses look for certainty of supply so a failure to meet demand can lead to lost goodwill. A customer who cannot be supplied may never return to buy. Businesses generally attempt to hold as little inventory as possible in order to minimise the costs while taking advantage of the benefits.

Progress questions

6   Explain three reasons why a business might hold as little inventory as possible.
7   Supermarkets often hold as little as two days' sales in inventory. A steel fabricator may hold up to eight weeks' sales in inventory. Explain the difference in the way these two industries hold inventory.

Managing inventory

Managing inventory is a major part of business activity. Many businesses use IT systems to do this so that inventory management is linked to other functions including sales, ordering, distribution, employee work allocation and the production process. Many inventory-managing procedures are based on the buffer inventory model. This is based on a business holding inventory "just in case". Buffer inventory is the products or raw materials of an organisation maintained on hand or in transit to stabilise variations in supply, demand and production. The inventory control chart (discussed below) is a method for helping to control the quantity of inventory to minimise costs while still holding enough inventory to meet customers' needs.

Using inventory control charts including reorder and lead time

The buffer inventory model primarily deals with how a business decides to order raw materials, though it can be adapted to finished products. It considers the costs and benefits of holding inventory and assumes that there will be a minimum quantity of inventory (buffer inventory) that a business will wish to hold. As production occurs the inventory level of raw materials will fall as it uses up the materials. Inventory then takes time to arrive after it has been ordered; this is the lead time. This means that at some level the business must reorder so that inventory does not fall below the minimum level. The reorder level is this level of inventory at which more is ordered. The reorder quantity is the amount of materials or components in a purchase order.

Key terms

Buffer inventory: the products or raw materials of an organisation maintained on hand or in transit to stabilise variations in supply, demand and production.

Inventory control chart: shows the level of stock held over time.

Lead time: the time taken for inventory to arrive from supplier after it is ordered.

Reorder level: the level of inventory at which more inventory will be ordered.

Reorder quantity: the amount of materials or components in a purchase order.

This model can be shown graphically, as in Figure 3.4.3.

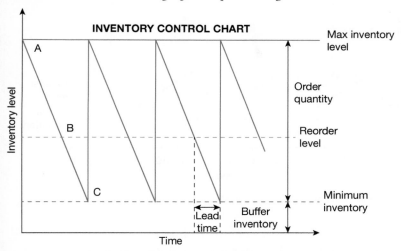

▲ **Figure 3.4.3**: Raw material buffer inventory, reorder level and lead time

Starting at point A the graph shows that the inventory level of raw materials falls as they are being used up as production takes place.

- The buffer inventory level shows the minimum amount of inventory the business needs to hold to maintain production to meet demand requirements.
- The lead time is the time taken for inventory to arrive from when it was ordered. This means that the raw materials must be ordered at B (amount to be ordered is the order quantity) so that they will arrive at C.
- The reorder level shows the level of inventory at which more inventory will be ordered. The buffer inventory is therefore always maintained.

The process of production continues and new raw materials are ordered each time the reorder level is reached. The quantity that is ordered is shown as being enough to take inventory above the reorder level and enable production to take place before there is a need to reorder. The graph shows smooth regular production. In reality many businesses face less regular, more complex production patterns, but the principle is the same.

Figure 3.4.4 shows this process numerically.

- Production starts at Week 0 with an inventory of 300 tonnes.
- Inventory is used up at the rate of 50 tonnes per week and at the end of Week 2 is at the reorder level of 200.
- The order quantity of 200 tonnes is ordered and this takes two weeks to arrive.
- At the end of Week 4 production reduces inventory to the buffer level of 100 tonnes.
- The new inventory arrives and takes the inventory level to 300 tonnes. The process is repeated.

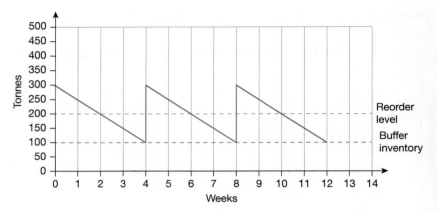

▲ **Figure 3.4.4**: Numerical example of an inventory control chart

Interpreting simple inventory control charts

Managing inventory levels means that decisions have to be taken about:

- The size of buffer inventory
- The maximum level of inventory
- The quantity to be reordered
- The level at which reordering will take place.

These decisions are made after determining production methods and levels, customer requirements, demand levels and the time it takes for orders to arrive. The steeper the gradient of the inventory level line the faster inventory is being used up. Tracking inventory levels on a chart enables a business to detect if there are variations that mean that reorders have to be made earlier or later than usual. The correct order size for regular orders can also be determined. The effect of changing the maximum and buffer inventory levels on reordering decisions can be measured.

Progress questions

The inventory control chart in Figure 3.4.4 comes from a business that is considering reducing the level of inventory it holds.

8 Predict the result of each of the following changes, assuming no change in any other variable:

  a Reducing lead time

  b Reducing buffer inventory

  c Reducing reorder level.

Inventory control methods: just-in-case (JIC) and just-in-time (JIT)

The appropriate values for the variables shown on the inventory control chart (buffer inventory, reorder level, order quantity, lead time) will be different for different businesses and industries.

Businesses can plan to achieve changes in these values to increase efficiency. Two extreme forms of inventory management are:

- Just-in-case
- Just-in-time.

Just-in-case (JIC) inventory control

Just-in-case inventory control involves maintaining large inventories to reduce the risk of failing to meet unexpected demand or an unexpected breakdown in supply. Large inventories make it possible to get round potential problems with unreliable suppliers and unexpected customer orders, and meeting demand without interruption. The business also relies less on the need for highly accurate demand forecasting, because it can use its buffer stocks when demand exceeds the expected or forecast level.

Inventory and just-in-time (JIT) production

The phrase just-in-time refers both to a production system, which is organised in such a way that products become available to customers just when they need them, and just-in-time inventory control, which refers to a system of managing inventories (raw materials or finished product) so that they are kept to an absolute minimum. JIT has been described previously in the context of lean production. In this section of the syllabus we are concerned with just-in-time inventory systems. Just-in-time inventory control involves operating with as low a level of inventory as possible, in some extreme cases no inventory at all.

Just-in-time involves:

- Raw materials being delivered only when needed
- Work-in-progress being kept to an absolute minimum through changes in production methods
- Finished products that are sent to customers as soon as completed.

JIT will require a very short lead time. It relies on being able to forecast customer demand as well as having an integrated production process. This way there is very little or no inventory of any type. It requires businesses to have complete confidence in, and co-operation from, their suppliers.

JIT inventory control can be achieved by changing the variables in the inventory control chart to achieve a smooth flow through the production process with a minimum of all types of inventory held.

Buffer inventory
This can be reduced because raw materials are only ordered when they are needed for production and finished products are immediately sent to the customer, not held in the business. The costs of holding inventory then become very small.

Order frequency
When materials are ordered from suppliers only when they are wanted, there will be more frequent and smaller orders than in traditional systems of inventory management.

Key terms

Just-in-case inventory control: involves maintaining high levels of raw materials and finished goods inventories, to ensure that the business is always able to meet customer demand, even when there is a disruption to material supplies or an unexpected increase in demand.

Just-in-time inventory control: involves managing inventories of raw materials, work-in-progress and finished products so that these are available exactly when they are needed and not before.

Lead time

This can be reduced by finding suppliers who can supply on demand with the right quantities of products of the correct quality. This will involve an integrated ordering system so orders are decided, dispatched quickly, with associated payment arrangements. The raw-material suppliers must be co-ordinated with the purchasing business, especially regarding expected quality assurance and standards as any shortfall here means there will not be enough raw materials for production.

The advantage of shorter lead times in JIT arrangements is that deliveries are likely to be more reliable than when lead times are longer.

Order quantity

This can be reduced by integrated production processes facilitated by IT systems. The order quantity will be determined by what is needed to be produced. This will depend on the customers' orders as in a JIT system products are only made to order, not for inventory.

Reorder level

This will depend not on the lead time before buffer inventory is reached but on when raw materials are needed for production. The quantity needed for production will be ordered.

It is difficult to see how inventory can ever be reduced to zero but achieving these changes can bring about a large reduction in the costs of holding inventory without compromising the benefits.

It is important to recognise that although there are significant benefits from using JIT, it is not suitable in a variety of situations:

- Small businesses may not be able to implement it due to lack of finance or facilities
- The business cannot risk being out of stock because of the damage caused through losing dissatisfied customers
- The business may not be able to rely on suppliers delivering on time
- The business may find holding inventory attractive particularly if the business anticipates significant cost increases in materials prices
- The product or service may be subject to unpredictable demand.

Activity

Research businesses, in your country or elsewhere, that operate a JIT system of production. What advantages do they gain from doing this?

Progress questions

9 Explain the difference between reorder level and reorder quantity.
10 Explain why an oil company always needs to hold buffer inventory of crude oil.
11 Give three situations in which JIT is not suitable.

Case study

Anixter helps cut inventory costs

A major manufacturer of medical equipment was having problems. It used two factories and had 2,000 inventory storage facilities in seven places in the two factories. It was ordering 900–1,000 different parts between 300 and 800 times a week. Delivery of parts was taking a long time from when they were ordered and the delays were leading to slower production. In response the business had increased its own on-site inventory holdings of components. To solve the increasing costs it approached Anixter, who not only supplied vital fasteners for medical equipment but also reorganised the inventories. An IT system linked to final orders forecast the demand for the components required. Anixter's distribution centre then pre-packaged 1,200 parts into easy-to-store-and recover bags. These bags were placed in the bins ready for production. The production forecasts gave a minimum and maximum demand for the components. This enabled much lower quantities of components to be stored in the factories and avoided all the delays that used to occur due to late delivery. Tracking customer orders and the components needed is now linked to the associated payments by customers and to Anixter. The costs of handling inventory have fallen significantly and there is much more inbuilt flexibility.

1   What problems were being caused by poor inventory control?
2   How did the solution by Anixter affect the following?
    a   Lead time
    b   Buffer inventory
    c   Reorder level.
3   Explain how the change in inventory control was related to JIT production.

The value of effective inventory control

Effective inventory control aims to eliminate problems and to maximise the advantages for a business. Holding the most appropriate amount of inventory can help to:

- Minimise the costs of holding inventory such as rent, insurance and security.
- Ensure that there is sufficient inventory to meet consumer demand however, there can be a problem if there is a sudden increase in consumer demand.
- Prevent inventory becoming out-dated or out of fashion while being held in store. Perishable goods such as food items often are wasted if they are not sold quickly.
- Prevent high-technology items becoming obsolete. This can happen very quickly and therefore if too much inventory is held, some of those items might become unsaleable.
- Ensure sufficient components and materials to allow a production line to function continuously and without any delay caused by a shortage of materials.

Influences on the choice of suppliers

There are several factors that can influence where a business will source its supplies. This can depend on the type of business in question. Some businesses require components and raw materials in order to manufacture goods while other businesses buy in finished goods to sell to the final consumer. A third category of business is those supplying services to customers but who still need to buy from suppliers; perhaps telephone and internet provision, computer hardware and software suitable for use in that specific business.

How will businesses choose their suppliers?

Businesses use a number of different suppliers. For its major items of purchase, or for purchasing one-off expensive items (such as new machinery), they should select their suppliers carefully.

Suppliers must have the ability to meet the specific needs of the business. A business will search for a supplier that can provide the materials, components, products or services that it requires. Some items of supply are more widely available than others. When there is only one supplier, which may be the case in some industries such as water supply and energy supply, businesses have no choice about which supplier to use.

The choice of suppliers can have an impact on how efficiently a business can operate. Suppliers can also have an impact on the financial success of a business.

Many businesses conduct supplier search exercises to identify suppliers who might be suitable for certain items of raw material or component (or service). Approved suppliers may then be added to a list or register, and only suppliers who are on the list are invited to submit quotations for orders that the business subsequently makes.

The main factors affecting the choice of supplier are sometimes referred to amongst procurement (buying) specialists as the 5Rs or "five rights". Preferred suppliers must be able to satisfy the business with regard to these 5Rs. See Table 3.4.4.

▼ **Table 3.4.4**: Selecting suppliers: the 5Rs

1	Right price	The selected supplier or suppliers must be able to provide items at an acceptable (or competitive) price. As a general rule, suppliers offering lower prices are often preferred to those asking for higher prices.
2	Right quantity	A supplier should be able to supply items in the quantities that the business needs. Even when a business uses more than one supplier, the capacity of suppliers to provide the items required in the quantities required is crucial.
3	Right quality	Suppliers are also selected on the basis of the quality of the items they supply. There is often a balance to be reached between price and quality, but suppliers with a reputation for quality are more likely to be selected in preference to others.
4	Right time	Suppliers are also selected on the basis of their reliability in delivering supplies at the agreed time. This is particularly important for a business that operates with a JIT purchasing and production system.
5	Right place	Suppliers must be able to deliver supplies to where they are wanted. This can be important in the case of international business and buying from suppliers in other (and distant) countries.

There are other factors that might affect the choice of suppliers such as:

- **Ethical or unethical business practices by the supplier**. In some countries, companies will not use suppliers that operate with unethical business practices, such as slave labour, child labour or unsafe working conditions for employees.
- **Flexibility in operating methods**. The choice of supplier might also depend on technical expertise and ability to adapt flexibly to changes or variations in the demand for products.
- **Financial strength**. In order to reduce the risks of a supplier going out of business and no longer being able to provide the required materials, a business might also select its suppliers on the basis of their relative financial strength.

The supply chain

A supply chain is the sequences or stages in the process of manufacturing and delivering a product (or providing a service). Some of these stages occur within the business itself, but others are performed by external suppliers.

Supply chain management is the process of obtaining all resources required by a business.

A supply chain often involves more than a business and its direct suppliers. For example, car manufacturers purchase tyres from specialist tyre manufacturers: these manufacturers in turn obtain supplies of synthetic rubber from their own suppliers. The supply chain can go back many stages. For example over 200 raw materials are needed for the production of car tyres, and car manufacturers use long supply chains for other components that go into the making of their cars, such as engines and all the items on a car dashboard. The supply chain ends with car distributors who sell finished items to customers.

A **supply chain** for the manufacture of processed food products begins with farmers and producers of other ingredients (such as herbs and spices) and ends with the sale of finished products in shops and supermarkets, or with the delivery of online purchases.

In today's global economy, supply chains can stretch around the world, making the problems of supply chain management very difficult.

- Businesses often monitor their main suppliers. When these are in other countries, a large amount of time and effort might be needed to monitor them (and occasionally visiting them).
- It is often more difficult to manage operations that are happening in other countries. For example, JIT purchasing systems operate internationally, but can be difficult to organise because of the delivery distances involved.
- With international supply, the cost of purchases can be affected by changes in an exchange rate. A change in an exchange rate can make the cost of buying in a foreign currency, when converted to the buyer's domestic currency, cheaper or more expensive (depending on how the exchange rate moves).

> **Key terms**
>
> **Supply chain management**: the process of obtaining all of the resources required by a business.
>
> **Supply chain**: the series of tasks involved in the production and movement of materials, components and finished goods from the original raw material suppliers to the final consumer.

The importance of managing the supply chain effectively

An effective supply chain is one that delivers goods or services to the end customers and meets their needs and expectations. When there are many links in the supply chain, from raw materials to sale of the end consumer product, there are many points where supply can break down and become unreliable. A supply chain is arguably only as strong as its weakest link.

It is sometimes useful to analyse a supply chain into three tiers of supplier. The Tier 1 suppliers of a business are its major suppliers that it deals with directly. Tier 2 suppliers are further up the supply chain, and these have dealings with the Tier 1 suppliers rather than the business: the Tier 1 suppliers need to manage the Tier 2 suppliers. Tier 3 suppliers are suppliers to Tier 2 suppliers, and are managed by Tier 2 suppliers.

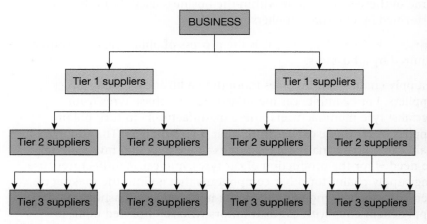

▲ **Figure 3.4.5**: Tiers of suppliers and supply chain management (simplified)

The main issues involved with effective supply chain management are concerned with achieving the "five rights" of price, quantity, quality, time and place, together with additional issues such as achieving flexibility in operations, ethical supply issues and using suppliers who are financially sound.

The importance of logistics

Logistics is the process of ensuring that the right products go to the right place at the right time, and in the right quantities.

Logistics are the operations involved in moving materials (or people) to where they are needed. In business, logistics management is an element of supply chain management, and it includes:

- Transporting materials, components and finished goods
- Warehousing
- Distribution of finished goods
- In international trade, activities involved in the shipment of goods, such as long-distance transport and warehousing, and customs clearance for exported and imported goods.

Logistics involves the management of the movement of materials, goods and (sometimes) people from the sourcing of raw materials, components and finished goods through to the delivery of a manufactured product (or a service) to the final consumer.

An important aspect of logistics management is organisation of the transportation of goods (sometimes referred to as freight).

Effective logistics management is important for business because the transportation and warehousing of goods affects:

- Reliability of delivery times
- The speed of delivery, when customers want to receive goods quickly
- Delivering goods to where they are needed and wanted
- Costs of operations: logistics operations can be expensive, especially when they involve the transportation of goods internationally.

Some businesses operate their own transport fleet for delivering goods by road, or they may use the services of a specialist delivery company. (Delivery companies such as DHL have their own transport fleet, including aeroplanes, and their entire business might be described as logistics services and logistics management.)

▼ Table 3.4.5: Elements of effective logistics management

Aspect of effective logistics management	Comment
Planning logistics operations	As with other aspects of operations management, effective logistics management requires careful planning, to ensure that the business has the capacity and the capability to transport planned volumes of output and deliver them on time to customers, at places where customers want to obtain them.
Co-ordination of operations	When the movement of materials and goods goes through several stages in a supply chain, effective logistics management ensures that operations between suppliers and transport companies are co-ordinated, avoiding delays, misunderstandings and errors.
Managing operating costs	Logistics can be a costly operation. Effective management keeps the costs of logistics under control, for example by choosing the most appropriate forms of freight transport and warehousing.
Arranging for speed of delivery when required	The speed of delivery can sometimes be important. Logistics managers may have to decide on the best method of delivering items to a customer. Over short distances, the best method of delivery might be for a business to use a vehicle from its own transport or the services of a logistics company. Over long distances and internationally, the quickest method of transport might be by air, but air freight is relatively expensive, and the capacity of aeroplanes to carry freight is less than for other modes of transport, such as ships, trains and trucks.
Keeping track of deliveries	Logistics managers should also be able to maintain control over operations by tracking the progress of goods. Digital systems for tracking and tracing goods are now used extensively.

Logistical problems arise when any of the necessary stages/processes do not happen as planned. When a situation occurs, such as the failure of a supplier to deliver on time the management team must have a plan B. This means that they should have planned ahead for every possible thing that could go wrong and should have a plan of action that will minimise its impact.

Progress questions

12 What is meant by "logistics" in a business context?

13 Explain two reasons why logistics management is important to a business.

Case study

The Global Oil Company

The Global Oil Company extracts crude oil from wells in its country of operations, and delivers them to oil refineries around the world.

The Big Chips Company manufactures and distributes IT digital equipment to customers around the world.

1 What are the similar concerns for both companies in ensuring effective logistics management for their goods?

2 In what ways do the logistical challenges differ between these two companies?

Exam-style questions

1 Explain why inventory control charts might be helpful for effective inventory control. (4 marks)

2 A café and restaurant is located in a village in the Swiss Alps. It experiences seasonal demand, with much bigger demand from customers during the winter skiing season than in the summer months.

Analyse the implications of seasonal demand for the business of this café and restaurant. (9 marks)

3 A building construction company regularly subcontracts aspects of building work to external suppliers. There is some disagreement, however, in how the company makes its choice of suppliers.

The newly appointed operations manager argues that the company should spend much more time on the pre-selection of potential suppliers before inviting any supplier to bid for work on a project. The managing director believes that this is an unnecessary and time-consuming activity, since there are many local subcontractors that can be invited to submit bids to undertake various aspects of the work.

Assess the arguments for and against whether pre-selection of possible subcontractors has an impact on the company's performance and make a judgement. (12 marks)

4 Major car manufacturers use just-in-time purchasing and production systems, but companies occasionally experience disruption to production due to supply problems. For example, BMW once experienced a hold-up of several days in production due to a shortage of steering systems from its supplier Bosch, which experienced production bottlenecks at a factory in Italy.

It has been argued that supply chains can be unreliable, making it preferable to switch to a just-in-case inventory management system rather than just-in-time.

Assess the arguments for and against JIT purchasing, and make a judgement. (12 marks)

Managing operations, human resources
and finance

4 Human resources

This section will develop your knowledge and understanding of:

→ The importance of managing human resources

→ Human resource planning and objectives

→ Internal and external influences on human resource plans, objectives and decisions.

This section looks at the importance for a business of managing human resources – people, or personnel. People have talents that can be developed into knowledge and skills and people who work for a business organisation can be described as its human capital. Assets for a business are something that enable it to make money or help to achieve its other goals, and the human capital of a business is the sum total of all the experience, knowledge and skills of the people working for it. People can give a business a competitive advantage, provided they are organised and managed effectively.

The importance of managing human resources

The purpose of human resources (HR) is to make sure that the business has the appropriate human resources to enable it to meet its objectives. Many large businesses readily accept that if they are going to be in a position to achieve ambitious goals, then their workforce must be fully committed to achieving those goals too. There must be enough people to do the work that is needed, but not too many of them; they need to have the right skills to do what is expected of them; and the workforce needs to adapt as the business environment changes. It is for such reasons that large companies regard the human resource department as essential.

The interrelationship between human resource decisions and other functions

All other departments and functions in a business rely on the support of HR to acquire and develop the people that they need. In a large organisation, the human resource (HR) department will provide employees to all functional departments, in other words, marketing, finance, production/operations, and sales and marketing.

The human resources department works with other departments to ensure that each of them has the right number of suitably skilled employees in the right locations. HR involves:

* Workforce planning: planning how many employees the organisation needs, in which locations they are needed, and what skills they should have
* Recruiting and selecting people with the required skills, or who have the potential to acquire the skills that are needed

Key term

Human resources: the business function of ensuring that the employees of an organisation are used in the most effective way possible to achieve optimum business performance.

Activity

Speak to two or three people you know who have been in work for some time, and ask them about the role that the HR department has played in their work experience to date. Make notes about what they tell you.

For example, ask them about how they found out about their job in the first place and how they were selected, how they found out about their pay and terms of employment, and what training they have received.

- Where there are gaps between the current skills of the workforce and the skills that are required, providing suitable training
- Retaining good employees, by offering suitable levels of pay.

An organisation may also seek to retain good employees by motivating them and winning their loyalty so that they do not leave and go to work somewhere else, but this is a responsibility for management throughout the organisation, not just the HR department.

How human resource decisions help improve the competitiveness of a business

Some businesses are capital intensive and rely on the efficiency of their machines and equipment to achieve business success. Manufacturing businesses that make extensive use of robots and automation are an example. However, many businesses provide services to customers, and competitive success depends on designing and providing services of a high quality that customers want to buy. Providing good service to customers calls for a motivated and suitably skilled workforce. Human resources – the people working for an organisation – can therefore be a key source of competitive advantage, and HR can play a key role in recruiting and developing a workforce that delivers the service quality that customers want.

Case study

Road Beaters

Road Beaters is a company that gives driving lessons to learner drivers from centres throughout the country in which it operates. It is highly successful and estimates that it has about 20% of the market for driving lessons. It relies on its small human resource management team to help maintain its strong competitive advantage.

1 In what ways do you think that the HR team might help to ensure that the company has a workforce that helps it to achieve and maintain its leading market position?

▲ **Figure 4.1.1**: Learning to drive is big business around the world

The impact of global business on human resource management

The functions of HR are similar in all business organisations, but the complexity varies enormously between businesses of different sizes, and particularly in global businesses. Global businesses operate in a number of different countries, and they employ people in each of them. The business should have a single identity as one company or group of companies, and develop a corporate culture, but at the same time they must allow for cultural differences among employees in the different countries. They are likely to have a large workforce, which means that labour turnover could be high, so that recruitment and selection of new employees is an ongoing task.

BMW

BMW is a major global manufacturer of cars. Its headquarters is in Germany, but it has operations throughout the world, in countries such as the USA and Australia. The company's policies include a requirement that all managers throughout the company and in all countries should communicate in English and not their native language if this is not English.

The company also expects its managers above a certain level of seniority to acquire work experience in different countries, as a condition of eligibility for further promotion in the future.

1   Why do you suppose that BMW applies these policies globally for the large numbers of managers that the company employs around the world?

Human resource planning and objectives

A key role of the HR department is to develop a plan for how many employees are needed in order for the business to function effectively.

This process is known as "human resource planning".

What is a human resources plan and why is human resource planning necessary?

A human resources plan is a plan for the numbers and skills that an organisation will need in its workforce in a future period, and it should include details of how these will be obtained and retained. Planning is made difficult by uncertainty. An organisation may estimate the numbers and skills of the people it will need, based on the best information available, and plan to acquire them but actual requirements may turn out differently from the plan.

Because of planning uncertainties, small businesses may have a "reactive" approach to obtaining and retaining the staff that it needs, taking measures to replace, recruit and train individuals as and when the need arises. Large organisations need to be more "proactive" and take measures in advance to ensure that it will have the people that it thinks it needs, because of the large size of the workforce and the range of skills and work locations involved.

Influences on the human resource plan

The way in which the HR department develops its human resource plan can be influenced by both internal factors and external factors.

▼ Table 4.1.1: Influences on the human resource plan

Internal influences	Example
Corporate objectives	If a company has a strategy to grow and expand its business domestically or globally it should plan to recruit the extra numbers of people it will need.
Operational strategies	If a retailing company develops a new strategy for online selling of goods, it may need to employ individuals with different skills, such as skills in IT and digital technology.
Financial strategies	If a company develops a financial strategy to reduce operating costs, it might need to plan for a reduction in the workforce, for example by outsourcing some activities to external suppliers.

External influences	Example
Technological changes	Technological changes, involving for example an increase in digital technology, will change the requirements that a business has for both employee numbers and skills.
Economic changes	A change in economic conditions, such as a period of economic recession, might affect sales revenues, so that a company needs to plan for some reduction in its workforce.
Changes in the market	The market for a company's products or services might change, or the nature of competition might change. For example, the business of traditional banks has been challenged by new companies offering digital financial services: banks are responding by developing digital businesses of their own, which need employees with the right skills.
Social changes	There has been an increase in some countries in flexible working and working from home. In countries with an ageing population, it may be necessary to plan for individuals to retire at a later age in order to sustain workforce numbers.
Political and legal changes	There may be changes in labour law, such as laws on maximum hours of working.

Progress questions

1. Why does the HR function need to work with every other department or function in an organisation?
2. How do the human resources of a business organisation contribute to the organisation's competitive advantage?
3. What is human resource planning?

Human resource objectives

In its human resource planning, a business should seek to achieve some key objectives, in other words, successful employee engagement, diversity in the workforce, a suitable number of employees with appropriate skills and the retention of employees.

Employee engagement

Employee engagement is about creating conditions in the workplace where employees are committed to the goals and values of the organisation, and to its success, and as a result give their best efforts every day. Employment engagement is far more than being happy or satisfied at work; rather, it means being willing to putting in extra effort to help the business to succeed.

Key terms

Diversity: in a workplace this means having a workforce drawn from a wide range of different backgrounds and characteristics, for example with differences in race, ethnicity, age, gender and sexual orientation.

Retention: with regard to labour, keeping existing employees so that they do not leave their job/employment.

Employee engagement: when an employee is fully committed to the business and views the attainment of their personal objectives as being beneficial to the overall business objectives.

Employee engagement can lead to many benefits for a business.

- A higher standard of work.
- Probably, a higher level of productivity (although engagement with work does not necessarily make an individual more efficient) and so higher profits.
- A higher level of customer care leading to higher levels of customer satisfaction.
- Increased customer loyalty and repeat purchases.

Employee engagement is more likely to have these effects in businesses where a positive attitude to work is most likely to affect performance. All of the above can be achieved as a result of engaged employees, but how can employee engagement itself be achieved?

- By making it an objective for the organisation.
- By providing work that is interesting and where individuals can see how it is contributing to the organisation's success.
- By involving employees in decisions: keeping them informed about what the business is doing.
- Asking for their opinions or allowing them to ask questions about any proposed changes.
- Encouraging them to make suggestions.
- Rewarding them for creativity and other achievements, so that individuals see that the success of the business is also a success for them personally.

The key is to make employees feel genuinely involved and an important part of the business, for which they are suitably rewarded.

Diversity

Diversity has become more important because many businesses operate in a global market. It can be very important that the range of employees in a business reflects the market in which the business operates. Diversity can also demonstrate that the business employs equality of opportunity in its recruitment process. In some countries there are requirements that, in particular large businesses, recruit employees from different cultures, ethnic groups and with disabilities and from different age groups. This approach can highlight the ethical and non-discriminatory values of a business which can give them a good reputation and perhaps some positive publicity.

It is widely accepted that a diverse range of employees can enrich the work experience of people working in that business.

Benefits of diversity include:

- Many languages spoken which can help when dealing with businesses in other countries
- It can help a business to understand the needs of consumers in different markets
- Gives employees an appreciation or awareness of different cultures
- Encouraging an understanding between employees from different backgrounds and attitudes to work

- Employees can learn from each other and can learn to accept and perhaps adopt different attitudes to work and life.

However, there can be some difficulties of a diverse workforce:

- When recruiting people from another country, there can be initial language problems. This can be avoided or reduced by some early language training.
- There might be a need for general diversity training to help existing employees recognise the benefits of working with people from different cultures, for example.
- A diverse workforce is not without its potential problems but a business must be ready to act quickly and firmly if any incidents of negative reaction occur. For example, if an older worker expresses resentment at the appointment of a younger person to a more senior level, or if discriminatory comments are made about a woman being appointed.
- The cost of training required either for the existing employees or for new recruits.
- Sexism, racism or any other form of discrimination should not be tolerated. This will require strong monitoring and enforcement of anti-discrimination policies.

Diversity in a workforce is not without potential problems but effective management of the workforce can result in deeper understanding and co-operation leading to better teamwork and increased productivity.

Number and skills of employees

An important part of a human resource plan is to predict the number and skills of employees that will be required, and to develop ways of ensuring that these numbers and skills are obtained. All businesses strive to have the number of employees that are needed in order to meet business objectives. As business objectives change, the number of employees required might also change. As well as the number of employees required, the skills that those employees are required to have might also change.

An HR department should always aim to have the correct number of suitably skilled employees at the time they are required.

Typically, the plan is produced by predicting the numbers of employees required in each type of job (for which particular skills might be required) and in each country and workplace location. These forecasts may be made for each six months, say, over the next two years and then annually from Year 3 to Year 5. An estimate should also be made of the numbers of employees within the organisation who are currently in those jobs, together with an estimate of how many might leave, to retire, to work elsewhere or because they will be promoted or transferred to a different job.

These forecasts will result in a gap in the numbers of people required, and in the skills required. The gap will usually be a shortage of employees, but may sometimes show an excess of employees in a particular job, where the organisation is planning to reduce workforce numbers.

The next stage of the human resource plan should be to decide on the action required to fill the shortfall in the numbers required. In order to fill the gap the HR department may:

- Retrain existing employees to acquire the skills needed to do the job
- Transfer employees with the required skills from a different part of the business
- Recruit individuals externally with the skills required to do the job.

The HR department should develop these plans in consultation and collaboration with management of the departments or functions affected.

A business might have made a decision to use more machinery and this will require its employees to have different skills in order to be able to operate or monitor the machines effectively. Some of the existing employees might be offered training to enable them to acquire the necessary skills. Some employees might be offered work in another part of the business that still requires their skills. However, there might be some employees who are not suitable for retraining and for whom there are no appropriate positions elsewhere in the company. These employees will be made redundant. Redundancy means that employees are asked to leave their job, not because they have done anything wrong, but because their job is no longer required.

When assessing the workers and skills required and in extreme cases making workers redundant it is important that the best workers are retained within the business.

Retention

Usually, businesses aim to keep the employees that they have, so that they do not leave the business. If a large number of employees leave a business it is often taken as an indication that the business is not a good place to work. Businesses that people want to work for will usually have a very low number of employees leaving their job.

A high rate of retention is desirable because when people leave their job:

- The business is losing their acquired experience and skills
- They must be replaced, which means having to spend more time and effort on recruiting new people from outside the organisation or retraining existing employees to do the work.

Case study

Planning for company change

A manufacturing company is planning to modernise the production system, introducing robots and other automated equipment to do work that has been more labour intensive in the past. The new production system will need fewer employees, some unskilled but some requiring a reasonably high level of competence in handling digital equipment.

1 What factors should influence the company's human resource plan to accompany the plan for investing in new equipment?

2 What measures would you take to plan for the changes in workforce numbers and skills required?

Even when a business has to make some employees redundant, the best employees must be kept in the business. How can this be achieved?

- Ensure that the business has an appropriate means of assessing the contribution of each employee and therefore know their value to the business.
- Make sure that the skills of employees are kept up to date with a well-planned and targeted training programme.
- Ensure that appropriate incentives are in place so that employees will want to stay with the business, in other words, use appropriate motivational techniques.

Not retaining the best employees can be very expensive for a business. For example, the cost of recruiting new employees and the training costs for new workers. There is also the loss of the skills and knowledge of employees who might have worked in the business for many years.

Internal and external influences on human resource plans, objectives and decisions

Resources

The human resources of an organisation are not just the number of people it employs, but also their talents, experience and skills. As explained previously, employees are the human capital of a business, and they help the business to make profits and achieve its other objectives.

The need for employees with various skills does not remain constant. It changes over time, so that organisations need more or fewer people with particular skills, or need employees with skills that were not needed previously. There have also been changes in social and environmental attitudes to working, and many organisations have adapted their working practices to the changes.

Developments in technology

In the twenty-first century, businesses exist in a world of rapidly changing technology. This can change the way in which goods are produced and services are provided and there will, therefore, be an impact on the type of employees needed. For example, the increased use of robotics in manufacturing has led to a change in the required skills of employees. Instead of requiring employees to have the skills to produce a product, a business now needs employees who can programme, monitor and maintain the robotic equipment.

Similarly, the payroll system has been computerised in many businesses. This change has removed the need for employees who can understand and complete the payroll calculations because now the business needs someone who knows how to input the data and the computer performs all the necessary calculations.

The increased use of computers in the workplace has meant that, in some cases, employees do not need to be at the actual place of business in order to do their work. The term "teleworking" refers to arrangements in which an employee works at an approved location other than the employer's premises. In recent years there has been an increase in working from home. As long as employees can connect to the internet and their employer's website, they can work.

Such developments have allowed businesses to reduce the number of employees based at the business premises and therefore to reduce the size of premises required. The HR department has had to recruit people who can work efficiently and effectively without the direct supervision of being physically at the workplace. Their work rate and contribution can still be measured.

Example

Uber Technologies Inc has been at the forefront of the developments in arranging car rides. Individuals who need transport from one location to another can arrange the transaction with Uber by using an app on a digital device and the fee for the ride varies according to the time of day and supply and demand in the area for rides. Payments are made by a method pre-selected by the individual obtaining the ride. The use of IT by Uber has made car rides easier to arrange, but it has also led to big changes in conditions of working, with drivers able to work whenever they want, but paid only for the rides they give, and they are not regarded as Uber employees.

▲ **Figure 4.1.2**: Ethical and environmental impacts

Ethical and environmental influences

In recent decades, consumers and the population in general have become more aware of the attitude of businesses to ethical behaviour and the potential environmental impact of business activity.

Many individuals and businesses now prefer to deal with businesses whose behaviour is ethical and environmentally friendly. Companies might try to recruit talent by promoting themselves as ethical employers, with ethical business practices. For example, some international firms encourage employees to take time off regularly from work to do charity work or volunteer work in their local communities.

Some major clothing and footwear companies have a supplier relationship policy that requires all its suppliers, in all countries, to treat its employees fairly, with reasonable pay, respect for human rights and healthy and safe working conditions. To remain as a supplier to such companies, suppliers must develop and implement their own ethical HR policies.

How does this affect the human resource plans, objectives and decisions?

Ethical influences might include:

- An ethical business would make sure that its recruitment policies did not discriminate against anyone due to their race, religion, disability, culture, sexual orientation, gender or age
- Training opportunities should be available to new and existing employees on a non-discriminatory basis
- The rewards offered to employees should be awarded in a fair and transparent way
- New jobs or promotion opportunities must be advertised in a way that allows all appropriate candidates an opportunity to apply.

Environmental influences might include:

- If a business has a strict environmental policy, the HR department will need to ensure that all employees, new and existing, are capable of following the requirements of the policy. This could influence the level of training required and the experience of any new employees recruited.
- Environmental policies might cause a significant change to the way in which the business works, which will impact on the workforce and skills required.
- Certain businesses might not be allowed to locate in their first choice of location. The nature of their business activity might require them to locate away from residential areas, for example, which could mean that the labour available to them is restricted.

Market conditions

Many elements of the market can affect human resource decisions and plans:

- When unemployment is low there is more competition between businesses for those who are applying for jobs.
- This increased competition can force businesses to increase the wages and/or other packages in order to attract employees. This competition is likely to be more intense in relation to jobs that require a specific and scarce skill.
- When unemployment is high it is often the lower skilled people who find it difficult to find work which can still leave a shortage of skilled applicants.
- Nowadays, people are more geographically mobile both nationally and internationally. This means that the local job seekers might be seeking work in other countries and equally applicants for work in one country might come from any part of the world. This is particularly so in the case of multinational companies whose employees might apply for a promotion that could require them to relocate to a different country.
- The skills and experience available in the local labour market might not be suitable for the work required by a business, in which case they will have to advertise internationally to find appropriate employees.
- Even in the case of the local labour market being highly skilled and qualified, the skills and qualifications might not match those required by a business.
- The HR department will need to be aware of the local labour market and then decide whether or not to advertise posts nationally or internationally. The requirement to offer a better package or benefits along with higher wages is another decision that they will need to take. They will have to keep aware of what other businesses are offering to employees doing a similar level of work and ensure that they, at least, match those offers if they are to obtain the required workforce.

All of the above points will have an impact on the decisions of the HR department, either in terms of the remuneration package to be offered or to the type of workforce that is available to them.

It might be decided to recruit locally and then to offer training to develop the skills of those new employees in order to meet the skill needs of the business. This is a slower process but can be cheaper than offering increased remuneration packages. The decision might depend on how urgently the workforce is required.

International competition and human resources decisions

International companies engaged in global competition will develop human resource plans that help to give them a competitive advantage over their global rivals. For example:

- Manufacturing companies may establish production facilities in countries where wages and labour costs are low. In the past, some international companies have moved production to China to benefit from low labour costs, but as labour costs have since risen in China, some companies are shifting operations to a different country with low labour costs, such as Vietnam.

- Some countries or cities that are regarded as major international centres for a particular industry and companies in these centres may develop HR policies for attracting individuals from around the world to work for them, competing with each other to attract the top talent. For example, Silicon Valley in California tries to attract individuals with IT skills from around the world; and London, a major international financial centre, has employed so many individuals from France that in 2017 it was called the sixth largest French city by French President Macron.

Exam-style questions

1 In some countries, there has been a large increase in the numbers of home workers or teleworkers employed by companies.

   Explain one of the reasons for this increase in teleworking. (3 marks)

2 An element of the human resource policy of many organisations is to achieve a high rate of employee retention.

   Explain one reason why a high rate of labour retention might be beneficial for a business organisation. (3 marks)

3 International businesses operate in many different countries and employ staff globally.

   Analyse how human resource policies can help an international business to compete effectively against its global rivals. (9 marks)

Using human resource data

All businesses will need to have some means of ensuring that all of their resources are working efficiently and effectively, including their human resource, the employees. The human resource department is responsible for recording and sometimes assessing the performance of employees.

Several of these measures are numerical calculations but they might also require other information to be used with them in order to give a thorough understanding of what the figures mean.

Labour turnover

Labour turnover is the number of employees leaving a business in a given time period. This is expressed as a percentage of the total number of employees.

The labour turnover rate is calculated by:

$$\frac{\text{Number of employees leaving in a year}}{\text{Average total number of employees}} \times 100\%$$

> **Key term**
>
> Labour turnover: the number of employees leaving a business in a given time period. It is usually expressed as a labour turnover percentage rate.

The total number of employees in an organisation can change over time, as the business grows or contracts, and the total number of employees at the beginning of the year is rarely the same as the total number at the year-end. The labour turnover rate should be calculated using the average total number of employees, and the best way to calculate this (approximately) is usually to take the average of the employee numbers at the beginning and at the end of the year.

Example

A company had 15,200 employees at the beginning of the year and 15,500 at the end of the year. During the year 1,640 employees left the company.

The labour turnover rate is calculated as follows:

$$\text{Average total number of employees} = \frac{(15,200 + 15,500)}{2} = 15,350$$

Labour turnover rate $= \left(\dfrac{1,640}{15,350}\right) \times 100\% = 10.68\%$. This might be rounded to 10.7%.

Employees leave for different reasons. Some move on to a job with a different employer, and others retire for reasons of age or ill health. Some might leave simply because they do not like the work or the pay. Except in very small businesses, some labour turnover is inevitable. The question for HR however is whether the rate of labour turnover is high or low, whether or not it is acceptable, and whether action should be taken to improve the rate.

The rates of labour turnover vary between industries, and a high rate of turnover can be a bigger concern in some industries than in others:

- The hotels and fast-food industries have a tradition of high labour turnover, with employees remaining only a very short time in their job. Students, for example, might take a short-term job in a hotel for the summer holiday before going back to university in the autumn.
- Organisations that employ highly trained individuals, such as hospitals, will be concerned about a high labour turnover rate because this leaves them with the problem of replacing the skilled individual they have lost, and this may be difficult due to a shortage of trained people looking for work.

▼ Table 4.2.1: Possible causes of a high labour turnover rate and action in response

Possible causes of a high rate of labour turnover	Action that might be taken to reduce the turnover rate
Better job opportunities with other employers	Improve terms and conditions of employment, for example by offering higher pay. A longer-term policy might be to make the work more enjoyable, and so increase employee engagement.
Employees reaching retirement age and leaving	Offer employees the opportunity to continue working: do not expect employees to leave when they reach a certain age.
Redundancies among the workforce	If a group of employees are made redundant, labour turnover will inevitably increase. The increase should be temporary, limited to the period of time when the redundancies occur.
Poor working conditions, poor employee morale	The organisation probably needs to look very closely at the failings of its human resource policies. Companies can earn a reputation as bad employers, putting off applicants for jobs as well as causing a high labour turnover rate.

Most businesses expect some employees to leave each year, which might be for personal reasons such as moving closer to family or because a person wants to try a new career. Such labour turnover would not indicate that there is a problem with the human resource management within the business.

If employees are leaving because of low pay, poor working conditions or low morale in the workforce, then the business would probably want to take action to prevent more employees leaving in the future.

What is a normal labour turnover rate?

A labour turnover rate is an approximate indicator of the average length of time that employees remain with their company. For example, if the labour turnover rate is 10% per year, this means that one in ten people leave each year, so the average length of time in employment is ten years (1/10%). If the labour turnover rate is 25% per year, this indicates that employees stay with their company on average for four years (1/25%).

A normal labour turnover rate might therefore be one that is consistent with the average length of time that employees might be expected to remain with their company.

Activity

The normal rate of labour turnover differs between businesses. Choose any four businesses (excluding hotels and fast-food chains) and put them into a descending order for labour turnover, with the business with the highest rate of labour turnover at the top and the business with the lowest rate of labour turnover at the bottom. You can search the internet for ideas.

Make a note of the reasons why you put the four businesses into your chosen order.

Labour productivity

Labour productivity measures the amount produced by an employee in a given time period. It is a measure of the efficiency of the workforce. Labour productivity is calculated as follows:

$$\text{Labour productivity} = \frac{\text{Output of the organisation in a period of time}}{\text{Average number of employees during the period}}$$

The period of time used for measuring productivity can be anything, from a minute to a year or even longer. Using the above formula, labour productivity is measured in output per employee per period of time. This can be expressed in a different way, as the average time to produce one unit of output. For example, if the average rate of labour productivity is four units per hour, this means that the average time to produce one unit is 15 minutes (1 hour/4 units).

The average number of employees in the period is usually calculated as the average of the numbers at the beginning and at the end of the period.

The output of the organisation might be measured in a number of ways, such as:

- The number of units of an item produced in the period. However this is only practicable when all the units produced are the same or very similar to each other.
- Sales revenue during the period. This measure can be used when the organisation produces a range of different items, or non-standard items, and when all items produced have a money value.
- There might be another way of measuring total output, such as the number of customers served in the period.

Example

A hairdressing business has four employees. In one working day of eight hours they carry out 96 haircuts and are paid $12 per hour. Labour productivity at this hairdresser is 96 haircuts/4 employees = 24 haircuts per employee per day, or 3 haircuts (on average) per employee.

Another way of stating productivity is to say that the average time per haircut is 20 minutes (1 hour/3).

The average cost of labour per haircut for each haircut is $4 (= 8 hours per day × 4 employees × $12 per hour, divided by 96 haircuts. Alternatively, it is the labour cost for 20 minutes, $12 × 20/60).

Importance of productivity

If productivity increases, employees produce more in a given period of time than they did before, which means that they produce units of output more quickly. As a result, if there is no increase in the rate of pay for labour, labour costs per unit produced will fall. This explains why productivity is such an important concept for businesses. In the example of the hairdressing business, if productivity can be increased so that each employee can do four haircuts in an hour instead of three, the average labour cost per haircut will fall from $4 to $3. The business can then:

- Reduce its price per haircut by $1 but maintain its profit margin per haircut, or

- Keep the price per haircut the same and increase its profit margin, or
- A combination of these, reducing the price by less than $1 and so increasing the profit margin per haircut.

Example

A retail store employs 50 people and during a year the store made sales of $4,000,000. The average profit on sales is 10% of sales value. Labour productivity is measured as the average amount of sales revenue per employee.

$$\text{Labour productivity} = \frac{\$4,000,000}{50 \text{ employees}} = \$80,000 \text{ in sales revenue per}$$

employee per year (a profit value of $8,000 per employee per year).

If sales revenue were to increase by 5%, say, with no change in employee numbers, total annual revenue would be $4,200,000 and

$$\text{labour productivity would be } \frac{\$4,200,000}{50 \text{ employees}} = \$84,000 \text{ in revenue per}$$

employee per year, and a profit of $8,400 per employee.

This example should illustrate how improvements in labour productivity can have a direct effect on a company's profits.

Improving labour productivity

One way of increasing labour productivity might be to improve employee engagement with the business and motivate them to work harder. In some cases, this approach to productivity improvements may work well. However, the most effective way of improving labour productivity is to invest more in capital (machines and equipment). Machines might be referred to as labour saving because when new machinery is installed, fewer employees may be required to do the work. However, new machines might also enable a workforce to produce more output in the time available, without reducing the numbers of employees.

- The increase in labour productivity will reduce the average labour cost per unit produced.
- However, the cost of machinery per unit produced will increase.
- This means that a higher rate of labour productivity reduces costs only if the reduction in average labour cost is greater than any offsetting operating costs, such as equipment costs.
- It is also important that any improvements in labour productivity are not achieved at the expense of a fall in the quality of output produced.

Employee costs as a percentage of turnover

Turnover is the number of sales times the price of sales, giving a total sales revenue or sales turnover for a business. Employee costs as a percentage of sales turnover is calculated as:

$$\frac{\text{Total employee costs in the period}}{\text{Total revenue in the period}}$$

A business with a high percentage of labour costs to total revenue is often called a labour-intensive business. A capital-intensive business should have a relatively low ratio of labour costs to revenue.

So what does this ratio tell us?

- When the information for other companies is available (for example, when competitors publish their financial statements) it is possible for a company to compare its own ratio with those of the other companies and use this comparison to assess whether its labour costs seem relatively high or low.

- Companies might set a target to reduce the ratio of labour costs to sales revenue, for example by making changes to improve labour productivity. They can then monitor progress over time towards achieving the target they have set themselves.

- When the ratio of employee costs to sales revenue is high, this might indicate that profitability would be at risk from a further increase in labour costs. The business might not be able to afford a big increase in wages and salaries for example, or might need to consider ways of reducing labour costs, for example by finding ways to reduce the total size of the workforce.

Any change in employee costs as a percentage of turnover will be the result of changes in either component of the calculation, total labour costs or total sales turnover – or both. Changes should be investigated in order to decide what action, if any, should be taken to improve the ratio.

Labour cost per unit

The (average) labour cost per unit produced is calculated simply as:

$$\frac{\text{Total labour costs in the period}}{\text{Units of output produced the in the period}}$$

Case study

Employee costs

The ratio of total employee costs to sales turnover differs between different types of business. In each of the following examples, decide whether the business is likely to have a high or a low ratio of labour costs to sales revenue. Give your reasons in each case.

1. A company designing and selling popular games for laptop computers and mobile phones.
2. A firm of professional accountants.

It can be used to measure labour costs as an alternative to the percentage of employee costs to sales revenue when the organisation produces just one product, or very similar products. The cost per unit will again depend on whether the business uses labour-intensive or capital-intensive methods of operating. A business which uses more capital than labour would expect their labour costs per unit to be lower than that of a business using labour-intensive methods.

Activity

Individually or in small groups list as many reasons for changes in the labour cost per unit. Then identify actions that could be taken to improve the figures where necessary.

It is also possible to calculate the cost per unit produced or sold for each different labour function, such as production labour, sales and marketing staff or administration staff.

Sales and profit per employee

Some businesses measure their labour efficiency by calculating the amount of sales or profit that is generated per employee. The results of such calculations could encourage businesses to change their method of working.

$$\text{Sales per employee} = \frac{\text{Total sales revenue in a period}}{\text{Average number of employees in the period}}$$

$$\text{Profit per employee} = \frac{\text{Total profit in a period}}{\text{Average number of employees in the period}}$$

Example

A small company providing car servicing and repair services had 12 employees at the beginning of the year and 16 employees at the year-end. During the year, its revenues totalled $1,330,000 and its profits were $106,400.

$$\text{Average number of employees} = \frac{(12 + 16)}{2} = 14$$

$$\text{Sales per employee} = \frac{\$1,330,000}{14} = \$95,000$$

$$\text{Profit per employee} = \frac{\$106,400}{14} = \$7,600$$

What does this data tell us?

If the sales and profit per employee are considered too low, ways to improve them should be considered. Such ways could include increasing the revenue per employee (for example, by increasing the prices charged to customers), reducing non-labour operating costs such as reducing the amount of money spent on advertising, or reducing labour costs by improving labour productivity.

The data also shows that if the business were to pay its employees an extra $7,600 per year each, the business profits would be wiped out.

As a general rule, sales per employee should be high when labour costs are high, such as sales for a firm of lawyers or a firm of management consultants. However this is not necessarily the case: a theatre company employs a large number of actors and theatre staff, for example, so labour costs can be quite high, but revenues may not exceed labour costs by much, and profits may therefore be low.

Employee engagement

As explained previously, employee engagement exists when employees are totally committed to helping the business to achieve its objectives. This concept can be difficult to measure but many businesses will use appraisal and/or questionnaires to assess the level of engagement of their employees.

However, there are difficulties with measuring employee engagement.

- It relates to how employees feel, and feelings are difficult to measure.
- The degree of engagement can change over time. For example, employees who are totally engaged but then do not get promoted when they expect to might change their attitude to the business.
- Employees might not answer truthfully when asked questions about their commitment to the company.
- Employees might be totally engaged until a change in the business takes place which might have a negative impact on the attitude of those working in the business. This could be a change in the senior management or even a merger or takeover by another business. If this results in a change in culture, attitudes of the employees might change.
- If a business changes its objectives, employees might not feel as committed to achieving the new objectives. For example if a business decided to abandon or ignore ethical or environmental issues, many employees might feel that they could no longer support the activities of the business as fully as they did previously.

It might be possible to assess employee engagement by asking them periodically to complete a questionnaire about their attitudes to their job and work, but a better measure is probably unofficial – word of mouth and the company's reputation as a good and exciting business to work for.

The extent to which employee engagement exists can depend on the corporate objectives of each business as well as the size of the business. Small businesses often have a close working relationship between the owners and the employees. This becomes more difficult as businesses become much larger and direct contact between owners and employees is much less likely.

Exam-style questions

1 Employee costs as a percentage of turnover are most likely to increase when:

   A   sales turnover is increasing

   B   the profit per employee is increasing

   C   employee engagement is high

   D   labour productivity is falling   (1 mark)

2 A manufacturing company produces kitchen light fittings. Its products are all similar to each other, and during a particular month it produced 256,000 light fittings. Its production workforce was 21 employees at the beginning of the month and 19 employees at the end of the month. Employees work a 160-hour month.

   What is the labour productivity rate for the month, in terms of output per hour and average time per unit produced?   (2 marks)

3 The motivation of a workforce might be judged in terms of employee engagement.

   Explain one reason why employee engagement is very difficult to measure reliably.   (3 marks)

4 The human resources management team in a company are reviewing labour productivity statistics for the past year. Data shows that during the year, sales per employee have risen compared to the previous year, but profit per employee has fallen.

   Analyse the possible reasons for these changes from the previous year to the current year.   (9 marks)

This section will develop your knowledge and understanding of:

→ Managing human resources

→ Influences on and effect of different organisational designs.

Managing human resources

This section explains how various methods of managing human resources contribute to the objective of achieving optimum business performance. In particular, it looks at the function of recruitment and selection, the value of training, reducing the size of the workforce to improve performance and organising the workforce within an organisational structure.

Effective recruitment and selection

Recruitment is the process of finding people to fill vacancies in the workforce or management team. It begins with the human resource plan, and estimating the gaps in the workforce that need to be filled. It goes on to advertise the job vacancies, then assess the job applications received. There may be interviews for a job vacancy before the preferred applicant is selected and offered the job with terms and conditions, such as job description, starting pay and holiday entitlement. The recruitment process might not end until the successful applicant has started the job and is gradually introduced into the company, in a "get-to-know-the-business" process called induction.

A key element in the recruitment process is selection. This is choosing the preferred applicant for a job vacancy, and making a successful job offer that the individual accepts.

What is effective recruitment and selection?

HR is about managing the workforce in order to achieve optimum business performance. Recruitment and selection contribute to this by attracting suitable candidates who might perform their job well, becoming skilled and experienced employees, by identifying the best person or persons for the job, and getting them to accept the job when it is offered to them.

Effective recruitment means making suitable people aware of job vacancies that exist and encouraging them to apply.

Effective selection means identifying the best candidate or candidates from among the applicants.

It might help to define effective recruitment and selection by looking at the meaning of ineffective recruitment and selection. Recruitment is ineffective when job vacancies are not brought to the attention of people who might be suitable applicants, or failing to persuade suitable applicants to apply. Selection is ineffective when the person chosen to fill a job vacancy is unsuited for the job.

> ### Key terms
>
> Recruitment: identifying the need for an employee, devising a job description and finding a person suitable to perform the job.
>
> Selection: choosing a suitable person to fill a job vacancy from among all the applicants for the job.

It might also be suggested that effective recruitment and selection means keeping the costs as low as possible. However, the amount of time and money that any business needs to spend on recruitment can depend on its rate of labour turnover. A business with a high rate of labour turnover will have to devote more time and resources to the recruitment and selection process.

Internal versus external recruitment

When one or more job vacancies occur, a decision has to be made between:

- Recruiting from outside the organisation: the person or individuals recruited may already be well qualified to do the job.
- Appointing someone from inside the organisation, possibly on promotion. An internally recruited person may need some training after appointment to enable them to do the job.

There are some advantages and disadvantages to each of these approaches, particularly when the post is a promotion.

▼ Table 4.3.1: Advantages and disadvantages of internal recruitment

Advantages	Disadvantages
• The candidate is known to the business.	• Can cause dissatisfaction for those not promoted.
• Can be motivating to others if they feel that they might be rewarded with promotion in the future.	• Can cause line management problems for the promoted person if they now supervise former colleagues.
• Can be less expensive as the recruitment and selection process will be shorter and also less training might be required.	• There might be a better applicant externally.

▼ Table 4.3.2: Advantages and disadvantages of external recruitment

Advantages	Disadvantages
• Brings in "new blood" and new ideas.	• The new employee does not know the internal structure of the business as well as someone who already works there.
• Possibly fewer line management issues.	• Internal applicants might be unhappy that a "stranger" has got the job. They might feel undervalued by the business.

Progress questions

1   Explain the difference between internal and external recruitment.
2   Discuss possible reasons why external recruitment might be more beneficial to a business than internal recruitment.

The recruitment process

There are several steps in a recruitment process. Mistakes or shortcomings in any of these steps could make the recruitment process ineffective:

- **Job description**. Unless one exists already, a job description should be prepared, setting out (briefly) the job title and what the job consists of. It is essential to understand what the job involves in order to identify individuals who should be able to perform it well. A job description should also set out what the pay scale is likely to be and how many days' holiday the jobholder would be entitled to. The job description also usually states who the successful applicant would report to and, in the case of a business with more than one location, it should also specify where successful applicant will be expected to work.

- **Person specification**. A person specification may also be prepared. This sets out the qualities and characteristics that the successful applicant will be expected to possess.

- **Advertising the job vacancy**. The job vacancy (or vacancies) must be brought to the attention of individuals who might be expected to apply. Advertising can be both within the organisation and externally. It should be appropriate for the type of job that is being advertised. Possible methods of advertising a job vacancy include:

  - The company's website (or internal IT system)

  - Advertising in an appropriate newspaper or magazine

  - Using the services of a recruitment agency

  - Government job centres

  - Careers guidance and assistance offices at universities and colleges

  - Headhunting agency, to advertise a vacancy in a senior management position

  - Personal contacts or previous knowledge of the individual (for example, performance record as an employee).

The selection process

The selection process begins when the HR team receive applications from individuals applying for the job. There are several ways in which individuals might be selected for a job:

- For unskilled jobs, an organisation might agree to appoint someone who is referred to them by a recruitment agency or a government job centre, after a brief interview with a manager or supervisor in the department where the individual will be working. The selection process would not be rigorous, but the organisation might take the view that if the individual proves unsuitable in the job, he or she can be dismissed and easily replaced.

- For other jobs, applicants may be required to submit a job application form or complete an online application. The selection process would then begin with vetting all the applications received and choosing a limited number of applicants for interview.

- A shortlist of applicants might then be interviewed, and might also be asked to take an aptitude test or psychometric test. Aptitude tests are usually related to the skills required by the job in question: they can include practical tests requiring the applicant to perform some part of the work for which they are applying. Psychometric tests are designed to give more information about the applicant's personality. They are often a written or online test asking a series of questions designed to assess the applicant's attitudes and decision-making ability.

- Interviews are a two-way process: the organisation wants to appoint the best person for the job, but the interviewees may need convincing that the job is something that they want.

The selection process ends when an individual is offered the job and accepts, and the terms of the appointment are set out in a formal **employment contract**.

Problems with selection methods

All of these methods are designed to give the business more information about each candidate and to assess who is the most suitable person for them to employ. However, none of these methods are perfect and it is still possible that when a new employee joins a business the appointment proves to have been a mistake. This can happen for a variety of reasons:

- The person performed well on the day of interview or test but has not been able to sustain a high level of performance once actually employed.

- The person appointed might find that the job is not as interesting or fulfilling as they thought it would be.

- Any tests administered might have failed to reveal other shortcomings in the person. For example, they might be good team members and physically capable of doing the job but they might be consistently late for work or frequently absent from work.

- If an unsuitable appointment is made this can prove very costly to the business. It will have to dismiss the employee and it must make sure that the way in which they are dismissed complies with the laws regarding employment.

Case study

Recruitment and selection methods

A major retail company is seeking to make some appointments to fill job vacancies within the organisation.

Which methods of recruitment and selection would you consider the most appropriate for filling a job vacancy for the following?

1 Stores assistant
2 Stores manager
3 Information technology (IT) manager.

Key term

Training: providing employees with work-related skills.

Staff training and development

Employees gain experience and acquire new skills by performing their job. In other words, individuals learn by doing the job. However, there are situations where individuals need training to help them improve their skills, or to acquire knowledge and skills more quickly than they otherwise would do.

The purpose and value of training is to develop the skills of employees so that they can contribute more effectively to the activities of the business. Training for employees is usually arranged by the human resource department.

- Training might be provided internally, by the organisation's own training managers, or externally, for example at a technical college or business school.
- Training (or education) might take place outside working hours, in the individual's free time. More often, training is provided during working hours.

Training might be "on the job" or "off the job".

On-the-job training often involves providing individuals with an experienced supervisor to show them how the job should be performed: what to do and how to deal with problems that may arise. Training therefore takes the form of passing on knowledge and experience on a one-to-one basis.

Another form of on-the-job training is job rotation. When an individual is recruited into a department of the company, such as the marketing department or the accounts department, he or she might be given a brief experience (perhaps three months or so) in each of a number of different teams within the department. This is intended to make the individual familiar, as quickly as possible, with the various different aspects of the department's work.

Off-the-job training is training provided away from the individual's job. It can take the form of:

- Short online programmes, lasting perhaps an hour or so: this form of training might be suitable to remind employees about health or safety measures at work
- "Classroom" courses, ranging in length from a half day up to one or two weeks
- Day release to attend a weekly course at a local college or business school, or a business seminar
- Block release, lasting several weeks or even months, to complete a course at a college, training school or business school.

To be effective in developing the skills and knowledge of employees, training should be planned and carefully targeted at the people who will benefit, and it should also be provided at a time that the employee is most likely to benefit. The chosen training method should be the one that is most likely to be effective in the circumstances – bringing the employee to the level of knowledge or skill that the training is intended to achieve. The value of training should take prominence over the mechanics of it.

Training needs can arise for a variety of reasons:

- When a person is appointed to work for a business they are often given induction training.
- Employees might also need specific task-related training if their work changes in some way, such as a new product being introduced. The production of the new product might require some new skills to be acquired due to new production processes being involved.
- There may be a legal requirement to provide training in some industries, such as health and safety training in manufacturing businesses or training in anti-money laundering procedures in banks.

- An employee could be underperforming and therefore may be judged to be in need of some additional training in order to be faster or more accurate in their work or perhaps both.

- When an employee is promoted, training is often needed to enable the promoted employees to make the change to a more responsible post. There may be aspects of the new post that they have not had to undertake in their previous work. For example, they might need some training in how to supervise people effectively if supervising employees had not been part of their work before the promotion.

- Some employees may need training to obtain a professional qualification, for example in accountancy or procurement and supply, so that they acquire the technical knowledge and skills to do their specialist jobs better.

Case study

Training new staff

A major global company has a policy of recruiting about 40 university graduates each year, with the intention that a proportion of these will eventually rise to senior management positions in the company during the course of their career. The HR department has the task of providing appropriate training for each year's intake of successful job applicants for these management trainee positions.

1 What training do you consider should be provided to these individuals, to bring them to a level of knowledge or skill where they can start to contribute value to the company as soon as possible?

Reducing the number of employees

Having discussed the recruitment of employees it is also important to consider times when a business might need to reduce the number of its employees. This might occur when a business introduces new machinery or new methods of working which causes a reduction in the number of employees required. Changes in methods of working can also result in more efficient working practices and cause some jobs to be no longer required.

It might be that a business relocates some of its operations to a different city or country, reducing the amount of work that is done in the original location and so requiring fewer employees there.

You might suppose that if an employer no longer needs some if its employees, it should be able to dismiss them. In most countries, however, when a business no longer needs some of its employees, it must make them redundant, and not simply dismiss them without compensation.

Redundancy

Redundancy occurs when the business no longer requires employees to do a particular job, or needs fewer employees to do the work. As a consequence, a number of employees lose their job. It is important to remember that it is the job that is no longer needed, not the person doing the job. It is often inevitable that when the requirement for a job no longer exists, the person doing that job will no longer be employed. However, many businesses will try to find alternative work for employees whose jobs have become redundant, and:

- Transfer them to a different job where vacancies exist, and
- If necessary, provide them with training to do this job.

In many countries, businesses are required to discuss possible redundancies with the appropriate trade union before making their plans known publicly. There are also legal requirements relating to making employees redundant. Employees who are made redundant are entitled to certain rights.

When employees are to be made redundant the process is usually handled by the HR department.

When a particular job is no longer available and the worker(s) doing that job are to be made redundant there are some additional issues to be considered:

- Make sure that the redundancies are lawful, for example, a job cannot be declared redundant and then the exact same job advertised. Any job advertised must be different in content than one that has been stated as being redundant.

- Make sure that all necessary procedures have been followed, for example appropriate discussion have taken place with trade unions and/or worker representatives

- Sometimes it is possible that the skills of an employee are no longer required in their current job but there might be employment opportunities elsewhere in the business. When employees are moved from a redundant post to one where their skills are still required this is known as redeployment.

- It can help the reputation of the business if they help those employees who are to be made redundant by helping them to find alternative work or by offering training for other posts within the business wherever possible.

- Appropriate redundancy payments must be made to those employees who lose their job. The law may specify the minimum amounts of redundancy pay.

- When a reduction in the number of employees is necessary, businesses must make sure that they keep the best workers. This means that a reduction of numbers must be accompanied by a careful analysis of who should go and who should stay. Many businesses operate a "last in, first out" policy but this might cause them to get rid of some of their best workers.

Get it right

Do not confuse redundancy with dismissal. Dismissal occurs when an individual has behaved in an unacceptable way, for example, fighting at work or acting in an aggressive or discriminatory way against work colleagues. Dismissals are of individuals. In contrast, redundancy usually applies to a group of employees, whose jobs (through no fault of their own) are disappearing.

Activities

1 Investigate the current legislation regarding redundancies in your country.

2 Find out what would justify instant dismissal from employment according to the current legislation in your country.

Case study

Jobs to go at Brevia plc

Brevia plc has announced that 10 per cent of its workforce will be made redundant when the current government contract for waste disposal comes to an end in April next year. The company currently employs 750 workers and is advertising 50 new posts in its new waste processing department. The new department will concentrate on recycling waste materials rather than disposing of waste into landfill sites as previously. The employees will need to have technical experience of recycling processes whereas the employees who will be made redundant are unskilled. Some of the employees who face the possibility of redundancy are claiming that this is unlawful because there are jobs available in the business.

1 Explain whether or not the redundancies are lawful.

2 Briefly explain if there are any actions, other than redundancy, that Brevia plc can take.

Organisational design

The efficiency and effectiveness of a workforce can depend on how jobs within the organisation are structured, and how authority, responsibility and accountability are distributed throughout the organisation. For example, who makes the decisions within a business, and who do individuals take their instructions from?

Organisation designs vary, and depending on the circumstances of the business, some designs are likely to be more suitable than others, in the sense that better decisions are made and employees perform their work more efficiently and effectively.

Several features of organisation design that affect the efficiency and effectiveness of an organisation and the people working within it are: span of control and levels of management hierarchy; delegation of authority for decision-making; and centralisation or decentralisation of decision-making.

The extent to which a business needs to have a formal structure can depend on the size of the business. An organisation structure shows everyone their place in the business and provides a framework for decision-making.

Key term

Organisational design: the framework of a business indicating the lines of authority and communication, and responsibilities for decision-making.

Span of control: the number of people that a manager, supervisor or team leader is directly responsible for.

Span of control

Within any organisation, some people are put in charge of others. The person in charge may be called a manager, a supervisor or a team leader, with responsibilities for decision-making in a particular area of the business operations.

The span of control refers to the number of people that a manager, a supervisor or a team leader is responsible for. For example, if a manager in an office has four supervisors reporting directly to him or her, the manager's span of control is four. And if each supervisor is responsible for ten workers, their span of control is ten each.

Example

Span of control can be illustrated in a simplified example as shown in Figure 4.3.1. Suppose that a department employs 144 workers. The figure shows how the organisation of the department will be structured if the span of control at each level of management or supervision is (a) 4 or 6 or (b) 12 (a wider span of control).

This simplified example illustrates that:

- In an organisation where managers or supervisors have a span of control, there is a hierarchical structure of authority or chain of command that goes down from senior management to employees at the bottom
- There are different levels of management or supervision within this hierarchical structure when the span of control is wider, the number of levels in the management hierarchy is less. In this example, when the span of control is 4 or 6 at each level in the hierarchy, there are three levels of management and supervision (with 29 managers and supervisors), but when the span of control is 12, there are just two levels of management and supervision (with 13 managers and supervisors).

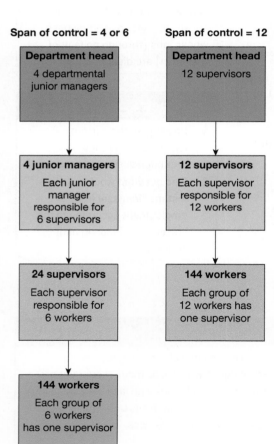

▲ Figure 4.3.1: Department organisation with span of control as narrow or wide

What is the most suitable span of control?

The most suitable span of control is one that enables the organisation to function in the most efficient and effective way. Managers or supervisors are responsible for getting their subordinates to do their work in the best way possible.

- When subordinates all perform routine tasks, a supervisor is probably able to manage a fairly large number of workers, and the span of control can therefore be quite wide.

- However, when a manager has subordinates whose work is more complex or varied, it may be difficult to manage a large number of them, and a narrower span of control is appropriate.

- When a manager has to spend a lot of time personally on complex tasks, there is less time for oversight of subordinates, and a narrow span of control is probably appropriate.

The efficiency of the span of control is also related to the number of levels in the organisation's management hierarchy.

▼ Table 4.3.3: Advantages and disadvantages of a narrow span of control

Advantages	Disadvantages
• Each manager will have fewer employees to be responsible for. • Close supervision of employees is possible. • Communication might be easier as there are fewer people for each manager or supervisor to contact.	• It is often associated with centralised decision-making, which means that employees are given very little opportunity to contribute to decisions. • Communication is often one way.

▼ Table 4.3.4: Advantages and disadvantages of a wide span of control

Advantages	Disadvantages
• It can allow employees to have some input into decisions made. This can help employees to feel more involved and therefore to derive more satisfaction from their work. • Fewer supervisors or managers are required, which can be a financial saving for the business.	• It can be difficult for supervisors and managers to supervise the larger number of employees in their span of control. Close supervision is unlikely to be possible. This can lead to errors going undetected. • Each supervisor/manager has a larger number of people to communicate with and this can be time-consuming.

Levels of hierarchy

In a large company there are different levels of management seniority, from the chief executive officer (CEO) at the top to the most junior managers and supervisors at the bottom.

- In a simple hierarchical structure, there may be a CEO and a number of functional or departmental managers; within each department there may be business sections, each with their section manager; and within each business section there maybe middle-ranking managers and below them junior managers.

- In many companies there is also a geographical or regional structure, with regional managers beneath the CEO and area managers beneath each regional manager.

The number of levels in the management hierarchy will depend on:

- the size and complexity of the organisation, and
- the spans of control within the management structure.

An organisation design with a large number of different management levels is known as a tall organisation, and an organisation design with a small number of different management levels is a flat organisation.

> **Key term**
>
> Hierarchy: in an organisation, a structure in which there are different levels of authority and seniority of management.

▼ **Table 4.3.5**: Advantages and disadvantages of a tall organisation structure (and narrow spans of control)

Advantages	Disadvantages
• Decision-making responsibilities are distributed between several levels and therefore usually have several management levels.	• Too many decision-makers can mean that the most senior managers lose some control of decisions made. This can lead to business objectives being more difficult to achieve. This can also result in bad decisions being made because the managers lower down the organisation might not have the overview of the business that the senior managers will have.
• Having many levels in a business can mean that employees see the range of opportunities that are possible for promotion. Small promotion steps are possible.	
• Having several levels of people making decisions can reduce the burden of decision-making on senior management.	• Tall structures tend to be very bureaucratic. Decisions and instructions need to be passed through many levels and this can be extremely time-consuming and can delay the receiving of information.
• There is potentially a narrower span of control for each manager or supervisor.	• As with any hierarchical structure there is a danger that there is a lack of contact, and therefore communication, between the various departments or divisions within the business. This can lead to duplication of effort or a lack of co-ordination between the different departments.

▼ **Table 4.3.6**: Advantages and disadvantages of a flat organisation structure (and wide spans of control)

Advantages	Disadvantages
• Fewer levels through which information and decisions need to be passed therefore making this less time-consuming. This can be an advantage to a business that exists in a highly competitive market when decisions might need to be made very quickly if a competitive advantage is not to be lost.	• There are fewer opportunities for promotion. This can be a demotivating factor because a promotion is likely to be a much bigger step in terms of authority and responsibility.
• There are a smaller number of managers and this is believed to reduce the feeling of "them and us" within an organisation.	• There is usually a much wider span of control. This can make it difficult for a manager to be able to communicate directly with their staff. This can be overcome with the use of frequent meetings but this is not always well-received by employees.
	• The absence of some layers of management can place a greater burden for decision-making on the remaining levels.

Progress questions

3 Explain the term "span of control".

4 Give one disadvantage of a tall organisational structure.

5 Why might it be difficult to manage a flat organisational structure?

Delegation

Authority within an organisation design refers to the decision-making powers of a manager or level of management. The chief executive officer of a company has the supreme authority for decision-making, but it is usually impractical, except in small organisations, for one person to exercise all authority personally.

Authority is therefore delegated down through the organisation structure. At each level in the management hierarchy, some authority is retained by the manager, but some authority is delegated to subordinates.

Delegation is essential in some organisations in order for them to function most effectively. When a task is delegated to an employee by a manager, the employee may be given authority to make decisions relating to the task, but he or she is accountable to the manager for what they do. Tasks and decision-making authority should only be delegated to an employee who is capable of completing the work to the desired standard.

> **Key term**
>
> Delegation: giving authority to make decisions and perform tasks to someone lower in the organisation hierarchy.

The difference between authority and responsibility

Although authority to make decisions and perform tasks can be passed down the hierarchy, the final responsibility for the successful execution of the work remains with the manager who delegates the work. It is the manager's responsibility to ensure that the employee has the required skills and experience to carry out the work. So whereas authority can be delegated, final responsibility cannot.

Issues of control and trust with delegation

Delegation requires an element of trust. Trust on the part of the manager that their employee will carry out the work as required. Trust on the part of the employee that the manager will not interfere once the work has been delegated.

When managers perform a particular task themselves they have complete control about how and when it is done and the standard to which it is done. They must accept that they will lose some control over the work if it is delegated to a subordinate. If a task is delegated but the manager is constantly checking up to see if the work is actually being done and that it is being done to the required standard, then the employee will sense a lack of trust and may no longer be willing to accept responsibility for the task. Constant checking by the manager is also wasting the time that could have been gained by delegating the task. However, if the manager does not keep checking, how do they know that the work is being done and is being completed to the required standard?

This is the dilemma faced by people who delegate some of their work to others. There is a relationship between the amount of control that a manager retains and the level of trust. A desire to maintain a high level of control by the manager indicates a lack of trust in the employee. High levels of trust in the employee would be demonstrated by a reduction in the level of control exerted over the employee.

▼ Table 4.3.7: Advantages and disadvantages of delegation

Advantages	Disadvantages
• Employees can acquire more confidence and skills through being given the authority to perform different tasks.	• Time might not be saved if the manager does not have sufficient trust in the employee and spends too much time checking that the work is being done correctly.
• Delegated tasks can make an employee feel that their manager respects and trusts them and their work.	• The manager might feel a loss of control over the task that has been delegated.
• Time is freed up for the managers to use perhaps on key strategic issues.	• Managers can feel threatened if the delegated task is performed better than if they had completed it themselves.
• It can allow managers to see which employees are perhaps ready for and capable of being promoted to a more responsible post.	• Problems of jealousy could occur if some employees feel that they should have been given the delegated task.
• Delegation can prepare employees for promotion by exposing them to some of the tasks that they would be expected to perform in a higher-level post.	• Delegation can cause tension among a group of employees if one of them is given the authority to oversee the completion of a group task. An employee can be put in charge of some co-workers for the purpose of a particular task. The roles within the group would necessarily change and this may cause relationship problems within the group perhaps causing a fall in efficiency.
• Tasks can be completed quicker and therefore the business can be more efficient.	
• It can be a strong motivator for employees.	• The employee chosen might not have the necessary skills and experience to be able to complete the task to the desired standard and therefore time and resources might have been wasted.

Delegation of authority and motivation

Delegation of authority can act as a motivator, and can lead to the employee developing a more positive attitude to their work and to the business. Delegation can be motivating for the following reasons:

- Giving authority and responsibility to an employee for a task that would normally have been done by their manager usually causes the employee to feel that their manager believes them to be capable of completing a wider range of more complex tasks than their current role entails

- Subordinates may begin to believe that if they do the task well they may justify promotion

- Delegated tasks can also provide an employee with a feeling of self-esteem and importance, contributing valuable work to the organisation

- The fact that an employee is given the authority to perform a delegated task can also lead to them gaining the esteem of their colleagues.

Activity

Low-cost airline companies such as EasyJet and Ryanair fly passengers between many different countries. Their popularity is due largely to the attractive prices they charge for flights.

Prepare two lists: one should be a list of the types of decision that will be made in these companies that are likely to be taken at a senior management level, and the other should be a list of decisions that you would expect to be taken at a lower level within the organisation.

Centralisation and decentralisation

Decentralisation is the delegating of decisions to lower levels in the organisation. Centralisation means that much of the decision-making is kept at the top of the organisation. In a centralised organisation design, only a limited amount of decision-making is therefore delegated down to lower levels of management (such as departmental heads, product managers or regional managers within the business).

Centralisation and decentralisation are matters of the degree to which authority is delegated. In a centralised organisation, some authority is delegated – if no authority is delegated, there would be no need for any managers below the top level. And in a decentralised organisation, some decision-making is retained by senior management at the top of the organisation.

Changing the degree of centralisation or decentralisation

The amount of centralisation or decentralisation of authority within a business should be such that decision-making by management is efficient and effective – that decisions do not take too long to reach, but that decisions are in the best interests of the organisation as a whole. For example:

- When an organisation is growing in size, or is expanding operations into new geographical regions, it may be necessary to increase the decentralisation decision-making to some extent, because senior management may no longer have the time to exercise as much control as in the past.

- A greater amount of decentralisation may be appropriate when management need to make decisions quickly. If "local managers" have the authority to make decisions, they do not need to spend time referring a problem to their senior manager for a decision.

- When an organisation operates in many different countries, it can be important to respond to the differing needs of customers in each country or region. Local managers should have better knowledge of local conditions and customer requirements. If they are given sufficient authority, they can respond accordingly.

- If an organisation is struggling, and may be in danger of financial collapse, senior management may take on more decision-making themselves, because tighter control is needed to prevent a collapse.

Key terms

Decentralisation: delegating decisions to people at lower levels in an organisation.

Centralisation: the process by which decisions are made within an organisation. When they are centralised they are made at the top level of the organisation.

▼ **Table 4.3.8:** Advantages and disadvantages of centralisation

Advantages	Disadvantages
• Decisions made will be consistently across all departments or divisions.	• Centralisation places a greater burden for decision-making on a few people at the centre of the business.
• A business image can be maintained due to the consistency of decisions.	• The best ideas might not always be enacted due to a possible limitation on the involvement of departmental and divisional managers. Some decisions made centrally might even be detrimental to the success of some products or regional decisions.
• Decisions should be made quicker due to the limited involvement of fewer senior managers.	
• All departments and divisions will be working toward the stated aims of the overall business; there is less opportunity for elements within the business to pursue their own aims, e.g. regional division that might want to develop a slightly different business image.	• Managers lower down the hierarchy are less likely to develop their decision-making skills. This could prove to be a problem if they are later promoted to a more senior decision-making role.

Exam-style questions

1 Explain one advantage of interviews as a method of selecting an individual for a job vacancy. (3 marks)

2 Explain the connection in an organisation design between span of control and the number of levels in the management hierarchy. (3 marks)

3 Companies have sometimes needed to abolish existing jobs due to advances in digital technology.

Explain one of the measures that a company might take to deal with employees who are losing their jobs in this way. (3 marks)

4 One of the functions of a Human Resource department is the recruitment and selection of individuals to fill job vacancies.

Analyse the reasons why it is important for a company to have effective recruitment and selection procedures. (9 marks)

5 The fast-food company McDonald's operates in many different countries around the world.

Analyse the benefits to a global fast-food company of a having a decentralised organisation. (9 marks)

4.4 Motivation and engagement

This section will develop your knowledge and understanding of:

→ The benefits of motivated and engaged employees

→ How to improve employee engagement and motivation

→ The use of financial methods and non-financial methods of motivation and engagement.

The benefits of motivated and engaged employees

Motivation at work is an enthusiasm and energy in individuals to do their job, and to work willingly as hard as they can. Motivation is associated with employee engagement: engaged employees are highly motivated.

Motivation comes from within the individual, but management may be able to take measures that motivate the people working for them.

Key term

Motivation: a desire to do something; to develop a drive to achieve a goal.

What are the benefits of motivated and engaged employees?

- Higher levels of productivity – motivated employees will work harder, and by working harder they may also be more productive.

- Better-quality products or services provided to customers – more attention will be paid to the way in which work is carried out, and the quality of the work.

- High levels of customer service – motivated employees will be trying to do the best job possible, and when this includes customer service this is likely to be of the highest standard possible. A motivated employee will recognise that a happy customer is likely to be a repeat customer and also that the reputation of the business rests not only on the goods produced but on the quality of aftercare that their customers receive.

- More loyalty from employees – this will demonstrate itself in lower absenteeism and lower labour turnover as employees feel that they want to give their best to the business. Employees are less likely to be absent unless they are genuinely unfit for work. Employees who are not motivated are likely to take time off when it is not absolutely necessary.

- Lower staff turnover – happy employees are less likely to look for work elsewhere. If they feel valued and trusted in their current job they might feel that their efforts will be rewarded and therefore they do not have any need to look for work elsewhere.

- Increased likelihood of achieving business objectives – when employees are working as hard as they can the business will have the best chance of achieving any stated objectives. Motivation in employees often means that they want to achieve something, and that they will make whatever effort is necessary to succeed.

In summary the benefits of a motivated workforce come from having more effective or efficient employees, so that the organisation is more successful in achieving its objectives. Management can take a variety of measures to improve employee motivation. Some measures may be more effective than others.

Motivation theories

There are a number of different theories about what motivates people at work. If management understand motivation and its causes, they might be able to develop policies for improving or maintaining the motivation of the workforce. You need to be familiar with the motivation theories of Taylor, Maslow, and Herzberg.

Taylor – Economic man

Taylor was a US engineer in the early twentieth century, who is considered be the founder of scientific management. Scientific management is concerned with applying scientific techniques of analysis and experimentation to improve the efficiency of work. Taylor was not interested in motivation: he believed that scientific methods were sufficient for achieving a highly efficient workforce.

Taylor's approach was to analyse the tasks that individuals perform at work, and:

- Break them down into smaller units of work
- Employ specialists to do each of these smaller units or tasks, selecting individuals with the characteristics or skills to perform the task well, and
- Increase efficiency through division of work and specialisation.

Taylor is considered the originator of "time and motion study" – finding from observation the quickest and most efficient way of getting jobs done. He is best known for experiments on productivity at a steel works, achieved by:

- Analysing the tasks involved in shovelling coal
- Experimenting with different types of shovel (for example, shovels of different sizes and with different handle lengths) and the amount of coal that should be shovelled in a single action, and
- Introducing work specialisation within the shovelling operations.

Scientific management has been strongly criticised because it results in dull, repetitive, and monotonous work. Tasks are reduced to such small units, such as tasks on a large production line in a factory, that they demoralise the workers who do the jobs. There is a risk that when employees are doing dull, repetitive work, their motivation and efficiency will be low.

Taylor also believed that people were motivated by money and that they should be paid according to the output that they produce. He argued that employees should be paid a fixed rate for each unit of output they produce – a piece work rate – and that people will work hard in order to receive the highest pay possible, in other words, that they are driven by the desire to earn money.

It is acknowledged that this approach to motivation is more likely to be successful when employees are striving to satisfy their most basic living needs such as the need for food and shelter. An employee who is struggling to feed and clothe their family is more likely to be driven by the need for money than to worry about whether they actually enjoy the work they are doing.

Maslow – Hierarchy of needs

In the 1950s, Maslow developed a theory of the motivation of individuals at work. He argued that individuals have five "in-built needs", and his theory was concerned with the power of each of these needs to motivate individuals in their work.

The five needs can be arranged in a hierarchy of levels. Maslow suggested that an individual's needs start at the lowest of the five levels. A need at a lower level is dominant until it has been fully satisfied. When the need at one level has been satisfied – and not until then – the need at the next level becomes dominant.

- A need that has not yet been satisfied motivates the individual.
- A need that has been satisfied no longer motivates the individual.
- The highest of the five levels of need – self-actualisation – can never be fully satisfied.

The hierarchy of needs (the five levels of need) is usually drawn as a pyramid.

Basic (physical) needs

These are the desire to be able to access food, clothes and shelter; the most basic of human needs. Maslow believed that these needs would be the driving force behind the actions of any person who feared that they might not be able to secure these for themselves. Such needs can be met by having the money to buy what is needed, in other words, being paid for work done enables the purchase of essential food and other products. Employees might not only be aiming to satisfy their own basic needs but they might also need to provide for a family.

Get it right

Some similarities can be seen in the ideas of some of the theorists and, in some questions, these can provide the basis for an analysis of motivation theory in a given situation.

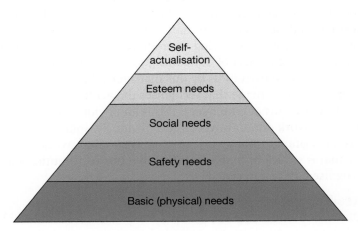

▲ Figure 4.4.1: Maslow's hierarchy of needs

Maslow believed that the other needs in the pyramid were irrelevant to a person who was struggling to satisfy these essential physical requirements. Only when they have ensured that they will not go hungry or lack suitable clothing or shelter will they look to the next level.

Safety needs

Once a person has made sure that their basic needs have been satisfied they will look for some security that they will be able to meet those needs in the future. This can be satisfied by having a contract to work; this provides job security at least in the short term. A person will be unlikely to be motivated by anything other than meeting their basic physical needs if they fear that they will not be able to continue to meet them in the future. If an employee feels that their job is threatened they will not be concerned with anything higher on Maslow's pyramid of needs until they feel confident that they will continue to receive the means to provide for themselves and/or their family.

Social needs

While not true of all people, it is accepted that most people enjoy contact with others whether at work or in their social lives. A large part of our lives is spent at work and so it is not unreasonable to feel that people benefit from some level of social interaction in their workplace.

Social groups can be formed due to people being required to work in teams, or as a result of social activities undertaken by their employers. Many businesses arrange social activities outside of normal working hours which can enable people to have contact with employees from different parts of the business. Alternatively it allows those who work together to get to know each other better beyond their working relationship. It is hoped that meeting the social needs of employees will lead to them performing better when at work.

Esteem needs

Esteem needs recognise that people need the approval and respect of others. These can be met in the workplace by employees being given positive feedback from their managers. Esteem needs can also be satisfied by co-workers showing their appreciation for the work of their colleagues. The respect of our colleagues can be just as important to us as any respect shown to us by our managers. Some businesses work with an award scheme that recognises the achievement of individuals or teams of employees; this is an obvious form of recognition for work done. However, less obviously, sometimes it might just be a simple "thank you" or "that is excellent work" from someone that is sufficient to make us feel that our contribution has been recognised and appreciated.

Self-actualisation

Self-actualisation means the opportunity for an individual to be able to fulfil their own potential. Within a workplace this means that people need to be able to develop their skills and therefore will need to be able to progress beyond their current level of skill and responsibility. This can be achieved by having training and staff development opportunities available and also by internal promotion.

Progress questions

1 Explain one weakness in Taylor's theory.
2 Explain one similarity between the theories of Taylor and Maslow.
3 Explain why social needs might be important in the workplace.

How can a business meet these needs?

▼ Table 4.4.1: Maslow's needs and how business can respond

Need	Business action
Basic (physical) needs	The payment of a wage or salary that allows employees to buy the essentials for life.
Safety needs	Job security through a contract of employment; follow health and safety guidelines for a safe work environment.
Social needs	Encourage team work, social activities and communication between all levels of employees.
Esteem needs	Give recognition for good work. Show appreciation, e.g. "employee of the month". Job titles give some employees status and meet this need. Promote people or give added responsibility.
Self-actualisation	Meet the need for a feeling of achievement perhaps through assigning more difficult and challenging tasks. Allow for further training and progression within the business.

Possible weaknesses of Maslow's theory

- It is very difficult for a manager to know for sure which level on the hierarchy each employee is on.
- Each employee is likely to be at a different level of the pyramid, which makes motivating them as a group very difficult, if not impossible, as each person will have different needs.
- It is also possible for a person not to desire the approval of others and therefore, once their "safety needs" have been met, self-actualisation might be their next goal.
- The idea that individuals are motivated by just one need at one level might simply be wrong.
- Maslow did not demonstrate that there is any direct connection between the motivation for self-actualisation needs and better performance at work. In other words, even if individuals are motivated by a need for self-esteem, does this necessarily mean that their work performance will improve significantly?

Case study

Fashion company

A company designs and manufactures fashion clothing, which it markets and sells worldwide under a well-known brand name. Its head office is in Europe, where the design work takes place, and it succeeds in attracting top-quality individuals to work for it. It also has factories that manufacture the fashion clothing: these are located in Bangladesh and Vietnam. The company's management

believe that the success of the company depends to a considerable extent on having a well-motivated workforce.

1 In what ways do you think that the ideas of Maslow might help the company's senior management to devise ways of motivating their workforce?

How can a manager know which level an employee is currently on? Perhaps at regular appraisal meetings the needs and wants of a member of staff could be discussed.

Herzberg – Two-factor theory

In the 1950s, Herzberg carried out some research into the motivation of individuals at work by interviewing 200 engineers and accountants, and developed a two-factor theory of motivation.

He identified two categories of factors or aspects of a job: those causing dissatisfaction with work and those causing satisfaction. He called these:

- **Hygiene factors** (the factors causing dissatisfaction) and
- **Motivator factors** (the factors causing satisfaction).

Case study

Bags By Design

▲ **Figure 4.4.2:** Helene and Lara still design the bags made in their factory

Helene and Lara had been designing and making fashion bags as a hobby for many years before starting their business Bags By Design. Over the last five years they have opened their own factory and now employ 30 people who make the bags that Helene and Lara still design. The bags are made using outer layers of cotton which are sewn together with a fibrous wadding in between the two outer layers. The fibrous wadding leads to lots of small particles in the air in the workshop and for this reason an air filtration system was installed to extract the wadding

particles from the air in the workroom. The extractor also cooled the sewing rooms which could be extremely hot due to all of the machines and the strong lights that were essential for the detailed work being done.

Helene and Lara know each of their employees by name and talk to each of them regularly in order to get feedback on the bag designs and on the fabrics that are being used. The employees feel as though they are part of the business and that their views matter to Helene and Lara. Recently the air filtering system broke down and it was ten days before the necessary parts to repair it could be delivered. The situation was made worse due to the breakdown occurring in August when the sewing rooms are usually at their hottest. During those ten days Bags By Design had a very big order to complete that needed everyone to produce maximum output to meet the delivery date. The order was completed on time despite the fact that the working conditions were worsened by the lack of the air filtration system.

1 Explain how the theories of Maslow and Herzberg related to the employees of Bags By Design when completing the large order.

▼ Table 4.4.2: Significant hygiene and motivator factors

Factors causing dissatisfaction	Factors causing satisfaction
Hygiene factors	**Motivator factors**
Company policy	Achievement
Supervision	Recognition
Relationship with the boss	The work itself
Working conditions	Responsibility
Salary or wages	Advancement
Relationship with colleagues	Growth

It might be supposed that factors causing dissatisfaction and factors causing satisfaction are opposites of each other, but Herzberg argued differently. He argued that:

- The opposite of dissatisfaction is not satisfaction: it is "not being dissatisfied"
- The opposite of satisfaction is not dissatisfaction: it is "not being satisfied".

The conclusion from Herzberg's analysis was that management need to deal with two different categories of factors affecting the motivation of employees.

- Hygiene factors must be given proper attention, so that employees are not dissatisfied. For example, employees need to feel that they are being paid well enough in order to prevent them from being dissatisfied, but paying them a good basic salary only prevents dissatisfaction, it does not create satisfaction.
- In order to motivate individuals, the motivator factors need to be satisfied. This means providing work that makes individuals feel a sense of achievement and recognition. According to Herzberg, motivation is achieved through **job enrichment** – making the work itself more interesting and fulfilling.

▼ Table 4.4.3: How businesses can satisfy hygiene factors and motivators

Hygiene factors	
	• Pay an appropriate wage/salary; what is an "appropriate" amount will vary from one person to another.
	• Make sure that working conditions are as good as possible; clean and at a suitable temperature. This might include providing canteen facilities or rest rooms.
	• Company rules should be reasonable and not too rigid.
	• Team work can be used to improve relationships between employees; two-way communication can improve the relationship between employees and their managers.
	• Employees who are less closely supervised are likely to feel less threatened and perhaps feel more relaxed at work.

continued overleaf ⟶

continued from previous page ⟶

Motivators	• Give positive feedback to employees.
	• Involve employees in decision-making.
	• Use delegation, which allows employees to enjoy more responsibility and to feel valued and trusted.
	• Ensure that the work is stimulating and rewarding. This can be achieved by allowing employees to work on complete units of work giving them a sense of achievement.
	• This might also mean varying the work (job rotation) or broadening the scope of the work (job enlargement and job enrichment).
	• Rewarding good performance. Perhaps by using internal rather than external promotion.

Progress question

6   Explain the difference between Herzberg's motivators and hygiene factors.

Case study

Alhambra Ltd

Alhambra Ltd produces components for cars. The employees work in teams. Recently there has been a higher than normal rate of defective components and also Ramone, the production manager, has noticed that the level of absenteeism is higher than normal. When he has questioned the employees they have said that their workplace has been too hot since the old air-conditioning unit was replaced. Ramone also recently introduced shift working for the first time in the history of Alhambra Ltd.

Ramone is puzzled by these changes because, after the introduction of quality circles, he believed that they would be more highly motivated due to having met their social needs.

1   Use the theory of Herzberg to explain why the level of defects and absenteeism might have increased.

Financial and non-financial methods of motivating employees

Ideas and theories of motivation have developed further since Taylor, Maslow and Herzberg. It is recognised that there are several ways in which employees can be motivated to work harder but not all employees will be motivated in the same way. For some people a financial reward is all they desire, but others seek recognition, appreciation and possible promotion.

There are many actions or incentives that the managers of a business might use in order to motivate employees that fall under the general headings of financial rewards and non-financial rewards.

Financial rewards

It is widely recognised that employees might be motivated by pay, although the way in which their pay (and other financial rewards, such as bonuses) is structured can be important. There are several methods of paying employees.

Key terms

Financial rewards: monetary incentives given to employees, for example, bonus payments.

Non-financial rewards: incentives given to employees other than those with a monetary value, for example, extra holidays, employee of the month recognition.

Piece rate

Piece rate payments made per unit or batch of units produced. This should ensure that employees produce as much output as possible but it does not necessarily mean that quality standards will be maintained. The focus will be on quantity rather than quality.

Commission

A **commission** is money paid according to the level of sales achieved. This method will inspire employees to achieve the highest possible level of sales. The danger with this is that the pursuit of sales might lead to the priority being to make sure that the sale takes place rather than to ensure that the product or service is the most appropriate one for the customer. While in the short term sales might increase, in the longer term customers might feel that their needs had not been properly considered. The salesperson might have wanted to make the sale so much that they did not fully consider whether the product was the best option for the customer. In such circumstances the customer is less likely to buy from that business in the future.

Salary schemes

A salary is an agreed amount paid monthly. This form of payment gives employees some level of security regarding the amount they will earn each month. (A fixed wage rate is similar to a **salary scheme**, except that wages are paid weekly and salary is paid monthly.)

Performance-related pay

Performance-related pay is a bonus paid for meeting or exceeding targets. However, targets that are set too high are unlikely to motivate; indeed they might have the opposite effect. In order for bonus payments to be made, the targets need to be measurable and the bonus must be seen to be fair. If employees are not motivated by money this form of incentive is unlikely to be successful.

Are financial rewards an effective motivator?

It is generally agreed that individuals need to be kept satisfied about their basic pay, in order to avoid feelings of dissatisfaction or inequality and unfairness. Dissatisfaction about pay will affect the attitudes and behaviour of individuals in their work. So pay can be described, in Herzberg's terms, as a hygiene factor.

It is not certain, however, whether offering performance-related pay incentives will increase the motivation of employees. Much will depend on whether the nature and the size of the incentive are sufficient. For example, two colleagues working together might each be paid an end-of-year bonus, one $10,000 and the other $25,000. The employee receiving just $10,000 might be angered at receiving less than the colleague, because of its comparative amount.

In other situations, employees may feel that although there is a performance-related pay scheme is in place, the employer is mean and does not pay bonuses that are high enough.

So if senior management want to motivate employees through performance-related pay, the scheme must be well-designed and seen by employees as fair.

Key terms

Piece rate payments: payments of a fixed amount per unit of work (per piece) produced.

Commission: payment made according to the number of sales achieved.

Salary scheme: method of payment in which individuals are paid a fixed annual amount, divided into 12 monthly payments.

Performance-related pay: payment made based on targets being met or exceeded.

Non-financial rewards
Team working

Team working, where groups of employees work together towards a shared goal, can be rewarding for employees as they are given the responsibility to produce a certain product. It is hoped that this will draw the employees together to pursue a common goal: the production of more products of a high quality. When this method is used it is not unusual for an element of competition to exist between different groups. Each group, or cell, then tries to outperform the others and to produce the highest number of products and of the highest quality. This group cohesion also meets some of the social needs as identified by Maslow because there will be constant interaction between the members of each cell. Other motivational needs are also frequently met by the use of team work including the desire to be trusted and to be given responsibility as such teams are also often expected to suggest ways in which their work pattern or method could be improved. This shows that their knowledge and abilities are being recognised.

Status rewards or recognition of achievement or effort

Some businesses achieve this by naming an "employee of the month" although the means by which such an employee is selected should be seen to be fair and unbiased. If any element of unfairness is suspected then this can demotivate the employees who are not selected. Giving an employee a recognised status in a business can be a strong motivator. This can be achieved by giving extra responsibility to an employee that to some extent raises their status in the eyes of other employees.

Promotion opportunities

Achievement can also be rewarded by giving a promotion to those who meet, and perhaps exceed, expectations in their performance. Sometimes only a small promotion is needed to give an employee the feeling that their efforts have been recognised and appreciated. One drawback to promotion is that there are a limited number of promoted posts available in any business. The belief that promotion is a possibility for those who perform well can be a strong motivator for some employees.

Promotion may be considered a financial reward as well as a non-financial reward, because individuals are usually paid more when they are promoted.

Job design

Job design involves deciding which tasks are involved in a particular role or job within a business. Jobs may be designed, or redesigned (amended) to make them more challenging and interesting for the employee. There are times when the job itself is the cause of dissatisfaction. It might be that the work is not challenging enough to motivate people or that the actual tasks are very monotonous and therefore the employee becomes bored. This can be costly to a business because a bored employee is more likely to lose concentration and to make mistakes. Jobs can be redesigned using job enlargement (giving the job holder more responsibilities and more things to do) or job

---

Key term

Job design: structuring jobs by deciding the tasks and responsibilities that should go with each job.

enrichment (giving the job holder more interesting things to do). Quality circles can also be used to make employees feel as though their efforts are appreciated and valued. Quality circles can consist of employees from all levels within the organisation who will meet to discuss problems and to suggest ways in which the problems can be resolved.

Empowerment

Many businesses now use empowerment as a means of motivating employees. This gives employees a feeling of importance and of being valued and trusted by their managers. This is a form of delegation, and as such it helps to relieve managers of the burden of some day-to-day decisions thereby giving them time to devote to more important matters.

Employee consultation

Employees often want to be recognised as having a good understanding of the business that they work in and also of the tasks that they are required to perform. Employee consultation recognises that employees are likely to have some worthwhile ideas to contribute to the business and that, in some instances, they might have a better solution to a problem than their managers. For example, the employees actually doing a job might be the ones who are most able to suggest how improvements could be made to how the work is done. They might be able to suggest a different way of working that could improve efficiency and possibly reduce costs for the business. By involving employees in this way they feel valued and appreciated and are likely to work harder for the business.

Key terms

Empowerment: the giving of power to employees so that they can make some of the decisions relating to their area of business activity.

Employee consultation: the involvement of employees in some business decisions.

Get it right

When answering a question on motivation remember that you must use the relevant motivation theories to explain "how" or "why" something might have happened or could be resolved. It is not sufficient to just describe the theories.

Get it right

If there is a context given in a question, for example, manufacturing or retail, make sure that you give examples in your answer that are relevant to that particular situation. Also take note if the question asks you to discuss "how" or "why" as each word requires a different approach.

Case study

P & A Textiles

Patrice and Adriana have run their T-shirt manufacturing business successfully for many years. However, over the past few months they have noticed an increase in absenteeism and also a rise in the number of employees leaving to take up work elsewhere. They are worried that this might be because of the growth that the business has experienced in the past three years. Three years ago they employed ten people and today they employ 45 people. Each employee makes complete T-shirts and they are all paid the same hourly rate. As the business has grown, Patrice and Adriana have relied on the more experienced employees to make sure that the newer members of staff are working to the required standard. They are becoming very worried because in the past three weeks four of their most experienced employees said that they want to leave as they have been offered work as supervisors in another local clothes manufacturing business. Over the last three or four months they have also noticed an increase in the number of faulty products being produced, which is costing them a lot of money due to the wasted time and materials. They have also noticed that productivity levels have begun to fall.

1 Explain two possible causes for the increase in absenteeism and labour turnover.

2 Explain two ways in which Patrice and Adriana might motivate their workforce.

3 To what extent might Patrice and Adriana benefit from treating their long-serving employees differently from those who have recently joined the business?

Exam-style questions

1   The management of a business may take measures to improve the motivation of employees.

Explain one non-financial method of motivation that might be used.   (3 marks)

2   Miguel owns and runs a small building company. He has plans to grow the business, but to do this he needs to expand the geographical area covered by the company's operations. He thinks that to win the support of his team of workers, and motivate them to support his expansion plans, he will need to offer them higher pay.

Is Miguel correct in thinking that higher pay will motivate his employees?

Assess the arguments for and against and make a judgement.   (12 marks)

3   Tamara owns and runs an internet dating agency. The business continues to grow successfully, but Tamara's second-in-command, Natasha, has now told her that she wants to resign from her job, which is no longer interesting or challenging.

Tamara wants to persuade Natasha to stay, and thinks that this will be possible by offering to redesign Natasha's job.

Is Tamara correct in thinking that job redesign will persuade Natasha to remain her company?

Assess the arguments for and against and make a judgement.   (12 marks)

This section will develop your knowledge and understanding of:

→ The value of employee involvement

→ The value of employee communication and good employer-employee relations.

▲ **Figure 4.5.1:** Communication is important in business

The value of good employer-employee communications and relations

Good communications between an employer and its employees are likely to result in good relations existing between them; but what do we mean by "employer" and what do we mean by "good communications"?

- Employees are likely to consider their "employer" as any person or group (for example, a board of directors or a management committee) that represents the interests of the business and its owners. This includes management at the most senior level, but on a day-to-day basis employees may consider any manager more senior than themselves as a representative of the employer.

- Good communications can be described as the open and transparent communication of information and ideas. The communications may be one-way, from management to employees, with management keeping employees informed about their plans and intentions and about events and developments within the business. Good communications may also involve a free two-way exchange of ideas and opinions, from management to employees and from employees to management, in which employees are treated with respect and their views and opinions taken seriously.

- It might be argued that good communications between management and subordinates also includes involvement by subordinates in decision-making within the business, but employee involvement is not a necessary pre-condition for good communications and relations.

The effects of good employer-employee communications can be any of the following:

- Employees should have a better understanding of what is expected from them.

- Employees (or their representatives) can contribute ideas and contribute to decision-making within the business.

- Employees can express concerns they may have about their jobs and working conditions, for management to respond.

- Two-way communications make it easier for each "side" – management and employees – to understand the position of the other: this makes it easier to discuss problems and respect each other's opinions.

- There are likely to be fewer disputes at work, and less strike action among employees who belong to a trade union: potential causes of conflict can be discussed and resolved in a constructive way.

- Labour turnover is likely to be lower than it otherwise would be, which means that the organisation should be more successful in retaining the skills and talents of its workforce.

Taking all these points together, good communications and relations should result in a business that functions better and more successfully.

Employee involvement in decision-making

Good relations between an employer and employees can be improved by involving employees in decision-making in the business. The nature of employee involvement can vary:

- Employees may be encouraged by managers and team leaders to contribute ideas and suggestions about what to do in their area of business activity. Involvement may take the form of team or group discussions, with the manager then making a decision on the basis of the ideas and suggestions that have been discussed.

- Involvement by employees might involve the input of technical know-how from a subordinate when the manager does not have the same level of technical knowledge. This can occur for example, in businesses making extensive use of digital technology, such as artificial intelligence.

- Representatives of employees may be involved in discussions with the employer about working conditions and rates of pay.

- In some organisations, representatives of employees may be involved in decision-making at a senior level, on matters of company policy and business strategy.

Methods of communication between employer and employees

The methods used for communication between employer and employees will depend on the group of employees. Employees may be relatively unskilled workers or technical specialists, and different methods of communication may be used for employees in different jobs and at different levels in the organisation hierarchy or team structure.

Methods of employee involvement include:

- Consultation
- Trade unions
- Worker directors.

Consultation
Meetings

These might take place on a company-wide regular basis, for example, monthly or quarterly staff meetings. The meetings might be used to update employees on whether the business is on target to meet its objectives or to explain any changes that will need to be made if targets are to be met. The employees might be asked for suggestions that might help the business to get back on target.

The meetings might be used to put forward ideas to the workforce and then to ask for feedback or allow for questions to be asked. This type of consultation allows for immediate feedback and also ensures that all of the employees receive the same information.

Questionnaires/newsletters

Some businesses circulate regular updates and news to their employees. Employees can be informed of any changes the business has had or of any successes the business has enjoyed, for example, securing a large order from a valued client or a new client.

Employees can be encouraged to contribute to the newsletter which encourages even more communication. In this way, the employees also feel part of the communication and can feel informed.

Questionnaires can be used by businesses to assess the feelings of their employees about issues facing the business.

Questions can be asked about the impact of any changes made to the working process or to the style of management.

Consultation can also take place during the appraisal process which is another opportunity for employees to give feedback to their line manager.

Worker directors

Worker directors are employees elected by their fellow workers to serve on the board of directors of their company. This practice has not been adopted in many countries but it is particularly popular in Germany, where there are two types of board: a management board that makes most of the business decisions about planning and strategy, and a supervisory board of directors which has general oversight of the business and its management. Directors on the supervisory board are not involved in the day-to-day management of the business – they are "non-executive". In Germany it is usual for as many as one third of the supervisory board of directors to be worker directors and as many as one half in some cases, but there are no workers' representatives on the management board.

There have been suggestions in the UK, however, that there should be legislation requiring large companies to appoint worker directors to the company's board.

▼ Table 4.3.1 : The advantages and disadvantages of having worker directors

Advantages	Disadvantages
By creating worker directors, it is hoped that employees will feel satisfied that their views are being represented at board meetings. However, there is no guarantee that the views of the employee directors will change the direction of any decisions made by the board. The extent of their ability to influence decisions will depend on the proportion of members on the board of directors who are worker directors.	There is also a possibility that once a worker has been elected to be a worker director they will begin to agree with the other board of directors point of view and might no longer represent their fellow workers as they had been expected to do.

continued overleaf ⟶

continued from previous page ➜

Advantages	Disadvantages
This format of governance does give a voice to the employees who have direct access to the board of directors and should be able to put forward any ideas or grievances from their fellow workers.	There is also the possibility that it would be difficult to discuss some sensitive matters with representatives of employees present. For example, if the business was finding itself in financial difficulty the senior managers might want to try to find a solution to the problem without worrying the employees. If they have the system of worker directors, then the information would be available to all.
	An added issue is that in some cases, it has been felt that some decisions have been made "behind closed doors" with the worker directors excluded. This, of course, should not happen.

Trade unions

Employees may join a trade union, which then arranges with employers that it should negotiate pay and working conditions with the employer, on behalf of all its members who work for the employer. This is known as "collective bargaining". A trade union works on behalf of its members to ensure that the rights of employees are satisfied while in employment. Trade union representatives will meet with representatives of any business to discuss issues related to trade union members employed by that business. These can be issues such as employment legislation that is not being followed as fully as it should be. For example, if a business is persistently asking its employees to exceed the maximum enforceable number of hours work per week, then the trade union might ask to discuss the matter with the business. Such discussions might take place with a representative from the HR department.

This relationship can be beneficial to both parties. By meeting with someone from the HR department a trade union representative can make the business aware that some departments are not working within the law. The HR department can then take action to ensure that all departments follow all employment laws and therefore can remove any cause of dissatisfaction among the employees.

If employees feel that they are not being treated fairly they are less likely to perform to the highest standards. However, if the issue can be resolved by meetings between HR and the trade union, their attitude towards their work may be improved, resulting in higher levels of productivity for the business.

The benefits to employers of trade union involvement in the workplace

- A business can benefit from the existence of trade unions by knowing that there is an external body that can intervene if it experiences certain problems with its employees. For example, if a group of employees decide that they will refuse to work until better canteen facilities are provided the business can ask a trade union to

> ### Key term
>
> **Collective bargaining:** negotiating by a trade union with employers on behalf of all the employees who are trade union members.

intervene. It can ask the trade union to explain to the employees that their actions are not lawful and that they must return to work.

- In the same way that a trade union can point out to a business that it is acting unlawfully, a trade union will also intervene to ensure that its members respect the employment laws, thus also aiding the employers.
- Employers can discuss issues with a representative from a trade union who will speak on behalf of the workforce rather than having to meet and discuss the same issue with numerous employees.

The benefits to employees of trade union involvement

- Employees have someone who can negotiate with employers on their behalf. Representatives from the trade unions will be more experienced in negotiating than the average individual employee.
- Trade unions will enjoy more power in negotiations than an individual employee would. They might collectively represent many hundreds or even thousands of employees and have the potential to cause major disruption to a business if they encourage strike action.
- Employees will have legal representation available to them if they are in dispute with the management/owners of a business.
- The trade union will provide them with up-to-date information about employment legislation that applies in their country.

Progress questions

1 What is meant by the term "collective bargaining"?
2 Explain two advantages to employees of their employer recognising a trade union.
3 Explain two benefits to a business of recognising a trade union.

The value of employee involvement

Many successful businesses use employee involvement in order to create better channels of communication and by doing so also improve employer-employee relations. Some benefits include:

- **Motivation and productivity**. Employees who feel that they have good relationship with their line managers are likely to feel more motivated, as a result of which they are likely to be more productive. The feeling that managers appreciate them can meet their need for recognition and the need to feel respected. Any increase in motivation and/or productivity can result in a reduction in costs and an increase in the competitiveness of the business.
- **Meeting business objectives**. Good communication can ensure that all employees are working towards the same objectives and that they all understand what they are working towards. This is also a result of having employees who are fully engaged with the business they work in.
- **Less resistance to change**. The increased communication can mean that employees have had some input to any changes that are to be made. If they have not been involved in any discussion they

Get it right

Remember when writing about trade unions that they also work with business owners and management; they are not always a negative force in a business.

Activities

1 Research any trade unions that operate in your country.
2 Make brief notes on what industry is represented by the trade union and, if possible, identify some of the roles performed by the trade union. There might have been some media reports of trade union action taken against a business or industry that can help you with your research.

will, at least, have been made aware of impending changes. This can make any resistance less likely and therefore changes can be implemented more smoothly.

Possible problems with employee involvement in decision-making

There can be some problems with employee involvement in decision-making within a business.

- The extra time taken by meetings for passing on information or for consultation.
- Employees might begin to believe that they should be informed or consulted about everything. There are some issues that would not be discussed with employees, for example, discussions about possibly relocating the business to another region, or when considering redundancies. In the early stages of considering such issues the senior managers might not want employees to know what they are discussing.
- It is not always appropriate to consult with employees, for example if a quick decision has to be made.
- In some circumstances and for some types of decision, employees may not have the knowledge or understanding of the business to contribute constructively.

Influences on the extent and methods of employee involvement in decision-making

The level of employee involvement can vary greatly between businesses and between different industries as can the methods used. Not all methods of employee involvement are appropriate in all business situations. The level and method of employee involvement can depend on:

- The leadership style adopted by senior managers. For example, managers who adopt a democratic style of leadership are likely to involve their employees in decision-making. Whereas, those managers who adopt an autocratic leadership style will keep decision-making at the centre of the organisation and will not involve their employees.
- The skill level of the employees. Highly skilled and educated employees are more likely to be able to make valuable contributions to business decisions and are more likely to be involved than those unskilled employees. For example, if a manager employs a laissez-faire style of leadership this is usually because the employees are highly skilled and can be relied upon to make their own decisions about how a task should be completed.
- The type of work being done. In a business where the work is highly automated, there might be fewer opportunities for employees to give feedback or to be involved in decision-making. In a business with little automation, the employees might be able to contribute ideas about how the work can be done more efficiently. However, where a high level of capital equipment is used, the opportunities to put forward suggestions for improved methods might be very limited.

- The sensitivity of the decision to be made. It is not appropriate for employees to be involved in discussion about whether or not workers will need to be made redundant. This type of subject would be discussed only by the senior managers in the initial stages. If employees were involved this could cause a lot of uncertainty and insecurity which could cause some employees to look for work elsewhere. This could result in some of the best workers leaving. Sometimes redundancies are a possibility but then alternatives are found that do not require any jobs to be made redundant. If this had been discussed openly with employees, in the early stages, they might have been concerned unnecessarily.

Progress questions

4   Explain two influences on the type of employee involvement that might be used.

Managing and improving employer-employee communications and relations

Employer-employee relations can be greatly strengthened by good communications which can be achieved largely through worker involvement. Such relationships can also be improved by managers taking an interest in the welfare of their employees.

Methods already discussed, such as worker directors and works councils, may be used as a way of allowing both sides to put forward and exchange their views. In some cases, this can lead to both managers and employees learning to understand the issues faced by others in a business.

The effectiveness of communications can depend on the leadership style within the business. Not all leaders think it is necessary to communicate with employees and that they should just follow orders. However, involving workers in some discussions and asking for feedback on ideas has proved beneficial to many businesses.

The HR department can play a big part in improving relations within the business with a key role being that of maintaining staff morale and welfare. This is yet another way of making sure that employees feel that they are important and that business thinks they are important.

Maintaining staff morale and welfare

The HR department will often deal with issues that can directly affect the morale of the employees. It is important that employees feel positive about the business that they work in. Any negative feelings can result in lower-quality work and an increase in absenteeism and labour turnover and a lack of punctuality, all of which can prove costly to a business. The welfare of employees is also important because any employee who is experiencing problems will not be able to fully apply themselves to their work. For example, an employee who has been told that they must move from their rented house at the end of the month will be very worried if they cannot easily find somewhere

Activities

1 Find out if your school has diversity and equality guidelines.
2 Use the internet or other methods to find out if a large business in your country has such policies.

else to live. A fall in the level of production can sometimes be caused by factors outside of the business environment. It is in the business's interests to help the employee to resolve such issues and thus help them to be able to concentrate when at work rather than worrying about issues such as housing.

Progress questions

5 Explain three ways in which a business can work to improve staff morale and welfare.
6 Explain two reasons why a business should want to improve staff morale and welfare.

Exam-style questions

1 In some companies, trade unions represent the interests of a group of workers in communications with their employer.

   Explain one of the advantages for a company of having workers represented by a trade union. (3 marks)

2 It has been suggested by some business analysts that large companies should be required by law to appoint a number of worker directors to the board of directors.

   Analyse the benefits to a large company of having worker directors on their board. (9 marks)

3 There is some disagreement among senior managers in a large international company about the extent to which employees should be involved in decision-making within the business. Some senior managers believe that by encouraging and allowing greater employee involvement, decision-making within the company, and business performance, will improve.

   Are these managers correct in their belief that greater employee involvement will improve business performance?

   Assess the arguments for and against and make a judgement. (12 marks)

Managing operations, human resources and finance

5 Finance

This section will develop your knowledge and understanding of:

→ The importance of managing finances
→ Financial objectives
→ External and internal influences on financial objectives.

The importance of managing finances

How financial decisions improve the competitiveness of a business

Competition between businesses is not always on price; sometimes they complete on quality, design, delivery or customer service. However, the price charged to customers is a key issue in remaining competitive; that is to maintain or gain an advantage over rival businesses.

Commercial businesses have an objective of making a profit. Businesses must be profitable in order to be competitive, and all the functions in a business organisation should act in a way that contributes to making profits.

Business operations need finance: there has to be money to pay for them. Money is earned from profitable operations, and businesses can also borrow, for example by obtaining a loan from a bank. Even so, supplies of finance are usually limited, and decisions have to be made about how best to use the money that is available.

Financial decisions made by the finance department or by the board of directors can have a clear impact on the activities and competitiveness of any business because they include decisions about:

• How to obtain finance to support business activities, and
• How to allocate the available funds between the different business functions.

The interrelationship between financial decisions and other business functions

Each department in a business might believe that they are the most important function within the business but, in truth, they all play their part in whether or not the business achieves its objectives. However, when it comes to the allocation of money to departments, financial decisions have to be made about the allocation of funds. Planning how to allocate funds between the different business functions is known as budgeting.

The relationship between financing decisions and business functions is illustrated in Figure 5.1.1.

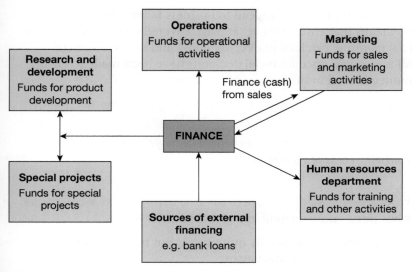

▲ Figure 5.1.1: The interrelationship between financial decisions and other functions

Finance provided to each business function is expected to be used to pay for activities that contribute value to the business.

For example:

- Spending on training to improve labour skills and productivity. When a business is facing spending cuts, training plans might have to be reduced or postponed. This can impact on the ability of the employees to increase productivity and/or to reduce the costs of production and so affect the competitiveness of the business.

- Financial decisions about the size of the marketing budget have an impact on the extent to which the marketing department is able to increase customer awareness of the business and its products – and sell them. Creating a brand image is often very expensive, requiring large sums of money.

- Financing decisions also affect the amount of resources available for research and development. Finance is needed to develop a new product or make improvements in the design of an existing one. The extent to which a business is able to develop successful new and innovative products affects its competitiveness. In a fast-changing technology market it can be essential for a lot of finance to be made available for research and development so that the business can stay ahead of its competitors.

Careful financial planning should ensure that money is available to pay for essential resources to operate the business, as well as to finance its growth. Departments cannot function without the resources they require, such as materials and components, people and physical space in which to work. If a production line does not have sufficient raw materials then work will stop. If there are plenty of materials but insufficient workers then the output will be lower than if the correct number of workers had been employed. If the finance for recruitment is cut this could result in the business not functioning effectively due to a shortage of employees.

Activity

In small groups discuss the resources needed to start up a café. The resources might include tables and chairs, for example. Decide, in your group, who will be responsible for which resource. Then allocate money to each of the resources required and explain why you gave what you did to each resource. You can set an overall amount of finance available but be realistic.

Lack of financial planning can lead to business failure. Financial success means that costs must be, at least, covered by income but poor financial planning can lead to over-spending and losses. Financial control is essential once financial decisions have been made to ensure that money is used in the most efficient manner.

> **Progress questions**
>
> 1 Explain one way in which a financial decision might improve the competitiveness of a business.

The impact of global business on the finances of a business

Many businesses now operate in a global market.

- Global businesses are usually quite large, and need much more finance than domestic businesses.
- Global businesses operate in many different countries, and buy materials from suppliers in many countries. To do this, they need finance in a number of different currencies.
- Global businesses have access to more different sources of external funding than domestic businesses, and in different currencies.

▼ Table 5.1.1: Some advantages and disadvantages of a global market on the finances of a business

Advantages	Disadvantages
The possible availability of lower-cost capital equipment, reducing production costs.	Transportation costs for equipment or materials purchased abroad can increase the overall costs of the business.
A lower wage economy might provide a cheaper workforce therefore the business might relocate to save on labour costs.	The lower-wage employees might not have the same skills or be able to produce the same quality of good.
Some governments will give financial incentives to a business to relocate to their country, e.g. tax benefits or grants.	After relocation, the business environment in the new country might change, removing the cost advantages of locating there.
	Change in the economic and/or political regime might change the costs and revenues of the business negatively.
Cheaper raw materials might be sourced from abroad.	The price will depend on the exchange rate at the time of purchase.
Purchases can be made when the exchange rate is most favourable therefore reducing costs.	Exchange rates can rapidly change, causing an increase in costs.
An increase in revenue due to more markets for goods and services.	Global businesses have to deal with different currencies, whose relative values are continually changing.

Advantages	Disadvantages
New ideas might be gained from other countries which might improve the brand image and enable prices and therefore revenue to be increased.	Marketing will need to be suitable for the new markets. Also marketing expenditure is likely to rise.
	An increase in competition from overseas businesses might force a business to lower its prices, causing a fall in revenue and profit unless costs can be reduced.

Financing global businesses: working with different currencies

Financing for a global business is made more complex by the fact that it must operate with different currencies, and that these currencies are continually changing in value relative to each other, often by small amounts but sometimes much more. Financing decisions they must make include:

- Which countries should we invest in?

- Where should we raise the finance to invest, and in what currency? For example, if a global company decides to invest in Nigeria, should it borrow in US dollars, the Nigerian currency (naira), or another currency?

- How many currencies should it hold to pay for expenditures around the world? If revenues are earned in one currency, should the company keep the money in the same currency, or should the money be exchanged into a different currency?

- Exchange rates are continually changing. Adverse movements in an exchange rate can result in financial losses. For example, if a global company based in the USA sells goods in China, and earns revenue in Chinese currency (renminbi), it will make less money than expected if the renminbi falls in value against the US dollar and the company wants to exchange its renminbi income into dollars.

- Are there any financial decisions we can make to reduce the risks from currency movements? (There are, but we do not need to know what they are.)

Financial objectives

All businesses set objectives in order to give some direction and focus to their activities. A financial objective is an objective set by a company that is expressed in financial terms. For example, a company's objective might be to make a profit, or to increase sales revenue and profits. For planning and control purposes, financial objectives are usually quantified as a financial target, for achievement during a period of time such as a financial year.

For commercial businesses, the main objective is usually a financial one – to make a profit. It is often assumed that the main aim of a commercial company should be to maximise profits. All other business objectives, such as increasing market share, improving operational efficiency and capacity utilisation and developing new products or services are all subordinate to the overriding objective of being competitive in order to be profitable.

Although the main financial objective of a company is often to make a profit, there may be other financial objectives too (see Figure 5.1.2).

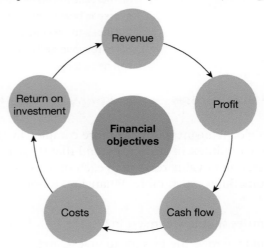

▲ Figure 5.1.2: Financial objectives

There may be other financial objectives, such as survival when the economy goes into recession and sales revenues fall.

The value of setting financial objectives

The purpose of setting business objectives is to specify what the business is trying to achieve. Objectives should be expressed as targets for achievement over a period of time, and targets should ideally be quantified, not qualitative. Objectives and targets enable a business to:

- Plan what it wants to achieve
- Monitor actual performance by comparing it with the target
- Take action ("control action") if necessary when actual performance is falling short of the target.

This applies to financial objectives and targets in the same way as to objectives and targets for other functions in the business.

- The main business objective is to make a profit, and it is appropriate to set a target for profit, perhaps as a percentage increase in profit over the previous year.
- Profits are made by selling goods or services, and by making a profit margin on the items that are sold. Financial targets for sales revenue and profit margin can be used as subsidiary objectives targets for the overall profit target.
- A business needs to have enough cash to pay for its expenditures, and to finance its plans for investment to grow the business. It may therefore be appropriate to set targets for cash flow.
- Businesses make investments in equipment, machinery and other assets in order to make profits and the amount of profit the

business earns should be sufficient to justify the amount of money invested. It might therefore be appropriate to set an objective of earning a suitable return on investment (or return on capital employed) and set a target for the required rate of return.

Revenue

Revenue is the amount of sales income that a business earns from its activities during a period of time. Revenue is also called "sales" and "turnover". (Strictly, turnover is revenue from sales of goods and services, whereas revenue can include income from other sources as well.)

Revenue should not be confused with profit. If a company sells an item for $1,000 and the item costs $600, its revenue from the sale is $1,000 and its profit is $400.

A business may set an objective for sales revenue. This aim can be linked to other corporate objectives such as increasing market share. A new business might accept a low revenue figure when it first enters a market but would expect that figure to grow as the business becomes more established. The business might have a financial objective of increasing revenue by 10% per year, which would have a knock-on effect for marketing objectives.

Example
A number of well-known "digital technology" companies have operated with large losses, financed by external investors who expect the company to grow and eventually become very profitable. Their financial objective in the short term is to increase revenues at a very fast rate. Companies such as Tesla, the manufacturer of electric vehicles, have yet to make a profit in any year in spite of being in business for a number of years. Twitter reported a profit for the first time in the first quarter of 2018, after being in business for nearly 12 years.

Cost of sales and other costs

"Cost of sales" is a term used in a number of industries, such as retailing and manufacturing. In retailing, cost of sales is the purchase cost of the goods that have been sold by the business in the period. In manufacturing, cost of sales is a **production cost** of the goods that have been sold in the period: this consists of the cost of the direct materials, production labour and other production costs (production overheads) for the goods that have been sold.

The cost of sales is just a part of the total operating costs of a business. There are other costs too, which can vary to some extent between different types of business. These other costs include:

- **Administration costs**: these are the costs of the administrative functions within the business, such as the human resources department and the accounts and finance department
- **Marketing costs**: also known as sales and distribution expenses: these are the costs of market activities.

Businesses do not usually set financial objectives for the cost of sales or other costs. Instead, they set objectives for sales revenue and profits. However, in a competitive market a business might set an objective to reduce its costs, in order to maintain or increase its profits.

> ## Key terms
>
> **Revenue (or turnover):** the sales income earned by a business during a period of time.
>
> **Cost of sales:** in retailing, the purchase cost of the items sold in a period. In manufacturing, the production cost of goods sold in a period: production costs consist of direct materials and components costs, production labour costs and other production overhead costs.

Key terms

Profit: the difference between revenues and costs. Revenues and costs do not always happen at the same time as cash receipts and cash payments.

Profit is the money left after total costs are deducted from total income.

Operating profit: the gross profit minus all other expenses required to bring that product to the customer.

Gross profit: turnover/revenue minus the cost of sales.

Profit margin: gross profit and operating profit are also calculated as a percentage of turnover/revenue; this is known as profit margin (gross profit margin and operating profit margin).

Link

Calculation and interpretation of gross profit, operating profit, gross profit margin and operating profit margin are covered 5.2 Financial data.

Profit: gross and operating profit

Profit is the difference between revenue and costs in a period of time.

- **Operating profit** is the difference between revenue and all the operating costs in the period. In retailing and manufacturing companies, operating costs include the cost of goods sold.
- When the cost of sales is measured, there is also a **gross profit**. This is the difference between revenue and the cost of goods sold in the period. Other operating costs (administration costs and sales and distribution expenses) are then deducted from gross profit to calculate operating profit.

Profit objectives can be expressed in terms of either:

- A target for total profit (which might be expressed as a target for gross profit and a target for operating profit)
- A target for profit margin.

Profit margin

Profit margin is sometimes used to mean profit. However, it is more accurately used to measure the amount of profit as a percentage of sales revenue.

- The gross profit margin is gross profit as a percentage of sales revenue.
- The operating profit margin is operating profit as a percentage of sales revenue.

The total profit of a business during a period is a function of sales revenue and profit margin. For example, if a company's sales revenue during a financial year is $2,000,000 and its operating profit margin is 5%, its operating profit is $100,000.

A business wanting to increase its profits might set as its financial objective for the next year the aim of:

- Increasing sales revenue
- Increasing the profit margin, or
- A combination of both.

High and low operating profit margins

Some businesses are willing to make a low profit margin and aim for high sales in order to make a high or satisfactory total profit. This is

Case study

Operating profit

In the current year, a company has achieved turnover of $12 million and an operating profit margin of 3.5%. It has set a financial objective of increasing turnover next year by 10% and increasing the operating profit margin to 4%

1   What is the operating profit in the current year?

2   What will be the operating profit next year if the target for turnover of $12 million is achieved, but the operating profit margin remains at 3.5%?

3   What will be the operating profit next year if the target of 4% for the operating profit margin is achieved, but turnover is again $12 million?

4   What will be the operating profit next year if both targets are achieved?

appropriate if the business is producing high-volume, low value items such as bottles of soft drinks. However, other businesses that produce a high-value item in small quantities might aim for a high profit margin in order to obtain their required total profit.

This is equally true of the service sector businesses. Some businesses provide services for large numbers of customers and might therefore be satisfied with a low profit margin, whereas businesses that provide a highly specialised service involving a lot of time and expertise would usually require a much higher operating profit margin. For example, a business that provides cleaning services to offices usually works on a low profit margin and hopes to obtain high revenues from a large number of cleaning contracts. A business that designs and installs sophisticated digital technology, however, will focus on fewer contracts but expect each of them to yield a high profit margin.

Cash flow

Cash flow is important to the survival of a business. Cash is needed to pay the day-to-day expenses incurred by a business. Most businesses would aim to have sufficient cash to meet daily requirements but would not want to hold too much cash, as this is money that could have been used more profitably elsewhere in the business.

Businesses might fail due to a lack of cash. Hence the need for cash flow objectives. A business can be profitable but can still fail if there is insufficient cash available to pay for day-to-day expenses. A profit is shown if a business has sold an expensive item/service but the money is not available to the business until the item has been paid for. In between selling the item and receiving payment for it, the business has a profit but does not have cash.

Most businesses aim to improve cash inflow and reduce cash outflow and to have a positive cash balance at the end of each month.

Return on investment

Some businesses must invest to grow while others must invest to survive. This can depend on the type of business. A business in the fast-moving technology market will be left behind by its competitors if investment does not take place.

In this section, we need to understand that, in simple terms, the return on the investment needs to cover the cost of the initial investment and also to provide some return/profit to the business. If a business only recovers the cost of the investment then it could be argued that it would have been safer to put the money into a bank account and to at least benefit from some interest on the amount. Businesses want a return on their investment sufficient to make the hard work and risk worthwhile. They may therefore set a target return on investment that they want to obtain from the investments they make. If a proposed investment is not expected to make a sufficient return, and exceed the target minimum return, the business should not invest in it.

> ### Key terms
>
> **Cash flow**: the flow of cash into and out of a business.
>
> **Return on investment**: the financial benefit gained from an investment, expressed as a percentage of the original investment.

> ### Link
>
> Cash flow is dealt with in more detail in section 5.5 Profit and cash.

Financial target setting

Tom has just left college and has decided to set up in business, providing grooming and care services for domestic pets. He thinks there is sufficient demand for pet care in his local area to make a business viable. Before he opens the business, he wants to think about the financial objectives and financial targets that the business needs to achieve.

1   Explain the value for Tom of setting financial targets for his business.

2   Explain with reasons what you consider to be the most important financial targets for his first year in business.

Progress questions

2   Where does a business obtain the finance that it needs for its business operations?

3   What is the relevance of financing decisions to the competitiveness of a business?

4   How does operating globally affect the financing of a business?

5   Why would a software company or an office cleaning company not calculate a cost of sales and a gross profit?

6   In general terms, what is return on investment?

External and internal influences on financial objectives

The previous section explained the possible financial objectives that a business might have. In this section we look at the various factors that can influence the extent to which those objectives can be achieved.

Resources

A business might have objectives for increasing total profit, or increasing sales revenue, but its ability to achieve those objectives is restricted by the limited amount of resources at its disposal. It cannot work at more than 100% capacity.

It might be possible to set targets for increased revenue and profits by hiring more employees, but there is a limit to the numbers of extra people that can be recruited and trained in a short time, and there may not be enough workspace in the business premises to accommodate additional employees.

Alternatively it might be possible to set targets for increased revenue and profits by investing in more machines and equipment, but a business must be able to raise the finance to pay for new resources. Without new investment, possibilities for growth are likely to be limited.

Developments in technology

Technological developments are having an impact on the financial objectives of a business. An objective of increasing profits and returns to company shareholders might not be possible in the short term due to increased expenditure caused by changing technology. The aim to improve cash flow might also be difficult to achieve. However, in a fast-changing technology based industry such expenditure might be essential to ensure survival.

Developments in technology can have an impact on how much money a business will want or need to spend, where funds will be allocated or on the possible sources of finance that it might use.

- If a business operates in a high-technology industry, such as manufacturing computers or mobile phones, large amounts of finance must be made available in order to keep pace with other businesses in the industry.
- In some industries, a huge financial budget must be allocated to research and development to produce new products that incorporate the new technology. This is evident in the car industry, where enormous investments are being made in electric cars and self-drive cars. For example, in 2018 Honda announced its intention to invest $2.75 billion with General Motors in a project to develop GM's Cruise model of driverless car.
- Large investments of this kind take many years to generate profits and a reasonable return on investment.

Some developments in technology can have the opposite effect, of making financial objectives more easily achieved. Many companies in recent years have been set up as internet companies, selling products or services such as computer games and online dating services.

- These start-up companies may need relatively small amounts of finance to get started, and if they are one-person or two-person businesses, their operating expenditures may be quite low.
- In addition, small businesses may be able to obtain finance from sources other than a bank loan, particularly when banks are unwilling to lend to high-risk business ventures.

For example, in recent years there has been an increase in the use of crowd funding, particularly for small businesses who have a business idea but lack the finance necessary to get their idea to market. It also allows awareness of sources of finance available internationally.

Developments in technology can also force businesses to rethink their business model, and reconsider how they should sell their products and what financial targets they should set. A notable example in recent years has been the development of online retailing. Many retailing, as well as manufacturing companies, have been forced to re-think how they should sell their products, and how much they need to invest in their online business. This has affected their financial planning and financial objectives for different parts of their business.

Ethical and environmental influences

Ethical and environmental influences can also influence financial objectives.

For example, if a business decides to reduce the amount of waste and pollution caused by the business, then it is possible that more expensive non-polluting equipment might be needed in its operations.

Key term

Crowd funding: obtaining funding for a business (or other venture), usually via the internet, from a large number of individuals.

This would have a negative impact on the business's ability to increase profit and return to shareholders.

Similarly, a business that has a strongly ethical approach to all its business activities might be less likely to replace employees with machines. This might reduce the possibility of reducing costs.

However, when customers see that a business is behaving in an ethical and environmentally friendly manner, they might increase their purchases from that business. This would possibly enable the business to meet its financial objective of increasing revenue.

Environmental issues

The impact on the environment is often considered by consumers when deciding which product to purchase or which business to buy from. Consumers are more aware of the activities of businesses partly due to the increased use of social media and the internet in general. If a business causes harm to the planet it might lose customers to businesses that advertise their commitment to reducing their impact on the environment. However, it is possible that a business striving to be environmentally friendly can have an accidental release of toxic substances. This has the danger of destroying the image of the business in a short space of time. The impact might depend on how quickly the damage is rectified.

Ethical attitude of business

The ethics of businesses is now under continual scrutiny making potential customers more aware of the moral conduct of the businesses they deal with. Some businesses will only deal with other ethical businesses. This might appear to be a restriction at first, but when we consider the publicity given to unethical businesses it seems that there are large gains to be made by behaving in a morally acceptable way.

As with environmental damage, if a business is found to be unethical either in its business dealings or in the way that employees are treated, the reputation of the business can be quickly tarnished. A good reputation can take years to achieve but it can be destroyed overnight if actions are taken that go against the stated ethical and environmental policies and they become known to the public.

Market conditions and domestic and international competition on financial objectives and decisions

Financial objectives and targets usually aim at maintaining the competitiveness of the business in its markets, and profitability; however financial plans and objectives can be affected by changing market conditions or by the activities of competitors.

Market conditions. The market for a product might be growing or in decline, and financial targets should be adjusted accordingly. For products with strong growth, additional investment might be needed for revenue growth and to maintain market share, but profit targets might be raised. For products in decline, the financial objective might be to remain profitable for as long as possible, but to plan for a profit fall.

The national or global economy maybe growing or in recession. Businesses should respond to current and expected changes in their markets as a result of the changing economic conditions, and adjust their financial targets to what seems reasonable in the circumstances.

Competition. Businesses respond to new competition in their market, and to new initiatives taken by existing competitors. The way that they act can affect their financial performance and so result in adjusted financial targets.

- It has been claimed occasionally that a dominant firm in its market has reacted to a new competitor entering the market by reducing its prices to a very low level until after the new entrant has been forced to leave the market because it is unable to make a profit.

- On a global scale, an initiative by a competitor to enter a new geographical market, such as Africa or China, might force a company to consider making a similar investment itself. This would require investment finance, and would have consequences for short-term profitability and short-term return on investment.

Activity

Draw up a table with the external and internal influences in this section down the side and financial objectives along the top. Then fill in which financial objective is likely to be influenced by which internal influence and how.

Exam-style questions

1 Commercial companies set financial objectives for themselves.

Explain one benefit to a company from setting financial objectives. (3 marks)

2 The main objective of many commercial businesses is to make a profit, but some businesses also set objectives for cash flow.

Explain one reason why a company may set an objective for cash flow (in addition to setting objectives for profit or sales revenue). (3 marks)

3 Recent advances in technology have led to the development of new products, such as domestic appliances, containing digital chips that respond to instructions via the internet from remote control devices. This new technology is called the Internet of Things (IoT), and many manufacturers are designing IoT products in order to remain competitive.

Analyse how financial decisions by manufacturers of Internet of Things products can impact on their competitiveness. (9 marks)

4 Setting financial objectives is more complex for global businesses than for companies operating in a domestic market. One reason for this is the challenge of operating with several different foreign currencies.

Analyse the problems for financial decision-making by global companies as a result of financing their operations in different currencies. (9 marks)

This section will develop your knowledge and understanding of:

→ Using financial data.

Financial data is used both for planning and setting objectives, and also for monitoring actual performance. Since the main objective of a business is financial, and since businesses cannot operate without finance or compete successfully without being profitable, the importance of financial planning and the use of financial data should be apparent.

In this chapter we shall begin to look at how financial data is used for business planning and monitoring business performance.

Using financial data

Calculating and interpreting gross and operating profit

Businesses cannot plan effectively or control their operations without having data for profit. It was explained in Section 5.1 that profit can be measured as gross profit (in some types of business) and as operating profit. The method of calculating gross and operating profit is shown, with illustrative figures, in Table 5.2.1.

▼ Table 5.2.1: The method of calculating gross and operating profit

When gross profit is calculated			When gross profit is not calculated		
	$000	$000		$000	$000
Revenue		300	Revenue		250
Cost of sales		(120)	Operating expenses	90	
Gross profit		180	Administration costs	50	
Administration costs	70		Sales and distribution expenses	85	
Sales and distribution expenses	80				(225)
		(150)	Operating profit		25
Operating profit		30			

Gross profit and operating profit are money amounts that measure the overall financial performance of a business.

Targets may be set for gross profit and operating profit. For example a company may set a target of increasing gross profit by 4% in the next year and operating profit by 5%.

Actual profits are used to assess the success (or otherwise) of the company during a period just ended. Typically, the actual profit earned is compared with the profit for the previous period, to establish whether profits have gone up or fallen, and by how much.

Where businesses calculate both gross profit and operating profit, it is possible to look at the cost of sales separately from other operating expenses. If a company wants to increase its profits by cutting costs, should it try to do this by reducing the costs of sales, or should it look for savings in administration or marketing costs?

Calculating and interpreting gross and operating profit margins

Gross profit and operating profit figures are used to plan and monitor the financial performance of a company, but they are not useful on their own for comparing the profitability of different businesses, such as rival companies.

It may be difficult to determine whether or not a profit figure is good or satisfactory for a business, compared to other businesses. Is a profit of $100,000 for one company better than a profit of $50,000 for a competitor? The answer to this question will depend to a large extent on the relative sizes of the two companies. If one company made a profit of $100,000 on sales of $2,000,000 an the other made a profit of $50,000 on sales of $500,000, it can be argued that the company with the smaller profit performed better, in view of the size of its profit relative to its turnover.

Profit margins are used to make comparisons of profit between different companies, and are also used by businesses to plan and analyse their own profitability (for example, by comparing planned profit with actual profit, and the reasons for the differences between plan and actual).

Profitability ratios can provide more useful information for planning and analysis of actual performance than the gross profit and operating profit figures themselves.

Two profitability ratios are the gross profit margin and the operating profit margin. These were introduced in Section 5.1.

These are calculated as follows.

Gross profit margin

This shows the relationship between the gross profit of the business and the sales revenue (revenue) that generated the profit. Gross profit margin is expressed as a percentage.

The formula used for the calculation of gross profit margin is:

$$\frac{\text{Gross profit}}{\text{Sales revenue}} \times 100\%$$

If Delinge Ltd generated sales revenue of $20,000 and a gross profit of $5,000 the calculation would be as follows:

$$\text{Gross profit margin} = \frac{5,000}{20,000} \times 100\% = 25\%$$

This means that for every $1 of sales revenue the business earns a gross profit of $0.25.

The analysis of this result will include whether it is higher or lower than previous years. If the same business had consistently generated profits of 40 per cent or more in previous years then this year the business has not been as successful. The reasons for the change in gross profit margin must then be investigated. Has the cost of sales risen? Has sales revenue fallen? Is it a combination of both of these? What action can be taken to improve the situation for the future?

Progress question

1 A business has sales revenue of $40,000 and a gross profit of $15,000. Calculate the gross profit margin for the business.

Case study

Competing supermarkets and gross profit margins

There are two supermarkets in a town, competing with each other and selling similar products. One supermarket sells at lower prices than the other, and the most recent financial results for the two businesses are as follows.

1 Calculate the gross profit margin for each supermarket.
2 Analyse the difference in gross profit margins between the two supermarkets. What might the comparative gross profit margins suggest about their differing approaches to making profits and being competitive?

	Flint Supermarket	Diamond Supermarket
	$	$
Turnover	5,000,000	3,000,000
Cost of sales	4,000,000	2,500,000
Gross profit	1,000,000	500,000

Operating profit margin (sometimes known as net profit margin)

This shows the relationship between the operating profit and the sales revenue. Just like the gross profit margin this ratio is also expressed as a percentage.

The formula for the calculation of the operating profit margin is:

$$\frac{\text{Operating profit}}{\text{Sales revenue}} \times 100$$

If Delinge Ltd had sales revenue of $20,000 and an operating profit of $2,000 the operating profit margin would be:

$$\frac{2,000}{20,000} \times 100 = 10\%$$

This result means that for every $1 of sales revenue the business earns an operating profit margin of $0.10 after all overheads have been covered.

Just as with the gross profit margin you must now question whether the result of 10 per cent is good or not. What was the operating profit margin last year or the year before that?

Progress question

2   A business has a sales revenue of $90,000 and an operating profit of $15,000.

Calculate the operating profit margin for the business.

Analysis of gross profit margin and operating profit margin

When both of these ratios have been calculated, further analysis can take place. The relationship between the two ratios will provide further information to stakeholders. The operating profit margin will illustrate how efficient the business is at controlling its expenses. For example, if a business had a gross profit margin of 50% and an operating profit margin of 5%, this might indicate that the business has lost control of its administration or marketing expenses. However, it might also indicate that this is a business that naturally incurs a high level of marketing expenditures or administrative activities in order to generate sales.

A better indication is to look at the relationship between these two ratios over a period of time.

Example

The profits of a business over the past three years are shown in the table below, together with the gross profit margin and operating profit margin in each year.

▼ Table 5.2.2: Profits over three years

	2 years ago	Last year	Current year
	$	$	$
Revenue	2,000,000	2,200,000	2,500,000
Cost of sales	1,200,000	1,210,000	1,300,000
Gross profit	800,000	990,000	1,200,000
Other expenses	560,000	726,000	900,000
Operating profit	240,000	264,000	300,000
Gross profit margin	40%	45%	48%
Operating profit margin	12%	12%	12%

In this example, the business increased its revenue from $2,000,000 to $2,500,000 in two years, an increase of 25%. Its gross profit has risen from $800,000 to $1,200,000 and its operating profit from $240,000 to $300,000. This might seem to be a very good performance.

However, the figures are not as good as they might at first seem. The gross profit margin has risen from 40% to 48%. This indicates that the business is either selling its products or services at higher prices, or that it has been successful in reducing cost of sales as a percentage of revenue. But the operating profit margin has remained constant at 12%, in spite of the increasing gross profit margin. This

Case study

Manufacturing company

The profitability of a manufacturing company for the past two years is shown in the following table.

	Current year $	Previous year $
Revenue	5,000,000	5,500,000
Cost of sales	3,000,000	3,410,000
Gross profit	2,000,000	2,090,000
Other expenses	1,600,000	1,595,000
Operating profit	400,000	495,000

1 What was the gross profit margin and operating profit margin in each year?

2 What do the comparable figures for revenue and net profit for the two years indicate?

3 What do the comparable figures for gross profit margin and operating profit margin in the two years indicate?

4 If you were a manager in this business, what action might you want to take, **if any**, on the basis of what these figures might be telling you?

shows that the ratio of "other expenses" to revenue has increased from 28% two years ago (40% − 12%) to 36% in the current year (48% − 12%). Other expenses seem to be increasing at an alarming rate, and management should look urgently into the reasons for this increase. It would seem that measures might be needed to bring other expenditures under better control.

Return on investment

Businesses may set targets for the return on any investment they undertake. For example, a business might require a minimum return of 8% on any investment in capital equipment for operations.

The size of the return on investment required can depend on a number of factors: for example if an investment is financed through borrowing then the return should be greater than the rate of interest paid to the lender.

A simple calculation to determine the return on any given investment is to take the total return from an investment over its lifetime (this is the difference between the financial benefits from the investment minus the cost of the investment) and calculate this as a percentage of the original cost of investment.

For example, if a business undertakes an investment costing a total of $500,000 and this yields total benefits of $575,000 then the return on investment would be:

$$\frac{575,000 - 500,000}{500,000} \times 100\% = \frac{75,000}{500,000} \times 100\% = 15\%$$

Whether or not this is judged to be a good return will depend on several factors, such as the desired return, and the length of time needed to achieve that return. A return of 15% over one year might seem very good, but if it is earned over ten years, this would not be so good.

There are different ways of calculating return on investment. In the example above, return on investment is shown for the entire lifetime of the investment. Another method of measuring return on investment, which is more informative, is to calculate the average annual return on investment:

$$\text{Average annual return on investment} = \frac{\text{Average annual profit from the investment}}{\text{Original cost of the investment}} \times 100\%$$

The average annual profit is the total profit over the lifetime of the investment divided by the life of the investment in years.

Example

A company invested $1,600,000 in a new machine. It has estimated that over the five years of the machine's life, it generated total profits of $3,000,000.

The average annual return on the investment can be calculated as:

$$\frac{(3,000,000 - 1,600,0000)/5}{1,600,000} \times 100\% = 17.5\%$$

This actual return can be compared with the target return that the company expects from its investments.

Progress questions

3   Why is it more useful to measure return on investment as an average annual return instead of a return over the entire life of an investment?

4   Why is it easier to calculate the expected annual return on a proposed or planned investment than it is to calculate the actual average annual return that an investment has made over its lifetime?

Completing and interpreting budgets

The nature of budgets

Budgets are financial plans for the future. They are usually prepared each year, for the financial year ahead. Budgets are expressed in money terms, which means that the plans for what the business is expected to achieve in the future period is a plan for revenues, costs and profit.

> **Key term**
>
> Budget: a financial plan for the future.

First it is important to distinguish between "forecasts" and "plans".

Forecasts are what we *think* is going to happen in the future. We use forecasts, for example, to anticipate likely future problems and convince investors to invest in our business.

Plans are what we *want* to happen or intend should happen in the future – what we are going to aim for. We use plans, for example, to set targets in the workplace and as a mechanism for monitoring and controlling.

Budgets are prepared for each business function:

- **The sales budget:** A sales budget is a plan for what the business intends to sell during the financial year.
- **The production cost budget:** In a manufacturing company, there is a production cost budget, which sets out what the business expects the costs of production to be (materials, production labour and other production costs).

- **Departmental budgets:** There are budgets for all other planned activities, usually prepared for each business function, such as marketing (sales and distribution), accounting and finance, the human resources department, and so on.

Allocating resources

Budgets provide an opportunity for forward thinking and help in planning processes. When planning a major project, such as an expansion, or managing plans for the future operations of a business, it is important to have a clear "road map" of where the business is going and how it is going to get there. Producing a budget provides the right kind of discipline to help in the planning process, forcing managers in each business function to think very carefully about what resources they will need, when they will need them and how much they will cost. With a well-produced budget it will be easier to ask "What if?" questions that can help in the planning process.

The master budget

The sales budget and the budgets for different aspects of business activities are brought together into an overall plan or budget for the business. This may be called the **master budget**, setting out the planned revenues, costs and profit for the year ahead.

Progress questions

5 Explain the term "budget".

6 Explain why a budget is different from a forecast.

The purpose of budgets

Budgets are a financial plan. They help with the planning of future actual operations by requiring management to consider how business conditions might change and what targets the business can reasonably set itself for the future. Budgets also help to co-ordinate the activities of the organisation: for example, a sales budget includes figures for the amount of sales that the business expects to make, and this enables the operations function to prepare a budget for production costs or operating costs that is consistent with the plans for sales.

A budget has several purposes:

- It is a plan. Planning enables a business to think about what it should be doing in the future, and what each function in the business needs to do to enable the business to achieve its financial targets and objectives. Looking ahead also enables management to identify any potential problems it faces, such as a risk of falling sales and profits.

- As a financial plan it co-ordinates the activities of the entire business. It also plans where the business will obtain the finance or cash that it needs to carry out its planned activities.

- It is used to communicate plans to management, informing them what is expected from them and how much funding they will receive to carry out their planned activities.

- Arguably, a budget can be used to motivate management to achieve the targets that have been set in the budget. This is more likely to be true if individuals will be paid a bonus if budget targets for profit are reached during the course of the financial year.

- Budgets are also used to monitor actual performance throughout the year, for example each month, by comparing actual results with the budget.

- Using budgets to compare actual and planned sales and profits means that management receive data that enables them to identify any problem that has arisen, such as an unexpected increase in costs or a shortfall in sales, so that they can take measures to deal with the problem. This use of budgets is sometimes referred to as financial control.

Case study

Snazzy Clothes (SC)

SC is a family business that manufactures fashion clothes for men. After ten good years when profits continued to grow, the family were all shocked to find that this year was not looking good. The family, Pierre, Alan, Monique and Isabelle, met with their parents, Giscard and Eva, to discuss the situation. Pierre, the finance manager, produced figures to show that profits are expected to be 50 per cent down on last year. Alan, the production manager, said, "Well I've done my bit, the new machinery we bought earlier this year is more efficient than ever before – we've produced so much I've had to pay bonuses to all the production employees." "That's no good," said Isabelle who is in charge of sales and marketing. "It is no good when we can't sell what you produce. Fashions have changed and we haven't."

That comment upset Monique who did all the designs. "The problem is that the sales staff has not put the effort in," she said. Giscard and Eva looked distressed. They had hoped that, now they were getting older, they would be able to hand the business over to the children. "But with arguments like this I don't think we can," said Eva. Alan, the managing director, said, "We are victims of our own success. Because we've been lucky and had ten good years we haven't had to do any financial planning. Now things are tough we need to plan – and plan very carefully."

1   How might financial planning help SC?
2   What kind of plans could SC make to improve the situation in the future?
3   Who do you think is right?

Benefits and drawbacks of budgeting

Looking at the uses of budgets it should be fairly clear that budgeting can produce benefits for a business.

- Budgeting – careful planning – should lead to greater efficiency and hence reduced costs, and monitoring performance enables management to identify and deal with problems before they become serious.

- Monitoring performance can help the business to achieve its targets.

▲ Figure 5.2.1: Performance outstrips budget

However, there are potential problems with budgets. Budgets project the future, and the future is uncertain. Budgets could be unhelpful, indeed they could be a hindrance, if the expectations that a business has about the future (the assumptions) are unrealistic. This could happen for a number of reasons:

- **Circumstances change:** for example a budget might be built on the assumption of a period of economic growth, but instead there is a recession.
- **Lack of budgeting skills:** the usefulness of a budget depends on who produces budgets. Often they are produced at departmental level and not all managers are skilled in budgeting.
- **Manipulation of budgets:** managers might find it difficult to put in a budget figure lower than the previous year because they may not want it to look like they overestimated the previous budget. Budgets are very often overstated.
- **Human nature:** managers are likely to be over-optimistic in case they are criticised by senior managers.
- **Aggregation problems:** individual managers will only see part of the picture.
- **New projects:** it may be difficult to plan for new projects as the business may not have previous experience of these projects.
- **Lack of data or other information:** not all budgeting can be based on past costs or other data.

There may be other difficulties arising from budgets:

- **Demotivating:** unrealistic targets will not have the desired effect of motivating staff. If objectives are not achievable people may not try.
- **Inflexible:** if managers have to stick rigidly to budgets, but circumstances change, then managers may be unable to react to the change, causing problems for the business. For example, if the marketing budget of Business A is fixed, and a competitor suddenly increases its marketing budget, then Business A may lose sales to the competition unless it has the flexibility to increase its marketing budget.
- **Conflict:** managers may argue fiercely to protect their own budget. It may be in the business's interest to reduce costs, but an individual manager is unlikely to want to reduce costs in their own area of influence.

Despite these undoubted potential problems with budgeting, businesses can design budgeting systems that work well. Well-designed budgets will need to be:

- Realistic
- Flexible
- Agreed with managers
- Holistic (look at the business as a whole)
- Reviewed regularly

- Seen as supporting managers, not challenging them
- Set for the short term with long-term aims in mind.

It is important to remember: whatever the problems with budgets, a business is much better off with a well-planned budget than without any budget at all. This is because budgets give a sense of direction, so that management know what they are trying to achieve. And comparing actual performance to budget enables management to monitor the success (or otherwise) of the business in achieving its planning targets.

Controlling and monitoring a business

Budgets assign responsibilities to managers through the use of cost centres. They can also be used in setting targets. Budgets give managers a useful tool to help them control their area of business operations. With a budget a manager should have an idea of what they are trying to achieve and when. This will enable the managers to produce more detailed plans for themselves and their employees. Budgets can give a clear statement of managerial responsibility, which clarifies controlling functions. All of these things can help to improve efficiency, motivate staff and provide positive direction to the area of the business. This then provides a vehicle for resolving possible conflict when things do not go according to plan, or managers are unclear as to what their role should be. Priorities, too, might be an area of dispute which can be clarified through the use of budgets. Budgets can be used for communicating with employees and setting targets, which, in turn, may motivate employees. This can be seen as part of delegation.

Budgets also help the monitoring process. With the "road map" provided by the budget, the business will be able to see how it is progressing. Having set levels of costs and incomes, the business will be able to compare what it has achieved with what it planned to achieve. Analysis of the projections (budget) and the outcomes will enable managers to identify problems and make decisions about how situations can be improved (see variance analysis below). Review of budgets also helps businesses in their future plans and budgets for the business by identifying where results differ significantly from the budget and what went wrong.

Assessing the value of budgeting

Budgets have the practical role of turning business objectives into practical plans. Strategic and other objectives can be somewhat vague, so that the discipline of setting a budget can force a business to be more systematic and logical in its forward planning and objective setting. Budgets then become the mechanism, through monitoring and analysing outcomes compared with budgets, for reviewing whether objectives have been met – a key part of business appraisal. In this way comparing a budget with actual outcomes will help the senior management see whether marketing objectives are being achieved, manpower planning is effective and so on. Budgets also help senior management in their overall control: departures from budgets are often only allowed after negotiation with, and approval from, senior management. Sometimes major stakeholders will be provided with budget information, so that budgets become a means of helping them assess their involvement in the business and its future plans.

However, the key thing about any budget is the extent to which it is realistic. There is a huge temptation to overstate positive aspects of a business and understate negative aspects. Unrealistic budgets can at best be misleading, at worst unrealistic.

Variances and variance analysis

Budgets are not just plans. They are also used by management to help them control their area of business operations, by comparing what they are trying to achieve (the budget plan) with what they have actually achieved.

The difference between the target financial performance and the actual financial performance is known as a variance.

For example, the budgeted expenditure on marketing for a small retail business might have been $5,000 for a financial year, but in the event turned out to be $6,000. There is a variance of $1,000: actual expenditure has exceeded the budget by $1,000. Since actual costs are higher than the budget, performance has been worse than planned, and this excess spending on marketing costs is an adverse variance.

If, on the other hand, the business had forecast sales of $50,000, but actual turnover turned out to be $60,000, actual sales are higher than budgeted. Higher sales indicate better performance, so the variance in sales revenue is a favourable variance of $10,000.

An adverse variance is indicated by the letter (A) and a favourable variance is indicated by the letter (F).

Using variances

By calculating and examining variances (known as variance analysis) businesses will be able to:

- Identify problems and take positive action so that further problems can be prevented
- Assess the budgeting process in order to make future improvements
- Assess the performance of departments and managers in achieving targets
- Understand present costs and revenues and control future events.

Calculation and interpretation of variances

Consider the information for a business shown in Table 5.2.3.

▼ Table 5.2.3: Comparing budgeted and actual spend

	Budget		Actual		Variance
	$000	$000	$000	$000	$000
Revenue		17,000		16,400	600 (A)
Operating expenses	7,800		7,250		550 (F)
Administration expenses	2,800		2,680		120 (F)
Sales and distribution costs	5,700		5,750		50 (A)
Total costs		(16,300)		15,680	
Operating profit		700		720	20 (F)

The comparison between budget and actual results shows that the actual profit was $20,000 higher than budget, so total variances were $20,000 favourable. However, actual sales were $600,000 less than budgeted: the favourable operating expenses may be due to the fact that sales were below budget, and profits seem to have exceeded budget largely because of the $120,000 favourable variance for administration costs.

Variances indicate areas for investigation: they do not explain the reasons in detail what has happened. In this example, management should:

- Investigate the reason why sales were less than budget. Was sales demand less than expected? Or were sales affected by a shortage of resources, such as a shortage of skilled labour?
- Check why administration costs were less than budget. This may have been due to success by management in the administration functions to reduce spending.

Two final points to consider:

- Variances are calculated after actual results have been measured. If a business waits until the end of its financial year to calculate variances, there will be a long delay before control information is available. So in practice, businesses divide the annual budget into shorter control periods, of one month or four weeks each, and measure actual results and calculate variances at the end of each control period.
- One of the reasons why businesses maintain accounting records is to collect the data they need for measuring actual financial results.

Exam-style questions

1   A company budgeted sales of $6,700,000 and total costs of $6,400,000. Actual sales were $7,200,000 and actual total costs were $6,800,000.

    Calculate the sales revenue variance and the operating profit variance.   (3 marks)

2   A company is deciding whether to purchase a new item of equipment costing $150,000. It is estimated that the total additional profits that will be earned from the equipment over its four-year life would be $198,000.

    Calculate the expected average annual return on investment from this equipment.   (3 marks)

3   The capital invested in a planned project will be $60 million. Expected sales from the project are $75 million each year. The profit margin will be 6%.

    Calculate the expected annual return on investment on the project.   (3 marks)

4   The senior management of Keepdry Rainwear have just finished preparing the budget for next year. It has been a long and difficult process. Sanjay, one of the managers, has expressed the view that budgeting is a waste of time. Sales demand for the company's products are uncertain, because they depend to some extent on the weather, which is unpredictable, so planning can never be accurate. He argues that everyone in the company already knows their job, so they do not need to plan.

    Is Sanjay correct to think that budgeting is unnecessary?

    Assess the arguments for and against and make a judgement.   (12 marks)

This section will develop your knowledge and understanding of:
→ Internal and external sources of finance.

Short- and long-run sources of finance

Businesses are financed from a mixture of different sources. The sources that are used will depend on the circumstances and requirements of the business.

A distinction is commonly made between finance that is provided for a relatively short period of time, and finance for a longer term.

Short-run sources of finance are usually defined as those which are repayable within 12 months. Businesses will obtain short-term finance when they need some financing for the business, but only for a short time.

Long-run sources of finance are provided for a period longer than 12 months. As a general guide, short-run finance is obtained meet a short-term requirement, and long-run finance is provided to support the business over a much longer time.

Most finance is obtained from external sources – from sources outside the business itself. Most of the sources of finance described in this chapter are from external sources. However a business should also have internal financing. This is financing, known as retained profits, that comes from within the business.

The rest of this chapter describes various sources of finance and when each of them might be used.

Trade credit

Trade credit is credit provided by suppliers who give a business time to pay for the goods or services that they have supplied. For example, a supplier of materials might deliver materials to a business and ask for payment within 30 days or 60 days. When suppliers give credit, they are providing goods or services that a business needs, without yet being paid. This is a form of short-term finance.

Trade credit is the most common form of short-term finance in business.

Debt factoring

Selling goods or services on credit is common practice for business-to-business transactions. When a business sells products or services on credit, it sends an invoice to the customer. An invoice is a request for payment, and when credit is given the invoice specifies when the payment should be made.

A business might sell a large amount of goods or services on credit, so there might be a lot of invoices that have not yet been paid. If the business needs to improve its cash flow position, it might be able to

> ### Key terms
>
> **Short-run finance**: finance that is needed by a business for a short period of time, usually less than a year.
>
> **Long-run finance**: finance that is needed by a business for a longer period of time. Sometimes finance provided for one to five years is known as medium-term finance.
>
> **Internal finance**: finance from within the business: retained profits.

arrange to sell its invoices to a specialist debt factoring business. The debt factor will make an up-front payment for the invoices – usually about 80% of the value of the invoices purchased. When the invoices are eventually paid, the debt factor will pay the remaining 20% of the money, minus its charges (for interest on the finance provided and administration charges).

For example, if a business sells invoices to the value of $10,000 to a debt factor, the debt factor may pay $8,000 immediately for the invoices and the remaining $2,000, minus charges of, say, $500, when the invoices are eventually paid.

A debt factoring arrangement is therefore a form of short-term financing, provided by a debt factor, against the security of the business invoices.

There are problems associated with debt factoring:

- Less than 100% of the invoice value is received, because of the debt factor's charges.
- A business might not like its customers to make their invoice payments to a debt factor rather than to themselves. It might be an indication to customers that the business has cash flow problems.

Businesses may use the services of a debt factor only when they cannot borrow short-term with a bank overdraft.

Overdrafts

A bank overdraft is an arrangement between a business and its bank, in which the bank allows the business to draw more money from its account than it actually has in there. The bank will state the maximum amount of the permitted overdraft and the business will be able to use up to that amount but must not exceed it. Many banks allow customers to become overdrawn on their accounts (but not excessively so) without a formal overdraft agreement; it is advisable to make a formal agreement. Overdrafts that have not been agreed require a higher rate of interest to be paid to the bank.

An overdraft can usually be arranged quickly and is normally used for short-term day-to-day financial needs such as paying for salaries or wages, paying a supplier for materials or paying rent for business premises. Banks will usually agree to provide an overdraft facility to a business if the business can show that it will be receiving money into the bank account soon, so that the balance on the bank account moves between positive and negative (overdrawn) and does not exceed the overdraft limit at any time. The overdraft is often used to cover a short-term shortfall in funds **to pay for day-to-day operating expenses**.

After trade credit, bank overdrafts are the most common form of short-term finance for most businesses.

▼ Table 5.3.1: Advantages and disadvantages of overdrafts

Advantages	Disadvantages
• They are usually quick to arrange.	• They usually require a high rate of interest to be paid to the bank.
• The bank does not require any involvement in the running of the business in return for the finance provided.	• The bank can call in the overdraft, which means that the business can be required to repay the overdraft immediately. This can cause the business to be unable to meet its short-term obligations and therefore become illiquid.
• Overdrafts are flexible in that the full amount of the agreed overdraft does not have to be used if it is not required. This reduces the interest payments to the bank.	

Retained profits

Retained profits are an internal source of finance. They consist of profits earned by the business that have not been paid out (to lenders in interest, to the government in tax, or to the business owners as dividends or other payments). For example, a company might make a profit of $200,000 after interest and tax, and may pay dividends to its shareholders of $80,000. This will leave $120,000 as retained profits.

Retained profits are an addition to the finance provided to the business by its owners. They are regarded as long-term finance (although the business can, if it wishes, pay out retained profits to its owners as dividends or other payments at any time).

It is usual for profitable businesses to retain some profits for re-investment, and retained profits are the most common source of long-term finance for many businesses.

In order to grow, a business needs additional long-term funding. It can obtain some long-term funds externally, but retained profits are a simple way of obtaining additional finance, and it is possible for businesses to grow and expand using retained profits as their only source of long-term funding.

This is the profit that the business has earned in the past. In any business this is readily available for use.

> **Key terms**
>
> **Retained profits:** the profits of a business, after interest and tax, that are not paid out to the business owners but are kept within the business, usually as a source of (internal) long-term finance.

▼ Table 5.3.2: Advantages and disadvantages of using profit retained in the business

Advantages	Disadvantages
• It is available immediately.	• The amount of finance might be limited if the business has low profits (and is unavailable if the business is making losses).
• It is a permanent source of finance because it does not have to be repaid to anyone.	• Retaining profits means that less money is available for payment to the business owners (shareholders, in the case of a company).
• Obtaining it does not incur any interest payments or any other costs.	
• There is no reliance for funding on any person or organisation outside the business.	

Key terms

Share capital: finance obtained through selling new shares in a company. Share capital (equity) represents ownership of the company.

Share issue: the process of raising new equity capital by issuing new shares.

Stock exchange: a market where shares in public companies can be bought and sold.

Share capital (equity)

Share capital is long-term finance for a company that represents the investment by its owners, the shareholders, in the company. Shareholders share in the ownership of their company, in proportion to the number of shares they own.

Share capital is also called equity. New long-term finance can be obtained for a company by issuing new shares. Share capital can be raised in either of two ways. Both are a form of "**share issue**":

- Issuing new shares and selling them to existing shareholders.
- Issuing new shares and selling them to new investors who are not yet shareholders. If new shareholders are brought into the business, the proportion of the business owned and controlled by existing shareholders would change. This is known as the dilution of ownership.

Share capital is a source of finance for companies only. A sole trader or a partnership business cannot issue shares because share capital is unique to companies.

A shareholder can sell shares to someone else, but this does not raise any new finance for the company. Share capital is a source of long-term equity finance only when new shares are issued.

Private and public companies

Companies are either private or public companies. One of the differences between them is that private companies cannot issue and sell new shares to the general public: any new issue of shares they make must be a private arrangement. Public companies, however, can sell their shares to the general public – anyone who wants to buy them. All companies whose shares are traded on a **stock exchange** or other trading platform must be public companies.

This means that a big difference between private and public companies is that:

- The amount of new equity finance that a private company can raise by issuing new shares is restricted, because there is usually a practical limit to the amount of new funds that can be obtained privately.
- Large stock exchange companies are able to raise large amounts of new finance by issuing shares that are bought by the general public (including "professional investors" such as pension funds and insurance companies).

There are occasions when existing shareholders in a public company are given an opportunity to purchase additional shares at a discounted price. This is known as a rights issue.

Public companies often raise new long-term finance in very large amounts. They can do so either by issuing new shares to the general public or borrowing. When interest rates on borrowing are very low, companies often prefer to raise finance by borrowing rather than by issuing new shares.

▼ Table 5.3.3: Advantages and disadvantages of raising finance through issuing shares

Advantages	Disadvantages
• It provides long-term finance for the business. • It does not have to be repaid: it is permanent finance. • A share issue by a public company can raise a large amount of finance.	• Issuing shares to new investors "dilutes" the proportion of the company that existing shareholders own. • There may be practical limits to the amount of new finance that private companies can obtain by issuing new shares. • Only companies can raise new equity finance by issuing shares. Other forms of business cannot.

Loans

Loans are an important external source of finance for businesses. All types of business can raise finance by borrowing, often from banks.

Banks will provide either short-term or long-term loans depending on the financial background of the business requiring the loan and the purpose for which the loan money is to be used.

Short-term loans are repaid in full with interest at the end of the loan term. With longer-term loans, some interest is repaid at regular intervals throughout the term of the loan, and these regular loan payments may also include repayments of some of the borrowed capital.

Banks may ask for some form of security on a loan, as protection. In the event that the borrower defaults on payments on the loan, the bank can seek repayment from the item that has been given as security. For example, with a loan to buy a property (a mortgage loan), the borrower gives the property as security for the loan.

Short-term loans

▼ Table 5.3.4: Advantages and disadvantages of short-term loans

Advantages	Disadvantages
• Usually a lower rate of interest must be paid than for an overdraft. • The term of the loan is fixed. • Security is not always required.	• The money borrowed is a fixed agreed amount and cannot be varied as and when required, as in the case of an overdraft. The whole of the agreed amount must be drawn and interest paid on the full amount.

Link

Public limited companies are discussed in 1.2 Types of business ownership.

Key term

Loans: money lent by a lender to a borrower, usually for a fixed term, and on which interest is payable by the borrower.

An overdraft is obtained to finance day-to-day operating expenses, and overdrawn amounts are paid back when the business receives money in from its sales of goods and services. A short-term loan is usually obtained for a specific purpose other than day-to-day operational requirements.

Long-term loans

For companies, long-term loans are an alternative to issuing shares as a long-term external source of capital. Long-term loans might be appropriate if the business is embarking on a large project that might take some time to become profitable or if the sum of money required is large.

Interest is payable on the money borrowed and the rate of interest varies according to the amount borrowed and the length of time of the loan. The amount of security offered can also have an effect on the rate of interest demanded by the lender. The higher the risk to the lender, the higher will be the rate of interest that must be paid on the money borrowed.

▼ Table 5.3.5: Advantages and disadvantages of long-term loans

Advantages	Disadvantages
• A fixed sum of money can be borrowed for a specified time. • If the money is borrowed at a fixed rate of interest, and interest rates subsequently rise, the business will benefit from only having to pay the lower fixed rate. • Payments of interest and capital repayments are made regularly and this can help with budgeting. • With borrowing, there is no loss of ownership or control of the business.	• Interest must be paid on the money borrowed. If the interest rate is agreed at a fixed rate and interest rates subsequently rise, the business will have to continue paying the higher fixed rate. • Payments usually begin immediately the loan is taken out, but the returns from the project financed by the loan may not begin for some time. • If the business has difficulty repaying the loan then whatever asset it offered as collateral (security) will be sold and therefore will no longer be available to the business. • When a business fails to repay any loan, the lender is able to take legal action: in some cases this could lead to the collapse of the business.

Debentures

Debentures are another type of long-term loan that is available to companies. Debentures are more commonly known as **bonds**. Whereas most loans are obtained from banks, debenture loans may be provided by other investors; however, debentures are not equity and debenture holders do not share in the ownership of the company they lend to.

Debentures or bonds are issued for a specific length of time, at the end of which the loan capital must be repaid in full. During the term of the loan, interest is paid at regular intervals, typically every six or twelve months.

> **Key term**
>
> **Debentures (bonds)**: loans sold by businesses to raise finance from investors. They are like shares, in the sense that they can be traded, but bond investors do not have ownership rights.

Medium-sized companies may be able to arrange a debenture loan, but debentures (bonds) are more commonly associated with borrowing by large public companies. After they have been issued, bonds can be bought and sold by their holders (in the "bond markets"), but bond trading does not raise any finance for the company. Finance is raised from the initial issue of the new bonds.

▼ Table 5.3.6: Advantages and disadvantages of debentures

Advantages	Disadvantages
• The full amount of the loan does not have to be repaid until a specified maturity date. • Large amounts of money can be raised. • Issuing bonds to obtain long-term finance for investment can be very attractive for companies when interest rates are low. • The business does not sacrifice any ownership or control (unlike with equity share issues).	• A fixed amount of interest must be paid to debenture holders (bondholders) each year whether the business is profitable or not. • The debenture might be linked to an asset, in which case if the business cannot repay the lender when the debenture matures the asset will be sold to repay the debt. These are known as "mortgage debentures". • There may be a limit to the amount of debt finance that a company can issue safely by issuing bonds/debentures. This is because interest costs may be high, and if company profits fall, they may be insufficient to cover the cost of the interest payments.

Leasing

Leasing is another form of external finance. It can be for a short term or for a longer term. Short-term leasing is sometimes known as renting.

Leasing enables a business to have the use of an asset, such as an item of equipment or a car, without having to purchase it. The asset is paid for and owned by a provider of lease finance, such as a bank or leasing company. The business that leases the asset from the leasing company makes regular payments for using the asset over an agreed term of the lease.

For example, a business might choose to lease its vehicles, which means that it will not have to bear the cost of purchasing the cars and/or trucks that it uses. Instead the business will take possession of the cars or trucks, and use them in its business, and regular agreed payments to the leasing company. The asset remains the property of the leasing company at all times. There are some forms of leasing agreements where the leasing company also bears any repair and maintenance costs. This form of acquiring equipment is a means of a business having the use of much more equipment than it can actually afford to purchase and can allow new businesses to start out with a much larger range of assets at its disposal than if it tried to buy everything that was needed for the business to function.

Hire purchase is similar to leasing except the regular payments made to the financing company are larger, and ownership of the asset

Key term

External finance: finance from sources outside the business.

Leasing: rather than buying assets such as major machinery, vehicles, or buildings, a business can pay another business (a leasing company business) for the right to use the asset in return for a series of lease payments over the term of the lease. The leasing company retains ownership of the asset.

eventually passes to the hirer (unlike with leasing, unless the lease agreement provides for an option to purchase the asset at the end of the lease term).

Leasing is an alternative to buying. It might be the preferred option for financing assets when businesses do not have sufficient money to purchase the asset themselves. Leasing may possibly also be a cheaper option than purchasing, but this depends on circumstances.

Leasing may be a common form of financing in certain types of business. For example, in the past, leasing of printing machines as been popular with small printing companies that have preferred the option of leasing to buying expensive machinery.

Venture capital

Venture capital is capital raised for a high-risk business venture, usually a new or recently established business. It is provided by investors who are prepared to take a big risk in return for the prospect of high returns in the event that the business is successful. Venture capital may be provided by individual investors (sometimes called "business angels") but most comes from companies that specialise in providing venture capital ("venture capital companies").

Venture capital may be provided to a young company in the form of a mixture of equity capital (shares) and loans. Loans give the venture capitalist the right to regular interest payments, and the shares give it some ownership in the company, so that it can benefit from the increase in the company's value if it becomes successful.

Venture capitalists are often willing to provide finance to businesses that have been refused loans by other institutions perhaps because they are seen as too risky. However, venture capital comes at a price because, due to the higher degree of risk involved, a higher rate of interest is likely to be charged on any loan finance, and the venture capitalist may also want a large share of the equity capital and ownership of the company.

Venture capitalists are not long-term investors. They expect the finance they provide to enable the business to grow successfully and fairly quickly, so that they will be able to sell their shares at a profit at an appropriate time in the future (after just a few years).

> **Key term**
>
> **Venture capital:** finance provided by investors (individuals or businesses) who specialise in investing in risky business ventures such as start-ups.

▼ Table 5.3.7: Advantages and disadvantages of venture capital

Advantages	Disadvantages
• It might be available to a young business when all other sources of finance are not. For example, if a new business cannot prove that it has the resources to be able to repay a loan, banks might not be willing to lend.	• The venture capitalist might insist on some involvement in the running of the business.
• Sometimes business advice is available from the venture capitalist along with the finance.	• The finance is usually provided only if the venture capitalist is given part ownership of the business.
	• It may be difficult to find a venture capitalist that is willing to provide finance.

Micro-finance

Micro-finance (also known as microcredit) is the lending of small amounts of money to people (sometimes groups of people) who would not be able to get a loan from a bank or other financial institution. Micro-finance is usually provided to enable the individual or group to establish a small business.

The recipients of micro-finance usually have low incomes or are unemployed and are therefore seen as too risky to be given a bank loan. There are many economies worldwide where it is accepted that getting a job is so unlikely that the best chance a person might have is to become self-sufficient in some way. This can involve starting up a small business enterprise for which some initial finance would be required. Many of the borrowers have been women who have been left without any means of support for themselves and their family. Without the aid of a small loan they would have been unable to buy the equipment needed to start their business. Some loans have been for the purchase of a sewing machine or for the initial expense of buying a weaving loom. The equipment has then allowed a person or group to begin to make items for sale.

Another example is the purchase of woodworking equipment that has allowed a small group of men to begin making wooden furniture for sale. It is the initial injection of finance that makes these business ventures possible. Some micro-finance schemes are government backed in some countries. A good example of an organisation undertaking this type of lending is the Grameen Bank in Bangladesh.

▲ Figure 5.3.1: Micro-finance could help this business grow

Government grants

A government grant is money provided by the government to a business to help the business to finance a new venture, or to help an existing venture to grow. Grants may be made to encourage businesses to set up operations in a particular part of the country (one that is economically under-developed) or to invest in a particular industry that the government wants to expand. For example, a government may provide grants to energy companies to encourage them to invest in "green" forms of energy, such as wind farms or solar panels.

Key term

Micro-finance: a source of finance and financial services to small businesses that are unable to access conventional banking. It is more common in developing countries than in developed countries.

Key term

Government grant: an amount of money available from the government that does not require repayment.

A grant is money that is not repayable to the government, provided that it is used for its intended purpose. Grants are therefore long-term sources of (external) finance. Instead of offering a grant, a government may offer a loan, which is repayable.

Governments also help and support businesses, with advice as well as financial help.

The total amount of money available in the form of government grants is a matter of government policy. Individual business can apply for a grant, and the government will decide whether or not to provide one.

The financial help from governments can come in the form of loans or grants. Loans must be repaid whereas grants do not have to be repaid.

Grants are often linked to a specific form of business development, for example, for the introduction of new technology. Alternatively they may be given to businesses in order to persuade them to locate in a particular area. Grants are frequently used to try to encourage businesses to move to areas of high unemployment and to encourage a move of some industries away from residential areas into areas that have been designated as industrial sites.

The great advantage of a grant is that it does not have to be repaid, but it might be given with strict guidelines about how it must be used.

However, government grants are available only for business activities that the government is willing to finance, as a matter of its business or industrial policy.

Crowd funding

Crowd funding is when finance is acquired from a "crowd", in other words, numerous individuals pool money to support a business venture. The finance is usually raised through the internet.

Crowd funding may be used by new businesses seeking some start-up capital. A person might have a good business/product idea but lacks the finance to set up the business. The internet has provided a vehicle for potential entrepreneurs to reach out to people who might be willing to provide finance for their business venture and there are now many websites that facilitate the raising of finance in this way.

Many contributors are only committing a small amount of money, but with numerous contributions from a "crowd", the total sum can be large. The contributors will sometimes receive shares in the business therefore benefitting from future profit, or they might benefit from receiving some of the product being made, for example receiving copies of a new magazine or free download of a new software product that they help to finance.

This source of finance is available to businesses that find it difficult to get bank loans perhaps due to the fact they are seen as too new and therefore a big risk.

Low-budget films have been financed in this way. Another example of crowd funding is when a natural disaster occurs somewhere in the world charities appeal for funds to allow them to help the victims of the disaster. Many donations, some of them very small, are made by individuals to allow that work to take place, but the total amount raised can be huge.

Progress questions

3 Explain two reasons why a business would apply to the government for a loan.
4 Outline two situations when it would not be advisable to use a short-term source of finance.
5 Name two external long-term sources of finance.
6 Explain one disadvantage of using a venture capitalist as a source of finance.

Activity

Research two businesses that have used crowd funding and try to identify why this source of finance was used rather than a more traditional source such as a bank loan.

In small groups, discuss and make notes on the reasons why an individual might decide to make money available to businesses that are raising money through crowd funding.

The values or beliefs of the business owners

Some business people might be averse to debt of any kind and therefore would look to source finance internally. This might place restrictions on the amount available and therefore the level of investment that can be undertaken.

There are people within some organisations who would want to deal only with ethical businesses and therefore the ethical stance of financial institutions would be taken into account when seeking finance.

There are also religious or cultural issues to be considered such as the need for business people following the Islamic faith to raise finance in a way that complies with Islamic principles or Sharia law.

Factors influencing selection of sources of finance

Different sources of finance are appropriate in different circumstances. The chosen source of finance could be for any one of a variety of reasons.

The financial history of the business

If the business has been established for a long time and has a history of well-managed finances, banks might be willing to agree a loan. Shareholders might have the confidence to buy more shares or, in the case of a small sole trader or partnership business, friends or family might be willing to give some financial support.

However, if the business's financial records show evidence of poor financial management or of a previous inability to repay a debt then the choice of a source of finance might be very limited. Any bank or individual lending to a business with a poor financial history would seek some assurance that their money would be repaid. For example, they would demand some form of security or collateral.

The financial history will also include looking at any debts that the business already has. If a business has already borrowed money and is still repaying previous loans then a lender might consider whether another loan could prove too difficult to repay. This is known as "gearing".

Link

Gearing is not examined at AS Level and will be discussed in A Level Chapter 2 Analysing the existing internal position of a business.

Appropriateness of different sources of finance

Some methods of financing are alternatives to others, and the choice of financing method for a business may depend on circumstances such as the current availability of finance from each potential source, and the comparable costs of each. Retained profits are only available, for example, to a business that is making profits; debt factoring is only useful to businesses that sell extensively on credit; and the availability of bank loans depends on the creditworthiness of the business that wants to borrow.

A brief summary of the appropriateness of different sources of finance is shown in the following diagrams.

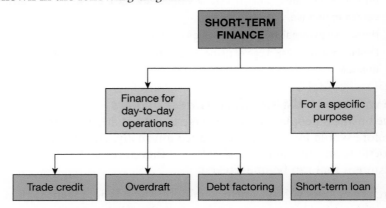

▲ Figure 5.3.2: Short-term funding

Short-term sources of funding are appropriate for businesses that need the finance for only a short time or to finance day-to-day operations. These sources of finance may not be available to start-up business that do not yet have an established track record.

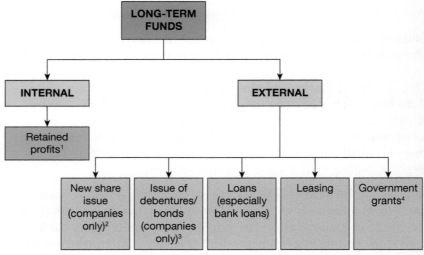

[1] Only if the business is profitable
[2] Large amounts of finance from equity issues usually only available to public companies
[3] Finance from bond issues may only be available to large companies
[4] Only if government grants are available

▲ Figure 5.3.3: Sources of long-term funds for established businesses

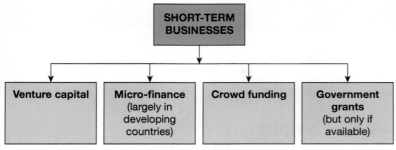

▲ Figure 5.3.4: Finance for start-up and young businesses

Case study

Stage Productions

Bacari and Agnes are the only shareholders in their company, Stage Productions. They organise venues for music and drama events. They will book the venue, organise all of the publicity and the printing and sale of tickets. They will also arrange for all of the sound and lighting equipment to be ready for the day of the event. Everyone who is employed to work at any stage of the preparation for the event or on the actual day of the performance is paid by Stage Productions. All that the musicians or actors have to do is turn up on the day of the performance! If the performances are popular Stage Productions achieves a good return on the money spent.

This business model has worked very well until now. The business is being asked to organise more events now than ever before and this is requiring it to spend more money

than it has ever had to. In the past the business might have been organising two or three events at the same time but recently it has had five or six in the planning stage at the same time. This has caused some financial worries because there have been times when it has only just been able to meet its weekly wage bill because of the money that needs to be spent in the preparation of any event.

The growth of the business means that it needs to buy more sound and lighting equipment because, at the moment, it is unable to accept work for events that are to be held on the same day due to needing the equipment at both venues.

1   Discuss the sources of finance that would be most appropriate for Bacari and Agnes to consider at this stage in their business development.

Exam-style questions

1   Most businesses need short-term finance. Explain one reason why they might want to obtain finance from a short-term source. (3 marks)

2   Some businesses obtain short-term finance by factoring their debts, but this method of financing has some disadvantages.
    Explain one of the disadvantages of debt factoring as a source of short-term finance. (3 marks)

3   Two friends are setting up a new business as a small company, and have each invested some of their own money in the business. After a few months, they realise that they need additional finance to sustain and grow the business, for which sales revenues are beginning to grow.
    Analyse the possible sources of new finance that might be available to the company. (9 marks)

4   The board of directors of a large public company are meeting to discuss future financing requirements for the business. They agree that a substantial amount of additional finance will be required. The finance director argues that the new finance should come from equity sources.
    Do you agree that equity financing is a more appropriate method of financing for a large company than debt financing?
    Assess the arguments for and against equity financing, and make a judgement. (12 marks)

This section will develop your knowledge and understanding of:

→ Break-even output.

Key terms

Break-even: the level of output and sales at which total revenue = total costs.

Fixed costs: costs that are the same fixed amount in total regardless of the level of output and sales.

Variable costs: costs that increase in total with increases in the volume of output and sales. It is normally assumed that the variable cost per unit is a constant amount.

Break-even output

Break-even analysis is a tool used to find the level of output and sales at which the total revenue from a product is sufficient to cover the total costs of producing that product, so that the business "breaks even" and makes neither a profit nor a loss. It is a technique that can be useful for financial planning and forecasting.

The use of the break-even method depends on separating total costs into fixed costs and variable costs.

Costs

Fixed costs (FC)

Fixed costs are costs that remain the same total amount in a period of time, and do not change with the level of output and sales in the period. For example, the rent for a factory will have to be paid every month regardless of whether any production has taken place or not. If in one month the business produces 1,000 units and the next month it produces 2,000 and the month after that it only produces 400 units, the rent of, say, $500 per month will remain the same. It does not double just because output has doubled. Nor does it fall if output is reduced. The business will have agreed an amount of rent to be paid and that amount will remain unchanged for the duration of the rental agreement. Salaries are also fixed costs because salaries must be paid to the employees regardless of how much work the employees do, in other words, it is usually a fixed amount per month.

Variable costs (VC)

Variable costs are costs that increase in total as the level of output and sales increases. It is normally assumed that the variable cost per unit produced and sold is a constant amount per unit. For example, if a business produces plastic buckets, the amount of plastic used and the total cost of the plastic will depend on the number of buckets produced. If a fast-food chain sells twice as many burger meals this month as it sold last month, then it will use twice as many bread rolls, twice as many burgers, twice as many fries and twice as much salad trimmings and sauces. Therefore the variable costs associated with producing the buckets or the burger meals will depend on how many are made, in other words, these costs will vary according to the level of production of these products. However, the variable cost per unit produced and sold is a constant amount. Wages that are agreed on "piece rate" are a variable cost because the employee is paid according to how many units have been produced, so the labour cost per unit is a constant amount.

Link

For more on piece rate, see 4.4 Motivation and engagement.

Total costs

Total costs are the total of fixed costs added to the total of variable costs:

TC = FC + VC.

A chart showing fixed costs, variable costs and total costs is illustrated in Figure 5.4.1.

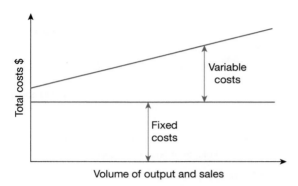

▲ Figure 5.4.1: Fixed costs, variable costs and total costs.

There are techniques for estimating the amount of fixed costs per period and the variable cost per unit produced and sold, but you do not need to learn them. For your examination it should be sufficient to know what fixed costs and variable costs are.

Break-even analysis can also be used to calculate the profit that will be made at any level of output and sales. If a business is producing at a level of output that is higher than the break-even level of output then the business will be making a profit. If it is producing and selling at below the break-even level, it is making a loss.

The break-even level of output can be determined by using a graph or by calculation.

The information that is required in order to find a break-even point is as follows.

Revenue (or turnover)

A break-even chart shows the total revenue at all levels of output and sales, in addition to costs. It is assumed that all items are sold at the same sales price, so that total revenue increases "in a straight line" on the break-even chart, from zero revenue at zero sales.

Total revenue = selling price × the number of units sold.

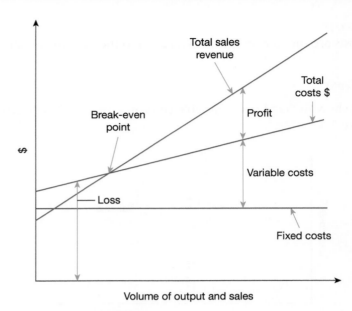

▲ **Figure 5.4.2**: Break-even chart

A break-even chart can therefore be drawn as shown in Figure 5.4.2.

A break-even chart shows that:

- If the business produces no output and makes no sales in a period, it will make a loss equal to the amount of fixed costs.
- As output increases, the loss will decrease up to a level of output and sales where total costs and total revenue are the same. This is the break-even point.
- As levels of output and sales increase above the break-even point, the business makes a profit and total profits increase as total sales increase.

Contribution

A break-even chart illustrates a simple calculation of profit at different levels of output.

Profit = Revenue – Total costs

Profit = Revenue – Fixed costs – Variable costs

Profit = (Revenue – Variable costs) – Fixed costs

(Revenue – Variable costs) is known as **"contribution"**. Contribution is a shorthand term for "contribution to covering fixed costs and making a profit".

Rearranging the above formula, we get:

(Revenue – Variable costs) = Fixed Costs + Profit

Total contribution = Fixed Costs + Profit

In other words, the total contribution in any period is the sum of fixed costs for the period plus the profit eared in the period (or minus the loss for the period).

At the break-even point, there is no profit and no loss, so at break-even:

Total contribution = Fixed costs.

The sales price per unit (S) and the variable cost per unit (V) is a constant amount, so the contribution per unit sold is also a constant amount (S – V). This is the **contribution per unit**.

We can express the total contribution in a period, where the quantity of items sold is Q, as

Total contribution = Q × (S – V)

Example

Dephton makes small poultry units (a wooden building for keeping hens and other poultry in). It has fixed cost of $24,000 per year. The selling price of each poultry unit is $195 and the variable cost per unit is $95.

1   How many poultry units will Dephton have to produce in order to break even?

2   What will be the profit or loss if Dephton makes and sells 400 units?

Every time Dephton sells a poultry unit for $195, the variable cost is $95 and the contribution per unit is therefore $100 (= $195 – $95). So the question is, how many $100 will be needed before the fixed costs of $24,000 have been fully covered?

The break-even point is $24,000/$100 per unit = 240 units (and sales revenue, at $195 per unit, of $46,800).

If the business sells 400 units:

	$
Total contribution (= 400 × $100)	40,000
Fixed costs	24,000
Profit	16,000

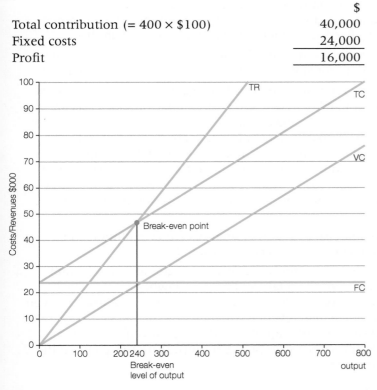

TR = Total revenue
TC = Total costs
VC = Total variable costs
FC = Fixed costs

▲ Figure 5.4.3: Break-even chart for Dephton Ltd

Margin of safety

The margin of safety is the amount by which output and sales (actual or budgeted sales) exceeds the break-even level. It is usually expressed as a percentage of the actual or budgeted sales.

For example, if a business produces 12,000 pairs of trainers per year and the level of output at which it breaks even is 9,000 pairs of trainers, the margin of safety is 3,000 pairs of trainers. This means that the business will continue to make a profit if the output falls but by less than 3,000 pairs of trainers per year. This can be reassuring for businesses during a recession when demand for their products might fall. They have an indication whether they will still be profitable at lower levels of production.

This will only be true if costs and revenue per unit remain unchanged.

The margin of safety could also be expressed as 25% (= (3,000/12,000) × 100%) of actual sales.

In the previous example, we calculated that Dephton needed to produce 240 units in order to break even. If it produced and sold 400 units per year it would be making 160 units more than it needed to produce to break even. This will give the business some security such that if demand falls it will still be profitable if the demand stays higher than 240 units. The margin of safety, at 160 units, is 66.7% (160/240) of actual output and sales.

Constructing a break-even chart

To construct a break-even chart:

- Prepare a graph in which the x axis represents the volume of output and sales and the y axis represents money (total revenues, total costs, fixed costs, total variable costs, loss and profit).
- Draw a line for fixed costs. This line should be horizontal to the x-axis, and it should meet the y-axis at the amount for fixed costs.
- Draw a line for total costs. This line begins at zero output and at the level of fixed costs. At zero output, total variable costs are zero, so total costs = fixed costs. As the total cost line is a straight line, you need to calculate only one more figure for total costs. For example, you might calculate total costs when output is, say, 1,000 units. At this level of output and sales, total costs = fixed costs + variable costs, which is fixed costs + (volume of output and sales × variable cost per unit). Mark this point on the break-even chart.
- Join this point to the point for total costs at zero output, and extend the line as far as seems appropriate.
- Draw a line for total revenue. This line begins at zero sales and zero revenue. As the total cost line is a straight line, you need to calculate only one more figure for total revenue. For example, you might calculate total revenue when output and sales are, say, 1,000 units. At this level of output and sales, total revenue = (volume of output and sales × sales price per unit). Mark this point on the break-even chart.

- Join this point to the point for zero revenue at zero output and sales, and extend the line as far as seems appropriate.

- You now have the break-even chart. The break-even point on the chart is the volume of output and sales at which total revenue and total costs are equal.

- If required, you can also show actual (or budgeted) output and sales on the chart, and the profit at this output and sales level.

Any level of output and sales below break-even point means that the business is producing at a loss as all the costs are not being covered. The extent of any loss can be seen by looking at the vertical difference between the TR and TC lines. At any level of production above the break-even level of output, a profit is being made.

From the chart, we can see the profit or loss that would be made at different levels of output by looking at the vertical difference between the total revenue line and the total costs line.

When the total cost line is above the total revenue line the business is making a loss whereas, when the total revenue line is above the total cost line, a profit is being made.

Manipulating break-even charts
A break-even chart also allows the effect of any changes to projected revenues and costs to be illustrated.

- For example, in the previous example, if the fixed costs of Dephton rose to $30,000, we could re-draw the total costs line in the break-even chart to show how many units would have to be produced and sold to break even.

- Alternatively, if the variable costs of production rose by $5 per unit we could re-draw the total variable costs line in the break-even chart to show how many units would have to be produced and sold to break even.

- If a competitor entered the market and Dephton was forced to lower the price of its poultry units to $175 per unit, we could re-draw the total revenue line in the break-even chart to show how many units would now have to be produced and sold to break even.

The uses of break-even analysis
A business might use break-even analysis to:

- Calculate the level of output that would be required to give a desired amount of profit. This can be determined either by reading from a break-even diagram or by calculation. If the calculation method is used this is done by adding the desired profit to the fixed costs and dividing this by the contribution per unit.

- Break-even analysis allows a business to see the possible impact of a change in costs. If a supplier has given notice that its prices are to be increased, then its customers could use the new cost figures to calculate the new break-even level of output. The increase in costs might mean that they will be unable to cover their costs and therefore will have to either find a cheaper supplier or perhaps increase the price of their products.

Get it right

You need to know how to construct, interpret and manipulate a break-even chart so that you are able to make changes to one that you are given. You must be able to interpret the information contained in any given break-even chart. Remember, break-even is the level of output, not the level of costs.

- It can test the impact of an increase in price on its break-even point and on its profits.

The limitations of break-even analysis

It is based on simple assumptions, such as a single product (or a fixed mix of products), a single selling price, a constant variable cost per unit and fixed costs unchanged a tall output levels. These assumptions can be varied to some extent, and the break-even chart can be "manipulated" to allow for some simple changes in assumptions.

- The conclusions drawn from break-even analysis will depend on the accuracy of the information that is used. In particular, estimates of fixed costs and variable costs per unit need to be reliable. If the estimates are inaccurate, the conclusions drawn will also be inaccurate.

- The revenue and cost lines are assumed to be linear when in reality this is not always true. For example, the business might be given a discount for purchasing in bulk when its order passes a certain level. This would have the effect of reducing the variable costs above a certain level of output. The fixed costs might also change with levels of output above a certain number. For example, using the current machinery a business might be able to produce 5,000 units of a product, but if output was required to be higher than 5,000 another machine would need to be bought. The fixed cost line in the break-even chart would increase to a higher value at that point.

- Break-even analysis can only be used for one product or a fixed sales mix of products. Therefore it would be of limited value to a multi-product business (unless the business makes each of its products at a different location).

Progress questions

1 Define what is meant by the term "break-even".
2 Give a formula for calculating break-even that includes contribution.
3 What is meant by the "margin of safety"?

Case study

Sports Alive

Sports Alive produces football boots and football shirts and shorts. The football shirts and shorts are sold as one complete kit. The fixed costs for Sports Alive are $24,000 per annum which are to be allocated equally between the production of both items. The variable costs for the football boots are $10 per pair and the selling price is currently $15 per pair. The variable costs of producing the football kits are $8 and the selling price for a complete kit is $12.

Sports Alive is eager to encourage young people to get involved in sport at an early age and has therefore just

announced that it will donate $1 from each pair of boots and each kit sold to local schools for the purchase of sports equipment.

1 Calculate the break-even level of output for the production of football boots before the $1 donation was announced.

2 Calculate the break-even level of output for the football kits after the announcement of the $1 per kit donation.

Exam-style questions

1 A company sells its product for $20 per unit. The variable cost of making and selling the product is $12 per unit. How much contribution in total will be earned from sales of $600,000 of the product? (3 marks)

2 A business has fixed costs per period of $1,000,000. The sales price per unit of the product is $90 and the variable cost per unit is $50. The budgeted margin of safety is 3,000 units. What is the budgeted volume of sales, in units and revenue? (3 marks)

3 Break-even analysis is used to assist management with planning and controlling costs and profits.

Analyse the ways in which break-even analysis might be used by management for planning purposes. (9 marks)

4 A company makes and sells a single product. Its budgeted fixed costs for next year are $400,000, and it expects to sell 30,000 units of the product at price of $20 per unit. The variable cost of production and sales is $10 per unit.

Analyse the measures that the company's management might take when faced with these budget estimates. (9 marks)

This section will develop your knowledge and understanding of:

→ Profit
→ Cash flow forecasts
→ Ways of improving working capital and cash flow
→ Ways of improving profits and profitability.

Profit

The meaning and significance of profit

Profit is the difference between revenue and costs incurred to achieve that revenue; the amount gained from a transaction after all expenses have been paid.

Profit = Total revenue – Total costs

The main objective of commercial businesses is to make a profit, and (often) to grow profits over time. The amount of profit that a business might seek will depend to a large extent on the size of the business, although some large businesses make low profits and some small businesses can be highly profitable.

Companies might be under pressure from their shareholders to increase the amount of profit earned. Shareholders invest money in a company in the expectation of receiving a return on their investment. Their return may take the form of an increase in the value of their shares, but shareholders usually expect to receive dividends on their shares, and dividends are paid out of profits. A company should therefore try to make sufficient profits to pay a satisfactory dividend to shareholders as well as to retain profits in the business to finance future investment and growth.

If a business is not profitable, and continually makes losses, its future existence may be at risk.

The distinction between gross profit, operating profit and profit for the year

Profit is measured and reported several ways.

Some businesses, such as retail businesses and manufacturing businesses, measure gross profit. This is sales revenue in a period minus the cost of sales. For a retail business, the cost of sales is the purchase cost of the goods that are re-sold. For a manufacturing business, cost of sales is a measure of the production cost of the goods that are sold.

Operating profit is the profit that a business makes on its operations in a period. This is measured as sales revenue minus all operating costs. Alternatively, it can be measured as the gross profit minus other operating expenses, such as administration expenses and sales and distribution costs.

Profit for the year is calculated by making some further adjustments to operating profit:

	$
Operating profit	X
Less: Finance charges (interest costs on borrowing)	(X)
Equals: Profit before taxation	X
Less: Taxation payable on profits	(X)
Equals: Profit after taxation	X

Operating profit is not a complete measure of profit for the year because there are costs (and perhaps some items of income too, such as interest earned on cash deposits) that are not included in the calculation of operating profit. The main examples of these costs are interest costs on borrowing and the taxation payable on profits.

It is important that you make clear which profit figure you are referring to. The word "profit" is a general term and often needs some clarification as outlined above.

The difference between profit and cash

An important fact that needs to be stated at the outset is that **cash** and profit are not the same thing! "Cash" is money that is received and paid out. It is useful to think of cash as the money that goes into and out of a bank account, and the balance on the account. "Profit" is the difference between sales revenue and costs.

There are various ways in which cash (or cash flow) and profit are not the same.

- Products might be sold on credit terms. A profit is made when the products are sold, but the cash is received only when customers eventually pay what they owe.
  Imagine that you buy a painting for $50 and then someone admires it so much that they buy it from you for $200, promising to pay you next week. When you make the sale, you have made a profit of $150 but you do not yet have any cash. Profit and cash flow do not happen at the same time, and they are not the same thing.

- A manufacturing business might spend money making goods that are held in finished goods store until they are sold. Until they are sold, the business does not make any profit, but it has spent money (cash) to make the goods.

- A company might borrow money from a bank. The borrowed money will add to the company's cash, but loans are not a cost chargeable against profit. Interest is charged against profit but not the amount of the loan.

- A company might pay a dividend to its shareholders. Dividends are payments of cash, but they are payments out of profits, and are not an expense in the calculation of profit.

- A business might spend $150,000 on a new machine, paying in cash. There will be some charge for the machine in calculating profit (known as a depreciation charge) but the full purchase cost of a machine is not charged in full against profit in the year that it is purchased.

> **Key term**
>
> **Cash**: legal tender used for making and receiving payments, and money held in bank accounts or in the form of banknotes and coins.

The difference between profit and profitability

There is a clear but perhaps subtle difference between the terms profit and profitability. Profit is a measurable and quantifiable amount. For example, we can say that a business has made a profit and we could check on the amount of that profit in monetary terms. Profitability is a relative amount: profitability might be high or low. For example, a business might make a profit of $50,000 but we cannot say whether this is good or not without making some comparison.

Profitability considers the profit achieved relative to the size of the business or the amount of sales revenue. If a business (Business A) makes a profit $5,000 on sales of $500,000 and a competitor (Business B) makes a profit of $20,000 on sales of $100,000, we can assess which business is more profitable by comparing their profit to their sales revenue.

Business A profitability = $50,000/500,000 \times 100 = 10\%$

Business B profitability = $20,000/100,000 \times 100 = 20\%$

Although Business A had a larger profit, Business B is more profitable because it is making bigger profits from the sales that it makes.

Cash and working capital

The importance of cash and working capital

Cash gives a business the ability to pay for everyday items such as wages and pay suppliers for raw materials or other products or services provided. Sufficient cash must be available to a business to enable it to meet short-term financial obligations.

- If a business does not pay its suppliers on time there is a good chance that the suppliers will refuse to supply the business in the future. The business would then be unable to function.
- If a business is unable to pay the wages and salaries of employees on time, the employees might look for work elsewhere. There are occasions when a business in financial difficulty might delay

▲ Figure 5.5.1: The possible result of poor cash flow management – closure payments of wages and salaries, but this can only happen in the short term. Employees need to be paid so that they can pay for things that they need such as food and other basic needs.

A business might be very profitable, but if it cannot meet its short-term financial obligations, it might be declared insolvent and could cease to exist.

However, there might also be a problem with holding too much cash. Cash in the bank is not serving any useful business purpose. (Interest might be received on a bank deposit, but this is not contributing to business operations.) A business holding cash should have a good idea of what it plans to do with the money, and when.

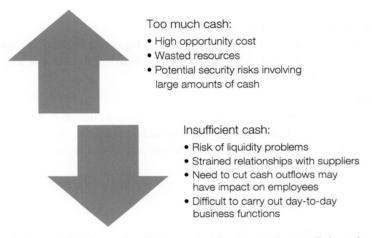

Too much cash:
- High opportunity cost
- Wasted resources
- Potential security risks involving large amounts of cash

Insufficient cash:
- Risk of liquidity problems
- Strained relationships with suppliers
- Need to cut cash outflows may have impact on employees
- Difficult to carry out day-to-day business functions

▲ Figure 5.5.2: The trade-off between holding too much or too little cash

Working capital

Working capital might seem an unusual term. It is the amount of long-term finance (long-term capital) that a business needs to support its day-to-day operations.

For day-to-day operations, a business needs to finance:

- Inventories, of raw materials and other supplies, work-in-progress and finished goods waiting to be sold
- Money owed by customers that has not yet been paid. Money owed by customers for sales of goods or services are known as trade receivables or trade debtors.

Inventories and trade receivables (debtors) are known collectively as current assets because they are assets of the business that will soon be converted into cash, as part of the business cycle.

Current assets must be financed. They are financed by a combination of long-term capital (such as equity finance and long-term debts) and short-term finance. The most common forms of short-term finance are trade credit and bank overdrafts. The amount of trade credit is known as trade payables or trade creditors. Collectively, short-term money owed is known as current liabilities.

Key terms

Working capital: there are different definitions of working capital. For the purpose of this chapter, working capital is the sum of the value of inventories and trade receivables minus the amount of trade payables.

Trade receivables: money owed to a business by customers who have purchased goods or services on credit and have not yet paid.

Trade payables: money owed to suppliers by a business for goods or services purchased on credit, which has not yet been paid.

Working capital is the amount of current assets of a business minus its current liabilities. It is an essential requirement of day-to-day business operations. Working capital can be measured in different ways, but for the purpose of this chapter, it is defined as follows:

	$
Inventory	X
Trade receivables (debtors)	X
Current assets	X
Current liabilities: trade payables	(X)
Working capital	X

(for the purpose of cash flow analysis)

Cash flows and working capital changes

It is important to understand the connection between profit and cash flows, and changes in working capital. The following example is a simplified illustration.

Example

A retail business buys five units of a product for $100 each, on credit. It then sells three units for $300 each, on credit, leaving it with two units in inventory. The working capital of the business is currently as follows.

	$
Inventory (2 × $100)	200
Trade receivables (3 × $300)	900
Current assets	1,100
Trade payables (5 × $100)	(500)
Working capital	600

Working capital is $600, but no money has been paid to suppliers and no money has been received from customers, so the cash position is $0. The profit on the sale of the three units is $600 (at $200 per unit), even though there has been no change in the cash position.

Now suppose that the customers who owe $900 pay for their purchases. The new working capital position is as follows.

	$
Inventory (2 × $100)	200
Trade receivables	0
Current assets	200
Trade payables (5 × $100)	(500)
Working capital	(300)

Working capital is negative at minus $300 and the cash position is $900. Working capital has been reduced by $900 but cash has increased by $900.

Now suppose that the business pays the $500 it owes to its supplier. The new working capital position is as follows.

	$
Inventory (2 × $100)	200
Trade receivables	0
Current assets	200
Trade payables	0
Working capital	200

Working capital has increased by $500, from minus $300 to $200 and the cash position after paying the supplier is $500 lower, at $400. Working capital has been increased by $500 but cash has decreased by $500.

The key point that this example demonstrates is that when there is any change in working capital (defined as inventory plus trade receivables minus trade payables) the cash position changes by an equal amount.

- An increase in working capital results in a reduction in cash.
- A reduction in working capital results in an increase in cash.

Case study

Understanding working capital (1)

At the beginning of a year, a company had $75,000 in inventory, $105,000 in trade receivables and $60,000 in trade payables. At the end of the year, it had $84,000 in inventory, $110,000 in trade receivables and $80,000 in trade payables.

1 Calculate the effect that the change in working capital during the year had on the company's cash position.

Case study

Understanding working capital (2)

A company buys goods costing $1,000 on credit and sells half of them for $1,600, all on credit.

1 What is the profit on the sale of the goods?
2 How much has the cash position changed?
3 What is the working capital (measured as inventory plus trade receivables minus trade payables)?

The company now pays its suppliers in full for the goods it purchased.

4 What is the cash position on the transaction now?

5 By how much has the cash position changed and by how much has working capital changed?

The company now receives payment in full from its customers for the goods they purchased.

6 What is the cash position on the transaction now?
7 By how much has the cash position changed and by how much has working capital changed?

Cash flow forecasts

A **cash flow forecast** is a forward-looking estimate of what a business expects its cash flows to be in the future.

The value of cash flow forecasts

Cash flow forecasts have many uses:

- Used for planning. Management are informed about what the cash position of the business is likely to be.
- Using the information in a cash flow forecast, management can decide whether the business will have a cash shortage (or a cash surplus).
- If a cash shortage is forecast, measures can be taken to improve the cash position, for example by negotiating a bank overdraft, or by taking measures to get customers to pay more quickly.

Constructing and analysing statements of cash flows forecasts

There are three stages to constructing cash flow forecasts:

1 Decide on the time span and time period or time intervals: often the time span will be 12 months, the time intervals will be one month.

2 Identify all of the cash inflows that are likely to occur, and in which time intervals (which months) they will happen. Cash inflows are likely to be:
   - Additional cash injections into the business by its owner or owners, as new long-term equity
   - Money received in the form of new bank loans
   - Money received from customers (both cash sales and payments of trade receivables).

3 Identify all the cash outflows that are likely to occur. These are likely to be cash payments for:

   - Payments to suppliers for purchases of goods or services
   - Payments of other operating expenses such as rental payments for property, the payment of wages and salaries to employees, payments for utilities such as electricity and water, and so on
   - Payments for purchases of capital items such as new equipment and machinery
   - Payments of interest on loans
   - Payments of dividends or drawings to the owners of the business.

A cash flow forecast can be very difficult for a new business to prepare because the business will not have any financial history on which to base its predictions. An established business can look back at what has happened before and can then build this in to a reasonably accurate forecast of cash flows in the future. It is important that a cash flow forecast is as realistic as possible. New businesses can sometimes be too optimistic about how successful they expect the business to be. Creating a "best", a "worst" and a "most likely" scenario is often a useful exercise for a new business when preparing cash flow forecasts before the business begins trading.

Example

Bellevue Hair Salon has several regular customers and can estimate, quite accurately, the cash inflow from customers each month.

The only cash inflow is from customers paying to have their hair styled.

The cash outflows are more numerous. There are two stylists who are paid each week. The shop is rented and the rent is paid monthly. Supplies of hair products are purchased every two months. Insurance premiums for the business are paid quarterly.

Cash inflows: Payments from customers.

Cash outflows: Wages; rent; payments to suppliers; insurance premiums.

The following simple format is often used to produce a cash flow forecast.

Cash inflows	$
Income from customers	500
Total inflow	500
Cash outflows	
Rent	200
Wages	150
Total outflow	350
Net cash flow	150

It simply lists:

- All cash inflows and shows a total for them
- All cash outflows and a total of outflows.

Then it subtracts the total cash outflows from the total of cash inflows to give a figure for the net cash flow.

Example

In the example the business has $150 more coming into the business than flowing out of the business. The difference between the cash inflow and the cash outflow is known as the **net cash flow**. This can be either positive or negative. In this instance Bellevue Hair Salon has a positive net cash flow.

Cash flow forecasts for a business, are fairly similar to the forecasts that many individuals make for themselves. In a household there is usually a need to list all of the income that can be expected and all the bills that need to be paid. The householder will then look at the closing balance to see if there is a need to draw on savings or take out a loan or an overdraft. This will depend on whether or not they expect the shortfall in cash to be short term or longer term.

Businesses do much the same thing when they prepare their cash forecasts.

Key term

Net cash flow: cash inflow minus cash outflow. This can be either a positive or a negative. figure.

However, the example above of the hair salon was for just one month of trading: there are other payments that need to be made such as the payments to suppliers every two months and the payment of insurance premiums every three months. The cash flow forecast will look different for those months. This is illustrated in the following example where the business also starts the period, at the beginning of May, with a cash amount of $50.

	May $	June $	July $
Cash inflows			
Income from customers	500	500	500
Total cash inflow	500	500	500
Cash outflows			
Rent	200	200	200
Wages	150	150	150
Supplies		50	
Insurance premium			50
Total cash outflow	350	400	400
Net cash flow	150	100	100
Opening cash balance	50	200	300
Closing cash balance	200	300	400

Even with the additional cash outflows in months 2 and 3 Bellevue Hair Salon still has a positive cash flow. The business is not going to be in a position where it cannot cover the necessary cash outflows.

If the calculation began without any figure being given for cash held at the start of the process then the balance to carry forward (closing balance) from the first month would be the same as the net cash flow.

Case study

Midi Computers

Jan runs a shop selling computers. The shop has done very well since it was set up two years ago. Jan has sold computers for home use. The profits have been good as he has been able to put a mark-up of 50 per cent on the price the computer manufacturers charge him. Jan buys the computers for an average of $200 and he is able to sell them for an average of $300. With other expenses averaging only $20 per computer that means a profit of around $80 per computer.

On the advice of a friend, Jan has recently started selling computers to business customers in Jan's town. He finds the business customers more demanding – they are much more skilled in negotiating lower prices and rather than

paying cash for the computers they expect two months credit.

Average prices for business customers are $250 so he should be making a profit of about $30 per computer.

However, Jan is very disappointed. Instead of the business's bank balance going up, he has an overdraft. "You want to get some credit from your suppliers" said Rose, one of Jan's business friends.

1   Why do you think Jan can make a profit on each computer and yet find himself with an overdraft?
2   How might getting more credit from suppliers help Jan reduce his overdraft?

The closing balance for month 1 is added to the net cash flow for month 2 to give a closing balance for month 2 and so on through all the months of the cash flow forecast.

It is important to remember that a cash flow forecast is just that: a forecast; a prediction. It is an estimation. It is not a statement of what has already happened but rather of what can reasonably be expected to happen in the future.

It is very important that a business carefully monitors the amount of cash that the business expects to have and this is achieved by preparing a cash flow forecast. The forecast will enable management to recognise whether there might be a cash flow problem – even if temporary – in the future, so that measures can be taken to ensure that cash (or an overdraft) is available.

The following example of a cash flow forecast covers a six-month period.

	January	February	March	April	May	June
	$000	$000	$000	$000	$000	$000
Cash inflows						
Cash sales	10	15	20	25	30	35
Payments of trade receivables	50	60	70	80	90	100
Total cash inflows	60	75	90	105	120	135
Cash outflows						
Lease payment	10					
Property rental payment	10	10	10	10	10	10
Payments to suppliers	25	35	45	55	65	75
Payments of wages and salaries	10	15	10	15	10	15
Other payments for operating expenses	5	5	5	5	5	5
Machine purchase			100			
Total cash outflows	60	65	170	85	90	105
Net cash flow	0	10	(80)	20	30	30
Opening cash balance	20	20	30	(50)	30	0
Closing cash balance	20	30	(50)	30	0	30

This cash flow forecast shows that although the business will increase its holding of cash slightly over the six-month period, there will be a cash deficit in March and April due to the spending of $100,000 to buy a machine in March. Management may try to finance the deficit by arranging a short-term loan with a bank. If the business is expected to have another negative cash balance later in the year, short-term borrowing by means of an overdraft might be preferred instead. (If a negative cash balance is expected for a long time, the business might seek additional long-term funding to eliminate the deficit.)

Activities

1 Draw up your own cash flow forecast for your personal income and spending. You can include any money that you might earn either at home or from a part-time job. You should also include any planned expenses such as a brother or sister's birthday present.

2 In small groups draw up what you think might be a cash flow forecast for an average or typical household.

Get it right

A high proportion of businesses fail in their first year. Most business failures, particularly of new businesses are caused by cash flow problems. Businesses get "easy" credit from suppliers but then find there is insufficient cash inflow to pay the suppliers at the right time. So cash may be more important than profit at times.

Key terms

Trade credit: when products can be purchased and payment for them is not required immediately. For example, 30 or 60 days might be allowed before payment must be made.

Cash inflow: cash flowing into a business from sales or loans.

Cash outflow: cash flowing from a business, for example, to pay rent or to pay suppliers.

Many new businesses fail due to poor cash flow and not because the business is not profitable. New businesses often find that their suppliers require them to pay for products or services in cash as soon as they receive them and it can be many months before suppliers give any trade credit to the business. However, the customers of the new business might expect to pay for the products or services at a later date because all the other businesses that they deal with allow them to purchase on credit terms. The problem is that the business would be paying money out immediately but would be having to wait for the receipt of cash from sales. This creates a potential cash flow problem - money flowing out but no money flowing in.

Analysing timings of cash inflows and outflows
What if there is a change to cash inflows and outflows?
The expected cash inflows and outflows of a business can change, in which case the cash flow forecast might need to be adjusted. Businesses should keep their cash position under continual review, so that they remain aware of any possible problem in the future, and take measures in advance to deal with it.

The best way of keeping the cash position (or liquidity position, as it is sometimes called) under review is to revise the cash forecast regularly.

Progress questions

1 What is meant by the term "cash flow forecast"?
2 Briefly explain the difference between cash and profit.
3 Explain one reason why cash flow is important to a business.
4 Explain two uses of a cash flow forecast.
5 Explain what is meant by a "liquidity problem".
6 Why might a business experience problems forecasting cash flows?

Interpretation of cash flow forecasts
From a cash flow forecast it is necessary to check for the following possibilities:

• Are there times of the year when a cash shortfall is forecast?
• If there are, how long is it predicted to last?

- What is the largest cash shortfall?
- What causes the cash shortfalls?
- In which months does the business have a cash surplus?
- How large do the surpluses become?

Knowing the answer to these questions can suggest strategies to deal with cash shortfalls. For example, should the business:

- Borrow to cover shortfall periods? Borrowing too much for too long would create an unnecessary cash surplus.
- Attempt to reduce cash outflows? How could this be done? Can some payments be deferred, or some receipts brought forward, to eliminate a short-term cash deficit in the future?
- Attempt to increase sales to increase cash inflows? This might work if it is done in the low sales months.
- Borrow to cover capital investment. This may work if the surplus is used to repay the debt later on.
- Do nothing. This may work in the short term and if the business has an overdraft facility, but if the shortfall is predicted get worse then action must be taken.
- Reschedule spending commitments. How critical are they to the business operations?

The answers to these questions may also lead to suggestions for strategies to deal with cash surpluses. However, the cash flow forecasts are based on forecasts and the answers to these questions are totally dependent on the assumptions made for these forecasts. This means that the forecasts are only as good as the assumptions.

This leads to the most important use of the forecasts: the "What if?" analysis. By varying the assumptions (in other words, asking "What if …?") the cash flow will show how sensitive the key outcomes (cash deficits or cash surpluses) are to the assumptions that have been made in the forecast. This means that informed decisions can be made with some regard to the uncertainties in forecasting.

Ways of improving working capital and cash flow

Cash forecasts can be used to predict cash deficits and take measures to prevent them from happening. Some measures to prevent a cash deficit would be to:

- Defer the purchase of new capital equipment
- Lease equipment instead of purchasing it: leasing involves lower payments when the asset is acquired, but lease payments (unlike a purchase cost) continue throughout the term of the lease
- Selling some assets that have a market value, such as a business property; however assets sales might have a negative effect on business operations, and a business might not have any assets that can be easily sold anyway
- Defer the payment of large dividends to shareholders, or reduce the amount of dividend payments.

Large "one-off" payments could possibly be deferred to improve the cash flow position, and this might be sufficient to deal with a potential

> ### Get it right
>
> You must be prepared to draw up a cash flow forecast or to calculate missing figures from a given forecast. You might be asked to make adjustments to a given cash flow forecast from given changes that are expected to occur. You should also be prepared to interpret a given cash flow forecast.

short-term cash shortage. However it might not be possible to deal with a cash shortage in this way, because there are no large "one-off" payments in the cash forecast.

Another way of trying to improve cash flows is to manage working capital – inventories, trade receivables and trade payables.

Managing cash and working capital

There are several ways in which managing working capital can help to ease cash flow problems and cash shortages. To understand how this is possible, you need to remember that changes in working capital result in a change in the cash position, as previously explained.

Managing inventory

If a business increases the amount of inventory it holds, its holding of cash will fall by the amount of the increase in inventory. Similarly, if a business is able to reduce the amount of inventory that it holds, its cash position will improve by the amount of the reduction in inventory.

This means that if a business needs to improve its cash flows and cash position, it could look for ways of reducing inventory levels.

However, reducing inventories is not always as easy as it may seem. If a business holds less inventory, it may be unable to produce goods quickly enough to meet sales demand. Inventory shortages can hold up operations.

Even so, many companies have improved their cash flows by entering into just-in-time (JIT) purchasing arrangements with suppliers, which dramatically reduces inventory levels. However, if a business already operates a JIT purchasing system, there will be little or no scope for reducing inventory levels further.

Managing trade receivables

If a business increases the amount of goods or services that it sells on credit, so that there is an increase in its trade receivables, its holding of cash will fall by the amount of the increase in trade receivables. Similarly, if a business is able to reduce the amount of trade receivable, its cash position will improve by the amount of the reduction.

This means that if a business needs to improve its cash flows and cash position, it could look for ways of reducing trade receivables.

There are several ways in which trade receivables might be reduced.

- A business could encourage more customers to pay immediately, when they buy goods or services. Increasing cash sales and reducing sales on credit would result in an earlier receipt of cash.
- A business might encourage customers who have purchased on credit to make their payments sooner, for example by offering a discount for early payment. Discounts for early payment, however, would reduce profits and might not be sufficient anyway to tempt customers to pay early.
- If customers are in the habit of paying late, a business might improve its efforts to get late payers to pay on time.

> **Key term**
>
> Inventory: stock of goods. These may be stocks of raw materials and other items purchased from suppliers, or part-finished production, or goods that have been manufactured (finished goods) but have not yet been sold.

A problem with measures to reduce trade receivables is that they might affect sales. In some industries customers expect to buy goods or services on credit. Any measures by a business to discourage sales on credit might have the effect of annoying customers, who might take their business elsewhere. A business needs to make sales in order to make profits, and selling on credit might be necessary.

Another way of reducing trade receivables is **debt factoring** – selling invoices to a debt factor. Debt factoring has the effect of achieving an early payment of customer invoices, but a disadvantage of debt factoring is the cost. Profits will be reduced by the debt factoring charges, so that in the longer-term, profits and cash flows will be worse.

Managing trade payables

If a business increases the amount of goods or services that it buys on credit or takes longer to pay its suppliers, so that there is an increase in its trade payables, its holding of cash will improve by the amount of the increase in trade payables. In effect, the cash position can be improved by deferring payments to suppliers.

A problem with increasing trade payables by paying later is that suppliers might not be willing to allow this to happen. If suppliers already offer reasonable credit terms, they will be reluctant to agree to a longer period of credit (in other words to allow a longer time for payment) and they will be annoyed if the business starts to pay its invoices late.

It might be possible to negotiate longer credit from some suppliers, but without the full agreement of suppliers, measures to defer payments could be unwise, because of the risk of worsening business relationships with suppliers.

Increasing sales

A completely different approach to improving the cash position is to try to sell more goods or services, or try to sell at a bigger profit. When sales volumes increase, there will usually be an increase in working capital, with more inventories and more trade receivables. However the increase in money received from higher sales should improve the overall cash position. Similarly, making a bigger profit on sales would also improve the cash position.

So how easy or how difficult might it be to improve profits and profitability?

Ways of improving profit and profitability and difficulties involved

Improving profits and profitability will not only improve cash flows. It will also make a business more successful in achieving its main business objective – to achieve profitability and grow profits. The management of a business should be looking continually for ways to improve profits.

- Total profits can be improved by increasing total sales revenue or reducing total costs. Total profits can be improved either by selling more at the same profit margin, or by improving profitability.
- Profitability is improved by achieving a higher ratio of operating profit to sales revenue.

Reduce costs

It might be possible to reduce costs, so that profit margins are increased. This would improve profitability and profits. Ways of reducing costs might be to:

- Improve labour productivity, for example by increasing automation in operations
- Reduce prices paid to suppliers: however, buying goods or services at lower prices could have an adverse effect on the quality of operations
- Be more rigorous in controlling various costs, such as the costs of electricity and energy
- Finding ways to operate more cheaply, such as moving to cheaper business premises, or cutting spending on training.

However, management should be trying to reduce costs all the time, and it might not be possible to improve profits by cutting costs further, without affecting the effectiveness of operations and damaging profits in the longer term.

Increase the prices of products or services sold

Another way of increasing profitability might be to increase the prices that are charged to customers. If customers are willing to pay the higher prices, both profitability (profit margins) and total profits would improve.

However, the effect of an increase in prices will depend on how competitors react. If there are a lot of competitors who do not increase their price, customers are likely to switch to buying from the competition, and sales volume would fall.

The effect on profit would depend on the amount of the fall in sales volume, and whether the fall in sales volume is more than offset by the effect of the price increase.

Businesses should consider planned price rises carefully, and assess the effect that they might have on sales volume, profitability and total profits, as well as on other business objectives (for example an objective of increasing market share, which might be badly affected by an increase in selling prices).

Case study

Lakeside hotel

Suzie and Ahmed run Lakeside, a small hotel. They offer bed, breakfast and an evening meal to their guests. They purchase frozen meat, vegetables and pastries from MPJ, a local supplier. After several increases in the price of those products over the past three years, Suzie and Ahmed decided that they could no longer afford to use their current supplier. The increased cost of food ingredients was having a negative effect on their cash flow situation. When a representative from MPJ telephoned for the weekly order Suzie told him that they were considering buying from a cheaper supplier. MPJ rang back within ten minutes to offer them a 10 per cent reduction in price on their orders. Profits and cash flow improved!

1 Why do you think that MPJ did not offer a 10 per cent discount to Suzie and Ahmed until they said they were about to buy from another supplier?

Case study

Carrefour

In 2011 Carrefour, a French supermarket chain, and one of the largest retailers in the world, reported a sharp fall in profits by 40%.

Faced with rising purchase costs for the products it re-sold, Carrefour increased its prices. However, other French supermarket chains did not follow, and Carrefour lost customers and market share. Carrefour responded by reversing its pricing policy and it reduced prices; however it was unable to recover sales revenues to their previous level and profits and profitability were poor.

Carrefour's further response to falling profits was to abandon a merger with a Brazilian supermarket chain, postpone major shop refurbishments and introduce redundancies throughout the workforce.

1 What do you think Carrefour hoped to achieve by increasing prices?

2 What do you think Carrefour hoped to achieve by reducing prices?

3 Why do you think neither policy achieved the desired effect of increasing profits?

4 What impact was Carrefour's response to falling profits likely to have had on cash flows and profits?

Increase sales volume

Profits might also be improved by increasing sales volume. Sales volumes might be increased by:

- Reducing selling prices, and attracting more customers; however, profit margins and profitability would decline and it is not clear that lower selling prices would have the effect of increasing profits.

- Expanding the business into new geographical markets, or developing new products; however strategies to develop the business and increase profits will take time to plan and implement.

- Spending more on marketing activities. More spending on marketing might result in more sales and bigger profits, but the benefits from higher sales might be offset by the cost of the extra marketing activities.

  Although it is possible to identify ways in which profits and profitability might be improved, achieving improvements in practice can be a difficult task, but one which management should be continually pursuing.

Exam-style questions

1 Explain one potential benefit to a business of preparing cash flow forecasts. (3 marks)

2 Bargain Basement (BB) is a business with several large retail outlets in many large towns selling household products and basic foods at very low prices. Two months ago the decision was taken to expand the range of items being sold to include plants and some small furniture items. It is hoped that the expanded range of products will bring many new customers to the shops of BB. The changes being made are not as a result of any feedback from customers but are because the managers of some shops feel that the extra items will boost overall sales. The management recognise that they will need to spend money to purchase the new items before they are able to put them on sale. They are worried that this will have a negative effect on the cash flow situation.

The management of Bargain Basement has prepared a cash flow forecast for the next three months. The new range of products will go on sale for the first time in June.

	April	May	June
	$000	**$000**	**$000**
Cash inflows			
Sales	23	22	25
Total cash inflow	23	22	25
Cash outflows			
Rent	5	5	5
Wages	4	4	4
Purchases	12	20	21
Total cash outflow	21	29	30
Net cash flow	2	(7)	(5)
Opening balance	7	9	2
Closing balance	9	2	(3)

BB has increased its purchase of items in May ready for the launch of the new products in June. If BB took the decision to reduce the purchases made in May to $16,000 what would be the effect on the closing cash balance in June? (3 marks)

3 At the beginning of its financial year, a business held inventories costing $25,000 and had trade receivables of $36,000 and trade payables of $22,000. At the end of the year it held inventories costing $41,000 and had trade receivables of $32,000 and trade payables of $29,000.

Calculate the effect on cash flows during the year (the increase or reduction in cash flow) arising from the change in working capital during the year. (3 marks)

4 Cash flow forecasts are based on estimates or expectations of future cash flows.

Analyse the difficulties that a new business might have when preparing a cash flow forecast. (9 marks)

5 The management of a company are considering ways of improving profit and profitability. A suggestion has been put forward that selling prices should be increased by 5%, although the likely effect of this would be a fall in sales volume (the quantities of items sold) by 5%.

Analyse the arguments for and against an increase in sales prices to improve profit and profitability. (9 marks)

6 A business has been expanding rapidly, with a large increase in sales. This has been accompanied by a large increase in working capital (inventories, trade receivables and trade payables) and spending on new equipment. Although the company is very profitable, it is facing a serious cash flow deficit.

The managing director of the business believes that the best way to overcome the potential deficit is to reduce the investment in working capital.

Do you think that managing working capital is an effective way of avoiding a cash deficit?

Assess the argument for and against and make a judgement. (12 marks)

Glossary

A

Adding value: the process of increasing the value or worth of a good or service.

Adverse variance: where the variance contributes to a lower than budgeted profit.

Agency employees: individuals who are employed by an agency. Businesses can hire workers from an agency to make up a shortfall in their own internal staff.

Average unit cost: total cost in a period divided by the number of units produced.

B

Barrier to entry: obstacles that make it difficult to enter a specific market.

Big data: very large databases holding vast amounts of data.

Break-even: the level of output and sales at which total revenue = total costs.

Budget: a financial plan for the future.

Buffer inventory: the products or raw materials of an organisation maintained on hand or in transit to stabilise variations in supply, demand and production.

Business objectives: the stated, measurable targets that provide the means to achieve business aims.

Business plan: a document setting out the objectives of a business and exactly how the business intends to achieve them in practical terms. It contains objectives, strategic and tactical plans, market information and budgets.

Business functions: the different areas of activity within a business.

C

Capacity (operating capacity or output capacity): the maximum output that operations can produce in a period, given their existing resources and normal methods of operating.

Capacity utilisation: the percentage of operating capacity that is used in a period of time.

Capital: the finance needed to run a business as well as the equipment used in production, such as computers, factories, offices and vehicles.

Cash: legal tender used for making and receiving payments, and money held in bank accounts or in the form of banknotes and coins.

Cash flow: the flow of cash into and out of a business.

Cash inflow: cash flowing into a business from sales or loans.

Cash outflow: cash flowing from a business, e.g. to pay rent or to pay suppliers.

Centralisation: the process by which decisions are made within an organisation. When they are centralised they are made at the top level of the organisation.

Charity: a non-profit or not-for-profit organisation that aims to provide a contribution to the social well-being of individuals or groups of people.

Collective bargaining: negotiating by a trade union with employers on behalf of all of the employees who are trade union members.

Commission: payment made according to the number of sales achieved.

Competition: in business, a situation in which two or more business organisations seek to persuade the same customers to buy their products or services in preference to those of rival businesses.

Concentration ratio: the ratio of the combined market shares of a given number of companies to the whole market size.

Confidence level: the probability that an outcome will occur.

Consumers: people who buy goods or services for personal use or personal consumption.

Contribution per unit: the sales price minus the variable cost per unit. Total contribution = the volume of sales multiplied by the contribution per unit.

Co-operative: a business owned by its members, who could be employees, customers or groups such as local farmers.

Correlation: relationship between the values of two variables, and how changes in the value of one variable relate to changes in the value of the other variable. Correlation may be positive, negative or non-existent.

Cost of sales: in retailing, the purchase cost of the items sold in a period. In manufacturing, the production cost of goods sold in a period: production costs consist of direct materials and components costs, production labour costs and other production overhead costs.

Crowd funding: obtaining funding for a business (or other venture), usually via the internet, from a large number of individuals.

Customer: the person/organisation that buys products or services. The final person/organisation in a chain is also known as the consumer.

Customer retention rate: the proportion of customers who continue to buy the product or service of a business from one year to the next.

Customer service: the process of providing a service to customers, before, during and after a purchase. The aim should be to deliver customer satisfaction.

D

Data mining: analysing big data, typically using techniques such as machine learning and artificial intelligence, to obtain new information.

Debentures (bonds): loans sold by businesses to raise finance from investors. They are like shares, in the sense that they can be traded, but bond investors do not have ownership rights.

Debt factoring: a method of short-term financing in which a business sells its customer invoices to a debt factor, and receives a proportion of the invoice value immediately and the rest, minus the factor's charges, when the invoices are eventually paid.

Decentralisation: delegating decisions to people at lower levels in an organisation.

Decision tree: a quantitative technique that can be used to distinguish the likely outcomes of different decisions.

Delegation: giving authority to make decisions and perform tasks to someone lower in the organisation hierarchy.

Diversity: in a workplace this means having a workforce drawn from a wide range of different backgrounds and characteristics, for example with differences in race, ethnicity, age, gender and sexual orientation.

Dividend: the reward paid to shareholders from the profits of a limited company.

Dividend per share: the reward per share that is paid to shareholders of a limited company.

Dividend yield: the rate of return that a holder of ordinary shares receives based on the market price of each share held. A dividend yield can be calculated only for companies whose shares have a market price; these are public companies whose shares are traded on a stock market. The dividend yield is calculated on dividends paid in the previous 12 months.

E

E-commerce: the conducting of business by digital means.

Efficiency: the rate at which a task is performed or output is produced. This can also be a measurement of the amount of resources that production uses relative to its output. Lower resource use for a given output is more efficient and less costly.

Employee consultation: the involvement of employees in some business decisions.

Employee engagement: when an employee is fully committed to the business and views the attainment of their personal objectives as being beneficial to the overall business objectives.

Empowerment: the giving of power to employees so that they can make some of the decisions relating to their area of business activity.

Enterprise: a person with enterprise has determination, ideas and vision and is willing to take risks in order to make the business happen.

Entrepreneur: a person prepared to take the risk of setting up and engaging in a business.

Ethical marketing: marketing that promotes ethical aspects of an organisation's products and activities. Ethics in business and marketing relate to issues such as environmental protection, social responsibility and employee welfare.

Exchange rate: the value of one country's currency relative to the currency of another country.

Exclusive distribution policy: policy of giving a distributor the exclusive right to distribute a product, typically within a specified geographical area.

Extension strategy: marketing strategy to extend the profitable stages of a product's life (growth and maturity).

External finance: finance from sources outside the business.

F

Family business: a business in which all of the owners are related members of one family.

Favourable variance: where the difference between budgeted and actual performance contributes to a greater than budgeted profit.

Financial rewards: monetary incentives given to employees, e.g. bonus payments.

Fixed costs: costs that are the same fixed amount in total regardless of the level of output and sales.

Flexible contracts: these allow the hours and days of work to be varied by agreement between employers and employees according to the needs of the business and/or the individual employee. These can include an agreement to allow flexible working hours within agreed parameters.

Full-time contract: a contract for a permanent job.

G

Goods: items that you buy, such as food, books, toys, clothes and make-up.

Government grant: an amount of money available from the government that does not require repayment.

Gross profit: turnover/revenue minus the cost of sales.

H

Hierarchy: in an organisation, a structure in which there are different levels of authority and seniority of management.

Human resources (HR): the business function of ensuring that the employees of an organisation are used in the most effective way possible to achieve optimum business performance.

I

Input: something that contributes to the production of a product or service.

Intensive distribution policy: policy of selling as much of a product as possible, in as many markets and as many locations as possible.

Interest rate: the cost of borrowing or the reward for saving.

Internal finance: finance from within the business: retained profits.

Inventory: stock of goods. These may be stocks of raw materials and other items purchased from suppliers, or part-finished production, or goods that have been manufactured (finished goods) but have not yet been sold.

Inventory control chart: shows the level of stock held over time.

J

Job design: structuring jobs by deciding the tasks and responsibilities that should go with each job.

Just-in-case inventory control: involves maintaining high levels of raw materials and finished goods inventories, to ensure that the business is always able to meet customer demand, even when there is a disruption to material supplies or an unexpected increase in demand.

Just-in-time: managing the flow of raw materials, work-in-progress, finished products in a production system so that items are available exactly when they are needed for production and not before.

Just-in-time inventory control: involves managing inventories of raw materials, work-in-progress and finished products so that these are available exactly when they are needed and not before.

K

Kaizen: processes to achieve continuous improvement.

Key performance indicators (KPIs): measures of business performance that are considered by management to be an important guide as to how well the company is doing.

L

Labour: the workforce of the business, made up of manual and skilled labour.

Labour productivity: the amount produced by an employee in a given time period.

Labour turnover: the number of employees leaving a business in a given time period. It is usually expressed as a labour turnover percentage rate.

Land: not just the land itself, but also all of the renewable and non-renewable natural resources on that land, such as coal, crude oil and timber.

Large business: a business that has a large number of employees, assets and turnover.

Lead time: the time taken for inventory to arrive from supplier after it is ordered.

Lean production: in manufacturing businesses, using resources as efficiently as possible by minimise waste and eliminating activities that do not add value, and at the same time ensuring quality.

Leasing: rather than buying assets such as major machinery, vehicles or buildings, a business can pay another business (a leasing company business) for the right to use the asset in return for a series of lease payments over the term of the lease. The leasing company retains ownership of the asset.

Limited liability: a situation in which the owners of a business can only lose the money they have put into the business and not their own personal wealth.

Loans: money lent by a lender to a borrower, usually for a fixed term, and on which interest is payable by the borrower.

Logistics: the operations involved in transporting goods to customers.

Long-run finance: finance that is needed by a business for a longer period of time. Sometimes finance provided for one to five years is known as medium-term finance.

M

Managers of a business: the people in charge of the business operations.

Margin of safety: the difference between the break-even level of output and the actual or budgeted output (when actual output is higher than the break-even level). It can be expressed as a quantity of sales units, or as a percentage of the actual or budgeted sales volume.

Market capitalisation: the total value of all the shares issued by a limited company at the current market price for the shares.

Market growth: the absolute or percentage increase in the size of a market.

Market leader: the biggest and most successful business in a specific sector.

Market mapping: using a chart (a market map) to position products or competitors in a market on the basis of how they rate according to two selected criteria.

Market segment: a part of a market that is distinctive in some way from the rest of the market.

Market segmentation: analysing a market and either dividing the market into segments for the purpose of marketing, or identifying attractive/distinctive sections within the overall market.

Market share: the proportion of total sales in a market obtained by the products of a business over a given period of time.

Market size: the total sales revenue or volume in the market.

Marketing: activities that promote and sell products or services.

Marketing budget: a financial plan, setting out the approved amount of expenditure on marketing activities for a financial year.

Market decline: the absolute or percentage decline in the size of a market.

Marketing mix: combination of policies and activities for achieving marketing objectives and targets.

Marketing objectives: aims for achievement through marketing activities, which should contribute to the achievement of overall business goals. Examples might be to increase sales (volume or value), increase market share or expand into new international markets.

Marketing strategy: a marketing plan for achieving marketing and business objectives.

Mass marketing: marketing a product to the entire market, without segmenting the market.

Micro-finance: a source of finance and financial services to small businesses that are unable to access conventional banking. It is more common in developing countries than in developed countries.

N

Net cash flow: cash inflow minus cash outflow. This can be either a positive or a negative figure.

Niche market: a very small section of the total market.

Niche marketing: targeting business activity (including marketing) on a small, specialised market.

Non-financial rewards: incentives given to employees other than those with a monetary value, e.g. extra holidays, employee of the month recognition.

Non-profit organisation: a type of organisation that does not earn profits for its owners.

O

Objectives: business objectives are the stated, measurable targets that provide the means to achieve business aims.

Operating profit: the gross profit minus all other expenses required to bring that product to the customer.

Operational budget: plan for operations expressed in money terms.

Operational flexibility: the ease with which a productive system can adapt to a changing market environment.

Operations function: the part of an organisation that produces goods or services and delivers them to customers.

Opportunity cost: the value of the next best opportunity that is lost by taking a particular decision.

Ordinary share capital (equity): the money raised by selling shares to shareholders.

Organisational design: the framework of a business indicating the lines of authority and communication, and responsibilities for decision-making.

Output: the quantity of products manufactured or services provided; something that occurs as a result of the transformation of business inputs.

Outsourcing: using another business (third party) to undertake some of the functions of a business (the host business).

Overdraft: a flexible source of short-term funding from a bank that allows a negative balance on the customer's bank account, up to a maximum amount or limit. An overdraft should be used to finance operating expenses when there is a short-term mismatch between money paid by the business and money coming in.

Owners of a business: the people that are entitled to the profits that the business makes.

P

Part-time contract: a contract of employment for a specified number of hours that is less than the number of hours worked by full-time employees.

Performance-related pay: payment made based on targets being met or exceeded.

Permanent contract: a contract of employment that does not specify a time period or have a termination date.

Piece rate payments: payments of a fixed amount per unit of work (per piece) produced.

Price elasticity of demand: a measure that compares the percentage change in demand for a product when there is a percentage change in the price. Price elasticity is usually either inelastic or elastic.

Price penetration: setting a low price for a product with the aim of winning market share.

Price skimming: setting a high price for a new product and gradually reducing the price over time, with the aim of getting as many customers as possible to pay a high price when the product is introduced to the market.

Primary sector: businesses that extract raw materials from the natural environment, for example, farming, mining, fishing, oil production, etc.

Private limited company: an incorporated business in the private sector where share ownership is limited to specified people, institutions or businesses. Shares are not available to the general public.

Private sector: the part of the economy that is owned by private individuals.

Product life cycle: stages through which a product's market progresses, from introduction to the market to decline and withdrawal from the market.

Productivity: a measure of efficiency, not simply a change in output. It is often expressed as a measure of how efficient labour is at production in a given time.

Profit: the difference between revenues and costs. Revenues and costs do not always happen at the same time as cash receipts and cash payments. Profit is the money left after total costs are deducted from total income.

Profit margin: gross profit and operating profit are also calculated as a percentage of turnover/revenue; this is known as profit margin (gross profit margin and operating profit margin).

Promotional mix: a specific combination of promotion policies and activities within the "promotion" element of the marketing mix. The promotional mix includes advertising, sales promotions and face-to-face selling.

Public limited company: a private sector incorporated business with the right to sell shares to the general public.

Public sector: that part of the economy that is owned by the government.

Q

Qualitative data: facts about the quality or value of something.

Quality: the fitness for use, customer satisfaction or conformance to requirements of an item.

Quality assurance: measures to prevent defects in quality from occurring.

Quality control: inspecting goods received from suppliers or inspecting items during the production process to check for defects, normally using sampling. The term may also be applied to inspecting finished goods from the manufacturing process, to check for defects before they are sold to customers.

Quantitative data: facts about the numerical aspects of something.

Quota sampling: non-random stratified sampling. This is used when the total population is divided into different categories or strata, but a sampling frame for the population is not available.

R

Random sampling: sampling in which every individual within a population has an equal chance of being selected for the sample. A sampling frame (a list of everyone in the population) is necessary for random sampling.

Recruitment: identifying the need for an employee, devising a job description and finding a person suitable to perform the job.

Reorder level: the level of inventory at which more inventory will be ordered.

Reorder quantity: the amount of materials or components in a purchase order.

Repeat sales: sales to customers who have bought the product or service previously.

Retained profits: the profits of a business, after interest and tax, that are not paid out to the business owners but are kept within the business, usually as a source of internal long-term finance.

Retention: with regard to labour, keeping existing employees so that they do not leave their job/ employment.

Return on investment: the financial benefit gained from an investment expressed as a percentage of the original investment.

Revenue (or turnover): the sales income earned by a business during a period of time.

Risk: a situation involving exposure to danger, harm or loss.

S

Salary scheme: method of payment in which individuals are paid a fixed annual amount, divided into 12 monthly payments.

Sales forecast: a quantitative estimate of sales demand in a future period.

Sales value: the amount of revenue from sales in a given period of time. It is always expressed as a money value.

Sales volume: the amount of sales of an item in a given period of time, commonly measured in units of sales.

Sampling: obtaining data from a small number of individuals in a population, in the expectation that the results from the sample will be representative of the population as a whole.

Secondary sector: businesses that manufacture and process raw materials, including those from the primary sector, for example producing electricity from coal, producing petrol and diesel from refining oil, the car manufacturing industry, cotton making, etc.

Selection: choosing a suitable person to fill a job vacancy from among all the applicants for the job.

Selective distribution policy: policy of distributing a product through selected outlets/distributors.

Services: actions such as haircuts, parcel delivery, car repair and teaching.

Share capital: finance obtained through selling new shares in a company. Share capital (equity) represents ownership of the company.

Share issue: the process of raising new equity capital by issuing new shares.

Share price: the price of one single share.

Shareholders: the owners of a limited company and other incorporated businesses.

Short-run finance: finance that is needed by a business for a short period of time, usually less than a year.

Simultaneous engineering: managing the processes for launching a new product so that various stages in development can take place at the same time instead of sequentially.

Small and medium-sized enterprise (SME): a business that has a limited number of employees, assets and turnover.

Social enterprise: a business venture whose main aim is helping people and/or the environment as opposed to making a profit.

Sole trader: a business owned by one person. The owner controls the business, often manages it and has usually provided all of the finance. There are no legal formalities needed to start up as a sole trader.

Span of control: the number of people that a manager, supervisor or team leader is directly responsible for.

Stakeholder: an individual or group who has an interest in a business. They can be affected by a business decision and/or have their views considered as part of the decision.

Start-up: a newly established business.

Stock exchange: a market where shares in public companies can be bought and sold.

Strategy: a plan of action designed to achieve a long-term aim or objective.

Stratified sampling: sampling in which a population is divided into categories or strata, and a sample is taken from each of the strata. Stratified samples should ideally be selected randomly.

Supply chain: the series of tasks involved in the production and movement of materials, components and finished goods from the original raw material suppliers to the final consumer.

Supply chain management: the process of obtaining all of the resources required by a business.

T

Tactic: a short-term course of action for the day-to-day management of a business or for trying to meet part of an overall strategy.

Tactical plans: actions to implement marketing strategy.

Target marketing: focusing business activity (including marketing) on one or more segments of the total market.

Temporary contract: a contract usually specifying a short-term period of employment, e.g. nine months, or until the completion of a project or order.

Tertiary sector: businesses that provide services, such as banking, retail, transport, tourism, etc.

Total contribution: the difference between sales revenue and total variable costs in a period. This contributes to covering fixed costs and making a profit. At break-even point, total contribution = fixed costs.

Total quality management (TQM): a structured approach to managing the quality of an organisation's products and services, involving the principles of "right first time" and continuous improvement, and involving all employees within the organisation.

Trade credit: when products can be purchased and payment for them is not required immediately. For example, 30 or 60 days might be allowed before payment must be made.

Trade payables: money owed to suppliers by a business for goods or services purchased on credit, which has not yet been paid.

Trade receivables: money owed to a business by customers who have purchased goods or services on credit and has not yet paid.

Training: providing employees with work-related skills.

Transformation process: the process of transforming "inputs" into "outputs".

U

Unincorporated: a private sector business that has not been registered as a company. Sole traders and partnerships are unincorporated.

Unlimited liability: a situation in which an individual or group of individuals are totally liable for the consequences of a course of action. For example, if a sole trader's business runs into trouble, the sole trader is personally responsible for paying all of the business's debts and could be forced to sell their personal possessions to pay their business's debts.

V

Variable costs: costs that increase in total with increases in the volume of output and sales. It is normally assumed that the variable cost per unit is a constant amount.

Variance: the difference between budgeted and actual performance.

Variance analysis: the process of calculating and examining variances in order to improve business performance.

Venture capital: finance provided by investors (individuals or businesses) who specialise in investing in risky business ventures such as start-ups.

W

Working capital: there are different definitions of working capital. For the purpose of this book, working capital is the sum of the value of inventories and trade receivables minus the amount of trade payables.

Z

Zero hours contract: a contract of employment where the employee does not have any guaranteed hours of work. Employees are only paid for the hours they are actually required to work, which might be zero in any given time period.

Answers

1.1 – progress questions, case studies, exam-style questions

Progress Questions

1. Capital items are machinery and equipment that a business continuously needs in order to produce goods and/or services. For a farm growing melons the capital items would include farm equipment to plant, fertilise, water and harvest the melons. Capital items also include other items such as farm buildings.

2. Outputs are the goods and services delivered, so the output from an office cleaning business is the cleaned offices.

3. A transport business makes a packet of tea more valuable by transporting it from the manufacturer or warehouse (where it is of little use to the final consumer) to the shop where the final consumer can buy it.

4. Value added is measured by taking the value of all of the inputs (usually the cost) from the value of the processed product (usually the price).

5. Opportunity cost is the benefit foregone when a decision is taken. So, for example, if I buy a new car I have lost the interest I would have got if I left the money in the bank earning interest.

6. Answer depends on the decision chosen. Discuss this with your class.

7.

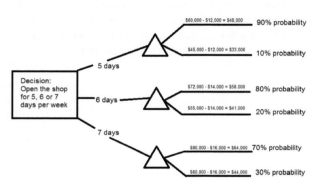

8. A business plan should include:
   - An executive summary or overview of the plan
   - An outline of the product or service that will be provided
   - Market analysis
   - A marketing plan
   - A production plan
   - An organisation plan (the people in the business)
   - A financial plan

9a. A new business needs a business plan to:
   - Set objectives and targets for what it is trying to achieve
   - Make sure that it has the money and other resources to achieve these objectives
   - Plan how it is going to achieve these objectives
   - Make the business think about all of the details and make sure that nothing is forgotten
   - Show to a bank or investors, to convince them that the business will be financially sound.

9b. A well-established, large business needs a business plan for similar reasons, to:
   - Review how things are currently done and what can be improved or changed
   - Decide what it wants to achieve further, in the future; for example to set out new business ideas
   - Make sure that it has the money and other resources to achieve these objectives
   - Plan how it is going to achieve these objectives
   - Show a bank or investors to convince them that the business will be profitable.

Case Studies

Sadie's new business
1. Ideas include: freedom, being her own boss, finding productive use of her savings.
2. Getting customers, setting right price, advertising, negotiating/buying equipment, supplies.
3. Plans for setting up the business, keeping track of customers/orders, keeping track of money, monitoring work progress.

Lee's restaurant
1. In addition to the cost of food ingredients, Lee also has to pay other costs such as staff wages, the cost of running the restaurant (the building, electricity, water) and charge enough to make a profit.
2. Lee might want to charge more to cover rising costs and/or to increase his profits.
3. Review your previous answer.

Stella's taxis
1. The total revenue ($11,000) minus the total costs ($8,500) leaves a profit for the month of $2,500.
2. If the total revenue was $8,000 the total costs would still be $8,500 (although fuel costs might be a bit less than $2,000 if there are fewer taxi journeys) so there would be a loss of £500 for the month.

Angelo's shirts
1. Angelo could be competitive by selling shirts more cheaply than the competition, or by selling something that the competition do not sell, for example, a different type/brand/colour/fabric of shirt to the competition. He could use discounts or special offers to attract customers. He could also consider the location of his shop and if this could be more appealing to customers.

At Home Store
1. The Thenins thought that a business plan was only for the benefit of the bank in order to get the loan, so was paperwork that they did not want to spend time on. They had an idea about what to do with the business and wanted to get going with it.
2. The business plan made the Thenins think about aspects of the business that they had not thought about before, and do research to better understand the market, which changed their plans. The business plan helped them to set objectives and have a longer-term goal, which they could measure if they achieved it. This helped them to be successful and to scope out further future ventures, such as the household consultancy business.
3. The Thenins learned the value of having a business plan, and how this helped them to set objectives, know their market, and plan for the future. Planning is an ongoing benefit for all businesses, which need to think all the time about where the business should be going, and how they can get there.

Volkswagen
1. To be the largest manufacturer of new electronic car products and self-drive cars, to be the best-known brand for new electronic car products and self-drive cars, to be known as the market leaders in new vehicle technologies.
2. The key performance indicators could be the growth in sales of new electronic car products and self-drive cars, the growth in profit from those sales, the company's share of the total market for electric and self-drive cars, and the growth in market awareness and brand recognition.
3. To be the first to market with new electronic car products and self-drive cars, to be competitive with pricing and offers, and by developing and selling cars that are different to the competition.

Sir Richard Branson
1. This will depend on where you are from. It is great to research people who have been successful near to you.
2. This will depend on the individual, but think about what they have achieved, what they have needed to do this, and how they have made their business a success.

Jumpstart Our Business Startups (JOBS) Act
1. Less risk, better guarantees and probability of repayment, known history – a "safer bet".
2. Small businesses will employ more people.
3. Banks might not lend, and other sources of finance to small businesses are limited.
4. Concern about increased competition, unfair competition.

Condor Copper

1. Three stakeholders (stakeholder groups) are employees, the community and the government.
2. Employees will benefit from having a job in the company. In a place with high unemployment, they might not easily find a job anywhere else. So CC offers the opportunity for a better future. The community will benefit from new roads and housing, and from higher employment in the area, all providing a better quality of life. However, the community may be concerned about the disruption of the project, including noise, pollution and traffic. The government will be keen for the community to benefit from the jobs and infrastructure, and will also be interested in the effect the project has on the economy and tax income, and also on the need for any new laws or regulations that might be required when the mine is opened.
3. The employees will likely have little say in the decision-making process. People in the community and community leaders may be consulted about decisions and asked for their opinion. The government will have more involvement in or influence over decisions because of its powers to pass laws and make regulations, and to tax business.

Exam-style Questions

1. D
2. C. A business must decide what it is trying to achieve (objectives) before it can decide on a strategy and detailed tactics for achieving them. Objectives, targets, strategies and tactics together make up the final business plan (although tactics can be decided after an outline business plan has been formulated).
3. There is a risk that business decisions will not be the best that could have been made, and that events may not turn out as well as expected. However, risk is unavoidable in business, since future results and events cannot be predicted with 100% confidence.
4. Only one function of a manager is needed for an answer. Answers can mention the functions of planning, controlling operations, communicating, co-ordinating or simply "decision-making". A brief explanation of the function should be included in the answer.
5. Answers might discuss:
   - Possible difficulties in obtaining the money to set up the business (such as to make an advance payment of rent on premises) and pay for stock: reluctance of banks to lend to new businesses
   - Winning customers. A new business might need time to become known and win customers. Need to sell enough to cover operating costs and costs of stock
   - High risks of selling goods in the clothing (fashion) industry
   - Difficulty of making progress against more established competitors (including sellers of clothing online)
   - Probable need to operate the shop with a small number of staff; the need for all staff to work hard and for long hours might be a problem.
6. The chief argument in favour of the view that entrepreneurs are only interested in making a profit is that the objective of a business should be to make a profit. If a business is not profitable, it will eventually run out of money and is unlikely to survive. However, an entrepreneur may be interested in other things in addition to making a profit:
   - Personal interest of the entrepreneur in the activities of the business
   - Personal challenge: wanting to be a business success
   - Wanting to provide employment for family members (many start-up businesses are family businesses).
   A judgement might be that entrepreneurs must want to make a profit if they want the business to succeed, but there are other considerations that make them want to develop their business.
7. This question can be answered in several ways. Here is a suggestion.
   - The function of a business entrepreneur is to have an original business idea, identify ways of turning the idea into practice, and take the risks of setting up the business (such as financial risks, in case the business fails). Some entrepreneurs have to work for a long time before their business succeeds.
   - An entrepreneur is needed throughout the period when the business is being established, contributing ideas, energy and money.
8. The benefits of new business start-ups. Only one should be discussed in the answer:
   - Although they begin as small businesses, they bring employment to the country: more people get jobs and wages or salaries
   - Many business start-ups will succeed and grow into bigger businesses. This will benefit the country as a whole, bringing more wealth and a better standard of living generally.

- Eventually, a successful business will grow to the stage where it has more extensive and larger-scale operations and employs many more people. A larger business needs more careful planning, co-ordination, control and 'people management'. Entrepreneurs are not always the right sort of individual for this type of management work.
- The sort of person needed to run an established business is therefore not the same sort of person that is needed to establish it.
- But when does a business reach the stage where it is sufficiently established and its entrepreneur founder is no longer needed?

Judgement (suggested). Entrepreneurs might be needed for more than just a 'short time' in order for the business to become successful. Answers might also mention that some entrepreneurs have remained successfully as leaders of their business (e.g. James Dyson, the industrial design engineer).

1.2 – progress questions, case studies, exam-style questions

Progress Questions

1. Advantages of operating as a sole trader include (choose any two):
   - Easy to set up
   - Easy to manage
   - Owner has freedom to manage everything
   - Decision-making is easy
   - Owner keeps all of the profits.
2. A sole trader business is **owned** by one person. The owner can employ as many people as he/she likes and this will not affect ownership.
3. Unlimited liability means that the owner is personally liable for any debts that the business might incur and the owner risks losing everything if things go badly wrong. This is a problem for the owner as it is likely to limit the risks that they will take with the business, and will limit the amount of personal finance that the owner will put into the business.
4. Limited liability is important in helping businesses to grow. Without limited liability, risk to owners is high, meaning owners, and others, are unlikely to invest large amounts for fear of losing personal possessions such as houses. With limited liability owners are only likely to lose, at most, the investments they put into the business. Owners, therefore, are more likely to expand and grow their business.
5. Disadvantages of being incorporated include loss of some of the benefits of being unincorporated:
   - Loss of freedom for the owner
   - Need to follow rules and regulations
   - Loss of privacy
   - Involvement of others in decisions, making decision-making more difficult.
6. Benefits of converting from a private limited company to a public limited company include:
   - Greater access to finance: a public company is able to invite the investing public to invest, if it wishes to do so
   - Higher profile
   - Better image
   - Better assurance for potential investors: shares in a public company are usually much easier to sell than shares in a private company.
7. A new business might not seek to be a public limited company from the outset because the costs of launching a public limited company are very high. The risk of such a large "set-up" cost would be too high. In addition, investors would know nothing about the business until it has been operating for a while. It is better to start more modestly and then convert to public limited status once established.
   There are few advantages in being a public company rather than a private company until the time comes when its owners want to issue new shares to the general investing public.
8. The public sector covers activities owned and managed by the government or "the State"). The private sector consists of businesses owned by private individuals, such as companies and sole trader businesses.
9. In most countries, supermarkets are not owned by the government so are privately owned. Therefore they are in the private sector.
10. "Social enterprise" is a term that covers a business that looks beyond making a profit as an objective. It may aim to help people or to improve the environment. Social enterprises have a "triple bottom line" – People, Planet and Profit.

11. "Social enterprises" have an overriding objective which is not profit driven, in contrast with traditional businesses which usually have "profit" as a central objective.

12. Small and medium-sized enterprises (SMEs) have the following advantages:
    - Today's small businesses become the successful businesses of the future: a large number of SMEs can be a sign of a healthy national economy
    - Create jobs contributing to the overall level of employment in the economy
    - Generate competition for larger businesses, which is good for consumers
    - Might supply a part of the market that has been ignored by large businesses
    - Can often respond faster to changes in the market than large businesses: SMEs are generally more innovative than established businesses
    - The service provided by small businesses is usually more personalised.

13. Some disadvantages of being a large business are:
    - Can be inflexible and therefore take a long time to reach decisions and react to market changes
    - May experience diseconomies of scale, such as difficulties in communicating with large numbers of employees or inefficiencies caused by the duplication of efforts
    - It can be argued that large businesses are run by professional managers, and so are less dynamic than smaller businesses run by entrepreneurs.

Case Studies

Mobile phone apps

1. The only significant disadvantage in becoming a private limited company is that there will be some additional administrative requirements that a private company must comply with (company regulations). However, these are not usually burdensome, and in some countries many individuals prefer to set up their private limited company rather than operate as a sole trader.

2. Miguel won't want to change to a public limited company as the costs of launching a public limited company are very high. The risk of such a large set-up cost would be too high. In addition, investors would know nothing about the business until it has been operating for a while. It is better to start more modestly and then convert to public limited status once established. Miguel does not need much more finance at this stage of the business development: becoming a public company only makes sense when the company needs to raise a large amount of finance from the general investing public.

Facebook in 2012

1. Selling shares to convert from the present business structure (e.g. sole trader, private limited) to a public limited company.

2. Competition, customers, employees might use the information for their own benefit.

3. Ensure retention of ownership and control of the business; attract a higher price from investors in the shares that are put up for sale. Ensure success of flotation, ensure continued control.

Social enterprises in Africa and South Asia

1. A business needs to make a profit over time in order to survive. (It might make no profit and no loss, but this can be risky.) If the business wants to grow, it will need additional finance to develop the business. Banks will not provide additional finance unless the company's owners provide some more finance too: additional finance for investment can come from the profits that the business makes.

2. Employment for employees, well-being of the community (the community is a stakeholder) in terms of facilities to play sport and better health.

The Gazania Organization

1. Some factors that have led to the success of the Gazania Organization include the strong leadership from Donald, who has key character traits to succeed in business (ambitious, smart decisions, risk taker), the delegation of expertise in the business to each of the three children, and the competitive desire to succeed that this inspires.

2. Being a risk taker can be a good or a bad trait in business. Donald is also described as "eccentric", which may mean that he does not follow others' rules so this could also be problematic in another business. But unless Donald is the business owner, he will find it difficult to get on with other people and other people might not want to work with him.

3. Family rivalry can be problematic as sometimes siblings feel that they are treated unfairly, or that favouritism is a factor in who earns the most money or is given the best roles. Bringing the children into the business in stages might help to create an order of seniority amongst them, reducing the risk that there will be a struggle for power between them. It also means that each child can be introduced to the business individually, rather than bringing them all in at the same time. However, a problem that could arise is that Aureli wants a bigger say in the business, even though Djamel is more "senior"; unless a way of giving Aureli more authority can be found, there is likely to be disagreement between him and Djamel at some time in the future.

Exam-Style Questions

1. B

2. C. Market capitalisation of a public company rises or falls with changes in its share price, which is currently $2.15 for 360 million shares.

3. Limited liability for a business (a company) means that the owners of the business (its shareholders) will not be personally liable for any unpaid debts of the business, except to the extent of the owners' capital already invested in the business. So if a company collapses because it cannot pay its debts, the shareholders will not be required to pay the debts out of their own money.

4. Total dividend = 4% × $240 million = $9,600,000. So dividend per share = $9,600,000/32 million shares = $0.30 per share.

5. Differences:
   - Charities do not have an objective to make a profit, unlike commercial companies, and so are not expected to make a profit. (They are allowed to make an operating surplus, however.)
   - Charities may not be established as a company
   - The finance for a charity comes from government sources and private donations, whereas companies get their finance from investors in shares (or lenders)
   - Some charities are established just for a short term and specific purpose (such as providing aid following a natural disaster)
   - Charities may have unpaid volunteers as well as paid employees
   - Regulation and government supervision of charities may differ from regulation of companies.

6. The objectives of a farming co-operative of small farmers is to carry on their business through sharing and mutual assistance. A number of small businesses acting collectively can achieve much more than many small businesses acting separately.

   In a farming co-operative, the famers can assist each other by working together and sharing labour, helping each other on their farms, for example during harvesting time. They can also share ownership of labour-saving equipment that they would not be able to afford to buy independently. In addition, they can share their marketing and distribution efforts, so that their crops are sold jointly – this can save costs and also result in obtaining better prices in the market.

   Another important characteristic of a farming co-operative is its constitution, and the rights and obligations of each of the co-operative members. For example, there must be clear rules about financial contributions and financial obligations to the co-operative, and procedures for assigning responsibilities for certain functions to individuals within the co-operative (such as responsibilities for the purchase of equipment, and for arranging the distribution and sale of crops).

7. Difficulties for small companies:
   - Limited resources and limited sources of finance. Bigger companies have more resources and more money to spend on activities such as marketing. Bigger companies usually find it easier to borrow when they need more finance
   - Bigger companies are often able to make products or deliver services at lower prices, because they can produce them at lower cost. (With their bigger size, larger companies may be able to spread costs over more output, and so reduce costs.)
   - Bigger companies are able to employ specialists, including professional managers, giving them an advantage over small companies that do not have specialists
   - Small companies may find it difficult to gain recognition from potential customers when they are competing with a larger and more well-known rival.

   However, answers might include the point that small companies can compete successfully, if they focus on a small market area or a specialised version of the product.

1.3 – progress questions, case studies, exam-style questions

Progress Questions

1. Barriers to entry are obstacles that make it difficult for a new competitor to enter a specific market. These obstacles may include the high costs of setting up the business, the response of competitors (for example, price cutting to make it impossible for a small business to make a profit), the long time it might take to win customers (customer loyalty to existing companies in the market) government regulations, or trademark and patent protections.

2. Possible suggestion: Depending on the barrier, the business may need to think creatively about how to compete in a different way to the main competitors. Technology might help with this.

3. The concentration ratio of the four large businesses is 24% + 20% + 12% + 10% = 66%

4. €25,000 divided by 1.15 (the exchange rate) = £21,739.13 to pay

5. €25,000 divided by 1.2 (the new exchange rate) = £20,833.34 to pay

6. A US company will usually want to convert all its income into US dollars and to make payments for all its purchases in US dollars. If a US importer buys in euros then if the exchange rate changes it will pay more or less in US dollars for the goods. If a US exporter sells goods into Europe in euros it will earn more or less in US dollars through selling the same goods, unless they change their prices to match the exchange rate.

7. Government could constrain activities on mining for the following reasons:
   - It has processes that may damage the environment
   - Local communities may suffer from mining activities in their area (e.g. health problems from waste and other output from the mines)
   - To make sure that standards are met for employees and their safety
   - The mining company may be a foreign company and the government may be worried about exploitation of the country's natural resources.

8. Education leads to people having longer, happier, healthier lives with more options and possibilities. Many believe that education is a right, so should be available to everyone all around the world. General education also means that the talents of the entire population can be developed, for the long-term benefits of the country.

9. If a key harvest failed it could mean that people are unable to feed themselves, or that the country is unable to make certain produce. The government might need to initiate a programme for ensuring that the population is properly fed (e.g. by obtaining assistance from other countries and governments).

Case Studies

Concentration ratio

1. The sales of the three biggest companies are growing each year, but the size of the market is growing at a faster percentage rate, so the market share of the three biggest companies is decreasing.

2. The sales for the biggest four companies is growing each year, at a faster rate than the overall rate of market growth, so the market share of the biggest four companies is increasing.

3. The fourth-biggest company must be growing as they have $60 million of sales in year 1, $132 million in year 2 and $200 million in year 3. This represents 7.5% of the total market in year 1, 15% in year 2 and 20% in year 3, so the market share of the fourth-largest company is increasing rapidly.

Exchange rates

1. If the exchange rate went from 1.3203 in June 2018 to 1.3150 in July 2018 we can see that the value of pound sterling has declined slightly in July 2018 by $0.0053 or 0.4% (0.0053/1.3203).

2. A fall in the Chinese currency means that Chinese exports become cheaper for buyers in other countries, and exports from other countries to China become more expensive for Chinese customers. The result will be an increase in Chinese exports and a fall in imports to China, improving the balance of trade for China. This might be a matter of concern to governments in other countries, and to companies in other countries that are competing against Chinese rivals.

Exam-style Questions

1. D

2. Year 2: ((712 − 672)/672) × 100% = 6.00%. Year 3: ((750 − 712)/712) × 100% = 5.34%

3. Likely problems:
   - High cost of buying or leasing aircraft. A substantial amount of capital would be required
   - Difficulty in finding landing slots at airports, without which it is not possible to have flights
   - Difficulty in attracting customers from other airlines: what can a new airline offer that existing airlines do not already offer?
   - It might be difficult to attract skilled staff (e.g. pilots) away from existing airlines, without offering much higher salaries.

4. When wages and salaries are rising at a faster rate than the rate of inflation, people have more money (in "real terms") to spend, so consumer demand will increase.

5. Likely consequences:
   - Natasha buys goods for resale in Japanese yen and has to exchange HK dollars to obtain the yen to pay for them. If the yen increase in value, the cost of purchases in HK dollars will increase
   - Natasha might try to pass on the higher costs to her customers by raising selling prices to customers in Hong Kong. This is likely to result in lower demand from customers, although the extent of the fall in demand might be difficult to predict. If demand falls, profits are likely to fall too
   - Alternatively Natasha can leave her prices to customers in HK dollars unchanged, so that the profit margin on the goods that she sells will fall, and her business profits will fall.

The extent of the fall in profit will depend partly on the extent to which the yen increases in value and the extent to which demand might fall in response to any increase in the HK prices of goods sold to customers.

2.1 – progress questions, case studies, exam-style questions

Progress Questions

1. Setting a marketing objective in terms of total sales volume is not possible for businesses that produce a range of many different products, or produce non-standard products or services. It is only possible for companies that produce a standard product such as oil or agricultural goods. Most companies set marketing objectives in terms of total sales revenue.

2. The total size of a market is often difficult to measure accurately, as this depends on having data from a reliable source. Such a source may not exist, which means that estimates of total market size may be inaccurate.

3. Customer retention means keeping existing customers. A customer retention rate is the percentage of customers who buy from a business again. Businesses most likely to set customer retention rates as a marketing objective are those that rely for their revenue on regular and repeated payments from customers, such as providers of media streaming services and providers of gas, electricity or phone services in a competitive market. (For example, the value of Netflix shares depends largely on growing subscriber numbers and customer retention rates.)

4. Setting targets for individual regions is of more practical value. Each region is given its own realistic targets for achievement, and it is also possible to make comparisons between the different regions.

5. Dynamic pricing is real-time pricing, where prices are continually adjusted up or down in response to market demand. Examples are foreign exchange pricing (buying foreign currency); continual re-pricing of organised holiday tours by travel companies in order to fill up a scheduled tour; and frequent re-pricing of airline seats in order to ensure that flights are full.

6. Relationship marketing is marketing activity aimed at building and retaining a good relationship with customers or potential customers, rather than activity aimed at getting customers to buy immediately. Loyalty card schemes are an example. However, digital relationship marketing is relationship marketing that involves digital communications between the business and customers/potential customers, such as through social media.

7. Social media can be used to persuade customers to buy the products or services of a business immediately, but it is used more commonly to build up consumer interest in the business and its products/services and to establish a positive relationship. Methods include providing regular new content to persuade consumers to keep visiting the media platform of the business; encouraging two-way communications (dialogue); and convincing followers to persuade friends to become followers too.

Case Studies

Zara

1. In order to respond at speed to changes in customer tastes for fashion, business activities need to be very closely co-ordinated. The marketing department needs to feed back information about what consumers are buying (and what they do not like) and how many units of an item customers are likely to buy, so that product designers can design new fashion products to meet current tastes and demand, and so that the production function can produce them in good time and in the quantities required.

   The marketing function also needs to work with the distribution (or 'logistics') function to ensure that fashion products that are produced are delivered to the sales outlets that need them.

   The marketing function also needs to work with the product design function, so that new products are priced to earn the company a profit, and can be produced at a cost that will earn the business a profit.

Sales objectives

1. Increase in sales = ((14m − 12m)/12m) × 100% = 16.7%

   Increase in market share = ((60m − 50m)/50m) × 100% = 20%

   The company succeeded in achieving its marketing objective for sales growth, but did not achieve its objective for market share.

Television subscriptions

1. The company is probably aiming to grow sales and profits. Marketing objectives can be set in terms of increasing subscriber numbers, customer retention rates, increasing revenues from subscribers and possibly increasing market share if there are competitors.

   Each of these objectives can be set for the business as a whole and also for each type of package.

   In addition, these objectives can be set for each country individually as well as for the business in total.

Premier League

1. The overall objectives of the Premier League might be to increase the total revenues from broadcasting rights, and to remain the exclusive representative of the Premier League football teams in negotiations with television companies and others. Marketing strategies to achieve these objectives are likely to focus on getting rival television and entertainment companies worldwide to compete with each other for broadcasting rights, pushing up the prices they pay in competitive bidding.

2. Individual football clubs might have an objective of increasing the share of the revenues paid to all the clubs by the Premier League. The amount received by each club will vary according to their position in the league, so an objective should be to finish as high in the league as possible.

   Football clubs will also have other marketing objectives, such as achieving a target number of attendances at their football matches, and for sales of replica football shirts and other sports items. Tactics for achieving these aims might be to spend money signing up new players to attract supporter interest, improving facilities at the football ground for visitors, and making sports goods available more widely, for example in specialist shops, department stores and online.

   Some clubs may also have an objective of attracting greater global support for the club, for example through public relations exercises such as team visits to other countries and measures to support grassroots football in under-developed countries.

Exam-style Questions

1. A. This is a general objective, not a strategy for achieving an objective.
2. B
3. C. (600,000/6 million) = 10% did not renew their subscription, so the retention rate is 90%.
4. Average employee numbers = 15,600 in Year 1 and 16,300 in Year 2.

   Sales per employee in Year 1 = $140 million/15,600 = $8,974.36

   Sales per employee in Year 2 = $150 million/16,300 = $9,202.45

   Sales per employee increased by $228.09 or (228.09/8,974.36) by 2.5%
5. Changes in the rules will affect the types of fish the company can catch, and the numbers that it can catch. This is likely to restrict the quantities that the company can catch. This is likely to affect marketing decisions about pricing fish, and deciding which markets/customers to prioritise for selling fish to. Marketing plans are likely to show a fall in annual sales revenue.
6. One benefit of preparing a marketing budget is to set a target for sales revenue that the business can aim to achieve, and to communicate this target to everyone in the business involved with marketing and selling. A budget also sets a time frame for achieving the target (the financial year) and enables the business to monitor progress towards achieving the target through the course of the year.

In addition, a marketing budget involves the allocation of a spending budget for marketing activities, and having a plan enables the marketing function to decide how best to allocate the available money to different marketing and selling activities.

7. Arguments for:
   - Expanding internationally increases the size of the market and offers prospects of selling more and making more profit
   - If the market for drones is becoming international, with foreign manufacturers competing for business, the company might need to become international to avoid losing some of its domestic market to competition
   - Customers in a global market are often international businesses themselves, that prefer dealing with international suppliers.

   Arguments against:
   - The costs of establishing international operations and investing in the resources required to operate internationally
   - If the strategy fails, the business will probably make heavy losses
   - Practical difficulties in setting up production facilities in other countries, such as difficulties in controlling operations that are geographically distant
   - Foreign exchange risks in an international business
   - Changing from a domestic business to an international business calls for a change in culture, which might be difficult to achieve successfully.

   Judgement:

   Make a judgement one way or the other. In general, companies choose to become international if they see strategic opportunities in a large global market.

2.2 – progress questions, case studies, exam-style questions

Progress Questions

1. To obtain information about a market, that will be useful to the marketing function, for example to prepare a marketing plan.
2. Published government statistics and statistics of global institutions; websites of companies and other businesses; research data from other organisations (universities, research institutes) and trade associations.
3. Face-to-face interviews; questionnaires (on paper or online); telephone surveys; opinions obtained from consumers online (e.g. via social media). Arguably, actual historical sales figures for a business are a source of primary data that can be used in marketing.
4. Estimates of sales are usually a starting point for planning other operating activities within a business, such as planning production capacity, employee numbers, purchasing quantities, finance requirements, and producing a budget. Business plans are therefore often based on sales forecasts. Continuing to produce sales forecasts throughout the year also helps a business to monitor actual sales performance against previous (forecast) expectations.
5. Obtaining marketing data from every person in the population would usually take too long and cost too much money.
6. A sampling frame is a list of every person in a population. A sampling frame therefore makes it possible to carry out "genuine" random sampling, and obtain what should normally be unbiased information from the sample.
7. Except when the population is small (so that a sampling frame can be constructed), or there is a record of every person in the population that can be used as a sampling frame, it is not possible to obtain a random sample.

Case Studies

Video advertising

1. Test by showing the video to an invited/selected panel of representative members of the public; then obtain their views by asking them to fill in a questionnaire. Answers can be assessed quantitatively or qualitatively. As this will take some time, the invited individuals will probably be offered a payment for their participation.

Motor boats

1. The business may overproduce and be unable to sell everything that it produces.

   Or there will be over-capacity, and some resources (machines, labour) will be idle for some of the time.
2. There may be a shortage of capacity, and the business may be unable to produce enough to meet sales demand (unless the business has spare capacity that would otherwise be unused).

The business might be able to find ways to increase capacity to meet the unexpected demand (e.g. put on an extra work shift) or hire temporary staff.

There might be a loss of business to competitors.

Developing a new biscuit

1. A sample will be taken from the north and another sample from the south. The size of each regional sample should be proportional to the sizes of the population in each region. Within each regional sample, 50% of the sample would be from among 18–25-year-olds, 20% from among 25+ to 50-year-olds, and 30% from people aged over 30. So if the sample size is 150 in each region, say, the sample would consist of 75 18–25-year-olds, 30 25+ to 50-year-olds, and 45 people aged over 30.

2. By gender; by ethnic groups; by lifestyle (e.g. sporty/active people and people who do not exercise).

3. Divide the sample into segments or strata, estimate the size of each segment as a proportion of the total population, and from this decide the sample size for each segment of the population. This is to reduce the risks from bias in the sample. Next, use a method of sampling that is as close to random as possible – for example in face-to-face market research by interviewing every 1 in 10 people in the street who fits into a segment until the quota (sample size) for the segment is full.

Ice cream

1. Correlation is positive, which means that higher sales of ice cream can be associated with higher temperatures. It cannot be proved, however, that higher temperatures cause higher ice cream sales. Also correlation is "perfect" when the correlation coefficient is 1. A coefficient of +0.83 is quite high, but by no means "perfect".

2. It is not clear that this information can be of practical use. The ice cream manufacturer would need to know what the midday temperature will be on each of a number of future days, and then adjust production quantities to meet the expected sales demand on those days. But since ice cream retailers stock ice cream for sale, there is no direct link between daily ice cream production quantities and daily ice cream sales.

Exam-style Questions

1. A.

2. Face-to-face interviews. Costly because of the time needed to carry them out, and the associated costs of interviewers (salaries/wages and expenses).

3. A confidence level is the probability that a certain outcome will occur. It is often expressed in association with a range of values. For example, if expected sales are between 1,000 and 1,200 units at the 95% confidence level, this means that there is an estimated 95% probability that actual sales will turn out to lie within this 1,000–1,200 range.

4. A market map is used to plot products or competitors on a graph, according to two characteristics such as price and quality. Having mapped existing products or competitors on the map, it is possible to identify possible gaps in the market. Examples of price/quality maps might be a map for the market for running shoes. Not all market maps look at price and quality. It might be possible, for example, to produce a market map for convenience off-the-shelf meals, rating them by time to cook and number of calories.

5. Data mining has been made possible by digital technology. It is now possible to capture much more information about the buying or shopping habits of consumers. It is also possible to use software to analyse this data at a level of detail that is not possible for humans (due to complexity and time required). Data mining might provide marketing information that more traditional methods of marketing research are unable to extract, for example by identifying particular buying preferences of particular types of consumer.

6. Pure random sampling is not possible because a sampling frame for the entire population cannot be obtained (and would in any case be too expensive to obtain). However, the sample should be as free from bias as possible. This is achieved by dividing the population into segments or strata, and estimating the proportion of the population that belongs to each segment. A total sample size is decided, and then divided into a sample size for each segment according to its relative size. When obtaining a sample (up to the quota limit) for each segment, a system of selecting individuals for the sample should be as free from bias as possible, for example by selecting every 1 in 5 or 1 in 20 people within each segment to respond.

7. Advantages:
   - Need to have an idea of sales in order to plan other activities, such as production and service levels.
   - Sales forecasts can be used to set a sales target. When they are used as a target, actual sales can be compared with the forecast throughout the period of the forecast.

   - Sales forecasts help a business to understand where it is going, in terms of growth/no-growth and in terms of which products can be expected to be more popular than others, and whether it might be necessary to develop new products or services – this helps long-term planning.

   Disadvantages:
   - Problems in producing reliable forecasts: reliability of assumptions used, e.g. about growth in the entire market for a product; where does the data come from to make a forecast?
   - Actual events may make a forecast out of date.

   Judgement:
   Planning is important in order to manage and control a business. Forecasts are a necessary part of planning and monitoring business activities and performance. (Judgements may differ, but they should express a sensible opinion.)

2.3 – progress questions, case studies, exam-style questions

Case Studies

Travel company

1. Answers to this question may vary: here are suggested answers.

   Demographic: Segment according to a combination of age group and family circumstances, e.g. single, couple with no children, couple with children (of varying ages).

   Geographic: Segments could be according to the region or area where people live, on the assumption that holiday preferences vary according to where people live. Alternatively, the market could be segmented according to geographical destination, such as domestic and foreign holidays.

   Income: Segment according to the income of customers, on the assumption that preferences for certain types of holiday (or quality of holiday) vary according to household income.

   Behavioural: The travel market might include customers who plan holidays a long time in advance (and so can be targeted with discounts for early booking) and customers who book holidays at the last minute.

   Psychographic: Markets may be segmented according to lifestyle, such as action holidays for active people; and cultural holidays for people who enjoy sights and culture; and beach holidays for people who want sun, sea and sand.

Perfumes

1. Suggestions: It might be possible to segment the market for perfumes by age, gender, price/perceived quality (income), frequency of use, geography.

2. Answers to this question can vary widely. However, the market segments chosen by this company should be consistent with the brand and brand image of its perfumes. An important segment might be customers who buy occasionally, typically at certain times of the year such as Christmas (when a large proportion of annual perfume sales occurs). The company may also target its products at women of a certain age and certain income.

Travel suitcases

1. The total market for bags and suitcases is segmented to a large extent by types of bag/suitcase, such as size (e.g. bags to fit into an overhead locker on a flight, rucksacks/soft bags). Within the market, most manufacturers will seek to position their products according to a combination of price and product quality/features, such as number of wheels on suitcases, weight of suitcase, durability of materials, branding.

Exam-style Questions

1. B.

2. Digital products can be delivered immediately, whereas physical products take time to deliver, especially internationally.

   There is no cost to deliver a digital product, unlike physical products.

   With physical products there are problems of arranging transportation, and export/import clearance, which do not exist with digital products.

3. Problems:
   - The size of the niche needs to be big enough to enable a business to sell enough products and make a profit.
   - There is a limit to the size of a market niche, which means that it might be difficult for a business to grow unless it expands into other segments/niches of the market.

- If the niche product becomes obsolete, or even if total sales decline, the survival of the business will be put in doubt.
- There may be competitors within a niche, which means that a business must make a decision about product positioning (price and product features) within its niche.
- Niche products may need specialist distributors, so there is a problem with making agreements with specialist distributors to sell the company's products.

2.4 – progress questions, case studies, exam-style questions

Progress Questions

1. The combination of factors/activities that a business uses to market its products or services. For physical products, the marketing mix is often described in terms of the 4Ps: product, price, place and promotion.

2. In which geographical areas should the product be sold?

   In what type of location should the product be sold (where can customers buy it?) and should the product be sold online?

   Marketing decisions about transportation and delivery of products to their market, or of goods sold online to their buyers.

   The distribution network used for selling to customers, e.g. specialist distributors, discount stores, supermarkets.

3. The impact on the customer of the physical environment where the service is delivered. For a service, the physical environment can have an effect on the willingness of customers to buy (and repeat buy) the service. Aspects of physical location include the decoration and furnishing of the room; comfort (e.g. when customers sit in a chair or rest on a couch to receive the service); size (e.g. space to move around can be important to users of gym services); room temperature.

4. Introduction, growth, maturity, decline. The stage that a product has reached in its life cycle can affect marketing decisions. For example, pricing decisions are likely to differ in each stage of the life cycle, and decisions about advertising and sales promotions, redesigning product features and the selection of distribution methods can all be influenced by stage in the life cycle.

5. A strategy aimed at extending the life of a product when it appears to be in the decline phase of its life cycle.

6. This is a model developed by the Boston Consulting Group that helps a company to analyse its product portfolio, and make marketing and investment decisions for each product. The model categorises products according to rate of growth in the total product market and the company's market share, and each product is placed in a 2 × 2 matrix according to market growth and market share. The amount of sales for each product can also be included in the analysis, by showing products in the matrix in different sizes according to sales revenues. Decisions about whether to invest more in a product, and how to market a product, can be made with regard to the categorisation of the product. For example, marketing decisions for "cash cow" products should be made with the aim of maintaining sales (and market share) through advertising, product redesign or new distribution initiatives.

7. Value of branding:

   Brand recognition. Customers recognise brands and will often buy a branded product where they recognise the brand rather than a non-branded product or a brand they do not recognise.

   Customer loyalty. Some customers develop loyalty to a brand, and buy the brand in preference to others. (Marketing efforts are often aimed at strengthening brand loyalty.)

   Pricing. It is often possible to sell products with a well-established brand name at a higher price than similar products without the same brand recognition.

   Extending the product range. If a company wants to grow its business by developing new products, it may be able to add a new product to the brand, and market it under the established brand name.

8. Price skimming is a policy of charging a high price for a new product when it first enters the market, and then gradually reducing the price as the market for the product becomes more mature (or grows). In this way, businesses can hope to maximise the profit margin for each unit of product that they sell. Price skimming has been used frequently by producers of electronic products, such as mobile phones and computer games hardware.

9. Price discrimination means charging different prices for the same product to different segments of the market, such as different prices for a train journey at different times of day, or lower cinema ticket prices for children or older people. Price differentiation means charging different prices for similar products to different market segments or on the basis of some differences in product design features.

Case Studies

Fitness centres

1. Answers to this case study can vary widely, although it might be difficult to find marketing measures for "place". Here are just a few suggestions.

   Price. Make a price initiative that rivals might not have taken. For example, reduce subscriptions to all members; offer reduced first-year subscriptions for new members; offer cut price membership for members in certain age groups.

   Product. Establish new categories of members, such as weekday members, weekend members, evening members; set up different categories of members according to fitness facilities they can use; provide a wider range of equipment than rivals.

   Promotion. Use local poster/billboard advertising; use internet search engines to attract visitors to the company's website; keep the website up to date.

   Physical environment. Keep refreshed in each centre: the décor, condition of equipment; condition of coffee bar; quality of music system or video entertainment system; ensure good-quality changing rooms and showers.

   People. Provide staff with fresh uniforms. Train staff in use of equipment and in customer service, complaints handling.

   Process. Make sure there is enough equipment to meet demand for use by customers. Make sure that there are enough trained staff to meet demand from customers for service/assistance.

Farm equipment

1.

	Tractors and harvesters	Televisions
Product	Efficiency/productivity of equipment	Ease/convenience of use
		Screen size, vision quality, sound quality
Price	Credit terms, and payment terms (instalment payments)	Possibly use of discounts during sales season
Place	Use of face-to-face selling	Online selling with home deliveries
	Selling at agricultural shows	Sales through selected distributors
Promotion	Physical demonstration of products, e.g. at agricultural shows, trade fairs	In-store displays, website displays
		Advertising (TV, magazines)

Increasing prices

1. Product A price elasticity of demand: 3%/5% = 0.6. Demand is inelastic. (Minus sign ignored)

   Product B price elasticity of demand: 8%/5% = 1.6. Demand is elastic. (Minus sign ignored)

2. Total sales revenue will change to (1.05 × 0.97) = 1.0185 or 101.85% of its previous level.

3. Total sales revenue will change to (1.05 × 0.92) = 0.966 or 96.6% of its previous level.

4. When the price elasticity of demand is inelastic, an increase in price will result in an increase in sales revenue.

   When the price elasticity of demand is elastic, an increase in price will result in a fall in sales revenue.

5. No conclusions can be drawn about the effect on profit of a change in price. Price elasticity of demand does not consider product costs or profit margins.

Promoting new products

1. Suggestions for answers to this case study might vary widely, but they need to be sensible.

   For example:

   Fast food outlets company. Redesign in-store menus and food displays to show this "health" aspect to the product range. Use TV and other advertising, promoting the healthy meal and at the same time the company generally. Encourage consumer responses and reaction through social media.

   Manufacturer of office equipment. Promote the new product through the company's online and paper catalogues, and through trade magazines. Promote the product features and benefits for users. Possibly sell to large customers at trade fairs and/or through product demonstrations.

Marketing a small shop

1. Suggestions:
   - Offer fresh products made each day (so promoting quality).
   - Advertise locally, e.g. on advertising displays in the railway station.
   - Use attractive displays for products in the shop; provide attractive shop décor and layout.
   - Provide quick and friendly service to customers; keep waiting times short.
   - Offer attractive prices.
   - Possibly offer to deliver food and drinks to customers at lunchtimes in local office buildings, when orders are received by email or online by a certain time each morning.

Exam-style Questions

1. C. Not an easy question. An extension strategy usually involves redesigning a product or how a product might be used, in order to extend its life.

2. A.

3. Price elasticity of demand = $1\%/3\% = 0.33$ (Minus sign ignored). Demand is price inelastic.
   Revenue with be $(1.03 \times 0.99) = 1.0197$ of current sales revenue. In other words, total sales revenue will increase by 1.97%.

4. A market penetration strategy is a strategy of selling a product at a low price to gain market or market share. It may be used by a company launching an entirely new product on the market, to establish a market. Or it might be used by a new entrant to a market, as a way of gaining a foothold in the market and some market share.

5. Price discrimination involves selling the same product at different prices to different segments of the market, such as selling train tickets to passengers at different prices, according to the time of day or day of the week that they travel.
   Price discrimination can be particularly beneficial for companies that provide services where the costs of service provision are largely fixed. For example, the costs of showing a film in a cinema are much the same whether there are 10 customers or 200 customers to see the film.
   This means that if a price change results in higher total sales revenue, it will also result in higher profits.
   So if the price elasticity of demand for a service is elastic, a reduction in price will result in higher sales revenue, and so higher profits.
   This is why price elasticity of demand is an important factor in deciding whether to have a policy of price discrimination. Lower prices should be offered to segments of the market only if the price elasticity of demand for the market segment is elastic.

6. Both office robots and mobile phones are products, so the 4Ps (rather than the 7Ps) should be considered for the marketing mix.
   Product. The product features will be important for both types of product. However, industrial buyers are more likely to be interested in productivity features and how the product will deliver commercial benefits. Consumer buyers of mobile phones will be more interested in product design features, such as size of screen.
   Price. Industrial buyers will be concerned most about the basic price of office robots, although they might also be attracted by generous credit terms. For new versions of a mobile phone, producers may be able to apply a price skimming policy, because some customers will want to have the "status" or prestige of being an early owner of the new model. Prices are likely to fall as a mobile phone model becomes more established in the market.
   Place. Consumers are likely to buy mobile phones at a specialist store, although some department stores also sell them. The phone producer has to make a marketing choice about which distribution outlets to use for its products. A producer of office robots is more likely to sell directly to large industrial buyers, and online for other buyers, and may not use distributors.
   Promotion. Consumer products such as mobile phones are promoted largely through advertising and social media. Office robots are more likely to be sold through product demonstrations, trade fairs and online catalogues, plus some advertising possibly in trade magazines.

7. There should be some consistency in marketing between different countries, in order to promote the global company and its brand name in a consistent way. However, there may also be some differences in the promotional mix between countries.
   Sales promotions should present the company's products or services to consumers: there will be some differences between countries because of the differences in menus. There can be some differences in the fast-food products that are sold and promoted.

There may also be promotional differences according to consumer attitudes to lifestyle and health: for example promotions in some countries may emphasise healthy products more than in other countries.
The promotional message may need to differ between countries. For example, in a country where fast-food outlets are "new" and uncommon, advertising and other promotions will need to present the benefits/pleasures of fast food to a relatively uninformed target market.
There may also be differences between countries in the use of handbills or brochures, possibly delivered by mail to consumers.

8.

	Advantages	Disadvantages
Intensive distribution	Products are made available to the widest possible number of potential customers, including low-price stores.	Most of these customers will not want to buy high-priced branded products. There will be a large amount of unsold/slow-moving stock in many sales outlets.
Selective distribution	Selected distributors, such as department stores, are consistent with the product image that the cosmetics company wants to present. Sales staff should have a reasonable knowledge of the products they are selling. Selected distributors are often popular with consumers at times of the year when perfume sales are highest – such as in the weeks leading up to Christmas in many countries.	Sales may depend on the location of the company's products within each store. Sales are also dependent on customers visiting the selected distributors. Consumer buying through department stores is falling in many countries.
Exclusive distribution	Sales outlets are cosmetics/perfume specialists. Sales staff should have a thorough knowledge of the products they sell. Customers visiting these outlets are specifically looking for perfumes and cosmetics, and may also expect to pay fairly high prices for the "exclusive" service they receive.	There is a limited number of exclusive distributors for any product. This means that the potential market for sales through these outlets is limited. Exclusive distribution is more suitable for high-priced products such as sports cars.

Judgement:
Selective distribution seems to be the most suitable method of distribution for perfumes and cosmetics, because this helps to promote the image of the products as quality products, as well as offering a reasonably large target market for the company's products. This is how expensive brands of perfumes and cosmetics tend to be sold.

3.1 – progress questions, case studies, exam-style questions

Progress Questions

1. The transformation process is the conversion or transformation of input resources into a business operation, and combining them to produce an output product or service.

2. The aims of business operations might be (only four required for a solution) to produce efficiently and economically (i.e. control costs); satisfy the customer; produce a good-quality product or service for the price it is sold at; speed of production or service delivery; flexibility in operations; or sustainable operations (e.g. operations should not cause damage to the environment).

3. Flexibility means being able to adapt the use of resources to meet differing requirements that may arise. Flexibility is sometimes referred to as "being nimble".

4. It is not possible to maximise the achievement of all operational objectives. Perhaps the most obvious example is cost and quality. It might not be possible to produce a high-quality product or service and at the same time minimise costs. Some compromise between the various objectives of operations is therefore necessary.

Answers

Case Studies

Entertainment company

1. The entertainments company presumably stages a variety of different events of different types. If its current focus is on holding a music festival, it might have insufficient resources within the company to do much else until the festival has ended.

   Some activities or departments within the company will be required to provide support for the music festival, without being directly involved in on-site operations. For example, a team in the company may need to acquire food, drink and other items for the stalls on site, and there may be a logistics unit that has to deliver all the equipment to the site.

   Decisions by different parts of the business therefore need to be co-ordinated, to ensure efficient and effective operations.

2. The same requirement for co-ordination of different teams or groups applies to situations where decisions by other teams can affect the operating function. For example, a different team might be responsible for signing up music artists for the festival and negotiating a fee with them. Decisions they make will affect who performs at the festival. Decisions by the finance function might affect ticket pricing.

   The key point is that different functions within a business interact, and decisions they make affect others. Co-ordination is necessary to ensure that the interaction is positive, and does not lead to arguments and lack of co-operation.

Hermès

1. Customers are willing to pay large amounts of money to buy a Hermès handbag, and wait a long time to obtain one. Silk scarves are more easily obtained, but nevertheless are associated with prestige and a high price.

   The objectives of operational management should be to support sales and marketing, in providing very high-quality products, with a top brand name association, to provide customers with a high level of satisfaction.

   Within the operations function itself, there should be objectives of careful and rigorous recruitment and training procedures for new craftsmen, and investment of money and skill in the design of new products.

Exam-style Questions

1. A number of different solutions could be given to this question. Here are some suggestions.

   The restaurant might have an objective of providing a high level of customer satisfaction, to compare favourably with competitors in the area. Customer satisfaction might be provided by the decor of the restaurant, standard of service, contents of the menu as well as the quality of the food itself.

   The restaurant might also have an objective of providing very high-quality food. At the top quality level, some restaurants try to achieve a Michelin star award.

   Alternatively, a restaurant might have an operational objective of maximising the number of customers that it serves; and to do this its objective might be speed of service. For example, if the same table can be used for two sittings of customers in an evening instead of just one, revenues might be doubled.

2. The transport company might try to compete on the basis of lower cost, and so lower its prices. In some countries, transporting goods by river is cheaper than transporting them by land, due to traffic congestion and the limited capacity of trucks for carrying goods. Competition on the basis of price, and therefore cost, is common in many industries; and barge operators might try to be operationally more efficient so that they can charge lower prices.

   The company may try to compete generally with other barge operators as well as road haulage firms on the basis of speed. Customers may value fast transportation for their goods, and if they do, the fastest operators are likely to be successful.

   The company may try to have more fleet capacity than rivals, so that it is capable to carrying more goods.

   Companies will also compete on the basis of the quality or features of the services they provide. For example, when goods have to be transported from a customer's premises to a loading point for barges on a river, the quality of this service could be an important competitive feature. Companies may also offer other service features for customers, such as a track and trace facility so that customers can find out at any time where their goods are.

3. The new generation of products means that manufacturers must develop new products to meet customer demand. Rival manufacturers compete to get successful products to market faster and at an attractive price. The operations function needs to work closely with R&D to develop ways of manufacturing the new products. There needs to be a way of producing the new products, with their unique

design features, in a way that is operationally efficient. To do this, collaboration between operations and R&D is essential.

The marketing function has the task of persuading consumers to buy the new products, by convincing them of their value. The products also need to be available when customers want to buy them. Close co-operation is needed between marketing and operations to ensure that the right quantities of the right products are produced, in order to meet the expected demand.

To make the new products, it will be necessary to invest in new manufacturing equipment and machinery. The operations function will therefore need to work with the finance function to identify how much the new equipment will cost and how much can be afforded. In addition, the marketing and finance functions may also have an idea of the price at which the new products should be sold – in which case the accounts function will need to work with operations to ensure that production costs are less than the planned selling prices.

3.2 – progress questions, case studies, exam-style questions

Progress Questions

1. Product: making products (or services) that customers want.
   Plant: having the capital equipment (machines etc.) to produce the output.
   People: having a sufficient number of people with the required skills to do the work.
   Process: using appropriate processes and operating methods.
   Programmes: having schedules for operations.
   Costs: keeping operating costs within acceptable limits.

2. There are two main ways that labour productivity can be measured:
   - Output produced per hour worked, or output per person per period. (When output is varied, it may be necessary to use sales revenue per hour worked as an efficiency measure.)
   - Time required to produce a unit of output.

3. Improving labour productivity depends on the cause of inadequate efficiency.
   - Lack of skilled employees to do the work: provide employee training or recruit people with the required skills
   - Lack of sufficient or suitable equipment: invest in new equipment
   - Too much idle time: improve management control over work scheduling
   - Poor planning and leadership: appoint better managers.

4. Land productivity is concerned with output from land, such as output per hectare of land. Land productivity may be used by managers in the agriculture industry.

5. Sales revenue might be used as a basis for measuring labour efficiency: sales revenue per operating employee per period. Efficiency targets might be set in the budget.
   In retailing, a target might be set for sales revenue per week per square metre of retail floor space.

Case Studies

Operating costs of a bus company

1. Bus miles travelled in the week = 20 buses × 30 journeys × 20 miles per journey = 12,000.
   Passenger miles travelled = 12,000 × 35 passengers per journey = 420,000.
   Cost per passenger mile travelled = $168,000/420,000 = $0.40.

Operations performance in call centres

1. The most likely reasons for long waiting times are:
   - Inadequate numbers of call centre staff
   - Lack of training for call centre staff in dealing with calls efficiently
   - Complexity of calls; therefore long average lengths of calls
   - Peak times for calls will explain long waiting times for individual calls, but not long average waiting times.

2. Recruit more call centre staff to deal with calls.
   Train call centre staff in dealing with calls, in order to improve their efficiency.
   Use automatic messages to tell callers how long they might have to wait, and ask if they would prefer to call back.
   Use automatic messages to tell callers how long they might have to wait, and offer them a call-back service, whereby the centre will call the caller when it is less busy.
   (Offering an online system for making complaints or asking questions is another possibility.)

Exam-style Questions

1. Average output per person per week = 2,800 units/20 people = 140 units

   Total hours worked in the week = 20 employees × 40 hours = 800

   Average time to produce one unit = 800 hours/2,800 units = 0.2857 hours per unit (= 17.14 minutes)

2. Capacity utilisation = (18,600/24,000) × 100% = 77.5%

3. One reason might be poor quantities of output, due to a poor harvest. If output is low for a given number of employees, productivity will be low.

   Another reason might be lack of machinery and equipment for employees to use. Productivity is higher when employees use efficient modern equipment.

   Inadequate training for employees would also be an appropriate reason.

4. Labour productivity may be measured as the amount of output per person per hour (or average time to produce a unit). Productivity should be greater among experienced and skilled employees than among new and inexperienced employees. High labour turnover probably means that experienced people are leaving and are being replaced by inexperience. They will be less productive until they acquire the skills and knowledge for the job. In addition, experienced employees might be given the task of mentoring and helping new employees. If so, their productivity will be reduced as well because of the time they spend helping their colleagues.

   Productivity may also be measured as output per employee per period of time. If absenteeism is high, output will be lower than it should be; therefore the output per employee per period will be lower.

5. Factory management may ask employees to work overtime. They might even put on an extra shift of working, although this would require the recruitment of a large number of new staff. Alternatively, it might be possible to recruit temporary labour (or ask employees on zero hours contracts to work more). However, it depends on the nature of the work: it is easier to recruit temporary staff for some types of work than for others.

   It might be possible to subcontract some work to an external firm. However, this will result in some loss of control over production, and the quality of work from a subcontractor may not be as good as the quality of work done internally.

   Depending on the nature of the work, it may also be possible to reduce the amount of scheduled maintenance work on equipment and machinery, so that they can be kept in productive use for longer. However, halting maintenance work for more than a short time could have adverse consequences in the longer term for equipment reliability and breakdowns.

3.3 – progress questions, case studies, exam-style questions

Progress questions

1. There are different ways of measuring capacity in a hospital ward. One approach is to measure capacity by the proportion of hospital beds that are occupied on average. However, hospital beds may be occupied by patients waiting to go home, and who are no longer being treated. If so, this measure of capacity is helpful only in measuring spare bed capacity rather than the capacity of hospital operations.

   Capacity might be measured in terms of nurses' hours or doctors' hours (although doctors might work on more than one ward), and actual hours worked as a percentage of budgeted hours. However, this would be measuring capacity in terms of input resources rather than output.

   Unfortunately, output from a hospital ward cannot be measured in a consistent way; so measuring capacity in terms of output produced is not easily achieved.

2. Improvements in efficiency normally result in lower operating costs. They might fail to do so when the cost of creating the productivity improvements (for example, by purchasing expensive new equipment) exceeds the benefit from the efficiency improvement.

3. • Excessive defects (or any defects at all) in production
   • Excessive stockholding: holding stocks does not add any value to operations
   • Waiting time: waiting to do something is a waste of time and resources
   • Excessive movement of items
   • Excessive movement of people: movement takes time but adds no value
   • Over-production: the over-produced amounts are waste
   • Inappropriate production

4. Kaizen is a term for continuous improvement. Improvements are small, but taken collectively and over time they can create substantial total improvements.

5. JIT stands for just in time. Just in time purchasing is an arrangement between a business and its suppliers whereby the supplier delivers fresh quantities of materials and other supplies at exactly the time that the business needs them for operational use. JIT purchasing is not easily achievable as there are so many unknowns, but it can succeed in some industries by reducing the time between ordering materials from suppliers and receiving delivery to a very short time.

6. As a general guideline, manufacturing businesses need to be capital intensive in order to produce output in the required quantities; and service industries are more labour intensive. A sports car manufacturer (even though just assembling kit cars) and a bottle manufacturer are likely to be more capital intensive than a board games manufacturer, but this will depend on the relative sizes of the businesses.

   A sports coach relies on their personal skills and needs relatively little capital equipment. Similarly an accountant needs IT equipment, but the value of their business is in personal knowledge and specialisation in farm accounts. These businesses will therefore be relatively labour intensive.

7. Capital intensive refers to an operation that relies mainly on capital (machinery and equipment) rather than on human effort. Labour intensive is the opposite: the term refers to a business that uses relatively little capital equipment and relies predominantly on human effort.

8. Quality control is a term for activities that involve checking items for faults or defects. Fr example, a business may check supplies delivered from suppliers for faults, and a manufacturing business may inspect production during and/or at the end of the production process, looking for faults. In some production process, quality control involves keeping production within certain tolerances (upper and lower limits) and rejecting output that exceeds these limits.

   Quality assurance is concerned with measures to prevent faults or defects from happening, for example by improving production methods or using better-quality materials in production.

9. One aspect of total quality management is "zero defects" or "right first time". The approach is intolerant of faults and defects in operations, and focuses on measures to ensure that output is of the required standard at all times. Quality assurance measures can prevent defects. In contrast, quality control is concerned with detecting faults and defects. From a TQM perspective, the ideal situation is one in which quality control is unnecessary.

10. An important aspect of TQM is Kaizen, or continuous improvement. An organisation should be looking all the time for small improvements that can be made to operations. This requires commitment from everyone involved. Individuals need to understand what is expected from them, and should take on responsibilities for improvements. Without commitment from everyone, including management, quality will not improve through Kaizen.

11. Sampling of output products is not 100% testing, and the results of a sample are typically that the level of output error is within a certain range, at a given level of probability. For example, sampling may be used to conclude that at the 95% level of probability, defects in production will be between 0.5% and 1%. This does not guarantee that all output will be of the required standard, because not all output is inspected and tested. Since defects may get through undetected, there are likely to be some customer complaints.

12. Products and services provide customers with a combination of quality and price. As a general rule, customers are willing to pay a higher price for better quality. People who are unable to or do not want to pay a high price for an item may be satisfied with a product of lower quality. An example is clothing: prices of clothing can vary considerably, and as a general rule groups of customer who want to buy fashion clothes for short-term use will not want to pay a high price; and ideas about quality among other customers will depend on the price they are expected to pay.

13. • Successful quality assurance will reduce the quantity of defective items in production, saving time (to put defects right) and cost.
    • Quality assurance may also result in the design of products of better quality.
    • If quality assurance results in better-quality products and fewer defects, the amount of customer complaints will fall, and customer satisfaction will be higher.

14. The internal customers of a department within an organisation are other parts of the organisation that make use of the department's output and operations. They can help to improve the quality of output or activities by the department by discussing their expectations and concerns, and making suggestions about how improvements in quality might be made. This is possible only if there is co-operation between the department and its internal customers.

15. There are many similarities between TQM and quality assurance, and quality assurance is a feature of TQM. However, TQM is broader in its perspective. For example, TQM promotes the concept of continuous improvement (Kaizen): things are never 100% perfect and improvements can always be made. In comparison, quality assurance is not associated with this commitment to continuous small improvements in ways of working.

Case Studies

Olympics 2020
1. A railway system is built to cater for peak capacity. Typically, this occurs during the working week, during the busiest times when people are travelling either to or from work. Arguably, some rail services operate at above 100% capacity at these peak times. However, there are many times during the day when the demand for rail services is below 100% capacity; so railways do not operate at full capacity because demand is variable and is often below full capacity level.
2. It might be possible to switch trains from routes that operate at low capacity and switch them to routes that will service the Olympics. A possible problem with this measure is that the routes servicing the Olympics might not be able to take many extra trains and services, for example for signalling and other technical reasons.

   There appear to be times when there is a shortage of employees rather than a shortage of trains. It may therefore be possible to recruit more (skilled) people in advance of the Olympics, although this would require a recruitment and training effort.

Habasit
1. Conveyor belts will improve productivity by automating the movement of items within a factory, and moving materials at a pace that is appropriate for operating requirements. Conveyors replace the movement of materials by hand, or by truck involving humans, and should be expected to speed up the process.

   As the case study indicates, the conveyors also reduce material wastage. Reductions in material wastage are improvements in efficiency in the use of materials.
2. Conveyor belts cost money to purchase, install and operate. These costs may exceed the benefits obtained from efficiency improvements in operations and materials usage. If so, efficiency will be improved, but at a higher cost.

GSEP Limited
1. When there is a culture of blame, individuals and groups within an organisation seek to blame someone else for anything that goes wrong. This leads to arguments and resentment, and a lack of unity and co-ordination within operations. This has an adverse effect on quality and efficiency.
2. The benefits of empowering employees is that employees might be motivated by having a closer involvement in decision-making within their area of working. Because they have a very good understanding of their work, they might see ways of getting a task done better, and if they have the power to take some work-related decisions themselves, they may be able to make improvements that would otherwise not be made.

   For empowerment of employees to be successful, employees must want to have empowerment which they might not – and they must also have the knowledge and skills to make sensible decisions. Not all employees are sufficiently knowledgeable to do this. Empowering employees will have a damaging effect if employees make poor decisions.
3. A greater amount of training should make employees more skilful in their work. This should result in fewer defects in output (less waste), possibly also a better quality of work, and improvements in productivity.
4. Lean production can be defined as cutting waste whilst maintaining or improving quality. This definition appears to apply to the situation described in the case study.

Jaguar
1. The case study seems to indicate several ways in which waste is eliminated: this is an objective of lean production. By organising work into small cells, it is possible that the physical movement of items in the workplace and also the movement of people are reduced. The entire production line is halted whenever a problem occurs anywhere, which means that there should not be a build-up of part-finished work (and so overproduction), all held up by a bottleneck further down the process. This reduces over-stocking. A just-in-time system also contributes to the avoidance of stocks.

   The workforce may be motivated by this system of working. This and the existence of discussion groups to find ways of eliminating waste should have some positive effect on efficiency, because eliminating waste means that more output is produced with fewer resources and less effort.

2. There may be some improvement in quality due to greater workforce involvement and motivation, but it is not clear from the information how improvements in the quality of output would be achieved. (Your view may differ, but the view here is that improvements in quality are not proved.)

Lean production and health service resource use
1. It is important to improve efficiency in the health service because the demand for health services is increasing and the resources available to provide those services are not increasing at the same rate. Efficiency improvements would make it possible to provide more services with the available funding and resources.
2. It may be argued that use of the term "lean" is inappropriate in the health service, but some improvements might be made that are consistent with the lean concept. Waste should be reduced or eliminated, although it is not clear here what "waste" means. There appear to be excessive stocks of unwanted items in storage rooms; avoiding these in the future may release more funds for essential items. Greater use of IT systems to record patient data would avoid the waste in the duplication of effort in interviewing and in providing information to doctors.

   Other improvements that might be made are not necessarily associated with a lean system, such as better use of bed space inwards, better information availability and making hospital facilities available for use for longer times in the day.

Starlight Fireworks
1. Only 1% of output is tested. This may be insufficient to obtain reliable statistical data about output quality. Staff are overworked, so they may not do a thorough job when testing samples of output for quality. Testing equipment may be old and getting less efficient.

   It is also surprising that Steve says that the deterioration in product quality happened after they had been inspected. This suggests that there is some fault in the quality control system, although it is not clear from the information available what this might be.
2. Quality procedures need to improve in order to prevent faulty products leaving the factory (or to reduce the percentage of faulty products leaving the factory). A high level of defects will lead to a high level of customer complaints, loss of reputation for the company and eventually loss of business. In a fireworks business, quality is a critical issue.
3. Steve should not be trying to shift the blame on to something or someone else when things go wrong. There is a need for a constructive and co-operative approach to dealing with problems that occur, and in this case improving product quality. Finding someone to blame does not provide solutions!

Managing quality of shirts
1. Design quality involves building quality into the design of the product, for example making an expensive range of shirts from high-quality cotton. Quality assurance involves other measures to ensure that products are made to their intended quality standard, so that items are not rejected during or after the manufacturing process; using suitable equipment to cut cloth the correct size might be an example. Quality control involves inspecting items with the intention of identifying defective items. For example, incoming cotton might be inspected for quality and shirts might be inspected for quality during or at the end of the production process.

KNOWHOW delivery services
1. Flexible delivery times enable customers to choose delivery times to suit their personal convenience and preference. (This is preferable to being told when to expect a delivery, without being given any choice.)
2. A problem might be that a large proportion of customers choose a particular time slot during the day, and not many choose some of the other time slots. If this happens, it will be difficult to schedule deliveries in a way that makes good use of delivery vans and drivers, and there may be times of day when demand for deliveries exceeds the ability of the company to meet it, and other times when drivers and vehicles are idle. This would be an inefficient use of resources.

   Scheduling will also be more difficult when delivery schedules are prepared in response to customer demand rather than the company's convenience.

   There will be a risk that due to scheduling and capacity problems, the company will be unable to keep its promises about guaranteed delivery times, damaging the company's reputation with customers.

Exam-style Questions
1. Quality control is concerned with identifying defective or sub-standard output. Quality assurance is concerned with improving quality and so reducing the incidence of defects.

2. One opportunity is that international expansion opens up more markets to the company and its products, so that it can expect to sell more to a larger number of customers. It will also enable the company to become an international company, which is often an important and necessary step in the expansion of a company.

There would be many challenges. One would be the problem of finding one or more locations for setting up production facilities in other countries, equipping it/them. Another challenge would be the need to recruit new employees in other countries where the company as yet has no direct experience of operating. In summary, international expansion creates problems of management and control.

(Other points could be made, such as the challenge of finding the finance to pay for the expansion in the business.)

3. The objective for total cost is probably to keep total costs within an acceptable level and to prevent total costs from increasing quickly. Fast response times probably require a bigger investment in drones, which will cost money. They may therefore be inconsistent with the objective of cost control.

There is no obvious way in which speed of delivery should affect the quality of the delivered product, unless the use of drones increases the risk of damage to goods (or theft) in transit.

Speed of delivery could be consistent with customer satisfaction, if customers value fast delivery of the goods that they order.

4. JIT purchasing and production methods reduce the need to hold stocks. One advantage is that this results in a lower investment in stocks, and so a saving in the finance costs of stockholding. A second benefit is that JIT reduces the need for storage space, saving operating costs of storage/warehousing, but perhaps more importantly for Daniel, freeing up more floor space for production operations.

JIT production methods may also enable a business to respond in a more flexible way to changes in customer demand for products.

JIT methods can have disadvantages too. If there is a delay with a delivery from a supplier, or if there is a breakdown in the production line, the business may be unable to meet customer orders. If this happens its reputation may be damaged and some customers may go to other furniture manufacturers in the future.

The company uses several suppliers, presumably for a range of different materials. Not all suppliers will agree to a JIT purchasing and supply arrangement. Some suppliers who agree to supply on a JIT basis may ask in return for higher prices on the materials they supply.

5. The benefits of successful implementation of a Kaizen system come from a series of small improvements in methods of working, that over time collectively provide improvements in quality and efficiency.

There are difficulties with introducing a Kaizen system. First, there must be the full commitment of the entire management and workforce, because the small but continuous improvements need to come largely from their suggestions. It may be difficult to persuade the workforce to commit themselves.

It may also be necessary to make radical changes in production methods, for example replacing a production line with a number of smaller work cells.

It may take a long time before continuous improvement has a big impact on quality and efficiency. Lisa will need to retain faith in the system and should not expect sudden and big improvements.

6. (The solution here is a suggestion. You may have different ideas.)

The company appears to have systems of quality control and inspection in place, but in spite of this the level of defective output appears to be high.

An effective way of improving the situation would be to improve quality assurance methods, to reduce the frequency of defects. One possibility might be to give employees training in shoe production methods, so that they learn how to produce better-quality boots and shoes. Another possibility might be to buy better-quality materials for the boots and shoes, so that there is less defective production. Quality assurance methods should be devised to meet the problems that appear to be causing the poor quality of work.

Better-quality materials would increase the cost of boots and shoes, but the savings from a lower level of defective output might justify the higher material costs.

The company's management should investigate a more extensive use of equipment to make boots and shoes. The company's operations are labour intensive because labour costs are low. Presumably, capital equipment for use in production would be expensive and add to costs. However, if the use of equipment improves productivity and reduces defects, there will be savings from a lower level of defects, and in the longer term the company's reputation with customers (due to better-quality products) might improve and total sales and profits might increase as a result.

3.4 – progress questions, case studies, exam-style questions

Progress Questions

1. Outsourcing can be arranged on either a long-term or a short-term basis. If it is on a long-term basis, an organisation decides that it will buy all the items that it needs from an external supplier, rather than make them itself. This arrangement will not help to match demand and supply for the company's products.

A short-term arrangement to buy items from an external supplier can help to match demand and supply when demand exceeds the capacity of a company to produce the item internally. However short-term outsourcing arrangements may create problems with quality and reliability.

2. The advantage to business is that it can call on available staff when it needs them, but does not have to pay them when it does not need them. This keeps labour costs down.

3. An advantage for an employee in having a part-time contract is that this frees up time for other purposes, such as more leisure time or additional and different work. Some individuals will enjoy having this flexibility and variation in their lives.

4. The main reason for holding inventory of materials or components is that items are available when needed, and there will not be any hold-up in production due to waiting for a re-supply of the materials.

The main reason for holding inventory of finished goods is that products are available to meet demand, and customers do not have to wait until the products they want are manufactured. If customers cannot buy what they want immediately, they may go to a different company to get it.

The need for inventory is reduced, but not eliminated entirely, by just-in-time purchasing and production arrangements.

5. Work-in-progress consists of part-finished items that are still going through the production process and have not yet been completed. Finished goods are items that have been fully produced and are ready for sale.

6. • By holding only a small amount of inventory, a business reduces the need for warehousing or storage space. This frees up space in its premises for other uses, or means that smaller premises are sufficient (and so premises costs, such as rental costs, are lower).

   • Inventory must be financed, and finance has a cost. Lower levels of inventory result in lower financing costs (such as lower interest costs on money borrowed to finance inventory).

   • Inventory may never be wanted, so that it becomes obsolete. Inventory may also deteriorate while it is held in store, or may be stolen. High levels of inventory could mean higher costs of obsolete, damaged and stolen goods.

7. Many of the goods that supermarkets sell are fresh food items with a sell-by date. Customers in general will be unwilling to buy items that are not fresh, which means that supermarkets need to sell these items quickly, very soon after they come into store and on to the supermarket shelves. If items are not sold quickly, they will take up room on the supermarket shelves earning no money for the company; supermarkets depend for their profits on the ability to turn over goods quickly. As they are resellers of goods made by manufacturers, they also are not concerned by a production schedule.

A steel fabricator is a manufacturing company and its production process is probably lengthy. If it held no inventories, it might be unable to meet customer orders quickly, and this could result in lost sales. It therefore needs to hold inventory so that it can meet orders that come in, all the time manufacturing more products to meet future demand.

8. **a** Reducing lead time. If the lead time for re-supply is reduced, the reorder level will also be reduced, but this will have no effect on average stockholding.

   b Reducing buffer inventory will reduce average stockholding levels, but will increase the risk of a "stock-out" in the period between placing an order for re-supply and receiving delivery from the supplier. Buffer inventory is intended to reduce the risk of stock-outs.

   c Reducing the reorder level without any reduction in the re-supply lead time means that it becomes much more likely that buffer inventory will be needed during the lead time period. Average stockholding will be lower, but the risk of stock-outs will be higher.

9. A reorder level is the level of stockholding at which a fresh order should be placed for the stock item. The reorder quantity is the quantity of the stock item that should be ordered when a new order is made. For example, a company might order 500 units of an item (reorder quantity) when the stock level falls to 100 units (reorder level).

10. There are a number of major oil companies. If one company runs out of stock of crude oil, customers will go to a different oil company to buy the stock they need. Buffer stock enables an oil company to meet orders in full and promptly when demand is higher than expected or when there are unexpected delays in extracting crude oil.

11. • When a company has a large number of suppliers, it may be difficult to arrange JIT purchasing with all of them, and not all suppliers may have production systems that are capable of JIT production. This may occur with some retailing organisations, such as department stores.

• JIT production is not practicable in industries where there needs to be a continual production of an item, and the production system cannot be easily switched on and off in response to changes in demand. Oil production is possibly an example of this.

• JIT production is also not possible in an industry where products are non-standard and are made to customer specifications. Work on production cannot begin until a customer's requirements are known, and products cannot be available immediately the customer places an order. Luxury boat-building is one example of this.

12. Logistics involves the flow of goods between their point of origin and their point of destination. It involves the transportation of materials to their place of manufacture and the transportation of manufactured goods to the point where they will be sold and/or delivered to the end customer. Logistics also includes warehousing activities for holding and handling items during this transportation process. Logistics is commonly associated with delivery trucks and vans, but it covers all forms of transporting goods, by rail, sea and air as well as by land.

13. Here are three possible reasons, but there are others too.

• The transportation of goods from point of origin to point of destination needs to be efficient, so that the costs are kept within control and do not become excessive

• The transportation of goods from point of origin to point of destination also needs to be effective, so that goods are available when they are needed, in the quantities that they are needed and at the time they are needed

• Logistics can be can an expensive aspect of operations. Like all operations, costs should be managed and kept within an acceptable limit. This requires control of all aspects of spending, not just efficiency management.

Case Studies

Outsourcing at Newtown Hospital

1. As far as possible, hospital management should try to forecast the demand for its various services and budget as far as possible with available funds and resources to meet that demand with internal resources. However, there will inevitably be some instances where the demand for services exceeds the ability of a hospital to meet them. It might be able to arrange with private hospitals to take on some of the excess demand.

Another possibility, as in the example of treating eye conditions, is that it might be possible to find an external organisation that is able to take over the administration and delivery of a specific range of treatments, so that the hospital can use its available resources for other work.

2. There are some practical difficulties. Private health services can be expensive, and if the state-funded hospital uses private hospitals to handle excess demand for treatments, this will take away finance that would otherwise be available for in-house treatments. It is therefore questionable whether a state-funded hospital can afford to pay for large amounts of private hospital assistance without limiting its own operational capacity.

A further problem with arranging for specialist companies to provide treatments on the hospital premises is that it would first of all be necessary to identify private companies that are capable of and willing to provide the treatments, and then it would be necessary to find space on the hospital premises for the service to operate in.

Delicaroma

1. Delicaroma would have a flexible workforce that it can adjust to meet demand from customers at all times. It could bring in staff when demand is expected to be high and operate with much lower staff numbers in quiet periods. In this way it could also keep labour costs low, since it would only pay staff for the hours that they actually work.

2. Employees would benefit from either a full-time or a part-time employment contract. This would provide them with some guaranteed income and so greater security in private life. An employment contract would also provide benefits such as entitlement to holiday and holiday pay. So in summary, individuals would be better off financially.

3. If employees have part-time or full-time employment contracts, it is likely that average staffing levels at the company's coffee shops will be higher. If this is the case, service levels should improve because there will be more people to provide service.

It might be argued that employees will be motivated better if they have a guaranteed number of hours of work and a guaranteed basic wage or salary; and if they are better motivated they may provide a higher level of service. There is no hard evidence, however, to suggest that this would happen.

Anixter helps cut inventory costs

1. There was a heavy administrative task in managing inventory and reordering and storing stock items. Much of the administrative work appears to have been inefficient, for example with seven different locations in the two factories for holding stock. Inefficient administration is an undesirable expense.

There were also delays in delivery of some stock items, resulting in delays in production.

There was also excessive stockholding, adding to costs of storage as well as finance costs of the investment in stock.

The system appears to have been inflexible, and unable to respond quickly to unexpected demand for certain stock items.

2. a By holding 1,200 items in easy-to-store-and-receive bags, lead times for producing some end products will have been reduced.

b By identifying minimum and maximum demand, quantities of components means that it should be possible to reduce buffer stock levels, sufficient to deal with maximum foreseeable demand but avoiding excessive stockholding above this maximum amount.

c Shorter lead times will result in lower reorder levels for stock items.

3. Just-in-time production aims to have items produced just in time to meet demand for them, so that in an ideal world there are no stocks of finished items waiting to be sold. This ideal is not easily achievable in practice, and the objective of a JIT approach should be to achieve a better balance between production and demand, so that inventories are reduced and kept as low as possible. In this respect, it can be argued that the manufacturer is working towards a production system with JIT features.

The Global Oil Company

1. Both companies will want to deliver the right quantities of their product to the locations where they are needed (for delivery to customers), at the time they are needed, and at an acceptable cost. An acceptable cost means having efficient systems for transporting the goods.

2. Global Oil will transport product in much greater quantities than Big Chips, and from more remote locations of the world (such as the desert or at sea). Big Chips will transport its finished goods from factory locations.

Methods of transportation will differ. Global Oil will use pipelines for transferring oil to locations for shipment, and will make extensive use of sea freight to deliver oil to distant locations. The products of Big Chips, because they are smaller in size, are more likely to be transported internationally by air or possibly road.

For road transportation, Global Oil will need special tankers, whereas Big Chips can use normal trucks and vans.

Global Oil may face problems of damaged pipelines and leaks that disrupt the flow of its oil. Big Chips is likely to have greater problems with protecting goods from damage in transit.

(Other comparisons between the logistics challenges of the two companies might be a valid answer.)

Exam-style Questions

1. Inventory control charts are likely to be produced within IT systems, and so might be of limited value for inventory control, since IT systems can present inventory control information automatically and in a non-graphical format. However, charts can give a useful pictorial demonstration of stockholding levels, and incidents of stock-outs, for important stock items.

(Your answer may differ in its assessment of control charts.)

2. Seasonal demand means that the café and restaurant will need to make most of its sales and profits during the winter months, but should try if possible to break even (or perhaps make a small profit) in the summer.

There are implications for staffing levels. More staff will be needed during the winter. The business therefore needs to consider arrangements for increasing staffing levels in winter from the full-time "core" staff by recruiting individuals who are willing and able to work for just the winter season.

There may also be implications for the food and drinks products that the business sells. Patterns of demand from customers for different types of meal or drink are likely to vary between winter and summer.

The café and restaurant may also change its opening hours, opening for a shorter time each day during the summer, or possibly even closing on some days.

3. (Answers may differ according to the judgement made at the end of the answer.)

A process of pre-selection of subcontractors has the objective of identifying businesses that have the capacity, resources and financial strength to meet any purchase requirements from the construction company. The shortlisted subcontractors will also have indicated their interest in being put on a pre-approved list and so their interest in working for the construction company. This means that a pre-selection process should mean that whichever subcontractors are selected to do work for the company, they will be competent, reliable and capable of delivering their wok to an acceptable quality standard.

Having a pre-selected list of subcontractors also means that the process of issuing invitations to tender or requests for quotations to do work, should be a relatively quick process. A small number of pre-approved suppliers can be invited to bid, making the process relatively quick.

An argument against the pre-selection of subcontractors is that the construction company will presumably do construction work at many different locations around the country. Local contractors may be able to deliver their products and services more quickly, and provide the required workers, than pre-approved suppliers in more distant locations (whose employees may be reluctant to work a long way from home).

There is also an argument that using local subcontractors has the added benefit of supporting the local economy in areas where the company does its construction work.

On balance, however, the pre-selection of subcontractors is preferable. There is greater certainty about the quality and reliability of pre-selected firms, and easier and quicker administration of bids to win contracts. Assessing bids from a large number of untested local subcontractors creates a risk that poor decisions might be made in awarding subcontract work, with adverse implications for the quality and reliability of construction projects.

4. When the supply of components and parts is uncertain and unreliable, there is a serious risk with JIT purchasing of stock-outs of key components when there is a delay in supply. This in turn will lead to hold-ups in production, loss of output and possibly loss of sales. This happened in the case of BMW and the shortage of steering systems.

The problem is made worse because a manufacturer may not deal directly with some important suppliers. In the BMW example, the delay in production was caused by supplier to Bosch, who has no direct connection to or dealings with BMW. JIT purchasing means that manufacturers may have to rely on an extensive supply chain with which they are not entirely familiar.

These risks suggest an argument in favour of "just-in-case" holdings of inventory, with manufacturers holding safety stock or buffer stock just in case there is a disruption to the supply of key components.

There are, however, strong arguments in favour of JIT purchasing, especially for large volume manufacturers who buy in an extensive range of different parts and components from external suppliers.

If a car manufacturer held safety stocks for all critical parts and components, it would need to hold large quantities of stock. This would require large amounts of extra warehousing space, and the need to invest in and manage extensive warehousing resources. There would also be a finance cost of investing in high levels of stock.

The administrative and management problems of a large storage/warehousing facility, and its associated cost, suggests that "just-in-case" stockholding would be too costly, and the benefits of a lower risk of production hold-ups would be outweighed by the costs.

4.1 – progress questions, case studies, exam-style questions

Progress Questions

1. The responsibilities of the HR function include the recruitment of new staff, employment contracts, training staff, maintaining employee records and the application of the organisation's employment policies. It may also be involved in performance reviews and promotion interviews. Staff work in all departments of an organisation, and the work of HR therefore affects every other department or function, for example making arrangements to recruit new staff or provide training.

2. Human resources of a business organisation contribute directly or indirectly to the outputs of an organisation – products or services. The efficiency and effectiveness of employees depends on their basic talent, plus their knowledge or skills gained from training or work experience. The work that employees do can affect the quality, quantity, speed and cost of their organisation's output; these can all affect the competitiveness of the organisation and give it a competitive advantage over rivals.

3. Human resource planning is a planning process for an organisation's human resources requirements that is linked to the organisation's strategic plans for the future. The aim is to ensure that (over the long-term planning period) the organisation will have a sufficient number of staff with the required qualifications, skills and competence to enable the organisation to achieve its goals and objectives.

Case Studies

Road Beaters

1. A competitive advantage for Road Beaters may be that it can provide driving lessons to meet the demand and at times to suit the convenience of customers, and also that it employs a team of highly skilled driving instructors. If so, the HR team can help to ensure that the company maintains its leading market position by ensuring that a sufficient number of driving instructors are recruited and retained, and that instructors have technical and theoretical skills to provide a high standard of teaching, and interpersonal skills that appeal to learner drivers. Where necessary, the HR team members can arrange for instructors to receive any training that might be appropriate (such as training in providing driving lessons for larger vehicles).

BMW

1. People in international companies employ people from many different countries, and also have business customers in many countries. In a global world there needs to be a universal language of business that enables individuals to communicate with each other, regardless of the country that they come from. English (particularly US English) is the global language of business. International companies require employees to communicate with colleagues in this language, so that there should be no serious communication difficulties. In addition, executives are able to communicate in a common language with business customers, many of whom will also speak English, either as their native language or as their language of business.

International companies often require executives to work in different parts of the world, so that they gain a broad knowledge of the company's business. It is difficult to manage an international company successfully without having some knowledge and experience of what it does around the world. Work assignments in other countries also help the people within the organisation to develop and share a common corporate culture, which helps to give the company a coherent identity.

Planning for company change

1. A starting point for planning should be to prepare a forecast of the numbers of employees who will be needed in the future, divided between unskilled and skilled, and when they will be required. This forecast should then be compared to the existing staff levels and their skills, to decide how many existing staff can be offered unskilled jobs and how many can be "upskilled" to take on more skilled jobs.

There will probably be a gap between available staff and staff requirements, so the human resources plan will also need to establish how many new skilled employees should be recruited (and when), and how many existing staff will need to be made redundant. The human resources plan may also include details of training requirements for upskilling employees, and possibly also rates of pay for both types of job, skilled and unskilled.

2. The measures that should be taken will follow on from formal agreement of the human resources plan. The HR department will need to plan a recruitment campaign to employ the numbers of skilled employees required, and a training programme for existing staff who will be offered the opportunity to take on skilled jobs. Discussions will need to begin with the representatives of employees who will be made redundant, so that arrangements for the redundancies can be determined. These measures need to be taken at times to coincide with the switch to the new production system.

Exam-style Questions

1. There are several reasons for the increase in home working/teleworking, but teleworking has affected office work more than manual jobs. Answers may include:

   - Advances in IT and communications. Employees can be connected to their bosses, colleagues and work files through the internet or by mobile phone. It is not necessary to work in a central office

   - A growing demand from employees to work from home, to avoid the time required (and expense) in travelling to and from work

   - Employers need less office space, so can save on accommodation costs.

2. Two reasons are suggested here.

Employees gain experience and develop their skills in their job, and over time many of them become more efficient or more effective in what they do. This makes them more valuable to their employer. A high rate of labour turnover would mean the loss of skills, which is likely to reduce the competitiveness of the organisation.

A high rate of labour turnover means that there will be a high rate of recruitment of new employees. Recruitment takes time and costs money. In addition, new employees may need time to get used to their job, and so may not be efficient or effective in their job until they get more familiar with it. A high rate of labour retention minimises these effects.

3. An international business recruits employees from many different countries. Some of the individuals are recruited for skilled jobs or for executive jobs with prospects for promotion to senior positions. Global companies compete to recruit the best talent, and recruitment by the HR department can enable a company to compete more effectively by attracting the best people.

HR is also responsible for training of employees throughout their career with the company. Well-designed training programmes raise the skills level of people in the organisation, and this will help to make it more competitive. Training for executives may also include programmes that help individuals to acquire the corporate culture, something that is important for large global companies.

In an international company, it is important that executives should have a good knowledge and understanding of the whole business, not just the business in one country. For this reason it is usual for international companies to require executives to work for several years in different countries, building their knowledge of the business. HR is likely to be involved in planning these work assignments for executives.

People within an international business must be able to communicate with each other, and to this end the company is likely to insist that all people at management level speak the same language. This is usually English. HR may be required to arrange language training for some individuals, to bring their knowledge of English up to the required level for efficient working.

4.2 – progress questions, case studies, exam-style questions

Progress Questions

1. Labour turnover is a measure of the proportion of employees who have left their employment with an organisation in a given period of time. A labour retention rate is a measure of the proportion of employees who have remained in employment with an organisation in a given period of time.

2. A large investment in new equipment or machinery is likely to result in a reduction in the number of employees required for the work. As a general rule, equipment (capital) replaces labour, because it improves efficiency. Since there will be fewer employees, it is likely that labour turnover measured by the number of employees leaving employment will fall. However, labour turnover measured by the percentage of employees leaving in a period may not fall (i.e. improve), but might even increase.

3. A labour-intensive business is one in which most of the work is done by humans without extensive use of equipment or machinery. It differs from a capital-intensive business where most of the work is done by machines and other equipment, with only a small amount of human involvement.

4. An improvement in labour productivity reduces the labour cost of producing an item (a product or a service). If there are no increases in other costs (such as an additional cost of labour-saving equipment) the lower labour costs will result in higher profits for the employer organisation. Employees can therefore argue that they should be awarded a share in the improved profits.

Case Studies

Employee costs

1. A company designing and selling computer games will employ software specialists. These are likely to be well-paid individuals (although many may be employed in a country with relatively low wages and salary levels). However, the company will need to invest heavily in IT and communications equipment and systems (including cyber security); and it is likely that much of its marketing and selling operations will be online and automated. The company sells large quantities of its games, and its total sales revenue will therefore be high. For this reason, it seems likely that there will be a relatively low ratio of labour costs to sales revenue.

2. Firms of accountants employ highly paid professional people, and much of the work of the firm will be labour intensive, because the skills needed to do the work are not easily automated. The firm will therefore have a high ratio of labour costs to sales revenue.

Exam-style Questions

1. D. (Falling productivity means that more labour time and cost is needed to produce the output of the organisation, so the ratio of labour cost to sales revenue will increase.)

2. Assumption: Number of employees = $(21 + 19)/2 = 20$

Total hours worked in the month = 20 employees × 160 hours = 3,200 hours

Output per hour = 256,000 fittings/3,200 hours = 80 fittings per hour

Average production time per unit = 3,200 hours/256,000 fittings = 0.125 hours per unit

3. Employee engagement with the work is a qualitative measure, to do with feelings and attitudes, so it is difficult to measure. Attempts to measure engagement, for example with a questionnaire, might not be reliable, and answers may be subjective or even untruthful.

4. There are three reasons why sales per employee may have risen. Sales prices may have risen, so without any change in sales volume or the number of employees, sales per employee will have gone up. A second reason is that sales volume may have increased, so without any change in sales price or in the number of employees, sales revenue per employee will have risen. The third reason, which links more directly to labour productivity, is that the company may have employed fewer people, and if there is no change in sales prices or sales volume, the lower employee numbers would result in higher sales revenue per employee. Producing and selling more with fewer people would be an improvement in labour productivity.

There are three reasons why profit per employee might have fallen. One is that the company might have reduced the sales price in order to achieve a higher sales volume. Revenue per employee might therefore have gone up (if sales revenue went up) but costs would be higher and profits perhaps lower, and as a result profit per employee would have fallen. Another reason is that costs in general might have gone up, reducing profits and so profit per employee. The third reason is linked to labour productivity. An increase in sales per employee might have been achieved by replacing labour with new equipment or machinery, and the additional costs of the capital invested and the running costs for the new capital equipment might have resulted in lower profits – so that even if there were now fewer employees and a higher sales revenue per employee, profit per employee might have fallen.

4.3 – progress questions, case studies, exam-style questions

Progress questions

1. Internal recruitment involves appointing individuals from inside the organisation (i.e. existing employees) to fill job vacancies that arise. It often means promoting someone to a more senior or better-paid position. External recruitment involves appointing people from outside the organisation to fill job vacancies that arise.

2. External recruitment will be preferable to internal recruitment when an organisation does not have suitable existing employees to fill job vacancies, or where there are better-qualified or better-experienced people outside to do a job.

A company might want to appoint people to new jobs requiring new skills, such as IT skills, and there may be a large number of suitable candidates externally, but relatively few internal candidates. Training internal candidates to fill the new job vacancies might be difficult.

External recruitment might also be preferable to an international organisation entering into a market in a country for the first time. It will be better to recruit a substantial number of people externally, from that country, and make relatively few internal appointments to the new jobs.

3. The term "span of control" is used with reference to the management and supervisory structure of an organisation. It refers to the number of subordinates reporting to a manager or supervisor. For example, a manager with a team of six people would have a span of control of 6.

4. (Several different points might be given as an answer here.)

A tall organisation is one with a hierarchical management structure, in which there are many different levels of management. Matters often have to be referred up through a number of management levels in order to obtain a decision, and the decision then has to be passed down through the management levels to the employees who put the decision into practice. As a result, decision-making can be very slow.

(Another point that could be made is that with a tall organisation structure, the people at the very top of the organisation are a long way from operations "on the ground" and so might not know enough about the business and its operations to make good decisions.)

5. A flat organisation structure is one in which there are few levels of management. If the organisation is fairly large, this would mean that the span of control for managers and supervisors would be large. When managers have a large number of people working for them, they can find it difficult to manage efficiently or effectively. There might be so many subordinates that a manager cannot give them all the time and attention they need so that work is not done or is not done as well as it should be. In addition, managers may spend so much time dealing with personal problems with subordinates that they have no time for other aspects of their job.

Case Studies

Recruitment and selection methods

The question asks for the most appropriate method of recruitment in each case, but in practice more than one method of recruitment and selection should be used.

1. Stores assistant. Recruit an individual through a local employment agency. (Alternatively, advertise the vacancy on a noticeboard in the store.)

2. Stores manager. Consider an internal promotion, advertising the job vacancy internally and inviting applications. The successful individual might then be selected on the basis of past performance record and an interview process. (Alternatively, advertise the job externally, possibly in a specialist trade journal or through a recruitment agency specialising in retail jobs. Selection would then be by application form/questionnaire and selection interview.)

3. IT manager. This is a job calling for specialist skills for which there is no suitable internal candidate, or at least not many suitable candidates. The recruitment process should look for candidates both internally and externally. The vacancy could be advertised on the company's website, or through a specialist recruitment agency for senior IT management. Selection would be on the basis of application forms and interview, with possibly also a practical test of IT skills.

Training new staff

1. The graduates should be given induction training when they first join the company. This may take the form of a training programme for about two weeks at the company's headquarters or training centre, with talks, seminars and activities. This will enable individuals to start learning about the company, and to get to know each other and other managers in the company.

   They should then be appointed to a department and country within the company to learn more and start to gain experience on the job; and they may be rotated through a number of jobs and countries.

   They should also be encouraged where appropriate to develop specialist skills or obtain specialist qualifications, for example in IT or in accounting, which they can bring to their job.

   The general principle should be that the sooner individuals are given relevant induction and training, the sooner they will be able to contribute value to the company.

Jobs to go at Brevia plc

1. The legality of the redundancies depends on the law in the country concerned. It would seem that if the company is losing a requirement for some unskilled staff but will be taking on a number of skilled staff, the redundancies are probably lawful. (It may depend, however, on how easily unskilled individuals might be retrained to do skilled work. It is assumed here that this would be very difficult.)

2. As previously mentioned, it might be possible to retrain some unskilled employees to do skilled work, but this will depend on the nature of the skilled work and the potential of the unskilled employees.

   There may also be some job losses from natural labour turnover before the end of April, for example with some individuals retiring or leaving to take up a job somewhere else. To the extent that employees are lost through "natural wastage", the number of redundancies required will be reduced.

   It is also possible that there are other unskilled jobs within the company, in different types of work, which might be offered to unskilled employees who would otherwise be made redundant.

Exam-style Questions

1. An advantage of using interviews to fill a job vacancy is that management of the organisation have an opportunity to meet with applicants, ask questions and make a judgement about the individual through face-to-face interaction. This can be particularly useful in selecting someone for a job requiring management skills or interpersonal skills.

2. When there is a narrow span of control, with managers in charge of a small number of individuals, there will be a large number of levels in the hierarchical management structure, especially in an organisation employing many people. When there is a wide span of control, with managers in charge of a large number of individuals, there will be a small number of levels in the hierarchical management structure.

3. It might be possible to retrain existing employees to acquire IT skills, so that they are able to take on any jobs that might be created by the switch to digitisation.

   (Alternatively, it might be possible to offer employees other jobs within the organisation, where vacancies exist. Answers might also choose making employees redundant as a possible measure.)

4. The efficiency, effectiveness and competitiveness of an organisation depend to a large extent on the skills of the people who work for it. Organisations should therefore seek to recruit the best talent available. They will often be competing with other employers for the same talent, therefore it is important that recruitment and selection procedures are well organised and well designed, so that individuals who are offered jobs will be likely to accept the offer.

   It is also important to find the right people to fill job vacancies. It is therefore important that the HR department should recognise and use the channels of recruitment that would be most suitable for each particular type of job vacancy. Individuals with different experience and skills are likely to use different channels for applying for jobs, and HR should match the type of job with the recruitment method used.

   Selecting individuals for job vacancies from among all those who apply is also important. Poor selection will result in the appointment of individuals who are unsuited to the job, who will perform the job badly, and who may well leave the organisation after just a short time. The method of selection that is most appropriate will depend on the nature of the job, but a face-to-face interview can often provide some reassurance that a suitable person is being chosen for the job.

5. A global company such as McDonald's must have some central control and unified identity, so decentralisation to some extent can have benefits.

   When a company operates in many different countries, the markets in those countries may vary widely in character. There are differences in language, but more importantly for a fast-food company there are differences in eating habits and preferences. The products sold in each country may therefore need to be adapted to local tastes and demand; this would be difficult with a centralised management structure.

   Similarly advertising and marketing activities might need to differ between countries, and decisions about this should be taken at a national level, and by managers who understand local conditions.

   There will also be day-to-day operational decisions to be taken at a national level or at the individual store level. Authority to make these decisions should be decentralised; it would take too long and would be inefficient to have to refer matters continually to senior managers at head office to make a decision.

4.4 – progress questions, case studies, exam-style questions

Progress Questions

1. A major criticism of Taylor's theory is that by dividing work into small repetitive tasks, jobs become monotonous and boring, so that the lack of motivation amongst employees to do their job well offsets the benefits of specialisation that time and motion study provides.

2. Taylor argued that workers are motivated by money, and should therefore be paid piece work to encourage them to work more productively. Maslow also argued that workers want to satisfy basic needs and security needs before they look for something extra from their job. In this respect, both theorists recognise the importance of money for workers. In other respects, however, the ideas of the two theorists are very different.

3. People spend a lot of their time at work, and it is reasonable to expect that during this time they will want social interaction with work colleagues in order to make their work more fulfilling. Maslow argued that when workers have satisfied their basic needs and needs for security, they will want to satisfy their social needs through their work. If these needs are not satisfied, they will not be committed to their work.

4. It is difficult in a supermarket to get workers to work together in teams, and so build up social interaction to satisfy social needs. A supermarket manager may therefore try to arrange social activities outside normal working hours for staff. Alternatively a manager may set aside a room in the supermarket where employees can take rest breaks, and mix socially with other people taking time out.

5. Esteem needs can be met in the workplace by employees being given positive feedback from their manager/boss. Jerome might do this by having a monthly reward scheme that recognises the company's employee of the month. Individuals who win an award will gain a sense of being respected. (A drawback to this idea, however, is that if any employees do not win an award, they might become resentful.)

6. According to Herzberg, hygiene factors are aspects of work that either demotivate employees if they are unsatisfactory or prevent employees from being demotivated if they are satisfactory. A pleasant physical working environment is an example. Motivators are aspects of work that can motivate individuals to work better if they are in place, or will prevent individuals from being motivated if they are not. Being recognised for performing well is an example of a motivator.

7. One type of financial reward is a basic salary or wage. Another is some form of bonus or commission, i.e. performance-related pay.

8. One form of non-financial reward is being given more responsibility for a task: this can motivate individuals who want to have greater authority and responsibility. Another form of non-financial reward is recognition by an employer for work well done – for example winning an employee of the year award. It can be argued that promotion to a more senior job is a form of non-financial reward, although individuals will expect an increase in their pay when they are promoted.

9. Financial rewards need to be fair, and seen to be fair. A scheme that rewards the manager of a team with a bonus without giving a bonus to any of the team members might be considered unfair. If so, it could demotivate the team members rather than motivate the team to do better, which is what the aim of the bonus scheme should be.

Case Studies

Fashion company

1. The company might consider that workers in the factories in Bangladesh and Vietnam want to satisfy their basic needs and need for security. By providing safe and reasonably pleasant working conditions, fair wages and secure jobs, the company might have a well-motivated workforce in the factories. The company is also successful at attracting talented individuals in other parts of the business. In order to attract individuals into jobs such as fashion design and marketing, it will be necessary (on the assumption that Maslow's theory is correct) to offer them social interaction, recognition of their value (for example through high pay and a performance-related bonus pay scheme) and a sense of personal achievement in the work that they are doing. This would require job design that enables individuals to get a sense of fulfilment from what they are doing in their work.

Bags By Design

1. Maslow argued that individuals are motivated at work by a hierarchy of needs, and that needs at lower levels must be satisfied before needs at a higher level can begin to motivate individuals. The poor working conditions during the ten days of the large order meant that the security needs of employees were not being met. In principle, this should have resulted in a demotivated workforce wanting an improvement in working conditions. However, social needs and esteem needs are being met at work, and if employees recognised that the poor working conditions were only temporary, the satisfaction of social needs and esteem needs at work would have been sufficient to motivate employees to meet the targets for the large order.

    Herzberg argued that hygiene factors, if they are unsatisfactory, can demotivate workers. Working conditions are a hygiene factor, and the poor working conditions should therefore have demotivated workers during the ten days of the large order. However, if workers recognised that the poor conditions were only temporary, other hygiene factors, such as a good social environment, might have been sufficient to prevent demotivation during this time. Herzberg also argued that motivator factors can make employees want to perform well at work. The sense of esteem that employees at Bags By Design appear to have would have been a factor in the success in meeting the targets for the large order.

Alhambra Ltd

1. According to Herzberg, there are hygiene factors at work that need to be satisfactory to prevent workers from becoming dissatisfied. Working conditions are an important hygiene factor. The replacement of the old air-conditioning system has made working conditions worse. Another hygiene factor is reasonable hours of working. The introduction of shift working means that individuals must to change their hours of working, which might be inconvenient for many and might affect their out-of-work living arrangements. Since hygiene factors have worsened, employees have become dissatisfied, with the result that both the level of defective items produced and worker absenteeism have increased.

P & A Textiles

1. The big increase in the number of employees might have made working conditions worse, with more people working in the same space that ten people used to work in. It is also possible that the large increase in employee numbers has meant that the social interaction amongst employees has worsened. These changes in working conditions might be sufficient to dissatisfy all employees, leading to an increase in absenteeism and labour turnover, and an increase in the proportion of faulty products. Payment of the same rates of pay to all workers, regardless of their experience, might also have caused dissatisfaction amongst the more experienced staff.

2. Pay can be an important motivator. For all workers, the company might introduce a bonus scheme based on performance in reducing the amount of defective production. A bonus scheme based on labour productivity and the quantity of output produced by individuals might help to reduce absenteeism and labour turnover.

    Management might also consider ways of improving the social atmosphere at work, and consider ways of improving social interaction between employees. A more pleasant social environment for working might help to improve job satisfaction and so reduce absenteeism and labour turnover and improve the quality of output.

3. The long-serving employees, being the most experienced, are likely to be the most skilled and most productive members of the workforce. They are also expected to provide training and assistance for newer members of staff. However, their experience and additional responsibilities are not recognised. P & A should therefore increase the pay of employees according to experience and time with the company; in other words, loyalty and experience should be recognised and rewarded. In addition, the additional responsibilities of experienced staff should be recognised, possibly by creating positions as supervisors within the company. Recognition through promotion might motivate individuals through a sense of recognition and esteem.

Exam-style Questions

1. One form of non-financial reward is being given more responsibility for a task; this can motivate individuals who want to have greater authority and responsibility.

2. Unless employees feel that they are being paid a reasonable amount, they are likely to be dissatisfied with their work. If Miguel is not paying a reasonable level of salaries or wages, it is likely that an increase in pay will reduce dissatisfaction. It is also probable that a remuneration scheme that rewards individuals for good performance will also motivate individuals. For example, bonus payments for achieving set targets for performance might motivate individuals to try to achieve those targets. It is also possible that higher basic salary levels will motivate individuals, because an increase in pay is a recognition of the worth and contribution of individuals. However, a remuneration scheme needs to be fair. If some individuals believe that an increase in the general level of pay is more favourable to some individuals than to others, the scheme may cause dissatisfaction rather than motivation. Other aspects of working affect the motivation of employees. Miguel wants to expand the area covered by his business, and this is likely to mean that employees have to travel more, perhaps spend more time away from home and work longer hours. If this is the case, higher pay will probably be essential to reward employees for the change in their working conditions. In summary, if Miguel wants to improve or maintain the motivation of his employees, at a time when the demands of work will increase, higher pay in some form or other will be necessary.

3. Motivation theorists such as Herzberg have argued that there are certain features of a job that can motivate an individual. One of these is job enrichment, whereby the tasks involved in the work provide personal satisfaction. Redesigning Natasha's job to make it more challenging and interesting for her might be sufficient to persuade her to stay with the business. Redesigning a job does not necessarily make it more interesting. To persuade Natasha to stay, the redesigned job would need to give here the fresh interest and fulfilment at work that she appears to need. However, Natasha might not want a job with more variety or responsibility. She might have lost interest in the internet dating business, or she might feel that she has been too long in the job. Although she says that she has lost interest in the job, it might be that her real dissatisfaction is with inadequate pay and rewards. Since Tamara wants Natasha to remain in the business, she needs to establish in more detail the reasons why Natasha wants to leave, and discuss with her what measures to redesign the job might be sufficient to persuade her to stay. On the basis of the information available, and without a better understanding of Natasha's thinking, this seems to be the only judgement that can be made.

4.5 – progress questions, case studies, exam-style questions

Progress Questions

1. Collective bargaining is a process in which the terms of working for a group of employees in similar jobs, such as pay, working hours and other working conditions, are negotiated with an employer by representatives of the employees, such as a trade union or a staff association.

2. When an employer recognises a trade union as representing a group of workers, employees benefit because skilled negotiators from the union will negotiate pay and working conditions on their behalf. In certain types of work, particularly unskilled work or work within large organisations, a union may be able to negotiate better terms than individuals bargaining with the employer by themselves would be able to achieve. Representation by a trade union is also likely to mean that terms and conditions of working negotiated for employees will be fair to all of them. Collective bargaining avoids a situation where employees might compete with each other for better pay or better working conditions.

3. An important benefit to an employer of recognising a trade union is that the union can negotiate pay and working conditions for the individuals as a group. This avoids the need, and the time and administrative effort, for the employer to deal with each of its employees individually. A second benefit is that if relations with the trade union are good, it may be easier to resolve any problems that arise at work. The trade union should be trusted by the employees concerned. The employer can discuss the problem with a trade union representative, and try to reach a solution.

4. Employee involvement in decision-making at work can vary in extent. One factor is the leadership style of the manager. Managers can differ in the extent to which they are willing to involve their subordinates in decision-making, and consult them before a decision is made. A second factor is the nature of the work: with complex work, a manager may need to discuss with subordinates problems that arise and ways of dealing with them. On the other hand, for jobs involving routine and repetitive work, employee participation is likely to be very limited. (Another point that could be made is that the extent of employee participation in decision-making depends on the skills and experience of the subordinates. Highly skilled employees are likely to have more influence over decision-making than unskilled or inexperienced workers.)

5. An employer may establish a job of staff welfare officer, who is available for employees to discuss problems outside work and help them to deal with them, such as problems with housing, travelling to work, or family life. Employers may also encourage employees to find a suitable balance between work and life outside work. In some types of job, individuals are encouraged to take time off from work (paid) to do charity work. Individuals might be discouraged from working excessive hours in the office. If there is dissatisfaction among some employees about discrimination at work, such as discrimination due to age, gender, race or disability, management should take measures to eradicate the discrimination, initially by setting an example themselves, and also by creating a culture at work where discrimination is not tolerated.

6. There is an ethical reason for wanting to improve staff morale and welfare. It can be argued that an employer has an ethical responsibility for the well-being of employees.

   Improving staff morale and welfare will also help to improve attitudes of people at work, reducing absenteeism, labour turnover and disputes in the workplace.

Exam-style Questions

1. An important benefit to an employer of recognising a trade union is that the union can negotiate pay and working conditions for the individuals as a group. This avoids the need – and the time and administrative effort – for the employer to deal with each of its employees individually.

2. By appointing worker representatives to a board of directors, an organisation will ensure that the views and interests of employees are represented on the top decision-making body within the organisation. This may be a particular benefit in cases where employees are not represented by a trade union, or where workers may have a particularly important role within the organisation, such as doctors within a private hospital company. Worker directors would also have some influence in persuading the board of directors to balance fairly the interests of workers and shareholders, for example by arguing against a large increase in dividend payments to shareholders when workers are given no increase in pay. A board of directors should reach a consensus in the decisions that they make. If there are one or more worker directors, decisions by the board will be seen as having the support of the worker representatives. This may help to reduce the risk of disputes between the organisation and its employees.

3. The aim of involving employees in decision-making at work should be to improve the performance of the company, in terms of improved decision-making and performance, or in terms of a reduction in disputes between employer and employees.

   Involvement by employees in decisions about working conditions should help to reduce the incidence of workplace disputes. By reducing dissatisfaction among employees, it might be expected that business performance will improve, even if it is simply through a reduction in absenteeism from work and in labour turnover.

   Employee involvement in decision-making may benefit a company and its performance, but this will depend on the nature of the decisions. For work of a routine and repetitive nature, employee participation in decision-making by management is unlikely to have a beneficial effect on performance.

   For work of a complex nature, especially where the work is organised on the basis of teams, involvement by subordinates in decision-making can be beneficial, if not essential, for achieving better performance. One example is in research and development work, where all members of a development team can contribute ideas about what should be done. Similarly with complex project work, managers will listen to advice and suggestions by subordinates before making decisions.

   Employees are also likely to have much more involvement in decision-making when they have particular skills or talents, such as long experience in the industry or technical skills or qualifications. This is because managers will consider carefully the advice that is given to them by subordinates that they respect.

   In summary, if employees are overlooked entirely and have no involvement in decision-making, there will be a low level of morale at work, with high levels of staff turnover and (probably) a poor level of efficiency and effectiveness in the work that is done. Involvement by employees in decision-making can improve morale and in many situations can help to improve the quality of decisions that are made. Better-quality decisions will lead to better business performance. However, the most suitable extent of employee involvement depends on circumstances and the nature of the work.

5.1 – progress questions, case studies, exam-style questions

Progress Questions

1. There are many different answers that could be given to this question. One suggestion is that a financial decision might be to allocate spending to a particular project, and if the project is successful, the business will be more successful and more competitive. Another suggestion is that a financial decision to allocate more money to marketing and sales activities could make the business more competitive if the extra money is spent successfully in winning more sales.

2. An important source of finance is retained profits. Many companies of all sizes also borrow from banks. Other sources of finance might be the issue of new shares, or borrowing from non-banks in the form of loans. Borrowing by very large companies may take the form of bonds, also known as debentures. In some circumstances, companies are able to obtain a grant from the government, for example to help pay for a new investment in a socially deprived area of the country.

3. Financing decisions are of two broad types: decisions about raising finance, and decisions about investing or spending. Decisions about raising new finance can add to competitiveness by providing funds for new investment in business ventures. Decisions about how to spend money affect competitiveness because businesses need to invest to compete and succeed, and some spending decisions are more successful than others.

4. Operating globally makes a business much more well known to foreign investors. This should make it easier for a business to raise finance because there are many more potential investors who might be interested in putting money into the business. Operating globally also means that the business will have business operations in different countries, so they need to obtain finance for operations in different currencies.

5. The cost of sales is a cost of producing something. It is calculated in manufacturing businesses. It can also be calculated in a retailing business, where "cost of sales" is actually the cost of goods purchased and resold. A cost of sales is not calculated for businesses that produce intangible items (such as software) or perform a service (such as an office cleaning company).

6. Return on investment is the financial gain that a business makes on the finance it has invested.

Case Studies

Operating profit

1. 3.5% × $12 million = $420,000
2. 3.5% × ($12 million × 1.10) = $462,000
3. 4% × $12 million = $480,000
4. 4% × ($12 million × 1.10) = $528,000

Financial target setting

1. Tom is setting up a new business and he needs to think about what he must do financially to set up the business and operate it successfully. He needs enough finance to buy equipment and possibly to rent a property for the business. In the early days, revenue will be slow to pick up, and Tom will need money to cover his expenditure whilst he is still making a loss. He also needs to feel fairly confident that he will have sufficient finance to meet his needs for at least a period of time.

   By making a financial plan and setting targets, he can monitor his actual progress when the business is set up, by comparing what he has actually achieved with his original target. This will tell him whether he is being successful, or whether things are not going as well as hoped, in which case he can think about what he should do before the situation worsens.

2. Tom's most important financial targets for the first year should be to:
   - Keep the business operating; this means having sufficient finance to cover all his spending
   - Have cash receipts in excess of operational expenditure
   - Build the business by achieving a target amount of revenue
   - If possible, make a small profit.

   His targets for the first year should not be excessively ambitious.

Exam-style Questions

1. Setting objectives gives a company a sense of direction, and understanding of what they want to achieve. Financial objectives may be to increase profits or revenue for example; however, broad objectives should be expressed in more "concrete" terms, as financial targets. Companies can monitor their actual performance by comparing it with their targets, and judging whether they are or are not on course to achieve their targets.

2. A company that does not have much cash, and possibly borrows from a bank, may set and objective and targets for cash flow. This is because if they spend more cash than they receive, they might run out of cash and have difficulty borrowing more.

3. When an important new technology emerges, businesses must either adopt the technology or lose competitiveness. Financial decisions about raising the finance to invest in the new technology can therefore have important implications for business survival.

   In addition, companies that invest more heavily in a successful new technology are likely to be more successful than competitors who invest less.

   When a large amount of new investment is required to develop new products, it can take a long time before the new products are developed and reach the market. When products reach the market, sales growth initially might be slow. If this happens, the business may be relatively unprofitable (and so relatively uncompetitive) in the short term.

   However, although spending on new investments might affect profits in the short term, if successful they will provide substantial benefits in time. In the longer term, a financial decision to invest should make a business more competitive and more successful.

4. A global business operates in many different countries, but it reports its profits in one currency and also pays returns (dividends) to its owners in that currency. However, the value of currencies is continually fluctuating, with exchange rate movements. In some cases, the value of one currency against another may change by a large amount in a short time.

   The profits that a global business reports therefore depend to a large extent on exchange rate movements. For example, if a US company makes a profit in France of €1,200,000, the profit that it reports will depend on the exchange rate between the US dollar and the euro. If the exchange rate is €1 = $1, the reported profit will be $1,200,000. However, if the exchange rate changes and the euro weakens to €1.20 = $1, the US company's profit will fall to just $1,000,000.

   The same problem applies with financing. If a global company borrows money, it will do so in a particular currency, but it is likely to exchange the money into other currencies for spending in its global operations. The ability of a company to repay its borrowing out of the profits from its global operations may depend on how exchange rates move.

Finally, there can be a problem with making a long-term investment in another country. For example, a UK company might invest in a long-term project in South Africa, where the project is expected to provide profits over a large number of years. The ability of the project to provide a suitable return will depend on how the South African currency (the rand) changes in value over time.

In summary, financial decisions by a global company are made difficult by the likelihood of foreign exchange movements, adding to the uncertainty about whether and where to invest.

5.2 – progress questions, case studies, exam-style questions

Progress Questions

1. Gross profit margin = ($15,000/$40,000) × 100% = 37.5%
2. Operating profit margin = ($15,000/$90,000) × 100% = 16.7%
3. Some investments last a very long time, and it would take too long to wait until they have reached their end before measuring the return that they have made over their entire life. Measuring return on investment as an annual amount means that information about return is provided more regularly. In addition, it makes it possible to compare returns on many different investments, to judge how they are performing.
4. When the proposed or planned average annual return on a future investment is calculated, assumptions are made about the costs that will be incurred as well as the revenues that the investment will earn. The expected return is based on reasonable assumptions. Looking back at an investment at the end of its life, it might be difficult to identify exactly the revenues, savings and expenditures that it incurred. Information systems in business are not built to provide this information.
5. A budget is a plan of operations (or capital investment), expressed in financial terms.
6. A forecast is a prediction about what will happen. A budget is a plan of what an organisation wants to happen and intends to achieve. When the budget is agreed, it is likely that the budget and current forecasts will agree with each other. However, over time and during the budget period, as circumstances develop, forecasts might change but the plan remains unchanged.
7. Budgets on their own are unlikely to increase the motivation of people working in the business. To motivate people, there must also be some incentive. For example, individuals may be told that they will be paid a bonus if the business (or their part of it) achieves or exceeds its budget targets.
8. Budgets could reduce motivation if the targets for achievement are unrealistic, so that individuals believe that there is no point in trying to work hard to achieve something that is not possible. A reduction in motivation would be even greater if management try to pressurise workers into improving their performance.

Case Studies

Competing supermarkets and gross profit margins

1. Flint Supermarket gross profit margin = ($100,000/$5,000,000) × 100% = 2%

   Diamond Supermarket gross profit margin = ($500,000/$3,000,000) × 100% = 16.7%

2. Flint Supermarket has made the larger gross profit, but Diamond Supermarket has made a higher gross profit margin. This indicates that it is adding a higher profit margin on to its costs than Flint Supermarket, and so making a bigger gross profit per $1 of sales. In comparison, Flint Supermarket is adding a lower profit margin to its costs, and this might explain its higher sales. In this example, the same gross profit has been earned by a lower gross margin and higher sales and by a higher gross margin and lower sales.

Manufacturing company

1. Current year gross profit margin = (2,000,000/5,000,000) × 100% = 40%

   Current year net profit margin = (400,000/5,000,000) × 100% = 8%

   Previous year gross profit margin = (2,090,000/5,500,000) × 100% = 38%

   Previous year net profit margin = (495,000/5,500,000) × 100% = 9%

2. The company has increased its sales but the gross profit margin has fallen. This means that gross profit did not increase by the same percentage amount as the increase in revenue. However, the company has succeeded in keeping other expenses slightly below the level of the previous year, and because revenue has increased, the result is an

increase in the net profit margin. With the increase in revenue and the increase in net profit margin percentage, net profit has increased by $95,000 or 23.75%.

3. It is difficult to draw any certain conclusion from the figures about the gross and net profit margins. It is possible that the company has had to reduce its gross profit margin slightly in order to obtain the higher sales. It would also appear that the company has been successful in keeping its other expenses low, at slightly less than the previous year's level. This explains the higher net profit margin despite the lower gross profit margin. However, we do not know why other expenses were as low even though revenue increased. It is perhaps worth noting that the percentage increase in revenue (by 23.75%) is exactly the same as the percentage increase in the net profit.

    (Note: An extreme view is that all other expenses of the business are "fixed costs" that do not change regardless of sales volume. However, this would be very unusual in practice.)

4. The answer to this question will depend on your personal point of view. One suggestion is that an increase in net profit by 23.75% is an excellent result, and the manager should aim for a similar performance next year. This means aiming to increase revenue, even if it means some reduction in the gross profit margin, and trying to keep other expenses at their current level.

Snazzy Clothes

1. The company needs to have a clear idea of what it is trying to achieve and what it needs to do to achieve its objectives. Financial planning would help the company to focus on the sales and profits it hopes to achieve, and what might be the obstacles to achieving them. Planning will also allow the company's management to co-ordinate their efforts, as well as set targets and monitor progress towards those targets. The focus should presumably be on profitability, and how the company needs to organise its activities in order to restore profits and prevent further profit decline.

2. The most useful financial plan would be a budget, setting out what the company should aim to achieve over the budget planning period. The budget would help the company to focus on sales and costs. Perhaps more importantly, a co-ordinated budget would enable the company to address the problem of the differences in production planning and sales, and what appears to be excessive production of products that the company cannot sell.

    Budgets should be prepared annually, and progress towards achieving the budget targets should be monitored regularly, probably every month.

3. The company seems to have operating capacity to produce goods efficiently. The problem seems to be that the company's products do not appeal to customers. Isabelle is probably correct in saying that the biggest problem is with product design. Without products that customers want to buy, the company will not be able to restore sales and profits. Alan is wrong to think that production can operate without any consideration for sales and profits, and the payment of bonuses to production staff do not appear justified in view of the company's poor performance.

Exam-style Questions

1.

	Sales	Costs	Operating profit
	$	$	$
Budget	6,700,000	6,400,000	300,000
Actual	7,200,000	6,800,000	400,000
Sales revenue variance	500,000 (F)		
Operating profit variance			100,000 (F)

2. Average annual profit = $198,000/4 = $49,500
    Average annual return = ($49,500/$150,000) × 100% = 33%

3. The expected annual profit = 6% × $75 million = $4,500,000.
    The expected average annual return = ($4,500,000/ $60 million) × 100% = 7.5%

4. Sanjay has two arguments in his favour. The first is that everyone in the business should know what their job is, and what they should be doing. If there were no budget, operations would not come to a halt. Secondly, since sales demand is uncertain, it is highly probable that the sales plan in the budget will turn out to be unrealistic, and budgets are usually based on the estimates for sales.

    However, there are several reasons why Sanjay is wrong, and why budgets should be prepared. A budget gives a business a sense of direction, and an understanding of what it is trying to achieve. It can

be used to communicate this sense of direction to everyone in the business, and it can ensure that the efforts of different departments or individuals are co-ordinated, so that they work towards the same goals. For example, a budget should help to ensure that the efforts of the production department are co-ordinated with those of sales and marketing.

Budgets can also be used to monitor progress. By reporting actual performance regularly, and comparing actual results with the budget plan, it will be possible to see when and why results are not going according to plan, and what results for the period are now likely to be unless corrective measures are taken. Where appropriate, control measures can be taken to put right anything that seems to be going wrong.

On balance, although the budget plan may not be achieved and although budgets are not essential, Sanjay's views are questionable. Budgets are a way of planning to achieve objectives, communicating intentions, co-ordinating efforts, and monitoring and controlling operations.

5.3 – progress questions, case studies, exam-style questions

Progress Questions

1. An important source of finance for a business is its own operations. It is usual to refer to retained profits as a source of finance, but cash received from business activities can be used to pay for continuing expenditures. Selling invoices to a debt factor enables a business to obtain cash sooner than it otherwise would. Instead of waiting for customers to pay what they owe, a business can get the cash more quickly, less the debt factor's charges.

2. One advantage of using retained profits as a source of finance is that it is obtained through normal business operations and does not require any particular effort to obtain. It may also be argued that it does not cost anything. In comparison, raising finance through a bank loan requires effort (negotiation with the bank) and has a cost (interest charges).

    A disadvantage of using retained profits as a source of finance is that retaining profits reduces the amount that is available for paying out to the business owners. (In the case of companies, retained profits reduce the amount available to pay out as dividends.)

3. A government might offer to lend money to businesses when it wants businesses to act in a particular way, for example invest in economically deprived areas of the country. Businesses might apply to the government for a loan in these circumstances when they want to invest but need to raise new finance to pay for the investment. Secondly, businesses might prefer to apply to the government for a loan, rather than apply to a commercial bank, because the rate of interest offered by the government is lower than for a normal commercial loan.

    (Note: Companies would prefer to obtain a grant from the government, because unlike a loan, a grant is not repayable.)

4. It is unwise to use short-term finance to support a long-term investment. A long-term investment provides returns over a long period of time, and a business should try to raise finance that is repayable over a long time (if it is borrowing) or where returns are paid over a long time (as in the case of dividends on shares). By borrowing short-term finance for a long-term activity, a business runs the risk of being unable to pay back the loan or re-borrow when the short-term loan becomes repayable.

    For similar reasons, a business should not use short-term finance when it needs the finance for a long time, because it will need to keep repaying short-term loans and borrowing again. This might be difficult for the reasons explained above. If a business needs long-term finance it should look for retained profits, new equity or new long-term borrowing.

5. New issues of shares.

    A long-term bank loan (or in the case of larger companies, an issue of debentures or other long-term bond).

6. A number of different answers might be given here.

    A venture capitalist will probably want to be awarded some shares in the business, reducing the proportion of the business owned by its founders and entrepreneurs.

    Venture capitalists expect a high rate of return on their investment, to compensate them for the risks that they are taking.

    Venture capitalists are not long-term investors. They will look for a way of selling their investment if and when the business becomes successful.

Case Studies

Stage Productions

1. External finance is needed because the business is growing, and profits and cash flow from business operations are insufficient to support the business growth.

    More specifically, finance is needed for two purposes.

    One is to invest in more sound and lighting equipment. This would be a long-term investment, so long-term finance should be obtained to pay for it. Bacari and Agnes are unlikely to have the money themselves, so they will need external long-term finance. This might be obtained from a venture capitalist or possibly from a medium-term bank loan.

    The business also needs finance to pay for day-to-day running costs, particularly wages. The finance required here might be short term. If it is a short-term requirement, with the business requiring cash to meet payments that fall due when it does not yet have cash coming in to make the payment, a short-term source of finance might be appropriate. This might take the form of an overdraft facility with Stage Productions' bank.

Exam-style Questions

1. The main reason for wanting short-term finance is to have the money available to make payments for day-to-day operational expenses, such as employees' wages, or to pay suppliers, when the business does not have sufficient cash immediately available to make the payments. Cash from sales will come in eventually, but there is a short-term deficit.

    This is a common situation in business, partly because businesses may not like to hold excessive amounts of cash in the bank. Cash is an idle resource, and is not earning any profit, so companies might keep their cash holdings as low as possible, and borrow (possibly on overdraft) short term when the need arises.

2. Debt factoring can be an expensive arrangement. The factor will charge interest on the money that it provides (i.e. the payments to the business that are made before the invoices are paid) and if it also takes over the administration of the invoicing and payments collection activities, it will charge for this service too.

3. A small but growing business needs both long-term and short-term sources of external finance, because it will not obtain sufficient profits and cash flow from its operations for the expenditures that it needs to grow.

    It needs long-term finance to pay for any new equipment that the business needs to grow its operations. It may also need finance to pay for day-to-day operational expenses, such as making payments to suppliers and paying for rental of a business property. This finance could be a combination of long-term finance and short-term borrowing.

    Long-term finance may be either equity or debt. New equity could come from the two friends and entrepreneurs themselves, if they have any more to invest. They may also be able to raise finance, in the form of equity or a loan, from family members or friends.

    The business appears to be achieving some success, since sales have been increasing, and it is possible that the owners may be able to obtain support and finance from a venture capitalist. However, a venture capitalist might want to see the business develop further before agreeing to put in any capital.

    If the business needs new equipment, it might be possible to arrange to lease it from a leasing company, rather than buy it outright. However, a leasing company would want some evidence that the business will be capable of affording the lease payments.

    It might be possible to obtain some short-term finance, in the form of a bank overdraft, to help with day-to-day expenditures and cash flows. Again, this will depend on the view that the bank takes about the business and its future prospects.

    In summary, it is not easy for a small and new business to obtain finance to grow. To raise finance from external sources, there has to be some evidence to convince investors or lenders that the business prospects are good, and that the business is a good investment prospect or a good credit risk.

4. Equity represents the ownership of a business. If a company raises finance by issuing new shares, it will be increasing or enlarging the ownership. The finance is "permanent" and does not have to be repaid; therefore in this sense it is a risk-free form of finance.

    Holders of shares in a company expect to receive dividends out of profits, but if the company is not making profits, it does not have to pay any dividends.

    However, there are some arguments against equity rather than debt as a source of new long-term finance. By increasing and enlarging the ownership of the company, additional equity also dilutes the ownership. The "old" shareholders do not own as much of the business, in percentage terms, that they did before.

A second problem is that equity shareholders do expect to receive dividends on their shares, and they may be angered by any failure of the company to do this. The amount of dividends that shareholders expect may well be more than the amount of interest that the company would have had to pay if it had obtained the finance by borrowing instead of issuing shares. There have been many occasions in the past when borrowing has been cheaper than issuing shares.

Most large companies are financed partly by equity and partly by debt, most of it long term. It would seem that the most appropriate approach to financing should be to have a suitable mixture of equity and debt.

5.4 – progress questions, case studies, exam-style questions

Progress Questions

1. Break-even is where sales revenue is exactly equal to total costs; therefore the business makes neither a profit nor a loss.

2. At break-even point: $F = Vx$

    Where F = total fixed costs, V = the variable cost per unit, and x = the number of units of product sold.

3. Margin of safety is the amount by which sales can fall short of the budgeted or expected amount before the business ceases to make a profit and just breaks even. If there is a bigger shortfall in sales than the margin of safety, the business would make a loss. The margin of safety is usually expressed as a percentage of budgeted or actual sales volume.

Case Studies

Sports Alive

The fixed costs are allocated equally between boots and kits; therefore they are $12,000 for each.

1. Contribution per pair of boots before the donation = $15 − 10 = $5.

    Break-even output and sales for boots (ignoring the donation) = $12,000/$5 per unit

    = 2,400 pairs of boots.

2. Contribution per kit after the donation (which is an additional variable cost):

    = $12 − 8 − 1 = $3.

    Break-even output and sales for kits (allowing for the donation):

    = $12,000/$3 per kit = 4,000 kits.

Exam-style Questions

1. Contribution per unit = $20 − $12 = $8

    The ratio of contribution to sales revenue (the "contribution to sales ratio") is constant.

    This is ($8/$20) × 100% = 40%

    So if sales = $600,000, total contribution = 40% × $600,000 = $240,000.

2. Contribution per unit = $90 − $50 = $40.

    The break-even point in units = $1,000,000/$40 per unit = 25,000 units.

    The margin of safety is 3,000 units; therefore budgeted sales = 25,000 + 3,000 = 28,000 units.

    Budgeted revenue = 28,000 units × $90 = $2,520,000

3. Break-even analysis can be used in the budgeting process. Break-even arithmetic is quite simple so it can be used to consider a range of different planning possibilities before the final budget is decided.

    It can be used to consider what profits would be if the selling price were higher or lower, or if the fixed costs or variable unit costs were higher or lower. For each possible outcome, it would be possible to calculate the expected profit (or loss) and margin of safety.

    Considering a range of different outcomes, with different sales prices, sales volumes, fixed and variable costs, and margins of safety, would be a form of risk analysis.

    In this way, break-even analysis can be used by a business to decide what it considers to be the optimum pricing policy for a product, balancing the expected profit with an acceptable level of risk (margin of safety).

4. The expected contribution per unit is $20 − $10 = $10

    The break-even point in units = $400,000/$10 per unit = 40,000 units. Since the budget is to sell just 30,000 units, this means that on these estimates the company will make a loss. (The expected loss would be $10 per unit, or $100,000 in total.)

This is clearly unacceptable and the company's management must consider what should be done to achieve a profit. Several possibilities could be considered. One is to raise the selling price per unit, increasing the unit contribution and so reducing the break-even point in units. However, by raising the selling price, sales demand might be less than 30,000 units, and it is not certain that a profit would be achieved.

Another possibility would be to consider ways of reducing costs, although a substantial reduction in costs would be necessary in order to achieve a profit. It might be possible to find ways of reducing fixed costs below $400,000 or reducing the variable cost per unit to less than $10.

However, on the basis of the expected figures there is an expected loss of $100,000 on sales of just $600,000 (30,000 units at $20 per unit). Management might therefore consider whether the company should cease production and sales of the product, in order to avoid the losses. Since it makes and sells only one product, this would mean closing down the business entirely.

In conclusion, the company is in a very dangerous financial position.

5.5 – progress questions, case studies, exam-style questions

Progress Questions

1. A cash flow forecast is a prediction of the future cash inflows and cash outflows of a business over a period of time, and changes in the cash position.

2. Profit is the difference between revenues and costs during a period of time. Cash flow is the difference between cash inflows and cash outflows. Cash inflows are not the same as revenues, since many revenues are sales on credit. Cash outflows are not the same as costs, for example because a business has to pay for inventory or capital assets.

3. Businesses owe money, to lenders, suppliers, the tax authorities and others. If a business does not have cash to pay the money it owes when the payment falls due, there is a risk that legal measures will be taken against it to obtain payment. These might lead to the financial collapse of the business. Problems with making payments will make lenders and creditors less willing to lend money or give credit in the future.

4. A cash flow forecast can be used to predict whether the business will have a cash surplus or a cash deficit at any time in the future.

   If the forecast indicates that there will be a shortage of cash, the business can take measures in advance to deal with the problem, for example by arranging a short-term bank loan or by deferring a large capital expenditure.

   If the forecast indicates that there will be a surplus of cash, the business can plan in advance how to make use of the money, for example by purchasing new equipment to improve operational efficiency and profitability.

5. Liquidity means cash or having ready access to cash (for example by means of a bank overdraft arrangement). A "liquidity problem" occurs when a business has insufficient cash or ready access to cash to meet its payment obligations when they fall due.

6. There are usually problems forecasting cash flows because there are uncertainties about the future, in terms of what sales and costs will be, what changes in working capital might occur, and what other cash receipts or cash payments might happen. It is also difficult to predict when cash flows will occur, as well as how large they might be. However, the difficulties in preparing cash flow forecasts should not put a business off from preparing them, so that it can establish its cash flow expectations and monitor its actual cash flow by comparing them with a previous forecast.

Case Studies

Understanding working capital (1)

	Beginning of year	End of year	Change
	$	$	$
Inventory	75,000	84,000	+ 9,000
Trade receivables	105,000	110,000	+ 5,000
Trade payables	60,000	80,000	(20,000)
Change in working capital			(6,000)

Working capital, defined as inventory plus trade receivables minus trade payables, has been reduced by $6,000 in total. A reduction in working capital has the effect of improving cash flow, so cash flows have been improved by $6,000.

Understanding working capital (2)

1. Profit = Sales – Cost of sales = $1,600 – (50% × $1,000) = $1,100
2. However, there has not yet been any receipt or payment of cash
3. There is remaining inventory of (50% × $1,000) = $500
   Trade receivables = $1,600
   Trade payables = $1,000
   So if we define working capital as inventory + trade receivables – trade payables, working capital = $500 + $1,600 – $1,000 = $1,100. (This is equal to the amount of the profit on the sales of the goods.)
4. The cash payment makes the cash position negative by $1,000.
5. The cash position has been reduced by $1,000. Ignoring cash, the working capital position has increased by $1,000, as it is now inventory $500, plus trade receivables $1,600 = $2,100. However, it can be argued that the negative cash position should be included in working capital (since definitions of working capital vary). If the negative cash is included, working capital remains unchanged at $1,100.
6. The cash position is improved by the payment of $1,600 received, so there is now $600 in cash.
7. The cash position is improved by $1,600. Ignoring cash, the working capital position has been reduced by $1,600 and is now $500 (inventory). Cash is $600, so the overall position is inventory $500 + cash $600 = Profit on transaction = $1,100.

Midi Computers

1. Profit and cash flow are not the same thing, nor the same amount. Cash flow differs from profit for several reasons. One of these is change in working capital, defined as inventory plus trade receivables minus trade payables. If working capital increases, cash flow will be less than profit by the amount of the increase. If working capital is reduced, cash flow will be better than profit, by the amount of the reduction.

   Jan's working capital has increased. The main reason is an increase in trade receivables, because the business is now selling computers on credit to business customers. So although selling to business customers is profitable, there has been a negative impact on cash flow, which will end only when the amount of trade receivables is no longer rising.

2. Getting more credit from suppliers will increase trade creditors, this will reduce working capital. As a consequence, cash flow will improve (be better than profit) by the amount of the increase.

Large increase in the failure of small businesses in Australia

1. Small businesses must have cash to pay for their expenditures. They could not borrow easily, so the cash would need to come mainly or wholly from cash flows from the business. If it runs out of cash, a business might collapse.

   By forecasting cash flows, a small business should be able to predict when it will have to make payments, and how much. In this way, it may be possible to improve cash flows by making arrangements in advance, for example by deciding to defer the purchase of more inventory, or asking customers for quicker payment, or arranging to defer some payments to suppliers and other creditors.

2. Cash flows might be improved by increasing profits. However, in the business conditions at the time, it would have been difficult for small businesses to raise their prices, and it might also have been difficult to reduce expenditures.

   A short-term measure to improve cash flows would have been to reduce working capital. As indicated above, this might have been possible by reducing holdings of inventory, or asking customers for quicker payment, or arranging to defer some payments to suppliers and other creditors.

   A more desperate measure would have been to try to sell capital assets of the business. However, although this might raise some cash in the short term, selling capital assets would have damaging long-term implications for the business.

3. For small businesses, most (or all) operating expenditures are essential, and few if any are discretionary (such as spending on advertising and sales promotions). Expenditures such as purchases of materials and payments of wages and salaries are essential to keep the business operational.

Lakeside hotel

MPJ presumably thought that Suzie and Ahmed had to obtain their supplies from MPJ, as the only local supplier available. MPJ was in effect a monopoly supplier to Suzie and Ahmed. Monopoly suppliers can usually charge higher prices because they do not have any competition.

The entry of a new competitor into the market, offering lower prices, means that MPJ must reduce its own prices or lose business (such as Suzie and Ahmed's) to the new supplier.

Carrefour

1. Carrefour would have hoped that by increasing the profit margin on all the items that it sold, it would increase profits. It might have expected some fall in sales due to the increase in prices, but not sufficient to offset the higher profits from the higher profit margins.

2. By reversing the price rises, Carrefour would have hoped to get back at least to the position it was in before. However, its previous increase in prices would have damaged its reputation, and customers who switched to cheaper stores or supermarkets would have had no reason to go back to Carrefour.

3. The increase in prices did not succeed because the fall in sales volume would have been more than offset by a fall in customers and sales. The reduction in prices would not have been enough to win a sufficient extra volume of customers and sales to offset the effect of the reduction in profit margins.

4. Falling profits would have the effect of making cash flows worse. In the short term the reduction in cash flow from lower profits might have been offset by a reduction in working capital (for example, lower inventory levels). In the long run, however, falling profits will lead on to worsening cash flows.

Exam-style Questions

1. Cash flow forecasts enable a business to predict whether it will have sufficient cash for its requirements, and if not, to take measures in advance to obtain the cash that it will need.

2. Purchases in May are paid for in June. In the cash flow forecast, there are forecast payments of $21,000 in June for purchases in May. By reducing purchases to $16,000, cash flows will improve in June by $5,000. Instead of having a negative cash balance of $3,000 at the end of June, BB would now have a positive cash balance of $2,000.

3.

	Beginning of year	End of year	Change
	$	$	$
Inventory	25,000	41,000	+ 16,000
Trade receivables	36,000	32,000	(5,000)
Trade payables	22,000	29,000	(9,000)
Change in working capital			+ 2,000

The increase in working capital during the year was $2,000. This would have had a negative effect on cash flows (by the same amount).

4. A problem for a new business is that it has no previous experience on which to base its assumptions for making a forecast.

In particular, it may be difficult for a new business to predict with confidence how many sales it will make at the prices that it is planning for its products or services. This means the estimates of sales revenues might be very uncertain.

If estimates of sales volume are uncertain, estimates of some costs will also be difficult to predict beyond the first few months. In particular, purchases of supplies will depend on the volume of sales.

There may also be uncertainty about the period of credit that customers will expect on sales, and the period of credit that suppliers will allow for purchases. So estimates of cash flows may be even more unpredictable than estimates of sales and costs.

Some costs, such as wages, rental costs of business premises and utilities costs (for example electricity and water) should be more predictable and less uncertain.

In spite of the difficulties, new businesses should prepare a cash forecast, because they need to ensure that they will have sufficient cash to survive. A cash forecast helps with planning and monitoring the cash position.

5. By increasing sales prices, the company would increase the profit margin on the goods that it sells (measured as profit per unit as a percentage of selling price). This might be a necessary measure when the profit margins are currently very low. Businesses can only survive on narrow profit margins if they make a large amount of sales.

However, higher prices almost invariably result in some loss of sales volume. In this example, sales volume would fall by 5%. As a result, total sales revenue would be $1.05 \times 0.95 = 0.9975$ or 99.75% of what it was before the price increase. Total revenue would fall and sales volume would fall, but we do not know what the effect on profit would be, because there is no numerical information about costs or profit margins. The business would need to expect an increase in profitability to justify the loss of revenue and sales volume.

It might also be added that the forecast of the fall in sales as a result of the price rise is only an estimate. The actual fall in sales volume might be larger than 5%, and profits might fall. Price increases therefore have an element of risk because of the uncertain impact on sales volume.

6. A business can improve its cash flows by reducing working capital. Some reductions should be possible if the business is holding excess amounts of inventory, or if it is inefficient in collecting payments from its credit customers. It may also be possible to arrange longer credit from trade suppliers.

However, there is probably a limit to the amount by which working capital can be reduced without affecting operational efficiency. A business needs working capital to function. The cash flow benefit from a reduction in working capital is only felt in the period when working capital is reduced. If working capital is subsequently held at the same level, there will be no further cash flow improvement.

There are other ways in which cash flows can be improved. Increasing profits, perhaps by reducing costs or increasing sales volumes, will improve cash flows over the longer term, and possibly in the short term too.

Cash flow can also be improved by raising new capital, such as borrowing from a bank, or by deferring capital expenditures.

In summary, some short-term improvement in cash flow can be obtained by reducing working capital, especially if working capital management is not as efficient as it should be. However, it is not a long-term solution to better cash flows: this must come from greater profitability. Other methods of improving cash flows can also be used. Working capital management may be a part of the answer to better cash flows, but it will be insufficient on its own.

Index